About this Book

Why is this topic important?

Sound management and effective leadership are vital at every level of an organization, from the executive suite to the middle-management ranks to the supervisory and team-leader roles. The key to effective leadership is great training—and great training begins with understanding. If leaders are to change their own attitudes and behavior or the climate and practices of the organization, they first must understand their current situation—what they are supposed to change *from*. This book contains surveys, questionnaires, and assessment instruments designed to provide that understanding. The assessments were specially selected as the best and most useful in the thirty-year history of the famous Pfeiffer *Annuals*. They provide data and insights that establish a fertile learning climate and lay a foundation for outstanding management training.

What can you achieve with this book?

This "book" is actually a working resource—a ready-made toolkit for trainers and consultants who teach leadership skills to managers and management candidates at any level of an organization. You are free to reproduce and use all of the instruments for legitimate training purposes. The assessments are complete, time-tested, and ready to administer. They provide hard data and key insights about the underlying beliefs that shape managers' current behavior, the behavior itself, and the organizational factors that mold attitudes and practices. The book includes assessments that can be used for a wide variety of training and development purposes, both in traditional instructional programs and in "action learning" initiatives that seek to develop leadership skills while bringing about actual, concrete changes in an organization.

How is this book organized?

The assessments are conveniently divided into three sections. The "Beliefs and Values" section includes instruments that shed light on the often-unexamined beliefs about working people and the management role that underlie an individual leader's approach to the job. Assessments in the "Present Performance" section provide data and insights into the manager's current behavior, both self-perceived and in the eyes of others. The final section, "Managing the Organization," offers instruments that measure the climate factors that shape the organization's current practices and will help or hinder any desired change in management behavior.

About Pfeiffer

Pfeiffer serves the professional development and hands-on resource needs of training and human resource practitioners and gives them products to do their jobs better. We deliver proven ideas and solutions from experts in HR development and HR management, and we offer effective and customizable tools to improve workplace performance. From novice to seasoned professional, Pfeiffer is the source you can trust to make yourself and your organization more successful.

Essential Knowledge Pfeiffer produces insightful, practical, and comprehensive materials on topics that matter the most to training and HR professionals. Our Essential Knowledge resources translate the expertise of seasoned professionals into practical, how-to guidance on critical workplace issues and problems. These resources are supported by case studies, worksheets, and job aids and are frequently supplemented with CD-ROMs, websites, and other means of making the content easier to read, understand, and use.

Essential Tools Pfeiffer's Essential Tools resources save time and expense by offering proven, ready-to-use materials—including exercises, activities, games, instruments, and assessments—for use during a training or team-learning event. These resources are frequently offered in looseleaf or CD-ROM format to facilitate copying and customization of the material.

Pfeiffer also recognizes the remarkable power of new technologies in expanding the reach and effectiveness of training. While e-hype has often created whizbang solutions in search of a problem, we are dedicated to bringing convenience and enhancements to proven training solutions. All our e-tools comply with rigorous functionality standards. The most appropriate technology wrapped around essential content yields the perfect solution for today's on-the-go trainers and human resource professionals.

Pfeiffer
www.pfeiffer.com   *Essential resources for training and HR professionals*

Jack Gordon, EDITOR

Pfeiffer's
CLASSIC
Inventories, Questionnaires and Surveys

FOR TRAINING AND DEVELOPMENT

Pfeiffer
A Wiley Imprint
www.pfeiffer.com

ISBN: 0-7879-7469-2

Acquiring Editor: Lisa Shannon
Director of Development: Kathleen Dolan Davies
Editor: Rebecca Taff
Senior Production Editor: Dawn Kilgore
Manufacturing Supervisor: Bill Matherly

Printing 10 9 8 7 6 5 4 3 2 1

How to Use This Resource

This handbook is intended as a working resource for trainers and consultants attempting to develop better leaders and managers for organizations in the business, government, and nonprofit sectors. It includes more than three dozen ready-made surveys, questionnaires, and assessment instruments that provide vital data and insights to lay the foundation for effective management-development initiatives. The instruments can be employed for a variety of purposes in conjunction with training efforts that address top-level executives, middle managers, supervisors, team leaders, or candidates for management positions.

You are welcome to reproduce and administer the assessments in your training sessions and workshops. They come complete with all necessary background material, validity data, scoring instructions, and interpretive information. They are offered as a set of tools to select and employ in a wide range of management-training situations.

This is a top-of-the-line toolkit. The assessments included here were specially selected as the best and most useful leadership-development instruments published in the thirty-year history of the legendary Pfeiffer *Annuals*.

The assessments are divided into three categories according to the kind of data they are designed to gather: "Beliefs and Values," "Present Performance," and "Managing the Organization." Here are two examples to illustrate how trainers and consultants can put this resource to work.

Situation 1

Suppose you are conducting a workshop to teach a group of managers how to take a more creative approach to their jobs. You could simply present a grab bag of creativity techniques and hope for the best. But a better approach might be to personalize the learning and drive home its relevance to every individual by opening the workshop with a self-scoring questionnaire that encourages trainees to examine their own habits and attitudes with regard to creativity and innovation.

In the "Beliefs and Values" section of this book you'll find just such an instrument: Inventory of Barriers to Creative Thought and Innovative Action. Reproduce the questionnaire, administer it, discuss the insights it yields—and you have just set the stage for a far more productive training session.

Are you planning this workshop as part of a broader organizational initiative to encourage innovation in the management ranks? In that case, you might want to start with a wider view of the company's current climate and practices, if only to find out what you're up against. Check out the Innovation Capability Audit in the "Managing the Organization" section.

Situation 2

Suppose you're planning an "action learning" project in which leaders will develop new skills while working to solve an actual problem or capitalize on an actual opportunity facing the organization. As a logical first step, why not find out how various stakeholders perceive the problem?

The "Managing the Organization" section offers several instruments that could prove extremely useful. For instance, check out the Problem-Analysis Questionnaire or Why Don't They Do What I Want? Understanding Employee Motivation.

Choose Your Tools

Those are just two among hundreds of situations in which these assessments can add value. They address topics ranging from an individual manager's aptitude to serve as a mentor to the unspoken norms and beliefs that shape the leadership practices of an entire organization.

Begin with the particular training challenge you face, and peruse this book for instruments that could help. To speed your search, thumbnail descriptions of the kind of information yielded by each assessment are included in the three section introductions.

If knowledge is power, this book is an extraordinarily powerful resource. The information and insights these instruments offer can help you provide better management training, help managers benefit more from the training they receive, and help organizations flourish as a result.

Contents

Section 2: Present Performance   165

Section 3: Managing the Organization 331

Introduction

Training in the working world is always aimed at bringing about some kind of change. When an organization sets out to impart new knowledge or build new skills or encourage new attitudes in a group of employees, the effort presupposes that the organization wants them to do something differently from the way its being done now. They are supposed to move from Point A, present performance, to Point B, desired performance. That is why good trainers and consultants insist on knowing as much as possible about what "desired performance" looks like before they do any training.

But if you want to take people from here to there, it also helps to know where "here" is. What skills and knowledge and attitudes do the trainees currently possess, and which ingredients in that stew do you propose to change?

In addition, there are environmental factors to consider. What forces in the organization have shaped these people's present behavior and held it in place? How difficult will it be to change individual behavior unless you also change certain things about the organization?

These are not simple questions, particularly when it comes to management and leadership development. To answer them, trainers and consultants need as much help as they can get.

This book is a practical, working resource created to provide that help.

The Best of Thirty Years

The surveys, questionnaires, and assessment instruments in this handbook are investigative tools designed for use in conjunction with management training initiatives. They usually will be administered at the beginning of a workshop or before a training program is designed. Some help to define and clarify what "desired performance" would look like for individual managers and for the organization as a whole. But most are intended to shed light on the "here," not the "there."

These tools were specially selected as the best and most useful in the thirty-two-year history of the famous Pfeiffer *Annuals*. Since 1972, trainers and consultants have relied on the *Annuals* as a treasure chest of resources for a wide range of training and organization-development needs. From that mother lode, we have compiled in this book what we believe are the most valuable surveys and instruments pertaining to common challenges in management and leadership training.

We chose the instruments not only for quality but with an eye toward serving a broad range of objectives. You will find assessments designed to support training for people at all levels of an organization's management hierarchy: top executives, middle managers, team leaders, and candidates for first-time supervisory positions. You'll also find instruments that serve a variety of functions, yielding information about many different facets of the individuals you intend to train and the environment in which they operate.

The Sections

The assessments are divided into three categories, based on the kind of information and insights they are designed to unearth. Thumbnail descriptions of every instrument are included in the section introductions, but here is an overview.

In the first section, "Beliefs and Values," we have included assessments that ask managers to examine and evaluate the underlying views and attitudes that shape their behavior and their approach to the leadership role. These beliefs are often unspoken and sometimes unconscious, but in many training situations the learning environment can be greatly enhanced if they are brought to light.

For example, in the "Beliefs and Values" section you will find self-scoring questionnaires that delve into an individual manager's fundamental beliefs about working people and the way they must be led. You'll also find instruments that shed light on questions such as: Do the manager's personal values match the organization's? What is the manager's learning style, and why does it matter? What do individuals' personality traits suggest about the best way for them to get organized and to manage their time?

The second section, "Present Performance," turns from the underlying attitudes that shape behavior to the behavior itself. Here you will find instruments that allow individuals to assess their own current performance, as well as instruments that reveal what that performance looks like to others.

Assessments in the "Present Performance" section provide information useful in a variety of training and development applications. Do individual managers encourage honesty, unity, and trust in the work groups they oversee? Do they communicate effectively with people from different cultures? Does a management candidate display the aptitude for a leadership role? Is an executive in danger of "burning out," and if so, what might be done about it?

The final section, "Managing the Organization," includes surveys and instruments that examine the climate factors that influence or dictate the behavior of every manager in the organization, regardless of what any particular training program may encourage them to do. The benefits of such knowledge are obvious, beginning with the wasted training it can prevent.

Some assessments in the "Managing the Organization" section may serve more direct purposes. In "action learning" initiatives, for example, managers learn new skills while working on actual projects to address real problems or opportunities in the organization. An instrument such as the Problem-Analysis Questionnaire might serve as a good starting point for such an initiative. Indeed, several surveys in this section could prove invaluable in any situation where a management development program is connected to a larger change underway in the organization.

The boundaries among the three sections can be blurry, so please do not limit your search for the right instrument to a single category. For instance, the book contains two assessments dealing with mentoring relationships. The Aptitude for Becoming a Mentor Survey is in the "Beliefs and Values" section because it addresses a manager's generic aptitude to serve as a mentor. The Mentoring Skills Assessment is in the "Managing the Organization" section because it requires two particular people—a prospective mentor and a protégé—to clarify their expectations for a specific relationship. This assumes that the relationship is part of an active development campaign underway in the parent organization.

A Toolbox

When we refer to this book as a working resource, we are speaking literally. This is a toolbox. Every assessment is a complete package, ready to be taken out of the box and put to work. Each includes everything that you and your participants need in order to administer, complete, and score the instrument, and to interpret the results. Background information, including reliability and validity data provided by the surveys' authors, also is included. You are free to duplicate the instruments and administer them for any legitimate purpose having to do with training or organization development.

There are only two exceptions to that liberal copyright policy. If noted, reprint permission must be obtained from the primary sources. And if the materials are to be reproduced in publications for sale or are intended for large-scale distribution (more than one hundred copies in twelve months), prior written permission is required. Please contact Pfeiffer if you have questions.

These time-proven assessments provide information and insights that enable leaders to improve their own skills and to build healthier, more effective organizations. In the hands of capable trainers and consultants, they offer invaluable assistance in the challenge of guiding managers and organizations from here to there.

Jack Gordon
Editor

Part 1
Beliefs and Values

Trainers and consultants are in the business of encouraging behavioral change. But a lot of behavior is shaped by fundamental attitudes and values that develop over time without much conscious thought—unspoken, unexamined, and unchallenged. Even if managers *want* to change their approach to the job, the task can be difficult or impossible without first bringing these underlying beliefs to light.

Another way to put it: If you want to become a better leader, it's best to begin with an accurate picture of who you are, what you value, and what you honestly assume to be the proper relationship of leaders and followers. In short, first know thyself.

Are you temperamentally suited for a management role in this company? What values and fears cause you to act the way you do? If you are doing something that prevents subordinates from giving you their best thought and effort, and you can't seem to stop doing it, why might that be?

The thirteen instruments in this section are designed to provide insights into those questions and more. They can be used to lay a foundation for more effective learning in workshops and other training applications addressing topics ranging from career development to time management.

Here are capsule descriptions of the assessments we have grouped under the heading of "Beliefs and Values."

- The Supervisory and Leadership Beliefs Questionnaire—Managers examine their underlying assumptions about the way employees must be supervised or led.

- Organizational Profile: Determining a Match—Career-development tool allowing managers and others to determine whether their personal traits and preferences make them a good match for their current organization.

- Motivational Analysis of Organizations—Behavior (MAO-B)—What motivates your own behavior at work? Which of six factors influence the values and fears that drive you?

- Managerial Work-Values Scale—Identifies and measures the things you value about a job or a working environment. Are you in the right job and the right company to assume a leadership role?

- Locus of Control Inventory—Management candidates and others rate the degree to which they have an internal or external locus of control ("I largely control what happens in my life and surroundings" vs. "Events are mostly out of my hands.")

- Supervisory Behavior Questionnaire—Describe the behavior of the most- and least-effective bosses you've had in your career. What does that tell you about the kind of leader you want to be?

- Inventory of Barriers to Creative Thought and Innovative Action—Individuals examine personal habits and attitudes that may inhibit their ability to create and innovate.

- The Learning Model Instrument—Managers gain insight into the meaning of "learning styles" and the characteristics of their own preferred style.

- Time-Management Personality Profile—Self-rating instrument highlighting five personality factors that suggest the best ways for individual managers to get themselves organized.

- The TEM Survey—A different approach to identifying habits and attitudes that affect one's time-management ability.

- Aptitude for Becoming a Mentor Survey—Rates a manager's aptitude to serve as a mentor for another person.

- Manager or Scientist: An Attribute Inventory—Designed especially for technical specialists, helps determine whether a candidate should become a manager or remain an individual contributor.

- Supervisory Attitudes: The X-Y Scale—Managers or management candidates measure their own assumptions about workers before learning about Douglas McGregor's Theory X and Theory Y models.

1 The Supervisory and Leadership Beliefs Questionnaire[1]

T. Venkateswara Rao

Summary

One of the most important tasks of a manager is to manage human resources. Effective management of human resources requires understanding the capabilities of subordinates, assigning them appropriate tasks, helping them to acquire new capabilities, maintaining their motivation level, and structuring the work so that people can derive some satisfaction from doing it. As one goes up the managerial ladder, he or she is required to spend an increasing amount of time interacting with people. These interactions may be on the shop floor, in group meetings, in face-to-face encounters with one other person, through telephone conversations, or in formal or informal gatherings. Many managers spend more than 50 percent of their time interacting with their subordinates.

The effectiveness of the manager depends on both the content of the interaction and the manager's style. The manager's technical competence, functional knowledge, skills, and information are very important in determining his or her effectiveness in managing subordinates. A capable manager is able to influence a subordinate by providing technical guidance and clear directions when needed. However, if the manager is not sensitive to the emotional needs of subordinates and does not use the appropriate styles of supervision and leadership, there is a great danger of crippling the growth of the subordinates. For example, an authoritarian manager may arouse strong negative reactions by continually dictating terms to capable subordinates but may do extremely well with

---

[1]Adapted from T.V. Rao, "Supervisory and Leadership Styles." In U. Pareek, T.V. Rao, & D.M. Pestonjee, *Behavioural Processes in Organisations*. New Delhi, India: Oxford & IBH, 1981.

subordinates who are dependent and who are just beginning to learn their roles. Similarly, a democratic manager may be liked by capable subordinates but seen as incompetent by dependent subordinates. It is necessary, therefore, for managers to interact differently with different people.

Major Supervisory Functions

The objective of supervision is to ensure that subordinates do what they are supposed to do. The manager can accomplish this through:

1. Continually striving to understand the style of operation and needs of each subordinate;

2. Continually evaluating the activities of each subordinate in terms of results and the goals toward which that subordinate is working;

3. Guiding subordinates in planning activities;

4. Evaluating the outcomes of activities;

5. Helping to plan future activities on the basis of past experiences; and

6. Rewarding subordinates for satisfactory or superior work.

Understanding the Needs of Subordinates

An effective supervisor understands how individual subordinates are motivated and what their needs are. Such understanding helps in assessing their tasks and performance and then later in guiding future activities.

Continual Evaluation

To guide subordinates effectively, a supervisor must observe their activities. Because a manager may have a very limited amount of time to observe all subordinates, a mechanism should be developed for obtaining and maintaining information about their various activities. Periodic discussions with individual subordinates can be helpful in obtaining such information.

Guidance in Planning Activities

Supervision also involves helping subordinates to plan their activities. This may include providing information and helping to set goals and priorities.

Providing Rewards

Managing also has a motivational aspect: rewarding workers when they accomplish something worthwhile. When a supervisor fails to do this, employees' motivational levels drop. Rewards need not always be monetary; receiving greater responsibility or a verbal expression of appreciation can be highly rewarding to subordinates.

Styles of Supervision

Although every supervisor is unique in some way, certain supervisory styles are characteristic of the majority of managers. Any manager may incorporate more than one of these styles into his or her own, depending on the situation.

Authoritarian and Democratic Styles

Lippitt and White (1943) identify two types of leaders: authoritarian and democratic. The authoritarian leader determines all policies and strategies, decides on the composition and tasks of the work teams, is personal in giving praise and criticism, and maintains some personal distance from employees. In contrast, the democratic leader ensures that policies and strategies are determined by the group, gives technical advice whenever the group needs it, allows freedom to group members to choose their work teams, tries to be objective in providing rewards and punishments, and participates in discussions.

When Lippitt and White compared these two styles of management in their experimental studies, they found that authoritarians produced (a) a greater quantity of work, (b) a greater amount of aggressiveness toward the leader, (c) less originality in work, (d) less work motivation, (e) more dependence, (f) less group feeling, and (g) more suppressed discontent.

Task-Oriented and Employee-Oriented Styles

Blake and Mouton (1964) developed the concept of task-oriented and people-oriented leadership. The following paragraphs explain the differences between these supervisory styles.

Task-Oriented Supervisor. A task-oriented supervisor emphasizes the task, often believes that ends are more important than means, and thinks that employees need to be supervised closely in order to accomplish their tasks. This type of supervisor becomes upset when tasks are not accomplished. The concern for task is so high that the human aspect is likely to be neglected in dealings with subordinates. This type of supervisor is likely to have difficulty in human relations and may appear to be a "tough" person. A task-oriented supervisor may frequently question or remind subordinates about their tasks, warn them about deadlines, or show a great deal of concern about details.

Employees who work with an excessively task-oriented supervisor often develop negative attitudes about their work and their supervisor. They may be motivated only by fear and may feel job dissatisfaction. They may develop shortcuts that, in the long run, affect the organization's performance.

Employee-Oriented Supervisor. In contrast, the employee-oriented supervisor believes that a concern for subordinates' needs and welfare promotes both the quality and quantity of work. This concern may be reflected in attempts to keep subordinates in good humor and in frequent inquiries about their problems (even those unrelated to work). In the extreme, this type of supervision also leads to inefficiency. Subordinates may perceive this type of supervisor as too lenient and may take advantage of the supervisor's concern.

The task-oriented and employee-oriented styles may not be present in pure forms, and one manager may demonstrate combinations of the two styles. The effectiveness of the styles also may depend on factors such as the nature of the task or the nature of the subordinate.

Subsequent work by Fiedler (1967) indicated that the effectiveness of task-oriented or people-oriented styles is contingent on situational factors such as the power of the leader, acceptance of the supervisor by subordinates, and the way in which the tasks are structured.

Benevolent, Critical, and Self-Dispensing Styles

Another way of looking at supervisory and leadership styles (Rao & Satia, 1978) has been used in various countries with satisfactory results. This classification was influenced by McClelland's (1975) work on institution builders and institutional managers and by Stewart's concept of psychosocial maturity (McClelland, 1975). In this concept, leadership or supervisory styles stem from three mutually exclusive orientations: benevolent, critical, and self-dispensing.

Benevolent Supervisor. This type protects subordinates, continually tells them what they should and should not do, and comes to their rescue whenever needed. Such supervisors cater to subordinates' needs for security and generally are liked by their employees. They are effective as long as they are physically present. In their absence, workers may experience a lack of direction and motivation. Such supervisors tend to have dependent followers, and initiative-taking behavior may not be reinforced.

Critical Supervisor. This type takes a critical approach to employees and does not tolerate mistakes, low-quality work, undisciplined behavior, or individual peculiarities. Finding mistakes, criticizing subordinates, and making them feel incompetent are characteristic behaviors of critical managers. Subordinates may produce acceptable work out of fear, but they do not like this type of manager.

Self-Dispensing Supervisor. This type has confidence in the subordinates, helps them to set broad goals, and allows them to work on their own. Guidance is provided only when requested by subordinates. Competent workers who have this kind of supervision are likely to feel confident about their work. They are free to work both independently and interdependently with their colleagues.

Institutional Supervisor

Closely related to the self-dispensing supervisor is what McClelland and Burnham (1976) refer to as an institutional supervisor, because this type is involved in developing the department or unit. Such supervisors are also called institution builders, because they ensure the growth and development of their units and subordinates by incorporating processes that help people to give their best and to grow with the organization. McClelland and Burnham identify the following characteristics of institutional supervisors:

1. They are organization oriented and tend to join organizations and feel responsible for building them.

2. They are disciplined to work and enjoy their work.

3. They are willing to sacrifice some of their own self-interests for the welfare of the organization.

4. They have a keen sense of justice.

5. They have a low need for affiliation, a high need to influence others for social or organizational goals, and a disciplined or controlled way of expressing their power needs.

Such supervisors often aim at a self-dispensing style but are flexible in their use of styles. They are likely to create highly motivating work environments in their organizations.

Implications of Supervisory Styles

No single supervisory style is universally effective. The effectiveness of the style depends on the employee, the nature of the task, and various other factors. If a new employee does not know much about the work, a benevolent supervisor is helpful; a critical supervisor may be frightening; and a self-dispensing supervisor may cause bewilderment. On the other hand, a capable employee may feel most comfortable with a self-dispensing style of supervision and resent a benevolent supervisor who continually gives unwanted advice.

Employees with low self-discipline probably could be developed best by critical supervision, at least on an intermittent basis. Continual use of critical supervision, however, is unlikely to be effective. Flexibility and perceptiveness about when to use each style are useful attributes for leaders or supervisors.

Leadership Styles and Motivational Climate

The effectiveness of any leadership lies in the kind of climate that is created in the organization. Supervisors may find the following suggestions helpful in creating a proper motivational climate.

1. *Create a climate of independence and interdependence rather than dependence.* A self-dispensing supervisor promotes an independent and interdependent climate for subordinates and does not interfere unless it becomes necessary. The subordinates are trusted and given freedom to plan their own ways of doing their work. They are expected to solve problems and to ask for guidance only when it is needed. By providing freedom of work, encouraging initiative, and supporting experimentation and teamwork, a supervisor also helps to satisfy the subordinates' needs for belonging, affection, and security.

Some supervisors allow their subordinates to come to them continually for advice and guidance and, in the extreme case, may not allow them to do anything on their own. If every subordinate must check with the supervisor and obtain approval before taking any action, the supervisor is creating a climate of dependence and the subordinates will not be able to take any initiative. When problems arise, they may hesitate to look for solutions; and when something goes wrong, they may not accept responsibility. Learning from experience becomes difficult, because they have always turned to their supervisor for advice. Thus, the supervisor becomes burdened with responsibilities and problem solving. Not only are the supervisor's energies wasted, but so are those of the subordinates.

2. *Create a climate of competition through recognition of good work.* Employees look forward to being rewarded for good or innovative work. Financial rewards are not always necessary; even a word of appreciation has a great motivating value. Although appreciation given indiscriminately loses its value, a supervisor should not withhold appreciation until the formal appraisal reports. Many other ways of recognizing good work can be very rewarding. Giving praise in the presence of others, giving increased responsibility, and writing letters of commendation and recommendation can be used in addition to financial rewards. Such recognition and public acknowledgment help employees to value work and to derive a sense of satisfaction and a feeling of importance. These go a

long way in motivating people to do better work. They even create a sense of competition among employees.

3. *Create a climate of approach and problem solving rather than avoidance.* Some supervisors approach problems with confidence, face them squarely, work out mechanisms to solve them (often with the help of others), and constantly work to overcome problems. They derive satisfaction from this struggle—even if the outcomes are not always positive—and they inspire subordinates to imitate their initiative.

Some supervisors, however, see everything as a headache and postpone solutions to problems or delegate them to someone else. Workers also are quick to imitate this avoidance.

4. *Create an ideal climate through personal example.* Just as supervisors are imitated in their approaches to problem solving, they are viewed as models for other work habits. In fact, the supervisor's styles may filter down the hierarchy and influence employees several grades below. Therefore, good supervision and good work habits make the supervisor's job easier in two ways: His or her own tasks are done more efficiently, and a climate is created for making the department or unit more efficient.

5. *Motivate people through guidance and counseling.* The foregoing discussions point out some general strategies that supervisors can use in creating the proper motivational climate for their subordinates. However, because individual workers have individual needs, individual counseling also can motivate subordinates. Within a group of workers, a supervisor may find very efficient workers, poor workers, problem creators, cooperative employees, and so on. Therefore, the supervisor should be sensitive to subordinates' individual differences.

Research Findings from the Supervisory and Leadership Beliefs Questionnaire

This instrument was administered to eighteen senior executives and was followed by a ninety-minute session on supervisory styles. Scores were fed back and the discussed in the class. A week later, when the executives were retested, dominant styles remained the same for fifteen of the eighteen participants. Similarly, the least-dominant style did not change for fifteen of the eighteen participants. Thus, style stability seems to exist in 83 percent of the cases. The three participants whose dominant style changed reported that they were influenced by the feedback and subsequent discussions.

Jain (1982) used this instrument to study the supervisory beliefs of six district collectors (Indian administrative service officers), who were also rated by their subordinates (N = 70) with the same instrument. The average scores of the perceptions of the subordinates differed from the self-assessments of the district collectors in only two of the six cases. This indicates that self-assessments of supervisory beliefs do tend to reflect the styles perceived by others. The self-dispensing style in this questionnaire should be considered close to the nurturant task-leadership style outlined by Sinha (1980). Sinha's research indicates that such a style leads to greater group productivity, satisfaction of group members, and work involvement.

Administering the Instrument

The Supervisory and Leadership Beliefs Questionnaire should be used for training purposes only. The instrument could be used for a short session (ninety minutes) on supervision and leadership or as part of a one-day workshop on supervisory/leadership styles. It is advisable to administer the questionnaire before any theoretical input is made. Scoring and interpretation should follow the theoretical input. Interpretation should focus on style flexibility and the need to use different styles with different employees, depending on the situations; however, the overall target should be the self-dispensing style. For a full-day workshop, role plays and simulation activities may be useful.

Scoring and Interpretation

The three scores obtained from this instrument are for benevolent, critical, and self-dispensing supervisory (or leadership) styles. The score of each style is obtained by transferring the points from the instrument to the scoring sheet and totaling each column on the scoring sheet. The sum of the three totals should equal 18. The column with the greatest total indicates the dominant supervisory orientation of the respondent. Scores above 9 normally indicate stronger style orientations, and scores near 0 indicate a lack of that supervisory orientation. For example, a benevolent score of 10, a critical score of 3, and a self-dispensing score of 5 would indicate that the respondent has a fairly strong benevolent orientation and less tendency to use the other two.

Scores are indicative of the strength of the beliefs or orientations underlying each style. However, a supervisor who was strongly oriented toward a certain style would probably use that style. Beliefs lead to behavior, although situations can create gaps between beliefs and behavior.

When one style strongly dominates a profile, style flexibility may be weak. In such a case, it is important for the respondent to examine his or her dominant style and the extent to which his or her flexibility is being hampered.

A higher self-dispensing score is desirable, particularly for managers who work in organizations with competent human resources. High critical scores may hinder human resource development and institutional development. The benevolent style is useful when the task is less structured, when the subordinate or the unit is new, or when the employees have high needs for dependence.

References

Blake, R.R., & Mouton, J.S. (1964). *The managerial grid.* Houston, TX: Gulf.

Fiedler, F.E. (1967). *A theory of leadership effectiveness.* New York: McGraw-Hill.

Jain, U. (1982). *Life styles of Indian managers: An exploratory study of the images, experiences and impact of collectors in their districts.* Unpublished fellow program dissertation, Indian Institute of Management, Ahmedabad, India.

Lippitt, R., & White, R.N. (1943). The social climate of children's groups. In R.G. Baker, J.S. Kounin, & H.F. Wright (Eds.), *Child behavior and development.* New York: McGraw-Hill.

McClelland, D.C. (1975). *Power: The inner experience.* New York: Irvington.

McClelland, D.C., & Burnham, D.H. (1976). Power is the great motivator. *Harvard Business Review, 54*(2), 100–110.

Sinha, J.B.P. (1980). *The nurturant task leader.* New Delhi, India: Concept Publishing.

Originally published in *The 1986 Annual Handbook for Faciliatators, Trainers, and Consultants.*

The Supervisor and Leadership Beliefs Questionnaire

T. Venkateswara Rao

Instructions: This instrument contains three sets of statements, and each set contains three statements. You are to distribute six points among the three items in each set. Distribute these points according to how strongly you agree with each statement. For example, if you strongly agree with the first statement and strongly disagree with the other two, the six points should be assigned to the first statement and zero points should be assigned to the other two. You may assign three points to one statement, two to another, and one to the remaining statement, or any similar combination. The assignment of points is governed simply by the degree to which you agree with each statement.

In these statements, the term "employees" refers to those employees who report to you or for whom you conduct the appraisal. If you supervise a department that is divided into subunits, all members of your department are considered your employees.

1. (a) Employees are capable of working on their own, and there is no need to supervise them. They need to be helped only occasionally. _____

    (b) Employees are generally lazy and avoid work unless they are closely supervised. _____

    (c) Employees need to be guided and helped continually. They need an affectionate supervisor who understands them and continually tells them what to do and what not to do. _____

2. (a) A good supervisor gives a great deal of freedom to employees and has faith in them. _____

    (b) A good supervisor treats employees as a parent would: continually advising them and telling them what to do and what not to do. _____

    (c) A good supervisor keeps a close eye on employees and makes them feel that they should be careful because they are being watched. _____

3. (a) How well employees work depends a great deal on
   how well their supervisor provides continual guidance. _____

   (b) How well employees work depends a great deal on
   how strict their supervisor is with them. _____

   (c) How well employees work depends a great deal on
   how much their supervisor trusts them, gives them
   freedom to experiment, and helps them to learn
   from their mistakes. _____

The Supervisory and Leadership Beliefs Questionnaire Scoring Sheet

Instructions: Transfer the points you have assigned to each statement to the appropriate blank below. Then total each column.

Item	Score	Item	Score	Item	Score
1 (c)	_____	1 (b)	_____	1 (a)	_____
2 (b)	_____	2 (c)	_____	2 (a)	_____
3 (a)	_____	3 (b)	_____	3 (c)	_____
Total	_____	Total	_____	Total	_____

Highest score here indicates a *Benevolent* supervisory orientation.

Highest score here indicates a *Critical* supervisory orientation.

Highest score here indicates a *Self-Dispensing* supervisory orientation.

2 Organizational Profile:
Determining a Match

Scott B. Parry

Summary

This instrument helps employees determine whether they work in an innovative, bureaucratic, or supportive organization and determine their own needs for power and control, achievement, and affiliation. A high match between organizational type and personal needs leads to higher job satisfaction.

As old hierarchical structures give way to team-based environments, many people feel out of place in their own organizations. This instrument was designed to help employees see what type of organization theirs is and to match their own needs with the climate of the organization.

Managers also can control to some extent the type of company they are helping to run, at least in terms of employee affiliation needs. This is because the degree to which employees see their organizations as supportive depends primarily on the degree to which their managers show a personal interest in them, their growth and development, and their feelings. When the work is routine and lacking in challenge and opportunity to achieve, management should welcome employees with high affiliation needs and provide the supportive climate that will nurture and meet these needs.

Description of the Profile

The Organizational Profile presents twenty-four phrases that could be used to describe an organization. Respondents are asked to rate each phrase according to how well it fits the organization, from "never true" to "always true." Respondents then score their profiles to determine the degree to which their organization is bureaucratic, innovative, or supportive. They then display their results on a bar graph to show to what degree each applies. Five questions provide topics for discussion when the assessment is used as part of a group learning experience.

Types of Organizations

Organizations have "personalities" that have been formed in response to many factors, such as the management style of their leaders, the nature of the work, the economic environment, the culture of the country, and so on.

Participants' responses to the list of twenty-four phrases indicates the degree to which their organization is bureaucratic, innovative, or supportive. Typically, an organization displays characteristics of all three, although one is usually dominant. Help the respondents to look at each of the types described below:

Bureaucratic

Bureaucratic organizations have lots of rules, regulations, policies, systems, and procedures. There are many controls on what employees can and cannot do. Static rather than dynamic phrases such as "We've never done anything like this before" are spoken as a warning, rather than as an exciting challenge.

In situations in which the work is well-defined and not subject to much change, the bureaucratic organization has many advantages. It is stable; decisions are predictable; and people know where they stand. For employees who are most comfortable working for a paternalistic organization (that is, management-worker relationships are similar to parent-child relationships), the bureaucracy provides comfort. Examples of such organizations are public utilities (electric, gas, telephone companies), the military, and government at all levels.

Innovative

Innovative organizations are dynamic, creative, progressive, exciting, and ambitious. Risk taking and entrepreneurial activities are encouraged. Such organizations attract high achievers, who welcome the opportunity to excel and move at their own pace. Innovative organizations tend to be at the cutting edge of their fields.

Taken to the extreme, an innovative organization can become an "ulcer factory," as high expectations and the demand to produce are too stressful for many. One's personal lifestyle and need for time with one's family may be more important than the need to achieve. Examples of this type of organization include advertising agencies, marketing firms, TV production, and technology industries (both hardware and software design).

Supportive

Supportive organizations promote friendly, nurturing, warm, helping relationships among employees. People with a strong need to develop friendships and have close ties with other employees are attracted to this kind of organization. "We're one big happy family" is the motto of a supportive organization.

How bureaucratic or innovative an organization is lies outside the control of most managers. This is influenced in large part by the nature of the work. However, all managers can strongly influence how supportive the organization is for employees. Thus, supportiveness can be seen as high or low in a bureaucratic organization and high or low in an innovative organization.

Organizational Trends in Corporate America

The past decade has seen a lot of downsizing, reorganizing, and flattening of organizations. Self-directed teams, empowerment, and fewer levels of management attest to the move away from bureaucratic organizations in favor of flatter, more innovative and supportive organizations.

Many factors explain this shift from the hierarchical organization to a flatter, more flexible one. Some of them are listed below:

- Leaner organizations are more profitable;

- Change can take place more rapidly when fewer people are involved;

- Technology makes it possible to produce more with fewer employees;

- A better educated workforce makes innovation and quality everyone's job;

- Increased competition from overseas forces innovation;

- Supportive organizations are more competitive in a tight labor market; and

- Employees want a greater say in decisions affecting their work.

The old hierarchical organizational structure and a new team-based structure are illustrated in Figures 1 and 2.

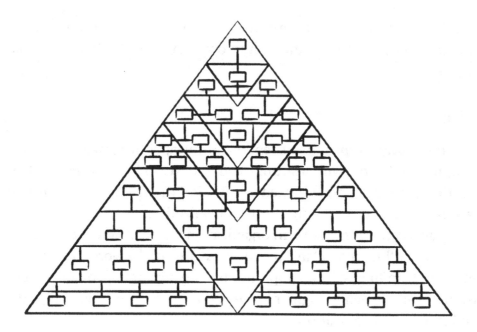

Figure 1. Traditional Hierarchical Organization

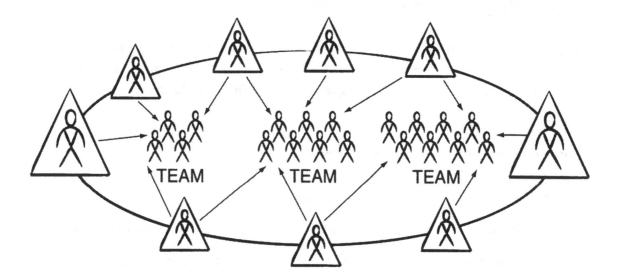

Figure 2. A Team–Based Organizational Structure

Design of the Instrument

The twenty-four phrases that make up the Organizational Profile are divided into three groups of eight that describe each of the three types of organization. These phrases are interspersed so that the respondent does not know what type of organization is being described until the assessment is scored. Thus, the validity of the instrument depends on the respondent's agreement with the eight phrases as being truly descriptive of the organization:

- Bureaucratic organizations are seen as systematic, careful, rules-governed, stable, hierarchical, controlling, predictable, and bureaucratic.

- Innovative organizations are seen as progressive, exciting, creative, entrepreneurial, dynamic, leading-edge, ambitious, and innovative.

- Supportive organizations are seen as friendly, fair, open in terms of relationships, warm, encouraging, harmonious, helpful, and supportive.

Interpreting the Results

The Organizational Profile can be completed and self-scored in ten to fifteen minutes. When the instrument is filled out as part of a group session (for example, a training class or staff meeting), you can ask the participants to write their scores on a sheet of paper and turn them in (anonymously). You can then calculate the group's average so that (1) individuals can compare their scores with the norm, and (2) participants can discuss the implications of organizational style in response to the five questions at the end of the Organizational Profile Interpretation Sheet.

References

McClelland, D.C. (1961). *The achievement society*. New York: Van Nostrand.

Originally published in *The 2000 Annual: Volume 2, Consulting.*

Organizational Profile

Scott B. Parry

Directions: The list below contains twenty-four phrases that could be used to describe an organization. Circle the letters in the column after each phrase that indicates how well that phrase fits your organization, using the following continuum:

Never True	Somewhat True	Frequently True	Always True

My organization is:

1.	Systematic, with well-established systems and procedures.	NT	ST	FT	AT
2.	Progressive and forward-looking.	NT	ST	FT	AT
3.	Friendly and supportive of my work.	NT	ST	FT	AT
4.	Careful and avoids taking risks.	NT	ST	FT	AT
5.	Exciting, as new things are often happening.	NT	ST	FT	AT
6.	Fair, in that employees are treated with respect.	NT	ST	FT	AT
7.	Rule-oriented, and regulations and policies govern behavior.	NT	ST	FT	AT
8.	Creative with lots of fresh, new ideas.	NT	ST	FT	AT
9.	Open with a healthy level of trust in relationships.	NT	ST	FT	AT
10.	Stable with infrequent and slow change.	NT	ST	FT	AT
11.	Entrepreneurial with new ideas and services.	NT	ST	FT	AT
12.	Warm with supportive relationships.	NT	ST	FT	AT
13.	Hierarchical, with many levels of management.	NT	ST	FT	AT
14.	Dynamic, with frequent changes.	NT	ST	FT	AT
15.	Encouraging of my efforts.	NT	ST	FT	AT
16.	Controlling and restrictive of employee behavior.	NT	ST	FT	AT
17.	Leading edge, encouraging of innovative thinking.	NT	ST	FT	AT

	Never True	Somewhat True	Frequently True	Always True			

18. Harmonious as employees work together.   NT   ST   FT   AT

19. Predictable with few surprises.   NT   ST   FT   AT

20. Ambitious with challenging goals that require
employees to stretch.   NT   ST   FT   AT

21. Made up of helpful people who are also friends.   NT   ST   FT   AT

22. Bureaucratic and heavily organized.   NT   ST   FT   AT

23. Innovative and encouraging of risk taking.   NT   ST   FT   AT

24. Supportive, with an environment that is positive
and reinforcing.   NT   ST   FT   AT

Organizational Profile Scoring Sheet

Scoring Your Profile

Directions: First circle the numbers that correspond with your answers to each question (never true, somewhat true, frequently true, or always true) on the following grid.

	NT	ST	FT	AT
1.	0	1	2	3
2.	0	1	2	3
3.	0	1	2	3
4.	0	1	2	3
5.	0	1	2	3
6.	0	1	2	3
7.	0	1	2	3
8.	0	1	2	3
9.	0	1	2	3
10.	0	1	2	3
11.	0	1	2	3
12.	0	1	2	3
13.	0	1	2	3
14.	0	1	2	3
15.	0	1	2	3
16.	0	1	2	3
17.	0	1	2	3
18.	0	1	2	3
19.	0	1	2	3
20.	0	1	2	3
21.	0	1	2	3
22.	0	1	2	3
23.	0	1	2	3
24.	0	1	2	3

Next, total your scores by first adding together the numbers in the eight rows of boxes that are not shaded. Put the total for these eight boxes in the box beside "Bureaucratic Total" below. Your responses to these eight phrases indicate the degree to which you regard your organization as bureaucratic.

Bureaucratic Total:

Now, add the numbers that correspond to your answers from the eight rows of boxes with the light shading and put the total in the "Innovative Total" box below.

Innovative Total:

Now, follow the same procedure for the most heavily shaded rows to obtain a total for the "Supportive" Total box below.

Supportive Total:

Profiling Your Organization

Now locate the numbers for each organizational type on the scale below and make a profile of your organization. Connect the numbers to create a line graph, or make them into a bar chart.

Bureaucratic	Innovative	Supportive
24	24	24
22	22	22
20	20	20
18	18	18
16	16	16
14	14	14
12	12	12
10	10	10
8	8	8
6	6	6
4	4	4
2	2	2
0	0	0

Organizational Profile Interpretation Sheet

Because the characteristics of bureaucratic and innovative organizations are quite different, it is not likely that your organization will have a high score on both at the same time. However, it is possible to rate your organization high on either of these scales and also to rate it high on the supportive scale.

Carefully read the three paragraphs below that describe an individual's need to achieve, to affiliate, and to have power. Decide which is your strongest need and how this need relates to the type of organization you work for.

Relating Organizational Profiles to Human Needs

David McClelland of Harvard has identified three needs that are present in all humans to a greater or lesser degree. They are described below.

Need to Achieve

Persons with a high *need to achieve* require lots of recognition and respect. Their satisfaction comes from the act of achieving rather than from external rewards (for example, money, awards). They tend to set goals that are moderately challenging, neither too easy nor too difficult. Achievers have a strong need for concrete, specific feedback on how well they are doing so that they can continually strive to be better.

Need to Affiliate

Persons with a high *need to affiliate* tend to derive greater satisfaction from the people they work with than from the work itself or the act of achieving goals. The feedback they seek is related to their attitudes, their loyalty, their importance to the organization, and the quality of the relationships they have cultivated with customers and other employees. Competition and the opportunity to achieve may actually be seen as threats to the person with high affiliation needs.

Need for Power

Persons with a high *need for power* want to influence the behavior of others. Sometimes this influence is desirable, as with teachers, ministers, lawyers, architects, and leaders in all fields. At other times their need to influence is dangerous, as with dictators, corrupt politicians, and gangsters. Persons with high power needs measure their success by the number of persons they are able to influence, either directly or through others.

These three human needs are associated with the three types of organizations in the following ways:

- People's need to achieve is best met in innovative organizations;

- Their need to affiliate is met best in supportive organizations; and

- Their need for power is satisfied most often in bureaucratic organizations.

Answer the following questions either individually or with your group to help you think about the "fit" between your personal needs and the organization for which you work.

1. Were you surprised by the three scores you gave your organization? Why or why not?

2. How do your perceptions compare with others in your group? Was there close agreement or was there a wide range of opinions about your organization?

3. Have you seen any changes in your organization's "personality" during the past five to ten years? Has it become more or less bureaucratic? Innovative? Supportive? Decide as a group.

4. What future forces and events do you anticipate that might change the personality of your organization? In what direction is it likely to go?

5. If you were running the organization, what would you regard as the ideal scores for the organization to have? Why?

3 Motivational Analysis of Organizations—Behavior (MAO-B)

Udai Pareek

Summary

A person's behavior is the result of several factors or motives. A knowledge of the typical, primary motivators of the behavior of people in a work setting can help managers and consultants to deal more effectively with those people. The first step in developing such knowledge is to become aware of ones own patterns of organizational behavior and to identify ones own primary motives. The Motivational Analysis of Organizations—Behavior (MAO-B) instrument enables the respondents to identify which of six primary factors motivates their own behavior in their organizational settings. The instrument can be used in managerial and supervisory training, as part of a human resource development (HRD) or team-building program, and for personal growth and development.

Rationale for the Instrument

Murray (1938) developed a long list of human motives or needs. Murrays work inspired further studies, which have produced different lists of significant behavioral motives. McClelland, Atkinson, Clark, and Lowell (1953) suggested three important motives (achievement, affiliation, and power) and also suggested elaborate methods for measuring them. McClelland subsequently demonstrated the importance of the achievement motive for entrepreneurship and marketing (McClelland, 1961; McClelland & Winter, 1971) and of power as a motivator in management (McClelland, 1975; McClelland & Burnham, 1976). He further attempted to identify a pattern of leadership motivation in which power plays a critical role (McClelland & Boyatzis, 1982). Litwin and Stringer

(1968) used the three motives of achievement, affiliation, and power in their study of organizational climates and found these motives useful for the study of organizational behavior.

Although McClelland's study of achievement and affiliation motives showed them to be rather simple variables, he found the motive of power to be a complex one. As he suggested during his study of power (McClelland, 1975), the desire for power contains both an urge to control others and an urge to make an impact. McClelland called these variables personalized power and socialized power. Thus, McClelland seems to suggest three different elements in the power motive: the need to control others (personalized power), the need to make an impact on others, and the need to use power in doing something for other persons and groups—such as in organizations (socialized power). It is helpful to make clear distinctions among these three. Control seems to be focused around keeping track of developments according to an agreed-on plan to be informed about "how things are going." This seems to be an important need or motive in managerial behavior. The so-called socialized dimension of power (reflected in the use of power for the benefit of others) seems to be a separate need or motive. Pareek (1968a, 1968b) suggests that this need is important for social development and calls it the extension motive.

Another motive that is relevant for organizational behavior is that of dependence. Although it generally has been regarded as a negative force, McGregor (1966) recognized the positive value of dependence in management, and Kotter (1979) further drew attention to its importance. Levinson (1982) pointed out the importance of dependence in the development of managers. This need is acknowledged in the process of mentoring (Levinson, 1982), which has received considerable attention in the recent management literature (e.g., Kram, 1985).

Thus, six primary needs or motives that are relevant to an understanding of the behavior of people in organizations have been identified. These are as follows:

1. *Achievement:* Characterized by concern for excellence, competition with the standards of excellence set by others or by oneself, the setting of challenging goals for oneself, awareness of the hurdles that stand in the way of achieving those goals, and persistence in trying alternative paths to ones goals.

2. *Affiliation:* Characterized by a concern for establishing and maintaining close, personal relationships, a value on friendship, and a tendency to express ones emotions.

3. *Influence:* Characterized by concern with making an impact on others, a desire to make people do what one thinks is right, and an urge to change matters and (develop) people.

4. *Control:* Characterized by a concern for orderliness, a desire to be and stay informed, and an urge to monitor and take corrective action when needed.

5. *Extension:* Characterized by a concern for others; an interest in superordinate goals; and an urge to be useful to larger groups, including society.

6. *Dependence:* Characterized by seeking the help of others in ones own self-development, checking with significant others (those who are more knowledgeable than oneself or have higher status, experts, close associates, etc.), submitting ideas or proposals for approval, and having an urge to maintain an "approval" relationship.

All these needs or motives can be used in explaining the behavior of people in organizations. However, each of these motives can have two dimensions: approach and avoidance. Atkinson (1953) first suggested the concept of avoidance behavior in discussing the achievement motive. It was further elaborated by several authors (Birney & Burdick, 1969; Heckhausen, 1967), and "fear of failure" emerged as an important component of the achievement motive, distinct from "hope of success," the other component. Much research has been done on fear of failure, which has been found to be dysfunctional although related to the achievement motive. For example, Varga (1977) showed that hope of success versus fear of failure (approach versus avoidance) was the most important intervening variable in explaining who benefited from achievement-motivation training programs as measured by an increase in entrepreneurial activity. People who were high in achievement motivation but also had a high component of fear of failure failed to start new businesses, in contrast to those who had a high component of hope of success. The concept of approach versus avoidance also is applicable to components of other motivators.

The six motives of achievement, affiliation, influence, control, extension, and dependence have been used in studying the behavior of people in organizations, and no further important managerial motives have been identified. Table 1 summarizes the approach and avoidance dimensions of each of the six motives. The behavior of a manager or employee thus can be analyzed not only in terms of the six primary motives but also from the perspective of (positive) approach or (negative) avoidance, reflected by hope or fear.

An employee's effectiveness may result from the existence or lack of a particular motivator or from the extent of the approach or avoidance dimension of a particular motivator. The motive, however strong it may be, may be made ineffective by a high degree of fear, i.e., high avoidance behavior. Thus, a high score for a motive on the MAO-B instrument must be assessed in relation to the number of avoidance items in the total score. High avoidance clearly can reduce an individuals effectiveness.

Table 1. Approach and Avoidance Dimensions of Six Motives

Motives	Approach (Hope of)	Avoidance (Fear of)
Achievement	Success	Failure
Affiliation	Inclusion	Exclusion
Extension	Relevance	Irrelevance
Influence	Impact	Impotence
Control	Order	Chaos
Dependence	Growth	Loneliness

The Instrument

The Motivational Analysis of Organizations—Behavior (MAO-B) instrument was developed to study manager or employee behavior in an organization. The MAO-B contains sixty items, five for each dimension (approach and avoidance) of each of the six previously discussed motives.

Scoring

The total score for each dimension (approach and avoidance) of the six motives can range from 5 to 20. The respondents operating effectiveness quotient (OEQ) for each of the six motive-specific aspects of behavior, defined by the net score of approach dimensions, can be obtained by using the formula

$$\frac{P-5}{P+V-10} \times 100.$$

"P" and "V" represent total scores for approach and avoidance dimensions, respectively, of a motive-specific behavior. Table 2 can be used to find the OEQ for each motive-related behavior.

Table 2. Operating Effectiveness Quotients

Avoidance Scores	Approach Scores															
	5	6	7	8	9	10	11	12	13	14	15	16	17	18	19	20
5	0	100	100	100	100	100	100	100	100	100	100	100	100	100	100	100
6	0	50	67	75	80	83	85	87	89	90	91	92	92	93	93	97
7	0	33	50	60	67	71	75	78	80	82	83	85	86	87	87	88
8	0	25	40	50	57	62	67	70	73	75	77	78	80	81	82	83
9	0	20	33	43	50	55	60	64	67	69	71	73	75	76	78	79
10	0	17	28	37	44	50	54	58	61	64	67	69	70	72	74	75
11	0	14	25	33	40	45	50	54	59	60	62	65	67	68	70	71
12	0	12	22	30	36	42	46	50	53	56	59	61	63	65	67	68
13	0	11	20	27	33	38	43	47	50	53	55	58	60	62	64	65
14	0	10	18	25	31	36	40	44	47	50	53	55	57	59	61	62
15	0	9	17	23	28	33	37	41	44	47	50	52	54	56	58	60
16	0	8	15	21	27	31	35	39	42	45	48	50	52	54	56	58
17	0	8	14	20	25	29	33	37	40	43	45	48	50	52	54	56
18	0	7	13	19	23	28	32	35	38	41	43	46	48	50	52	54
19	0	7	12	18	22	26	30	33	36	39	42	44	46	48	50	52
20	0	6	12	17	21	25	29	32	35	37	40	42	44	46	48	50

Reliability

The test-retest reliability coefficients for the six dimensions of role behavior (based on a sample of fifty, two months apart) are as follows:

MAO-B Variable	Reliability Coefficient	Level of Significance
Achievement	.61	.001
Affiliation	.61	.001
Influence	.58	.001
Control	.68	.001
Extension	.53	.001
Dependence	.45	.001

All of the coefficients are very high, significant at the .001 level. The instrument is thus a highly reliable one.

Internal Factors

The MAO-B scores of about 500 employees of a large bank were factor analyzed, rotated by the varimax method. Only those factors with an eigenvalue of 1 or above were taken, extracting in all five factors.

The five factors showed that the MAO-B has one factor of personal responsibility, one factor reflecting fear of responsibility, two positive factors related to people (one of personal growth with the help of others and the other encompassing human concern), and one factor of integration and centralization of tasks. Achievement, influence, and control contributed to the personal responsibility factor, whereas dependence and affiliation emerged as independent factors. Extension motivation was distributed into the various factors. Three motives emerged in the behavior of employees; these can be called the achievement motive, the task motive, and the affiliation (or human relationship) motive.

Validity

The relationship between effective role behavior (as reflected by the operating effectiveness quotient) and some personality variables was found in a study of five hundred employees, a sample of the employees of a large multi-locational firm. The levels of significance of the correlations appear in Table 3.[1]

As can be seen from the table, all dimensions of effective role behavior are positively correlated with role efficacy (see Pareek, 1980a, 1980b). It can be said that people who experience higher role efficacy use more effective role behavior on all dimensions. The same is true of the two dimensions of locus of control, internality and externality (see Pareek, 1982). Two types of external locus of control were discovered using the scale by Levenson (1972, 1973): externality events caused by others and externality events caused by chance. The correlation values were significant in the expected direction for all dimensions of role-behavior effectiveness. However, the correlation between the control dimension and internality was not found to be significant. It can be concluded that, on the whole, people having a higher external locus of control show less effective role behavior, and those having a higher internal locus of control show more effective role behavior (except, perhaps, on the control dimension).

As can be seen in Table 3, effective role behavior had a significantly negative correlation with the total role-stress score (see Pareek, 1983). Of the total for role stress, four of six correlations were significant at the .001 level; for the "extension" dimen-

---

[1]A minus sign indicates that the correlations were negative.

sion, the correlation was significant at .004; and for affiliation, it was at .002. The correlation value of both of these dimensions (which are of an interpersonal nature) with two role stresses (role isolation and role erosion) were not significant. The correlation value of role ambiguity and of role stagnation was not significant respectively with the extension and affiliation dimensions. In summary, people who use more effective role behavior in general experience less role stress. This is particularly true of work-oriented role behavior.

Table 3. Level of Significance of Correlation Between Role Effectiveness Dimensions and Other Variables

Other Variables	Role Effectiveness Dimensions (—Indicates negative correlation)					
	Achievement	Influence	Control	Extension	Affiliation	Dependence
1. Role Efficacy	.001	.001	.001	.001	.01	.001
2. Internality	.001	.003	—	.045	.001	.001
3. Externality (Others)	-.001	-.001	-.005	-.080	-.002	.001
4. Externality (Chance)	-.001	-.001	-.001	.001	-.003	-.022
5. Externality (Total)	-.001	-.001	-.001	-.004	-.001	-.001
6. Role Stress	-.001	-.001	-.001	-.004	-.002	-.001
7. Coping Strategy (Avoidance)	-.001	-.001	-.004	-.014	-.036	-.044
8. Coping Strategy (Approach)	-.002	.001	.004	.018	—	.014

Table 3 also shows the values of correlation between effective role behavior and strategies for coping with stress (avoidance and approach strategies). Effectiveness (OEQ) for all dimensions of role behavior had significant negative correlation with avoidance strategies and significant positive correlation with approach strategies (except for the affiliation dimension, for which the value was not significant). For the avoidance strategies, the correlations were significant at .001 for achievement and influence; at .004 for control; at .014 for extension; and at .036 and .044 for affiliation and dependence. For the approach strategies, the values were significant at .002, .001, and .004 for achievement, influence, and control, respectively, and at .014 and .018 for dependence and extension. It can be concluded that people who demonstrate effective role behavior generally use approach strategies in coping with role stress.

Norms

The mean values for the MAO-B scores of a sample of five hundred employees from four banks (Sen, 1982) for the approach and avoidance dimensions and the OEQ are shown in Table 4. These tentatively can be used as cutoff points for interpretation of the scores. However, norms should be developed for different groups. The mean values for different levels of employees, as well as different age groups, are shown in Table 5a and 5b.

Table 4. Mean Values for a Sample of Five Hundred Bank Employees

Dimensions	Approach	Avoidance	OEQ
Achievement	16	10	68
Influence	14	10	65
Extension	15	13	56
Control	15	12	63
Affiliation	15	11	64
Dependence	15	11	65

Administering the MAO–B Instrument

The MAO-B instrument can be administered in a group. The participants should be told that the instrument is meant to provide a profile of motivational aspects of role behavior and that there are no right or wrong answers. If the instrument is used for HRD purposes, the instrument results can be used to help individuals and the group to plan for increased effectiveness in their roles.

If the instrument is used with students of management, they should be asked to respond to the instrument as they would if they were in managerial positions in an organization. The scores can then be discussed to show the motivational trends of the students.

Table 5. Mean Values for Levels and Age Groups

Dimension	Levels				Age Groups						
	Top Mgmt.	Senior Mgmt.	Super-visory	Tellers	<25	26–30	31–35	36–40	41–45	46–50	>50
Achievement	73	70	67	65	64	66	68	65	71	68	72
Influence	70	67	65	61	62	64	63	63	67	68	69
Extension	58	58	56	54	52	55	57	56	56	57	58
Control	68	65	62	60	59	61	61	62	64	65	66
Affiliation	67	64	62	66	61	65	64	66	64	64	66
Dependence	66	67	64	64	64	63	64	64	67	67	67

If the instrument is used with students of management, they should be asked to respond to the instrument as they would if they were in managerial positions in an organization. The scores can then be discussed to show the motivational trends of the students.

The concepts underlying the instrument should be presented after the respondents have obtained profiles of their motivational tendencies.

Use of the MAO-B Instrument

The MAO-B can be used for self-analysis, for individual counseling, and for organizational and human resource training and development. A respondent can examine his or her scores and then plan to reduce the avoidance behavior of a motive for which he or she received a low OEQ score by examining the related items on the instrument and inferring the behavioral implications. In counseling work, both the counselor and the client can complete the instrument from the clients perspective; then the counselor can help the client to plan new behavior.

In an HRD or OD training program, the participants can look at their profiles, request feedback from other participants, and then discuss in trios ways of increasing their effectiveness by reducing their avoidance behaviors for the relevant motives. The instrument also can be used in organization development and consulting work to obtain group profiles, to search for organizational factors to explain the profiles, to develop organizational strategies to improve the profiles, and to develop individual strategies to increase employees operating effectiveness for the various motives.

References

Atkinson, J.W. (1953). The achievement motive and recall of interrupted and complete tasks. *Journal of Experimental Psychology, 46,* 381–390.

Birney, R.C., & Burdick, H. (1969). *Fear of failure.* New York: Van Nostrand Reinhold.

Heckhausen, H. (1967). *The anatomy of achievement motivation.* New York: Academic Press.

Kotter, J.P. (1979). Power, dependence, and effective management. In *Harvard Business Reviews on human relations.* New York: Harper & Row.

Kram, K.E. (1985). Creating conditions that encourage mentoring. In L.D. Goodstein & J.W. Pfeiffer (Eds.), *The 1985 annual.* San Francisco: Pfeiffer.

Levenson, H. (1972, August). *Distinctions within the concept of internal-external control: Development of a new scale.* Paper presented at the meeting of the American Psychological Association, Honolulu, Hawaii.

Levenson, H. (1973, August). *Reliability and validity of the I, P, and C scales: A multi-dimensional view of locus of control.* Paper presented at the American Psychological Association convention, Montreal, Canada.

Levinson, H. (1982). *Executive* (rev. ed.). Cambridge, MA: Harvard University Press.

Litwin, G.H., & Stringer, R.A. (1968). *Motivation and organizational climate.* Boston: Harvard Business School.

McClelland, D.C. (1961). *The achieving society.* New York: Van Nostrand Reinhold.

McClelland, D.C. (1975). *Power: The inner experience.* New York: Irvington.

McClelland, D.C., Atkinson, J.W., Clark, R.A., & Lowell, E.L. (1953). *The achievement motive.* New York: Appleton-Century-Crofts.

McClelland, D.C., & Boyatzis, R.E. (1982). Leadership motive pattern and long-term success in management. *Journal of Applied Psychology, 67*(6), 737–743.

McClelland, D.C., & Burnham, D. (1976). Power is the great motivator. *Harvard Business Review, 54*(2), 100–111.

McClelland, D.C., & Winter, D.G. (1971). *Motivating economic achievement.* New York: The Free Press.

McGregor, D. (1966). *Leadership and motivation.* Cambridge, MA: MIT Press.

Murray, H.A. (1938). *Explorations in personality.* New York: Oxford University Press.

Pareek, U. (1968a). A motivational paradigm of development. *Journal of Social Issues, 24*(2), 115–122.

Pareek, U. (1968b). Motivational patterns and planned social change. *International Social Science Journal, 20*(3), 464–413.

Pareek, U. (1980a). Dimensions of role efficacy. In J.W. Pfeiffer & J.E. Jones (Eds.), *The 1980 annual.* San Francisco: Pfeiffer.

Pareek, U. (1980b). Role efficacy scale. In J.W. Pfeiffer & J.E. Jones (Eds.), *The 1980 annual.* San Francisco: Pfeiffer.

Pareek, U. (1982). Internal and external control. In J.W. Pfeiffer & L.D. Goodstein (Eds.), *The 1982 annual.* San Francisco: Pfeiffer.

Pareek, U. (1983). Organizational role stress scale. In L.D. Goodstein & J.W. Pfeiffer (Eds.), *The 1983 annual*. San Francisco: Pfeiffer.

Sen, P.C. (1982). *A study of personal and organizational correlates of role stress and coping strategies in some public sector banks*. Unpublished doctoral dissertation, Gujarat University.

Varga, K. (1977). Who gains from achievement motivation training? *Vikalpa, 2*(3), 187–199.

Originally published in *The 1986 Annual Handbook for Faciliatators, Trainers, and Consultants.*

Motivational Analysis of Organizations— Behavior (MAOB)

Udai Pareek

Instructions: This inventory can help you to understand how different motivations can affect your behavior and your performance at work. There are no "right" or "wrong" responses; the inventory will reflect your own perceptions of how you act at work, so you will gain the most value from it if you answer honestly. Do not spend too much time on any one item; generally, your first reaction is the most accurate.

For each of the statements, refer to the following scale and decide which number represents how often you engage in the behavior or have the feeling described. Then write that number in the blank to the left of the statement.

Rarely/Never	Sometimes/Occasionally	Often/Frequently	Usually/Always
1	2	3	4

_____ 1. I enjoy working on moderately difficult (challenging) tasks and goals.

_____ 2. I am overly emotional.

_____ 3. I am forceful in my arguments.

_____ 4. I refer matters to my superiors.

_____ 5. I keep close track of things (monitor action).

_____ 6. I make contributions to charity and help those in need.

_____ 7. I set easy goals and achieve them.

_____ 8. I relate very well to people.

_____ 9. I am preoccupied with my own ideas and am a poor listener.

_____ 10. I follow my ideals.

_____ 11. I demand conformity from the people who work for or with me.

_____ 12. I take steps to develop the people who work for me.

_____ 13. I strive to exceed performance/targets.

Rarely/Never	Sometimes/Occasionally	Often/Frequently	Usually/Always
1	2	3	4

_____ 14. I ascribe more importance to personal relationships than to organizational matters.

_____ 15. I build on the ideas of my subordinates or others.

_____ 16. I seek the approval of my superiors.

_____ 17. I ensure that things are done according to plan.

_____ 18. I consider the difficulties of others even at the expense of the task.

_____ 19. I am afraid of making mistakes.

_____ 20. I share my feelings with others.

_____ 21. I enjoy arguing and winning arguments.

_____ 22. I have genuine respect for experienced people.

_____ 23. I admonish people for not completing tasks.

_____ 24. I go out of my way to help the people who work for me.

_____ 25. I search for new ways to overcome difficulties.

_____ 26. I have difficulty in expressing negative feelings to others.

_____ 27. I set myself as an example and model for others.

_____ 28. I hesitate to make hard decisions.

_____ 29. I define roles and procedures for the people who work for me.

_____ 30. I undergo personal inconvenience for the sake of others.

_____ 31. I am more conscious of my limitations or weaknesses than of my strengths.

_____ 32. I take interest in matters of personal concern to the people who work for me.

_____ 33. I am laissez faire in my leadership style (do not care how things happen).

_____ 34. I learn from those who are senior to me.

_____ 35. I centralize most tasks to ensure that things are done properly.

Rarely/Never	Sometimes/Occasionally	Often/Frequently	Usually/Always
1	2	3	4

_____ 36. I have empathy and understanding for the people who work for me.

_____ 37. I want to know how well I have been doing and I use feedback to improve myself.

_____ 38. I avoid conflict in the interest of group feelings.

_____ 39. I provide new suggestions and ideas.

_____ 40. I try to please others.

_____ 41. I explain systems and procedures clearly to the people who work for me.

_____ 42. I tend to take responsibility for others' work in order to help them.

_____ 43. I show low self-confidence.

_____ 44. I recognize and respond to the feelings of others.

_____ 45. I receive credit for work done in a team.

_____ 46. I seek help from those who know the subject.

_____ 47. In case of difficulties, I rush to correct things.

_____ 48. I develop teamwork among the people who work for me.

_____ 49. I work effectively under pressure of deadlines.

_____ 50. I am uneasy and less productive when working alone.

_____ 51. I give credit and recognition to others.

_____ 52. I look for support for my actions and proposals.

_____ 53. I enjoy positions of authority.

_____ 54. I hesitate to take strong actions because of human considerations.

_____ 55. I complain about difficulties and problems.

_____ 56. I take the initiative in making friends with my colleagues.

_____ 57. I am quite conscious of status symbols such as furniture, size of office, etc.

Rarely/Never	Sometimes/Occasionally	Often/Frequently	Usually/Always
1	2	3	4

_____ 58. I like to solicit ideas from others.

_____ 59. I tend to form small groups to influence decisions.

_____ 60. I like to accept responsibility in the group's work.

Motivational Analysis of Organizations— Behavior (MAO-B) Scoring Sheet

Instructions: Transfer your responses from the MAO-B inventory to the appropriate spaces on this sheet. If you entered the number 2 in the blank to the left of item 1, enter a 2 in the blank after the number 1 below; if you entered a 4 as your response to item 13, enter a 4 in the blank to the right of the number 13 below, and so on until you have entered all your responses in the spaces below.

A	B	C	D	E	F
1. ____	3. ____	5. ____	10. ____	12. ____	8. ____
13. ____	15. ____	17. ____	22. ____	24. ____	20. ____
25. ____	27. ____	29. ____	34. ____	36. ____	32. ____
37. ____	39. ____	41. ____	46. ____	48. ____	44. ____
49. ____	51. ____	53. ____	58. ____	60. ____	56. ____
A	**B**	**C**	**D**	**E**	**F**
Total ____	Total ____	Total ____	Total ____	Total ____	Total ____

a	b	c	d	e	f
7. ____	9. ____	11. ____	4. ____	6. ____	2. ____
19. ____	21. ____	23. ____	16. ____	18. ____	14. ____
31. ____	33. ____	35. ____	28. ____	30. ____	26. ____
43. ____	45. ____	47. ____	40. ____	42. ____	38. ____
55. ____	57. ____	59. ____	52. ____	54. ____	50. ____
a	**b**	**c**	**d**	**e**	**f**
Total ____	Total ____	Total ____	Total ____	Total ____	Total ____

Now sum the numbers that you have entered in each vertical column and enter the totals in the blanks provided. These totals are your scores for the approach-avoidance dimensions of each of the six primary motivators of peoples behavior on the job. Transfer these totals to the appropriate blanks in the two middle columns below.

Achievement	A (approach) _____	a (avoidance) _____	OEQ _____
Influence	B (approach) _____	b (avoidance) _____	OEQ _____
Control	C (approach) _____	c (avoidance) _____	OEQ _____
Dependence	D (approach) _____	d (avoidance) _____	OEQ _____
Extension	E (approach) _____	e (avoidance) _____	OEQ _____
Affiliation	F (approach) _____	f (avoidance) _____	OEQ _____

To compute your operating effectiveness quotient (OEQ) for each motivator, find the value for your approach (capital letter) score for the motivator along the top row of the table that follows, and then find your avoidance (lowercase letter) score for that motivator in the left column. The number in the cell that intersects the column and row is your OEQ score for the motivator. Transfer that score to the tally marked "OEQ" at the bottom of the previous page. Do this for each motivator.

Avoidance Scores	Approach Scores															
	5	6	7	8	9	10	11	12	13	14	15	16	17	18	19	20
5	0	100	100	100	100	100	100	100	100	100	100	100	100	100	100	100
6	0	50	67	75	80	83	85	87	89	90	91	92	92	93	93	97
7	0	33	50	60	67	71	75	78	80	82	83	85	86	87	87	88
8	0	25	40	50	57	62	67	70	73	75	77	78	80	81	82	83
9	0	20	33	43	50	55	60	64	67	69	71	73	75	76	78	79
10	0	17	28	37	44	50	54	58	61	64	67	69	70	72	74	75
11	0	14	25	33	40	45	50	54	59	60	62	65	67	68	70	71
12	0	12	22	30	36	42	46	50	53	56	59	61	63	65	67	68
13	0	11	20	27	33	38	43	47	50	53	55	58	60	62	64	65
14	0	10	18	25	31	36	40	44	47	50	53	55	57	59	61	62
15	0	9	17	23	28	33	37	41	44	47	50	52	54	56	58	60
16	0	8	15	21	27	31	35	39	42	45	48	50	52	54	56	58
17	0	8	14	20	25	29	33	37	40	43	45	48	50	52	54	56
18	0	7	13	19	23	28	32	35	38	41	43	46	48	50	52	54
19	0	7	12	18	22	26	30	33	36	39	42	44	46	48	50	52
20	0	6	12	17	21	25	29	32	35	37	40	42	44	46	48	50

When you have completed this process for all of your scores, you will have a numerical picture of what typically motivates your behavior at work, whether you respond positively (approach) or negatively (avoidance) to each of the six typical motivators, and how your responses to each motivator influence your operating effectiveness.

4 Managerial Work–Values Scale

T. Venkateswara Rao

Summary

The term *value* has been defined as "the excellence or the degree of worth ascribed to an object. Though ascribed to the object and reacted to as if external or objective, value is a function of the valuing transaction, not of the object" (English & English, 1958). By this definition, work value means "the degree of worth ascribed to a particular type of work, activity, or aspect of the work." This definition of work value makes the term distinct from occupational (or job) preference, because it refers to the degree of worth that is ascribed to it. Whereas preference indicates a general attitude, value implies a stronger attitude or a positive evaluation.

Review of Research

From the 1920s through the 1980s, hundreds of investigations were conducted on the question of work values or job attitudes. Douglass (1922) studied 2,844 high school seniors, who gave the following reasons for preferring a job: (1) a general impression of the advantages and attractiveness of the job; (2) the respondent's own fitness for the job; (3) the job's financial returns; (4) opportunities for service; and (5) the respondent's knowledge of his or her fitness for the work based on personal experience. Kornhauser's 1936 study of 350 Chicago males indicated that security and independence were the most strongly desired aspects of a job by members of lower- and middle-income groups; this contrasted with members of wealthy and upper-income groups, who most desired social approval (Centers, 1949).

Centers (1961), whose many studies stimulated research in this particular field, conducted a nationwide survey of U.S. Americans. Centers found that the respondents desired independence, self-expression, security, the opportunity to serve others, and interesting experience, in that order. They placed less value on dimensions of power, fame, esteem, leadership, and profits.

Centers also found significant differences in value patterns for different occupational groups. Large business owners' preferences for self-expression, leadership, and interesting experiences were in marked contrast to those of unskilled laborers, who chose security more frequently than any other value.

Ginzberg (1951) theorized that choices made before seventeen years of age were only tentative and that real choices were made only after age seventeen.

Gray (1963) compared the work values of fifty secondary-school teachers, fifty accountants, and fifty engineers. Teachers scored highest on their preferences for social rewards, whereas accountants scored highest on the value of prestige.

Significant gender differences in the ranking of occupational values were reported by Thompson (1966). In this study women placed significantly less emphasis on leadership, pay, and recognition than men did. Men, in contrast, placed less emphasis on self-expression and social service than women did. High achievers valued jobs that encouraged individuality more than low achievers did. High pay, leadership, and interesting and challenging jobs were the other preferences of high achievers.

Domenichetti (1970) found that work values also change as a function of vocational maturity.

Schein (1990) identified the following eight categories of career anchors:

1. Technical/functional competence;

2. General managerial competence;

3. Autonomy/independence;

4. Security/stability;

5. Entrepreneurial creativity;

6. Service/dedication to a cause;

7. Pure challenge; and

8. Lifestyle.

According to Schein, a career anchor represents a person's self-image of what he or she excels in, wants, and values. Although a person can have only one career anchor, the categories can be arranged in a hierarchy according to what that person would be willing to give up if forced to choose between two anchors.

Managerial Work Values

Values often are considered to be organized into hierarchical structures. The concept of a value system suggests a rank ordering of values along a continuum of importance. Two distinct types of values—instrumental (means) and terminal (end) values—make possible two distinct value systems, each with a rank-ordered structure of its own. These value systems are functionally and cognitively connected with each other as well as connected with a person's attitudes toward other specific objects and situations.

Theoretically, with large numbers of values, a large number of variations in the rankings are possible. It is, however, unlikely that all possible value patterns will exist, because social factors (such as culture, social system, gender, occupation, education, religion, and political orientation) sharply restrict the number of actual variants.

Values impact managerial interactions in a variety of ways. Values influence managers' choices; choices, in turn, are important in determining managerial effectiveness because they influence outcomes. For example, the values that managers hold may influence their choices of subordinates, their likes and dislikes for given jobs, or the extent to which they involve themselves with certain tasks. A manager may value scientific and theoretical knowledge so much that he or she unconsciously may prefer a thinker or a theorizer for a routine job. Another manager's preference for a particular machine may be more a result of aesthetic values than an awareness of the efficiency of that machine. A research-and-development manager may try to economize unnecessarily because of personal economic values, thus limiting his or her ability to experiment with new products. The values an individual holds about different aspects of life constantly affect that person's choices. Managers are likely to make better decisions in all situations if they act with an awareness of their reasons and with the knowledge of the extent to which their values direct their decisions.

Dimensions of Work Values

Because work values are the degree of worth a person ascribes to particular aspects or dimensions of work, identifying the dimensions of work helps in understanding work values. Dimensions of work include the opportunities the work offers for a person to satisfy the following needs:

1. To be creative;

2. To earn money;

3. To be independent;

4. To enjoy prestige and status;

5. To serve others;

6. To do academic work;

7. To have a stable and secure job;

8. To enjoy one's colleagues; and

9. To have good working conditions.

Managers who prefer academic work may excel as trainers, whereas managers who want to be creative might be more resourceful in research-and-development departments. Managers who prefer service may do well in public services, whereas managers who prefer independence might better join organizations that offer autonomy and freedom. Knowledge of one's own work values helps a person to choose a job that is congruent with these values and/or to make career decisions that reflect these work values.

The Instrument

The Managerial Work-Values Scale was first developed to measure the work values of medical doctors (Rao, 1976). Subsequently, the instrument was adapted to measure the work values of managers (Pareek, Rao, & Pestonjee, 1981).

The instrument has been further adapted here to focus more specifically on nine work values, using the paired comparison method to measure their relative strengths. The work dimensions included are creativity, economics, independence, status, service, academics, security, collegiality, and work conditions.

Of these dimensions, creativity, independence, service, and academics can be considered as *intrinsic* and the rest as *extrinsic* dimensions of work.

This instrument consists of thirty-six pairs of items. Each item in a pair represents one of the nine work dimensions. The respondent distributes three points between the items in each pair, based on personal preferences for that work dimension.

Because each work dimension is compared with eight other dimensions, the maximum possible score for any work value is 8 x 3, or 24 points. Thus, the score for any work value could range from 0 to 24.

Administration and Scoring

The Managerial Work-Values Scale can be self-administered. When the instrument is used in groups or for training programs, the administrator should have the respondents complete the instrument first, then discuss the concept of work values, and then help the respondents to score their own responses. Each respondent's scores on each item (1a, 1b, 2a, 2b, and so on) should be transferred to the scoring sheet. The score for each work-value dimension can be obtained by adding scores on all eight items of that dimension. The total of all scores on all work values totals 108 points.

Interpretation

Because this scale uses the paired-comparison method and because it is intended to prepare the work-value profile of the respondent, no norms are necessary. On the basis of the scores obtained by a respondent, the corresponding work values can be ranked in descending order of the scores. Thus the highest-scored dimension is the dominant work value of the respondent, and the lowest-scored dimension is the least-valued dimension of work.

Normally, scores between eighteen and twenty-four indicate strongly valued work dimensions. A respondent can have more than one dominant work value. In fact, results for some respondents tend to demonstrate clusters of work values scored as high or low. Explanations for each dimension are provided on the interpretation sheet.

Validity and Reliability

Two types of validity have been established for this scale in its original version: content validity and validation with self-ratings. The scale items were given to eighteen research psychologists working in university departments of psychology and other institutes of education and administration. These psychologists were given the definitions of each of the work values and were asked to classify the scale items into work-value categories. Each item was correctly classified into its work-value category by 89 percent of the experts. Eighty-eight of the original ninety items were correctly classified by seventeen or eighteen of the judges, representing 95 to 100 percent agreement, indicating a high degree of content validity.

Coefficients of correlation were computed between the scores on this scale and self-rankings assigned to the work dimensions by 120 senior medical students as follows:

- Creativity = .86;

- Economics = .64;

- Independence = .39;

- Status = .51;

- Service = .73;

- Academics = .68;

- Security = .65;

- Collegiality = .35; and

- Work conditions = .47.

Given the limitations of self-rankings, these coefficients of correlation indicate a high degree of concurrent validity; all coefficients are significant at the .01 level.

Cluster analysis of the coefficients of correlation obtained on this scale (N = 309 senior medical students from seven medical schools) indicated that the original ten work values fell into four clusters. The first cluster consisted of status, security, economics, and work conditions; the second consisted of creativity and service values; the third consisted of academics and independence values; and the fourth consisted of collegiality and rural. The first cluster consists of extrinsic dimensions, and the next three are more intrinsic in nature.

Test-retest reliability was established by using twenty-six respondents. The test-retest coefficients of correlation obtained were as follows:

- Creativity = .81;

- Economics = .61;

- Independence = .87;

- Status = .81;

- Service = .75;

- Academics = .57;

- Security = .51;

- Collegiality = .57; and

- Work conditions = .29.

Except for work conditions, all coefficients are significant at the .01 level.

Suggested Uses

This instrument has been used in postgraduate programs of management as well as in management-development programs. It is particularly useful as a value-clarification activity, and it can be used in conjunction with any career-development program.

An action plan can be created for helping respondents to bring their careers more closely in line with their work values.

References

Centers, R. (1961). *The psychology of social classes: A study of class consciousness.* New York: Russell and Russell.

Domenichetti, M. (1970). Work-values in adolescence as a function of vocational maturity. *Dissertation Abstracts International, 21,* 4-A.

Douglass, A.A. (1922). Interests of high school seniors. *School & Society, 16,* 79–84.

English, H.B., & English, A.C. (1958). *A comprehensive dictionary of psychological and psychoanalytical terms: A guide to usage.* New York: McKay.

Ginzberg, E. (1951). Towards a theory of occupational choice. *Occupations, 30,* 491–494.

Gray, J.T. (1963). Needs and values in three occupations. *Personnel and Guidance Journal, 42,* 238–244.

Pareek, U., Rao, T.V., & Pestonjee, D.M. (1981). *Behavior processes in organizations.* New Delhi: Oxford & IBH.

Rao, T.V. (1976). *Doctors in making.* Ahmedabad, India: Sahitya Mudranalaya.

Schein, E.H. (1990). *Career anchors: Discovering your real values* (rev. ed.). San Francisco: Pfeiffer.

Thompson, O.E. (1966). Occupational values of high school students. *Personnel and Guidance Journal, 44,* 850–853.

Originally published in *The 1991 Annual: Developing Human Resources.*

Managerial Work–Values Scale

T. Venkateswara Rao

Instructions: This questionnaire consists of pairs of statements related to work values. Read each pair of statements carefully and assess the relative values of the statements for you. Some alternatives may seem equally attractive or unattractive to you; nevertheless, you must choose between the alternatives. For each pair of statements, you have three points to distribute. For example, read the following pair of statements:

I prefer work in which:

_____   1a. I develop new ideas.

_____   1b. I am paid well.

In the blanks preceding items 1a and 1b, you would distribute points according to the explanations that follow.

- If you prefer "a" and do not prefer "b," mark the blanks as follows:

  3   1a.

  0   1b.

- If you have a slight preference for "a" over "b," mark the blanks as follows:

  2   1a.

  1   1b.

- If you have a slight preference for "b" over "a," mark the blanks as follows:

  1   1a.

  2   1b.

- If you prefer "b" and do not prefer "a," mark the blanks as follows:

  0   1a.

  3   1b.

Although you will see the same item more than once, proceed through the questionnaire and treat each pair of statements independently. Be sure to use only the combinations of numbers shown. Remember that first impressions are important.

I prefer work in which:

_____	1a.	I develop new ideas.
_____	1b.	I am paid well.
_____	2a.	I do not need to depend on others for help.
_____	2b.	I have a prestigious position.
_____	3a.	I solve others' problems.
_____	3b.	I have an opportunity to teach others what I know.
_____	4a.	I am paid enough that I can have all the things I want.
_____	4b.	I have a very secure position.
_____	5a.	People respect me.
_____	5b.	I teach and do research.
_____	6a.	I feel a sense of achievement.
_____	6b.	My colleagues and I get along well together.
_____	7a.	I have adequate freedom and independence.
_____	7b.	I solve others' problems.
_____	8a.	I have the opportunity to invent new things.
_____	8b.	I have no fear of losing my job.
_____	9a.	I do things the way I please.
_____	9b.	I do research.
_____	10a.	I can help others to be happy.
_____	10b.	I have all the physical facilities I need.
_____	11a.	I receive large financial rewards.
_____	11b.	I teach.
_____	12a.	I have high status.
_____	12b.	My physical surroundings are good.

I prefer work in which:

_____	13a. I help other people.
_____	13b. I am in no danger of being laid off.
_____	14a. I have a high salary.
_____	14b. I am respected by others.
_____	15a. I am an influential person.
_____	15b. Nothing can threaten my job.
_____	16a. I do unique things.
_____	16b. I do not need to depend on others for help.
_____	17a. I do things almost entirely by myself.
_____	17b. I do not fear losing my job.
_____	18a. I earn an adequate income.
_____	18b. I work in pleasant surroundings.
_____	19a. I solve the problems of others.
_____	19b. I have good associates.
_____	20a. I am respected by others.
_____	20b. My colleagues are people I like.
_____	21a. I invent new things and find new ways of doing things.
_____	21b. My surroundings are pleasant.
_____	22a. I have the freedom to do things the way I want to do them.
_____	22b. I am paid enough money.
_____	23a. I have the satisfaction of helping people.
_____	23b. I have good opportunities for salary increases.
_____	24a. I enjoy the company of my colleagues.
_____	24b. I can save money.

I prefer work in which:

_____   25a. I use my great potential.

_____   25b. I have an influential position.

_____   26a. I do things independently.

_____   26b. My coworkers are my friends.

_____   27a. I can be creative and use my intellect.

_____   27b. I have an opportunity to teach.

_____   28a. I have the freedom to do things the way I want to do them.

_____   28b. My physical surroundings are pleasant.

_____   29a. I serve others.

_____   29b. I have high status.

_____   30a. I am secure in my job at all times.

_____   30b. Superiors and subordinates get along well with each other.

_____   31a. I teach and do research.

_____   31b. I have adequate facilities.

_____   32a. I can feel I did the job well.

_____   32b. I satisfy a number of clients.

_____   33a. My job is secure.

_____   33b. I have adequate physical facilities.

_____   34a. I have a steady job.

_____   34b. I can be an academician.

_____   35a. I get along well with others.

_____   35b. I can explore theories of management.

_____   36a. I like my superiors and subordinates.

_____   36b. I have all the facilities I need.

Managerial Work-Values Scale Scoring Sheet

Instructions: Please transfer your scores from the questionnaire to this scoring sheet. Note that the blanks do not necessarily follow in order. Be sure to transfer your scores to the correct blank. When you have transferred all of your scores, total each of the nine columns.

Creativity	Economics	Independence
1a. _____	1b. _____	2a. _____
6a. _____	4a. _____	7a. _____
8a. _____	11a. _____	9a. _____
16a. _____	14a. _____	16b. _____
21a. _____	18a. _____	17a. _____
25a. _____	22b. _____	22a. _____
27a. _____	23b. _____	26a. _____
32a. _____	24b. _____	28a. _____
Total _____	*Total* _____	*Total* _____

Status	Service	Academics
2b. _____	3a. _____	3b _____ .
5a. _____	7b. _____	5b. _____
12a. _____	10a. _____	9b. _____
14b. _____	13a. _____	11b. _____
15a. _____	19a. _____	27b. _____
20a. _____	23a. _____	31b. _____
25b. _____	29a. _____	34b. _____
29b. _____	32b. _____	35b. _____
Total _____	*Total* _____	*Total* _____

Security	Collegiality	Work Conditions
4b. _____	6b. _____	10b. _____
8b. _____	19b. _____	12b. _____
13b. _____	20b. _____	18b. _____
15b. _____	24a. _____	21b. _____
17b. _____	26b. _____	28b. _____
30a. _____	30b. _____	31b. _____
33a. _____	35a. _____	33b. _____
34a. _____	36a. _____	36b. _____
Total _____	*Total* _____	*Total* _____

Managerial Work–Values Scale Interpretation Sheet

Instructions: Transfer your total score from each of the nine dimensions on the preceding page to the chart below.

Work Value	Score
Creativity	_____
Economics	_____
Independence	_____
Status	_____
Service	_____
Academics	_____
Security	_____
Collegiality	_____
Work Conditions	_____

The higher your score for a particular dimension, the more value you place on that dimension. On the lines below, list your top-ranked work value (the one with the highest score) on line 1, the second-ranked work value on line 2, and so on through line 9.

	Work Value	Score
1.	_____	_____
2.	_____	_____
3.	_____	_____
4.	_____	_____
5.	_____	_____
6.	_____	_____
7.	_____	_____
8.	_____	_____
9.	_____	_____

The following list explains what each dimension indicates:

1. *Creativity* reflects the extent to which the respondent prefers a job that allows opportunities for achievement and creativity, one in which he or she can use original ideas and have a sense of accomplishment.

2. *Economics* correlates to how much a person values the financial or monetary aspects of a job.

3. *Independence* corresponds to the respondent's preference for a job in which he or she can work without interference from others and/or without depending on others in order to do a good job.

4. *Status* relates to a person's values regarding status, prestige, and the need to be respected by others.

5. *Service* refers to the respondent's desire for work in which he or she can be of service to others.

6. *Academics* indicates a preference for teaching and research-related work.

7. *Security* points to the extent to which a person prefers a secure and permanent job as protection from an uncertain future.

8. *Collegiality* shows the degree to which a person likes to have co-workers, superiors, and subordinates who are friendly and easy to work with.

9. *Work Conditions* refers to the person's concerns about physical facilities and other work conditions.

Managerial Work–Values Scale Action Plan

Instructions: Use the data from the Interpretation Sheet to evaluate your current job. The work-value dimensions you value most may or may not be present in your job. The following action plan will allow you to outline ways to get more of the dimensions you value most. List your work values in rank order and then assess the degree to which your current job satisfies these values, using a scale of high, medium, and low satisfaction. As an option, you may choose to retake the Managerial Work-Values Scale, responding to the statements from the frame of reference of your present job. The results of the second survey then can be compared with the results of the first survey and an action plan created from that point.

	My Work Values	Degree to Which My Job Satisfies These Values:
1.	_____	_____
2.	_____	_____
3.	_____	_____
4.	_____	_____
5.	_____	_____
6.	_____	_____
7.	_____	_____
8.	_____	_____
9.	_____	_____

Action Plan

The outline on the next page allows you to look at the degree to which your job satisfies your work values and make action plans for maintaining the dimensions you like and for changing the dimensions you do not like. Perhaps you rated your job as "high" in satisfying most of your key work values; you might use the outline to make a plan for maintaining that satisfaction. If you rated your job as "low" or "medium" in its ability to satisfy certain work values, decide on the changes you desire and fill out the action plan accordingly.

Work Value	Change Desired	Assistance Needed	By Whom	Time Line

5 Locus of Control Inventory

Udai Pareek

Summary

There are two contrasting attitudes regarding the way rewards and outcomes are determined. Some people believe that we can neither predict nor influence significant events, whereas others believe that we can do both. Issues related to prediction and causation of social and personal matters have intrigued philosophers, politicians, behavioral scientists, and psychologists alike.

Review of Research

One of the most popular terms developed for discussing these issues is locus of control. This was suggested by Rotter (1954) and subsequently generated a great deal of research. The concept is based on the extent to which people perceive the contingencies that affect outcomes. Individuals who have low perceptions of such contingencies are said to have an internal locus of control; they believe that their own actions produce outcomes. Those who have high perceptions of contingencies are characterized by an external locus of control; they believe that outcomes are the result of contingencies rather than of their own actions. Internal and external loci of control are represented by the terms internality and externality, respectively. Similarly, people with high internality are called internals; those with high externality, externals.

Internality is related to effectiveness and adjustment. When compared to externals, internals have been reported to be more sensitive to new information, more observant, more likely to attend to cues that help resolve uncertainties (Lefcourt & Wine, 1969), and more prone to both intentional and incidental learning (Wolk & DuCette, 1984). The association of internality with various aspects of learning (for example, curiosity, eagerness to obtain information, awareness of and desire to understand situations and their contexts, and the ability to process the available information) seems to make good sense. For example, in order to influence or control outcomes, the person with an internal approach must acquire as much information as possible and then process that information as quickly as possible. Evidence supports the assumption that an internal locus of control leads to academic achievement (Crandall, Katkovsky, & Crandall, 1965; Harrison, 1968; Lessing, 1969).

Some studies have also shown a high and positive correlation between internality and perseverance, which is characterized by extra time spent on work (Franklin, 1963), continued involvement in difficult and complex tasks, and willingness to defer gratification (Mischel, 1966). Lefcourt (1976) summarized the research on the relationship between internality and deferred gratification. Involvement in long-term goals requires deferment of gratification; and persistence in effort requires undivided attention, which is not possible unless the temptation of immediate gratification is resisted. Because internals believe that their efforts lead to favorable outcomes, they can rely on their own understanding and predictability. In contrast, externals—perceiving a lack of personal predictability and fearing that unforeseen external factors will affect outcomes—may find it more attractive to seek immediate gratification than to try to achieve distant goals.

Internality was found to be an important characteristic of people with high achievement motivation (McClelland, 1961). It was further reported that internal locus of control generates moderate or calculated risk taking, and one study indicated that the correlation between achievement motivation and preference for moderate risk was significant and positive among internals but almost zero among externals (Wolk & DuCette, 1984).

Internality seems to be a cornerstone of the process of valuing, which includes awareness of ones own values, willingness to declare those values in public, and adherence to them and the behavior associated with them in spite of outside pressures. This process of developing ethical norms and using those norms even in periods of crisis has also been called inner-direction—the state of being directed by ones own, internalized standards rather than merely conforming to outside expectations, norms, or pressures.

Some studies have indicated a significant relationship between internality and morality, which leads to resistance of temptation (Johnson, Ackerman, Frank, & Fionda, 1968), helping others (Midlarski, 1971), and low Machiavellianism (Miller & Minton, 1969). Apparently internality is important in the development of standards for judging ones own behavior. Both personal autonomy and responsibility are involved in the process of valuing, which is necessary for the development of a healthy and proactive society.

One study (Mitchell, Smyser, & Wood, 1975) uncovered relationships between internality and certain organizational attitudes and behaviors. For example, internals experienced greater job satisfaction than externals did. Internals also preferred a participatory management style, whereas externals preferred a directive style. Further comparisons indicated that internals believed that working hard was more likely to lead to rewards and that they had more control over the ways they worked. Supervisors with an internal orientation believed that persuasive power was the most productive approach, whereas their external counterparts relied on coercive power. Furthermore, the use of rewards, respect, and expertise was seen by internally focused supervisors as the most effective way to influence subordinates; those with an external orientation saw coercion and their formal positions as most effective.

The sum of these findings indicates that internality plays an important role in human development and meaningful living. Nevertheless, the internal pays a price. Those who perceive their own abilities and actions as solely responsible for their failures are likely to experience stress and may become self punitive. Attribution of failure or negative conditions to external factors can help people to cope with adverse experiences more effectively, to perceive social reality in the proper perspective, to fight injustice, and to rectify undesirable situations.

Rotter (1966) developed the first instrument to measure internality and externality. Although Rotter's instrument has been used extensively in research and training, his unitary concept of internality has been challenged. On the basis of factor analysis of the responses on Rotter's instrument, several studies found multidimensionality in Rotter's instrument, which seemed to contain items related to control ideology, personal control, system modifiability, and race ideology (Gurin et al., 1969; Guttentag, 1972; McDonald & Tseng, 1971; Minton, 1972; Mirels, 1970). Levenson (1972) questioned putting three external factors (chance, fate, and powerful others) together. Levenson also proposed a new scale to measure internality and externality; instead of viewing these elements along a continuum, Levenson proposed to measure both internality (I) and externality (E). Furthermore, Levenson proposed two subscales for externality: one to measure perceived influence of chance (EC) and the other to measure perceived influence of powerful others (EO). Gutkin, Robbins, and Andrews (1985) reported factor analysis results of a health locus-of-control scale that revealed internal and external factors.

The Instrument

Although Levenson's scale has been used in many organizational studies, the instrument was not developed specifically for organizations. Therefore, Levenson's (1972) concept of locus of control was used to develop the Locus of Control Inventory, which was designed to measure internality and externality in the organizational context. An earlier version of this instrument contained Levenson's six-point scoring system and twenty-four items (parallel to Levenson's instrument). The current five-point system appears to be a superior measure; and the thirty-item version contains ten statements each for internality (I), externality-others (EO), and externality-chance (EC).

A locus-of-control orientation is reflected in the way a person views what happens in an organization; that is, how much control the person believes that he or she has in important organizational matters, how much control the person believes is held by certain others, and to what degree the person believes events are a matter of luck. The Locus of Control Inventory links the locus of control to seven areas:

1. General

2. Success or Effectiveness

3. Influence

4. Acceptability

5. Career

6. Advancement

7. Rewards

Using the Instrument

The Locus of Control Inventory can be used for both research and training purposes in human resource development, organization development, or training packages. It was developed, however, primarily for training purposes.

Scoring

Numbers that respondents have assigned to the instrument items are transferred to the scoring sheet and a total is computed for each column. Scores will range from zero to forty for each of the three columns (Internality, Externality-Other, and Externality-Chance).

Norms

Based on data from more than three hundred managers, mean and standard deviation (SD) values are presented in Table 1. High and low scores were calculated by adding or subtracting one-half SD value to or from the mean, respectively. Similarly, very high and very low scores were obtained by adding or subtracting one SD value to or from the mean. Such norms can be worked out for specific organizations for interpretation purposes.

Table 1. Mean and Standard-Deviation Values

	Mean	SD	Very High	High	Low	Very Low
I	25	8	33	29	21	17
EO	25	9	34	29.5	20.5	16
EC	19	9	28	23.5	14.5	10

Reliability

Levenson (1972) reported moderately high internal consistency, with Kuder-Richardson reliabilities (coefficient alpha) of .64, .77, and .78 and split-half reliabilities of .62, .66, and .64 for I, EO, and EC, respectively. Retest reliability for a one-week period for the three subscales were .64, .74, and .78, respectively. Reliabilities of the Levenson instrument were also moderately high in another study (Sen, 1982) in India.

Split-half reliability coefficients for the earlier version of the Locus of Control Inventory were .43, .45, and .55, and even-odd reliability coefficients were .41, .48, and .54 for I, EO, and EC subscales, respectively. The current version has similar reliability coefficients.

Validity

There was a high correlation (.89) between Levenson's instrument and the Locus of Control Inventory in a sample of twenty-six bankers. This finding indicates the validity of the Locus of Control Inventory. Using Levenson's scale, Surti (1982) reported a highly significant coefficient of correlation (.70) between EO and EC in a sample of 360 professional women and correlation values of .00 and .06 between I and EO and between I and EC, respectively. This finding shows the validity of Levenson's two-factor concept.

Twenty-seven managers responded to the Locus of Control Inventory, to Rotter's instrument of locus of control and an adaptation of that instrument (Rotter, 1966), and to Valecha's (1988) adaptation of Rotter's instrument. The data indicated acceptable validity of the Locus of Control Inventory, and other data have established construct validity for the instrument.

Correlates of Internality and Externality

In a study of four hundred bankers using Levenson's instrument, Sen (1982) found a high positive correlation (significant at the .001 level) between internality and role efficacy (see Pareek, 1980a and 1980b, for the concept) and a negative correlation (significant at the .01 level) between I and both EO and EC. Surti (1982) reported similar results when 320 professional women completed the instrument.

There is some evidence that externals, especially those who believe things are controlled by powerful others, experience higher role stress. When forty women entrepreneurs completed the Levenson instrument, Surti (1982) found positive correlation (significant at the .01 level) between EO and the following role stresses: interrole distance, role overload, result inadequacy, resource inadequacy, role inadequacy, and total entrepreneurial role stress. See Pareek (1990a) for the concept of entrepreneurial role stress. There were significant positive correlation (at the .01 level) between EC and inter-role distance and between EC and role overload. Surti also reported positive and negative correlations, respectively, between EC and avoidance style and between EC and approach styles (both significant at the .05 level). See Pareek (1987) for the concept of coping styles.

Using the Motivational Analysis of Organizations—Behavior (Pareek, 1986), Sen (1982) found positive correlations between internality and operational effectiveness of five motives. The levels of significance are shown in parentheses: achievement (.001), influence (.003), extension (.05), affiliation (.01), and dependence (.001). He also reported significant negative correlations (most of them significant at the .001 level) with both EO and EC and operational effectiveness of all six motives. This indicates that internals use the motivational behavior more effectively in organizations than externals do.

Using the Locus of Control Inventory with 212 managers in engineering firms, Keshote (1989) found negative correlations (significant at the .05 level) between both EO and EC and interpersonal trust, measured by the Rotter (1967) scale. Externals seem to have low interpersonal trust.

Keshote, using the Locus of Control Inventory and the Pareek (1990b) instrument to measure perception of and the need for coercive and persuasive power, found positive correlation (significant at the .01 level) between I and perception of having persuasive power and between EO and perception of having coercive and persuasive power. The EC scores had positive correlation (significant at the .05 level) with perception of having persuasive bases of power. These correlations indicate that internal managers use more persuasive bases of power, EO managers use more coercive bases, EC managers use less persuasive bases, and externals of both types want more coercive power.

When using the Locus of Control Inventory and an instrument to measure styles of managing conflict (Pareek, 1982a, 1983), Keshote found significant positive correlation between negotiation style and internality. Externals of both types showed preference for other styles. Regarding interpersonal styles (Pareek, 1984), EO managers were found to have lower operating effectiveness on task orientation; and EC managers, lower operating effectiveness on regulating, task-innovative, and confronting styles.

In summary, internal managers tend to have higher role efficacy, to experience less role stress, to use problem-solving approaches to stress and conflict, to use their motivational behavior more effectively, and to use more persuasive bases of power in working with their employees. Externals seem to do the opposite and to have lower interpersonal trust. Externals want more coercive power; EOs use more coercive bases of power while working with their employees, and ECs useless persuasive bases.

Development of Internality

Organizational climate and environments seem to influence the development of internality. Baumgartel, Rajan, and Newman (1985), using four indices of organizational environment (freedom-growth, human relations, performance pressure, and person benefit) with a group of 3,200 student respondents (78 percent men, 22 percent women) in a center for postgraduate management education in India, found clear evidence of the influence of organizational environments on locus of control as measured by the Levenson instrument. However, this effect was more striking for female than for male postgraduates. Regression analysis (based on data from 320 professional women) that used role efficacy as a variable indicated that out of the fourteen variables that finally emerged in the stepwise regression, organizational climate alone explained about 34 percent of the variance, showing a very large effect on role efficacy (Surti, 1982).

Administering the Instrument

The respondents complete the instrument by evaluating each statement according to a five-point scale ranging from zero (seldom or never agree) to five (strongly agree). The responses must be transferred to the scoring sheet, which presents three scores (internality, externality-others, and externality-chance).

If possible, the scoring sheets should be completed in advance, so that the mean and standard deviation can be calculated prior to a discussion of the scores. Norms can be created, as demonstrated in Table 1.

The facilitator leads a discussion based on the concepts and findings included in this article. Respondents are asked to predict their own levels (high, medium, or low) of the three dimensions. In very open groups, each member of a trio can estimate the levels of the other two trio members.

Completed scoring sheets are distributed to the respondents, as well as copies of the interpretation sheet. Trios are formed to discuss discrepancies between actual scores and both self-predicted and other-assessed levels. The discussions should be based on observed behavior.

The facilitator presents implications of internality for employee effectiveness and leads a discussion on how to increase internality and reduce externality. The discussion should include which organizational practices promote I, EO, and EC. Table 2 shows which of the thirty items in the Locus of Control Inventory are related to each of the seven areas addressed by the instrument.

Table 2. Distribution of Items in Locus of Control Inventory

	Internality	Externality (Others)	Externality (Chance)
General	1, 27	4, 30	7, 24
Success or Effectiveness	3, 10, 16	6, 19, 22	9, 13, 21
Influence	28	17	26
Acceptability	25	29	18
Career	2	5	8
Advancement	23	11	14
Rewards	20	15	12

Another important discussion would deal with how to increase internality among the employees (Pareek, 1982b). Material that would help the facilitator lead this discussion includes Baumgartel et al. (1985), Richard (1975), Mehta (1968), and DeCharms (1976).

References

Baumgartel, H.J., Rajan, P.S.S., & Newman, J. (1985). Educational environments and attributions of causality: Some exploratory research findings. *Quality of Work Life, 2*(56), 309–328.

Crandall, V.C., Katkovsky, W., & Crandall, W.J. (1965). Children's beliefs in their control of reinforcements in intellectual academic achievement behaviors. *Child Development, 36*, 91–109.

DeCharms, R. (1976). *Enhancing motivation: Change in the classroom.* New York: Irvington.

Franklin, R.D. (1963). Youths expectancies about internal versus external control of reinforcement related to N variable. *Dissertation Abstracts, 24*, 1684. (University Microfilms No. 63–6493)

Gurin, P., Gurin, G., Lao, R., & Beattie, M. (1969). Internal-external control in the motivational dynamics of Negro youth. *Journal of Social Issues, 25*(3), 29–53.

Gutkin, J., Robbins, R., & Andrews, L. (1985). The health locus of control scales: Psychometric properties. *Educational and Psychological Measurement, 45*(2), 407–110.

Guttentag, M. (1972). *Locus of control and achievement in minority middle school children.* Paper presented at the meeting of the Eastern Psychological Association, Boston, MA.

Harrison, F.I. (1968). Relationship between home background, school success, and adolescent attitudes. *Merrill Palmer Quarterly of Behavior and Development, 14,* 331–344.

Johnson, R.C., Ackerman, J.M., Frank, H., & Fionda, A.J. (1968). Resistance to temptation and guilt following yielding and psychotherapy. *Journal of Consulting and Clinical Psychology, 32,* 169–175.

Keshote, K.K. (1989). *Personnel and organizational correlates of conflict management styles.* Unpublished doctoral dissertation, University of Gujarat, India.

Lefcourt, H.M. (1976). *Locus of control: Current trends in theory and research.* Hillsdale, NJ: Lawrence Earlbaum.

Lefcourt, H.M., & Wine, J. (1969). Internal versus external control of reinforcement and the development of attention in experimental situations. *Canadian Journal of Behavioral Science, 1,* 167–181.

Lessing, E.E. (1969). Racial differences in indices of ego functioning relevant to academic achievement. *Journal of Genetic Psychology, 115,* 153–167.

Levenson, H. (1972). *Distinctions within the concept of internal-external control: Development of a new scale.* Paper presented at the meeting of the American Psychological Association, Hawaii.

McClelland, D.E. (1961). *The achieving society.* Princeton, NJ: Van Nostrand.

McDonald, A.P., & Tseng, M.S. (1971). *Dimension of internal vs. external control revisited: Toward expectancy.* Unpublished paper, West Virginia University.

Mehta, P. (1968). *Increasing achievement motive in high school boys.* New Delhi: National Council of Education Research and Training.

Midlarski, E. (1971). Aiding under stress: The effects of competence, dependency, visibility, and fatalism. *Journal of Personality, 39,* 132–149.

Miller, A.G., & Minton, H.L. (1969). Machiavellianism, internal-external control and the violation of experimental instructions. *Psychological Record, 19,* 369–380.

Minton, H.L. (1972). *Internal-external control and the distinction between personal control and system modifiability.* Paper presented at the meeting of the Midwestern Psychological Association, Cleveland, OH. 34, 226–228.

Mirels, H. (1970). Dimensions of internal vs. external control. *Journal of Consulting and Clinical Psychology, 34,* 226–228.

Mischel, W. (1966). Theory and research on the antecedents of self-imposed delay of reward. In B.A. Maher (Ed.), *Progress in experimental personality research* (Vol. 3). New York: Academic Press.

Mitchell, T.R., Smyser, C.M., & Wood, S.E. (1975). Locus of control: Supervision and work satisfaction. *Academy of Management Journal, 18*(3), 623–631.

Pareek, U. (1980a). Dimensions of role efficacy. In J.W. Pfeiffer & J.E. Jones (Eds.), *The 1980 annual* (pp. 143–145). San Francisco: Pfeiffer.

Pareek, U. (1980b). Role efficacy scale. In J.W. Pfeiffer & J.E. Jones (Eds.), *The 1980 annual* (pp. 100–105). San Francisco: Pfeiffer.

Pareek, U. (1982a). *Conflict and collaboration in organizations.* New Delhi: Oxford & IBH.

Pareek, U. (1982b). Internal and external control. In J.W. Pfeiffer & L.D. Goodstein (Eds.), *The 1982 annual* (pp. 174–181). San Francisco: Pfeiffer.

Pareek, U. (1983). Preventing and resolving conflicts. In L.D. Goodstein & J.W. Pfeiffer (Eds.), *The 1983 annual* (pp. 195–203). San Francisco: Pfeiffer.

Pareek, U. (1984). Interpersonal styles: The SPIRO instrument. In J.W. Pfeiffer & L.D. Goodstein (Eds.), *The 1984 annual* (pp. 119–130). San Francisco: Pfeiffer.

Pareek, U. (1986). Motivational analysis of organizations—behavior (MAOB). In J.W. Pfeiffer & L.D. Goodstein (Eds.), *The 1986 annual* (pp. 121–133). San Francisco: Pfeiffer.

Pareek, U. (1987). Role pics: Measuring strategies of coping with stress. In J.W. Pfeiffer (Ed.), *The 1987 annual* (pp. 91–107). San Francisco: Pfeiffer.

Pareek, U. (1989). Motivational analysis of organizations—climate (MAOC). In J.W. Pfeiffer (Ed.), *The 1989 annual* (pp. 161–180). San Francisco: Pfeiffer.

Pareek, U. (1990a). *Entrepreneurial role stress scale.* Unpublished manuscript.

Pareek, U. (1990b). *Persuasive and coercive power scale.* Unpublished manuscript.

Reichard, B.D. (1975). *The effect of a management training workshop altering locus of control.* Unpublished doctoral dissertation, University of Maryland.

Rotter, J.B. (1954). *Social learning and clinical psychology.* Englewood Cliffs, NJ: Prentice-Hall.

Rotter, J.B. (1966). Generalized expectancies for internal versus external control of reinforcement. *Psychological Monographs, 80*(1, Whole No. 609).

Rotter, J.B. (1967). A new scale for the measurement of interpersonal trust. *Journal of Personality, 35,* 651–665.

Sen, P.C. (1982). *Personal and organizational correlates of role stress and coping strategies in some public sector banks.* Unpublished doctoral dissertation, University of Gujarat, India.

Surti, K. (1982). *Some psychological correlates of role stress and coping styles in working women.* Unpublished doctoral dissertation, University of Gujarat, India.

Valecha, G. (1988). *A locus of control scale.* Unpublished manuscript.

Wolk, S., & DuCette, J. (1984). Intentional performances and incidental learning as a function of personality and task direction. *Journal of Personality and Social Psychology, 29,* 90–101.

Originally published in *The 1992 Annual: Developing Human Resources.*

Locus of Control Inventory[1]

Udai Pareek

Instructions: The following thirty statements represent employees attitudes toward their work in an organization. Read each statement carefully; then indicate the extent to which you agree with it by circling the appropriate number. There are no right or wrong choices; the one that is right for you is the correct answer. If the responses do not adequately indicate your own opinion, use the number closest to the way you feel. Use the following key:

Strongly Agree 4	Generally Agree 3	Agree Somewhat 2	Agree Only Slightly 1	Seldom or Never Agree 0

1. I determine what matters to me in the organization.

    4   3   2   1   0

2. The course of my career depends on me.

    4   3   2   1   0

3. My success or failure depends on the amount of effort I exert.

    4   3   2   1   0

4. The people who are important control matters in this organization.

    4   3   2   1   0

5. My career depends on my seniors.

    4   3   2   1   0

6. My effectiveness in this organization is determined by senior people.

    4   3   2   1   0

7. The organization a person joins or the job he or she takes is an accidental occurrence.

    4   3   2   1   0

8. A persons career is a matter of chance.

    4   3   2   1   0

9. A persons success depends on the breaks or chances he or she receives.

    4   3   2   1   0

10. Successful completion of my assignments is due to my detailed planning and hard work.

    4   3   2   1   0

[1]This instrument is based on the multidimensional locus of control scales developed by Hanna Levenson ("Differentiating Among Internality, Powerful Others and Chance,") in *Research with the Locus of Control Construct* (edited by H. Lefcourt), Academic Press, NY, 1981, pp. 15–63. The Locus of Control Inventory, written by Udai Pareek, applies these concepts to the organizational environment and is used here with the permission of Hanna Levenson.

Strongly Agree	Generally Agree	Agree Somewhat	Agree Only Slightly	Seldom or Never Agree
4	3	2	1	0

11. Being liked by seniors or making good impressions on them influences promotion decisions.　　　　4　3　2　1　0

12. Receiving rewards in the organization is a matter of luck.　　　　4　3　2　1　0

13. The success of my plans is a matter of luck.　　　　4　3　2　1　0

14. Receiving a promotion depends on being in the right place at the right time.　　　　4　3　2　1　0

15. Preferences of seniors determine who will be rewarded in this organization.　　　　4　3　2　1　0

16. My success depends on my competence and hard work.　　　　4　3　2　1　0

17. How much I am liked in the organization depends on my seniors.　　　　4　3　2　1　0

18. Getting people in this organization to listen to me is a matter of luck.　　　　4　3　2　1　0

19. If my seniors do not like me, I will not succeed in this organization.　　　　4　3　2　1　0

20. The way I work determines whether or not I receive rewards.　　　　4　3　2　1　0

21. My success or failure in this organization is a matter of luck.　　　　4　3　2　1　0

22. My success or failure depends on those who work with me.　　　　4　3　2　1　0

23. Any promotion I receive in this organization will be due to my ability and effort.　　　　4　3　2　1　0

24. Most things in this organization are beyond the control of the people who work here.　　　　4　3　2　1　0

Strongly Agree	Generally Agree	Agree Somewhat	Agree Only Slightly	Seldom or Never Agree
4	3	2	1	0

25. The quality of my work influences decisions on my suggestions in this organization.   4   3   2   1   0

26. The reason I am acceptable to others in my organization is a matter of luck.   4   3   2   1   0

27. I determine what happens to me in the organization.   4   3   2   1   0

28. The degree to which I am acceptable to others in this organization depends on my behavior with them.   4   3   2   1   0

29. My ideas are accepted if l make them fit with the desires of my seniors.   4   3   2   1   0

30. Pressure groups in this organization are more powerful than individual employees are, and they control more things than individuals do.   4   3   2   1   0

Locus of Control Inventory Scoring Sheet

Instructions: The numbers below correspond to the numbers of the items in the Locus of Control Inventory. Please transfer the numbers you assigned by writing them in the appropriate blanks below. Then total the numbers you transferred to each column.

Item Number	Number You Assigned	Item Number	Number You Assigned	Item Number	Number You Assigned
1	_____	4	_____	7	_____
2	_____	5	_____	8	_____
3	_____	6	_____	9	_____
10	_____	11	_____	12	_____
16	_____	15	_____	13	_____
20	_____	17	_____	14	_____
23	_____	19	_____	18	_____
25	_____	22	_____	21	_____
27	_____	29	_____	24	_____
28	_____	30	_____	26	_____
Column Total	_____	Column Total	_____	Column Total	_____
	I		**EO**		**EC**

Locus of Control Inventory Interpretation Sheet

The following information will be helpful in interpreting your scores. These scores represent the way you view what happens in your organization; therefore, no score has to be permanent. If you are not happy with the way you have marked the answers, you may create an action plan that will help to change the way you look at things. Select the column with the highest total. Then read the section below that pertains to that column. Next read the section pertaining to your lowest total. Then read the remaining section. The paragraph on ratios may also be helpful.

I (Internal)

A person with an internal orientation believes that his or her future is controlled from within. A total I score of 33 or above indicates a very high internality tendency. It represents self-confidence in a persons ability to control what happens to him or her in an organization. However, this person may sometimes be unrealistic in assessing difficulties and may ascribe personal failure to situations over which he or she had no control.

A score from 29 to 32 shows high trust in ones ability and effort and is likely to lead to effective use of these. A score of 18 to 21 indicates that the individual lacks such self-trust and needs to examine his or her strengths by using feedback from others.

A low score (17 or less) in this area represents little self-confidence and could hinder a person from utilizing his or her potential.

EO (External-Others)

A person with an external-others orientation believes that his or her future is controlled by powerful others. Very high EO scores (30 or higher) indicate dysfunctional dependence on significant other people for achieving ones goals. A score of 21 to 29 reflects a realistic dependence on supervisors, peers, and subordinates. A score of 17 to 20 shows an independence orientation, and a score below 17 indicates counter-dependence.

EC (External-Chance)

A person with an external-chance orientation believes that his or her future is controlled primarily by luck or chance. To an extent, the lower the EC score, the better, because a person with a low EC orientation is more likely to utilize another potential in trying to achieve goals. However, a score of 10 or below may reflect problems in coping with frustrations when unforeseen factors prevent achievement of goals.

Ratios of Scores

The ratio of your I and E scores can also provide information about your orientation. If your I/total E ratio is more than one (that is, if your I score is greater than the total of your E scores), you have an internal orientation. If your EO ratio is more than one, you have more internality than externality-other. If your I/EC ratio is greater than one, you are more internal than external chance. Ratios greater than one are beneficial, and action plans can be created to change ratios that are lower than desired.

6 Patterns of Effective Supervisory Behavior

Henry P. Sims, Jr.

Summary

The purpose of the Supervisory Behavior Questionnaire is to identify patterns of leader behavior and to describe them in terms of an operant theory of leadership (Mawhinney & Ford, 1977; Scott, 1977; Sims, 1977). This introduction to the instrument will present a conceptual approach to leadership theory that is different from the traditional approaches of consideration/initiating structure, managerial grid, and/or contingency theory.

Theory Underlying the Instrument

The instrument assumes a theory of leadership based on operant or reinforcement principles (Skinner, 1969). According to this theory, behavior within organizations is controlled by "contingencies of reinforcement." Figure 1 represents a positive reinforcement contingency, which consists of three parts. The first part is a discriminative stimulus (SD), which is an environmental cue that provides an individual with information about how behavior will be reinforced. A discriminative stimulus is environmental information that comes before individual behavior. The second part is the response or behavior of the individual. The behavior is followed by the administration of a reinforcer. A positive reinforcer (the third part) is a reward that is administered following a desired behavior; it has the effect of increasing the frequency of the behavior.

Reinforcers are frequently thought of as material benefits, that is, pay or some extrinsic incentive. In the supervisor-subordinate relationship, however, interpersonal reinforcers frequently are more potent (at least in the short term). Compliments or statements of recognition that are contingent on desirable behavior at work can have reinforcing effects that serve to increase future performance.

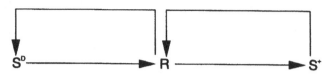

S^D = discriminative stimulus
R = response behavior
S^+ = positive consequence

Figure 1. Contingency of Positive Reinforcement

Another type of reinforcement contingency is punishment[1]—the administration of an aversive stimulus contingent on a specific response. In leadership practice, punishment typically is used to decrease the frequency of an undesirable behavior. In work situations, leaders typically use oral reprimands or undesirable job assignments in an attempt to eliminate behavior that is undesirable or detrimental to job performance.

Both positive reinforcement and punishment are actions of the leader that follow subordinate behavior. Obviously, the behavior of the leader also can have a substantial impact on the subordinates successive performance. Frequently, the type of behavior that occurs before subordinate behavior can be considered a discriminative stimulus (SD)—a cue that informs the subordinate of what behavior is expected in order to be reinforced. An example of this is a goal or objective.

These three types of leader behavior (positive reinforcement, punishment, and discriminative stimulus or goal specification) are basic elements in a leaders behavioral repertoire. Although these classes of behavior are not exhaustive, they form the key foci for any operant-based theory of leadership.

Purpose of the Instrument

The Supervisory Behavior Questionnaire[2] was developed for training purposes. The instrument is designed to direct the participants attention to three types of leader behavior: goal specification behavior (scale A), positive reward behavior (scale B), and punitive reward behavior (scale C).

The instrument is self-scored, and most participants can determine their own scores and derive a profile of the three scores with little or no assistance.

---

[1]"Punishment" is technically distinct from "negative reinforcement." which involves the *removal* of an aversive stimulus in order to *increase* a target behavior. However, punishment and negative reinforcement are both aversive control techniques.
[2]The roots of this instrument can be traced to a leadership instrument originated by Ronald Johnson, William E. Scott, and Joseph Reitz, and originally published in Johnson (1973). Other research using similar scales has been reported by Greene (1975), Reitz (1971), Sims (1977), and Sims and Szilagyi (1975). In general, these scales have been found to possess acceptable construct validity and reliability. People wishing to use these scales for research should *not* use the version reported here, which is intended to be a classroom exercise, but should consult the sources listed above.

Procedure for Administering the Instrument

Each participant is instructed to think about a job that he or she now holds or has held in the past (and, more specifically, about the supervisor on that job) and then to complete the questionnaire. Participants may need to be reminded that the questions refer to the supervisor.

After completing the questionnaire, the participants are directed to complete the self-scoring procedure and then to draw a profile of the scores of all three scales on the graph.

Debriefing and Discussion

The facilitator begins the debriefing by initiating a process to name the three scales and, after this is done, reads the descriptive name most often used to designate the characteristics that were measured. These are supervisory goals and expectations (scale A), supervisory positive reward behavior (scale B), and supervisory punitive behavior (scale C).

A few volunteers go to the newsprint flip chart and write the names of the jobs they described and their scores for scales A, B, and C, for both the most effective and least effective supervisors. The facilitator directs each participant to briefly describe the aspects of the supervisor that prompted the scores reported (e.g., "He tells me what I will be doing next"). The facilitator then attempts to develop patterns of differentiation of scores between highly effective and highly ineffective supervisors and between conditions leading to highly satisfied and highly unsatisfied workers. The facilitator can calculate mean scores for both the most effective and the least effective supervisors.

Finally, the facilitator presents a lecturette on the theory underlying the instrument. Material from the literature of supervisory development can be assigned as backup reading or used as handouts (Hammer, 1974; Jablonsky & DeVries, 1972; Luthans & Kreitner, 1975; Mawhinney, 1975; Mawhinney & Ford, 1977; Nord, 1969; Scott, 1977; Sims, 1977; Skinner, 1969).

Variation

An alternative way to use the instrument is to direct the participants to provide two scores for each question: one for the supervisor and the second for how the participant would behave as a supervisor. This variation provides a self-description component.

Value of the Instrument

This instrument provides an experiential introduction to leadership theory and allows the participants to examine leadership behaviors from the perspective of their own past experiences. This personal aspect induces substantially greater interest and involvement and longer retention of the underlying theory. In addition, several opportunities exist during the debriefing phase to describe the underlying theoretical principles in terms of actual past behaviors. If accompanied by significant exposure to principles of behavior modification (Brown & Presbie, 1976; Luthans & KreitneMr, 1975), the instrument offers a unique opportunity to demonstrate how leadership theory can be put into practice.

References

Brown, P.L., & Presbie, R.J. (1976). *Behavior modification in business, industry, and government*. New Paltz, NY: Behavior Improvement Associates.

Greene, C. (1975). *Contingent relationships between instrumental leader behavior and subordinate satisfaction and performance*. Proceedings of the American Institute for Decision Sciences.

Hammer, W.C. (1974). Reinforcement theory and contingency management in organization settings. In H.L. Tosi & W.C. Hamner (Eds.), *Organization behavior and management: A contingency approach*. Chicago: St. Clair Press.

Jablonsky, S.F., & DeVries, D.L. (1972). Operant conditioning principles extrapolated to the theory of management. *Organizational Behavior and Human Performance, 7*, 340–358.

Johnson, R.D. (1973). *An investigation of the interaction effects of ability and motivational variables on task performance*. Unpublished doctoral dissertation, Indiana University.

Luthans, F., & Kreitner, R. (1975). *Organizational behavior modification*. Glenview, IL: Scott, Foresman.

Mawhinney, T.C. (1975). Operant terms and concepts in the description of individual work behavior: Some problems of interpretation, application, and evaluation. *Journal of Applied Psychology, 60*, 704–714.

Mawhinney, T.C., & Ford, J.C. (1977). The path goal theory of leader effectiveness: An operant interpretation. *Academy of Management Review, 2*, 398–411.

Nord, W.R. (1969). Beyond the teaching machine: The neglected area of operant conditioning in the theory and practice of management. *Organizational Behavior and Human Performance, 4*, 375–401.

Reitz, H.J. (1971). *Managerial attitudes and perceived contingencies between performance and organizational response*. Proceedings of the 31st Annual Meeting of the Academy of Management, 227–238.

Scott, W.G. (1977). Leadership: A functional analysis. In J.G. Hunt & L. Larson (Eds.),

Leadership: The cutting edge. Carbondale, IL: Southern Illinois University Press.

Sims, H.P. (1977). The leader as a manager of reinforcement contingencies: An empirical example and a model. In J.G. Hunt & L. Larson (Eds.), *Leadership: The cutting edge.* Carbondale, IL: Southern Illinois University Press.

Sims, H.P., & Szilagyi, A.D. (1975). Leader reward behavior and subordinate satisfaction and performance. *Organizational Behavior and Human Performance, 14,* 426–438.

Skinner, B.F. (1969). *The contingencies of reinforcement: A theoretical analysis.* New York: Appleton-Century-Crofts.

Originally published in *The 1981 Annual Handbook for Faciliatators, Trainers, and Consultants.*

Supervisory Behavior Questionnaire

Henry P. Sims, Jr.

Instructions: This questionnaire is part of an activity designed to explore supervisory behaviors. It is not a test; there are no right or wrong answers.

Think about supervisors (managers) you have known or know now, and then select the most effective supervisor and the least effective supervisor (effective is defined as "being able to substantially influence the effort and performance of subordinates").

Read each of the following statements carefully. For the most effective supervisor, place an X over the number indicating how true or how untrue you believe the statement to be. For the least effective supervisor, place a circle around the number indicating how true you believe the statement to be.

Definitely Not True = 1	Slightly Not True = 3	Slightly True = 5	Definitely True = 7
Not True = 2	Uncertain = 4	True = 6	

Most effective . . . X

Least effective . . . O

1. My supervisor would compliment me if I did outstanding work.   1   2   3   4   5   6   7

2. My supervisor maintains definite standards of performance.   1   2   3   4   5   6   7

3. My supervisor would reprimand me if my work were consistently below standards.   1   2   3   4   5   6   7

4. My supervisor defines clear goals and objectives for my job.   1   2   3   4   5   6   7

5. My supervisor would give me special recognition if my work performance were especially good.   1   2   3   4   5   6   7

6. My supervisor would "get on me" if my work were not as good as he or she thought it should be.   1   2   3   4   5   6   7

Definitely Not True = 1   Slightly Not True = 3   Slightly True = 5   Definitely True = 7
         Not True = 2   Uncertain = 4   True = 6

7. My supervisor would tell me if my work
    were outstanding.   1   2   3   4   5   6   7

8. My supervisor establishes clear perfor-
    mance guidelines.   1   2   3   4   5   6   7

9. My supervisor would reprimand me
    if I were not making progress in my work. 1   2   3   4   5   6   7

Supervisory Behavior Questionnaire Scoring Sheet

Instructions: For each of the three scales (A, B, and C), compute a total score by summing the answers to the appropriate questions and then subtracting the number 12. Compute a score for both the most effective and the least effective supervisors.

Question Number	Most Effective	Least Effective	Question Number	Most Effective	Least Effective	Question Number	Most Effective	Least Effective
2.	+( )	+( )	1.	+( )	+( )	3.	+( )	+( )
4.	+( )	+( )	5.	+( )	+( )	6.	+( )	+( )
8.	+( )	+( )	7.	+( )	+( )	9.	+( )	+( )
Subtotal	( )	( )	Subtotal	( )	( )	Subtotal	( )	( )
	−12	−12		−12	−12		−12	−12
Total Score	___	___	Total Score	___	___	Total Score	___	___
	A	A		B	B		C	C

Next, on the following graph, write a large "X" to indicate the total score for scales A, B, and C for the most effective supervisor. Use a large "O" to indicate the scores for the least effective supervisor.

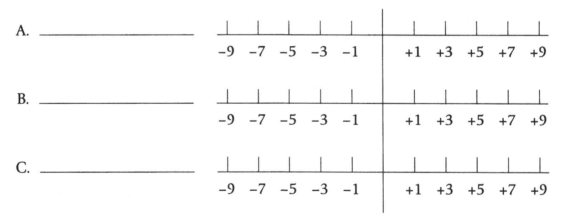

A. _____
   −9 −7 −5 −3 −1 | +1 +3 +5 +7 +9

B. _____
   −9 −7 −5 −3 −1 | +1 +3 +5 +7 +9

C. _____
   −9 −7 −5 −3 −1 | +1 +3 +5 +7 +9

7 Inventory of Barriers to Creative Thought and Innovative Action

Lorna P. Martin

Summary

Creativity was once widely held to be limited to a few talented individuals. However, "an impressive body of solid research over the past few decades has conclusively proved that most of us were born with rich and vigorous imaginations, and that creative ability is almost universally distributed" (Raudsepp & Hough, 1977, pp. 34). "Creativity as a fundamental trait is possessed by every person . . . [and yet] very few people make use of their creative potential" (Knecheges & Woods, 1973, p. 4). Raudsepp and Hough (1977) offer support to that notion by stating that "creativity is contingent upon the preservation of the curiosity and wonder we had in early childhood . . . [and that] unfortunately, . . . is the one thing that is conspicuous by its absence in most grownups" (p. 4).

Given the premise that most small children are very creative, one might wonder what helps or hinders creativity. Over time, the inhibition of creativity increases as children conform to the social pressures of the educational process and/or as they interact in society. Eventually, layers of behaviors are developed that thwart the creative potential. C.A. Doxidis (no date, p. 39) expands on this view and asserts, "Very often, a person's sense of creativity is not challenged. The spark does not emit as much energy. This spark shrinks and shrinks until no radiation emits from it. If a person's creative spark is not challenged or if this energy is restricted, this confinement becomes tighter and tighter until the spark is finally extinguished."

Raudsepp and Hough (1977) propose that an individual's creativity never really becomes completely lost. "By retraining ourselves to unstifle creativity," they contend, "we can unearth our hidden potentials and bring them to the surface again to make use of them for a more creative and fulfilling life" (p. 7).

Unearthing and enhancing human potential such as the ability to create or innovate is critical for the human resource development (HRD) practitioner, who attempts to increase both individual effectiveness and organizational performance and productivity. Increasing individual effectiveness requires increasing creativity in addition to unlearning nonproductive and self-defeating behaviors in oneself and in others. Creativity can be reawakened; indeed, "studies have revealed that there are certain factors that block the creative process and that a conscious effort to avoid or overcome these blocks can enhance creativity" (Ross, 1981, p. 129).

One natural starting point for an intervention designed to tap or enhance creativity has been to attempt to measure one's present level of creative ability (Dellas & Gaier, 1970; Golann, 1963; MacKinnon, 1965; Roe, 1952). Another approach to intervention has been to demonstrate and implement techniques that facilitate creative problem solving (Gordon, 1961; Osborn, 1953; Parnes & Brunelle, 1967). The identified studies reveal that both of these methodologies work. Yet both of these methods seem to put the cart before the horse. The literature clearly indicates that an alternative and, perhaps, more logical starting point might be the identification of specific barriers or blocks that inhibit an individual's creative effort. This information then can be used to prescribe strategies to reduce the immobilizing effects of such blocks. This approach enables individuals to free up their creative potentials by avoiding or altering blocking behavior and by implementing healthier and more creative alternatives.

Theoretical Framework

The Inventory of Barriers to Creative Thought and Innovative Action was designed to identify and to measure the degree of inhibitors affecting a person's ability to create and innovate. Its underlying hypothesis is that creative and innovative behavior will increase as a result of feedback obtained from the instrument and the subsequent awareness and understanding of a person's identified inhibitors.

Investigations of the factors associated with the creative process and the individual originated with Rogers (1959), who attempted to correlate characteristics of the individual and the environment to creative performance. He asserted that a relationship exists between an individual's internal psychological makeup and creativity; for instance, individuals who display creative behaviors generally are open to experience, lack rigidity in thinking, have the ability to deal with conflicting information, and are not unduly influenced by criticism or praise.

In addition to these internal psychological characteristics, Rogers (1959) also postulated external environmental conditions that would affect an individual's creative ability. For example, creativity would be increased when the external environment provided for greater psychological safety and freedom for the individual. In essence, Rogers believed that this could be accomplished by accepting the individual, by removing external evaluation, by using empathy, and by providing freedom for the individual to think and feel.

Other empirical studies are consistent with Rogers' view (for example, Golann, 1962; Pankove, 1967; Welsh, 1959). Although these studies identify creativity enhancers rather than barriers to creativity, one can conclude that if the factors associated with increased creativity are lacking, creativity will be decreased or inhibited. The barriers to creative thought defined in the literature can be categorized into the following three major groups:

- *Perceptual blocks,* or the way a person sees things;

- *Cultural blocks,* or the way a person ought to do things; and

- *Emotional blocks,* or the way a person feels about things.

These common barriers, humorously and uniquely depicted in a film, "Imagination at Work" (Industrial Management, 1959), can be described further as follows: *Perceptual blocks* include factors such as the following:

- Failure to use all the senses in observing;

- Failure to investigate the obvious;

- Inability to define terms;

- Difficulty in seeing remote relationships; and

- Failure to distinguish between facets of cause and effect.

Cultural blocks include influences such as the following:

- A desire to conform to an adopted pattern;

- Overemphasis on competition or on cooperation;

- The drive to be practical and economical above all things;

- Belief that indulging in fantasy is a waste of time; and

- Too much faith in reason and logic.

Emotional blocks include elements such as the following:

- Fear of making a mistake;

- Fear and distrust of others; and

- Grabbing the first idea that comes along.

Adams (1979, p. 11) describes barriers to creativity as "mental walls that block the problem solver from correctly perceiving a problem or conceiving its solution." His work identifies two major categories of inhibitors: *structural barriers*, which include psychological, cultural, and environmental blocks; and *process barriers*, which include elements related to cognitive style. (For an overview of Adams' work, see Ross, 1981.)

Morgan (1968) contends that the barriers that frustrate writers prove to be the same as those that thwart creative people in business and industry. He describes the barriers as primarily emotional blocks that constitute the most serious inhibitors to creative functioning. He identifies the principal groups of barriers as follows:

- *Personal feelings of security,* such as low self-esteem, feelings of anxiety, fear of criticism, fear of failure, or lack of curiosity;

- *Need for superficial security,* such as lack of risk taking or not trying new things;

- *Inability to use the unconscious,* such as not using visualization or fantasy;

- *Inability to use the conscious mind effectively,* for example, inability to organize data;

- *Work-oriented barriers,* such as "keep trying," "always prepared," "ready?"; and

- *Environmental barriers,* such as the need to find the proper setting, and to give oneself every advantage.

The work of Morgan actually sparked the development of this instrument that identifies barriers to creative thought and innovative action. The theoretical underpinnings of the instrument itself systematically integrate the literature on barriers to creativity and enhancers to creativity to provide the necessary framework.

The instrument, "Inventory of Barriers to Creative Thought and Innovative Action," measures elements that are both internal and external to the individual based on, but not limited to, the work of Rogers (1959). This instrument identifies barriers that inhibit creative thought in a personal sense, issues related to self-esteem, elements that deal with self-confidence, and behaviors associated with risk taking. It also examines the barriers that the environment might impose, such as factors related to the availability and use of time, issues of privacy, imposition of limitations, and physical facilities.

Additionally, the instrument was designed to take into account the cognitive style of the individual. The instrument identifies variables related to intuitive right-brain thinking, as well as elements typically associated with systematic or logical left-brain thinking. These factors were assimilated into the instrument using the work done by Botkin (1976), Bruner (1965), Keen (1975), and McKenney and Keen (1974), among others.

The instrument also was intended to consider various elements associated with independence and the need to conform on an internal or personal level as well as in a group or work-related setting. Based on, but not limited to, the work of Roe (1952), these factors have been incorporated into the instrument.

The Instrument

The instrument consists of thirty-six items, set up in a six-point Likert-scale format. These items identify and measure barriers in the following six categories or trait groups:

1. *Barriers related to concept of self.* These examine the variables most often associated with an individual's self-esteem, self-confidence, handling of rejection, and ability to confront differing opinions.

2. *Barriers related to need for conformity.* These examine the variables most often associated with an individual's inclinations to break away from tried and true patterns, to take risks, to express one's ideas, and to scrutinize traditional views and standard practices and policies.

3. *Barriers related to ability to abstract.* These examine the variables most often associated with an individual's tendencies to use the unconscious mind, to abstract, to view things in holistic or visual ways, and to rely on gut hunches or intuition.

4. *Barriers related to ability to use systematic analysis.* These examine the variables most often associated with an individual's tendencies to use the conscious mind, to apply logic, to think in linear or sequential ways, to organize oneself and one's ideas, and to rely on facts or data.

5. *Barriers related to task achievement.* These examine the variables most often associated with an individual's work patterns, persistence, attitudes toward others, and resourcefulness.

6. *Barriers related to physical environment.* These examine the variables most often associated with an individual's preferences as to physical surroundings, dealing with distractions, use of personal space, and need for privacy.

Validity and Reliability

The instrument has undergone statistical scrutiny and has been widely used in a variety of organizational settings with diverse populations. The instrument has a test-retest reliability of .89; it appears to have construct validity as demonstrated by factor analysis and content validity as demonstrated by expert ratings of the items as they pertain to the literature.

Administration

The following suggestions will be helpful to the facilitator who administers the instrument:

1. Distribute the instrument and read the instructions aloud as the participants follow on their copies.

2. Point out to the participants that the instrument is not a test that has right or wrong answers, but a device designed to indicate one's barriers to creative thought and innovative action.

3. Indicate to the participants that they should not spend a great deal of time pondering each response—the first guess is usually the best one.

4. When the participants have completed all of the items on the instrument, discuss the dimensions measured by the instrument. Have the participants estimate or predict the subscale categories in which they believe themselves to have barriers, as well as the categories in which they believe themselves to be relatively free of barriers.

Scoring

Each participant should be given a copy of the Barriers to Creative Thought and Innovative Action Scoring Sheet. The Scoring Sheet identifies six categories in columns labeled A through F. Each column contains the numbers of the items directly related to that column. Each participant should transfer his or her scores to the scoring sheet and add all values in each column to obtain totals for each column.

Each participant should be given a copy of the Barriers to Creative Thought and Innovative Action Profile Sheet. The participants will plot their scores on the graph.

The vertical axis represents the numerical scores; the horizontal axis, the categories of barriers. The participants then should draw lines connecting the plotted points. The final version will appear as a line graph; for example:

(A)   **(B)**   **(C)**   **(D)**   **(E)**   **(F)**

The high scores are the barriers or hurdles to overcome in order to increase one's creative thought and innovative action. For instance, in the example shown previously, Columns B and E are the two highest points on the graph and represent the barriers this individual needs to overcome.

Interpretation and Processing

When participants have identified their own individual barriers to creativity, this information can be interpreted and processed in two steps. First, the facilitator can publish his or her own scores for each subscale of the instrument. Participants then are asked to examine the column scores for significant divergence or variability among columns. For instance, the facilitator's scores might indicate a high degree of inhibition with regard to one column, with all other scores indicating relatively equal patterns. That score would be examined closely for its fit to reality and its significance for the facilitator.

Second, the participants are asked to form pairs and to exchange scoring sheets and profile sheets. The partners take turns interpreting each other's scores and follow this with a brief discussion of the instrument and the impact of the scores.

The participants may wish to post scores and discuss them as a group. Sample questions that might be asked include the following:

1. Which scores seem to fit? Which scores do not seem to fit?

2. Based on your knowledge of the other group members, which column scores would you have predicted? Which surprise you?

3. How can you use this information to work together more effectively?

Alternatively, each participant may be assigned a confidential code number. Graphs then are posted, identified only by code number. The group members choose the individual they think best fits that graph and offer a written or oral rationale for each selection. This activity offers an opportunity for further individual and group insight into the ways in which members stifle or cultivate their own or the group's creativity.

References

Adams, J.L. (1979). *Conceptual blockbusting: A guide to better ideas* (2nd ed.). New York: W.W. Norton.

Botkin, J.W. (1974). *An intuitive computer system: A cognitive approach to the management learning process.* Unpublished doctoral dissertation, Harvard University, Cambridge, MA.

Bruner, J.S. (1965). Some observations on effective cognitive processes. In G.A. Steiner (Ed.), *The creative organization* (pp. 106–117). Chicago, IL: Chicago Press.

Dellas, M., & Gaier, E.L. (1970). Identification of creativity: The individual. *Psychological Bulletin, 73,* 55–73.

Doxidis, C.A. (no date). Report of a national seminar: *Creativity—the state of the art.* Racine, WI: Thomas Alva Edison Foundation, Institute for Development of Educational Activities, and the Johnson Foundation.

Golann, S.E. (1962). The creativity motive. *Journal of Personality, 30,* 588–600.

Golann, S.E. (1963). The psychological study of creativity. *Psychological Bulletin, 60,* 548–565.

Gordon, W.J.J. (1961). *Synectics: The development of creative capacity.* New York: Harper & Row.

Industrial Management (Producer). (1959). *Imagination at work.* [Film]. Beverly Hills, CA: Roundtable Productions.

Keen, P.G.W. (1973). *The implications of cognitive style for individual decision making.* Unpublished doctoral dissertation, Harvard University, Cambridge, MA.

Knecheges, D.P., & Woods, M.E. (1973). Innovating for fun and profit. *The Creativity Review, XV*(2) 312.

MacKinnon, D.W. (1962). The nature and nurture of creative talent. *American Psychologist, 17,* 484–495.

MacKinnon, D.W. (1965). Personality and the realization of creative potential. *American Psychologist, 20,* 272–281.

McKenney, J.L., & Keen, P.G.W. (1974, May/June). How managers work. *Harvard Business Review,* pp. 79–90.

Morgan, J.S. (1968). *Improving your creativity on the job.* New York: AMACOM.

Osborn, A.F. (1953). *Applied imagination.* New York: Charles Scribner's Sons.

Pankove, E. (1967). *The relationship between creativity and risk taking in fifth grade children.* Unpublished doctoral dissertation, Rutgers, the State University of New Jersey, New Brunswick.

Parnes, S.J., & Brunelle, E.A. (1967). The literature of creativity. *Journal of Creative Behavior, 1,* 52–109.

Pfeiffer, J.W., Heslin, R., & Jones, J.E. (1976). *Instrumentation in human relations training* (2nd ed.). San Diego, CA: Pfeiffer & Company.

Raudsepp, E., & Hough, G.P., Jr. (1977). *Creative growth games.* New York: Jove.

Roe, A. (1952). *The making of a scientist.* New York: Dodd, Mead.

Rogers, C.R. (1959). Toward a theory of creativity. In H.H. Anderson (Ed.), *Creativity and its cultivation* (pp. 69–82). New York: Harper & Row.

Ross, M.B. (1981). Creativity and creative problem solving. In J.E. Jones & J.W. Pfeiffer (Eds.), *The 1981 annual* (pp. 129–134). San Francisco, CA: Pfeiffer.

Welsh, G.W. (1959). Preliminary manual: *The Welsh figure preference test* (Research ed.). Palo Alto, CA: Consulting Psychologists Press.

Originally published in *The 1990 Annual: Developing Human Resources.*

Inventory of Barriers to
Creative Thought and Innovative Active

Lorna P. Martin

Instructions: For each of the statements in this inventory, refer to the following scale and decide which number corresponds to your level of agreement with the statement; then write that number in the blank to the left of the statement.

Strongly Agree	Agree	Agree Somewhat	Disagree Somewhat	Disagree	Strongly Disagree
1	2	3	4	5	6

_____ 1. I evaluate criticism to determine how it can be useful to me.

_____ 2. When solving problems, I attempt to apply new concepts or methods.

_____ 3. I can shift gears or change emphasis in the abstract.

_____ 4. I get enthusiastic about problems outside my specialized area of concentration.

_____ 5. I always give a problem my best effort, even if it seems trivial or fails to arouse enthusiasm.

_____ 6. I set aside periods of time without interruptions.

_____ 7. It is not difficult for me to have my ideas criticized.

_____ 8. In the past, I have taken calculated risks and I would do so again.

_____ 9. I dream, daydream, and fantasize easily.

_____ 10. I know how to simplify and organize my observations.

_____ 11. Occasionally, I try a so-called "unworkable" answer and hope that it will prove to be workable.

_____ 12. I can and do consistently guard my personal periods of privacy.

_____ 13. I feel at ease with colleagues even when my ideas or plans meet with public criticism or rejection.

_____ 14. I frequently read opinions contrary to my own to learn what the opposition is thinking.

Strongly Agree	Agree	Agree Somewhat	Disagree Somewhat	Disagree	Strongly Disagree
1	2	3	4	5	6

_____ 15. I translate symbols into concrete ideas or action steps.

_____ 16. I seek many ideas because I enjoy having alternative possibilities.

_____ 17. In the idea-formulation stage of a project, I withhold critical judgment.

_____ 18. I determine whether an imposed limitation is reasonable or is unreasonable.

_____ 19. I would modify an idea, plan, or design, even if doing so would meet with opposition.

_____ 20. I feel comfortable in expressing my ideas even if they are in the minority.

_____ 21. I enjoy participating in nonverbal, symbolic, or visual activities.

_____ 22. I feel the excitement and challenge of finding a solution to problems.

_____ 23. I keep a file of discarded ideas.

_____ 24. I make reasonable demands for good physical facilities and surroundings.

_____ 25. I would feel no serious loss of status or prestige if management publicly rejected my plan.

_____ 26. I frequently question the policies, objectives, values, or ideas of an organization.

_____ 27. I deliberately exercise my visual and symbolic skills in order to strengthen them.

_____ 28. I can accept my thinking when it seems illogical.

_____ 29. I seldom reject ambiguous ideas that are not directly related to the problem.

_____ 30. I distinguish between the trivial and the important physical distractions.

_____ 31. I feel uncomfortable making waves for a worthwhile idea if it threatens the inner harmony of the group.

_____ 32. I am willing to present a truly original approach even if there is a chance it could fail.

_____ 33. I can recognize the times when symbolism or visualization would work best for me.

_____ 34. I try to make an uninteresting problem stimulating.

_____ 35. I consciously attempt to use new approaches toward routine tasks.

_____ 36. In the past, I have determined when to leave an undesirable environment and when to stay and change the environment (including self-growth).

Barriers to Creative Thought
and Innovative Action Scoring Sheet

Instructions: Transfer your inventory responses to the appropriate blanks below. Then add the numbers in each column, and record the totals in the blanks provided.

A	B	C	D	E	F
1. _____	2. _____	3. _____	4. _____	5. _____	6. _____
7. _____	8. _____	9. _____	10. _____	11. _____	12. _____
13. _____	14. _____	15. _____	16. _____	17. _____	18. _____
19. _____	20. _____	21. _____	22. _____	23. _____	24. _____
25. _____	26. _____	27. _____	28. _____	29. _____	30. _____
31. _____	32. _____	33. _____	34. _____	35. _____	36. _____

Column
Totals

_____   _____   _____   _____   _____   _____

Barriers to Creative Thought
and Innovative Action Profile Sheet

Instructions: Plot the scores from your scoring sheet onto the following graph. The vertical axis, which represents your numbered scores, ranges from 6 to 36. The horizontal axis, which represents the columns on your scoring sheet, ranges from A to F. The key at the bottom of this page identifies the barriers in each column. Connect the points you have plotted with a line. The high points represent your barriers.

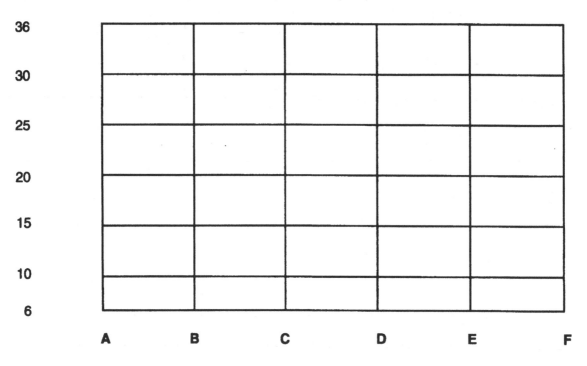

Keys to Barriers

A = Barriers Related to Self-Confidence and Risk Taking
B = Barriers Related to Need for Conformity
C = Barriers Related to Use of The Abstract
D = Barriers Related to Use of Systematic Analysis
E = Barriers Related to Task Achievement
F = Barriers Related to Physical Environment

8　The Learning–Model Instrument

Kenneth L. Murrell

Summary

Although the learning model presented here was not designed exclusively for managers, the versatility and flexibility demanded by a managerial career require a knowledge of and experience with a variety of learning styles. The Learning Model for Managers introduces four domains of learning based on a persons preference for cognitive or affective learning and the persons preference for concrete or abstract experiences. As it is important for managers to learn how to use a variety of learning styles, the manager is given special attention as the model and instrument are discussed.

Developing the Model and Instrument

The idea that people will be able to live a better life if they understand who and what they are goes back at least to the early Greek philosophers. Many aids and guides have been created to help people in today's world to learn more about themselves. After reading *Freedom to Learn* (Rogers, 1982) and studying various learning-style models and instruments (e.g., Kolb, Rubin, & McIntyre, 1974, and instruments described in Peters, 1985, and in Pfeiffer, Heslin, & Jones, 1976), I saw a need for a different type of learning model and self-awareness instrument. The following goals were important in developing this new model:

1. To create a model that will help to explain the cognitive and affective learning styles in such a way that managers and trainers can gain an appreciation for and understanding of the various ways in which learning takes place;

2. To clarify conceptually what a learning environment is so that participants in a learning program can gain an understanding of what the learning environment is and of how experiential-learning methods differ from other learning methods;

3. To create an instrument, based on the models assumptions, that will provide immediate self-awareness feedback to help individuals know more about how they learn;

4. To develop an instrument that will help individuals (a) to connect their awareness of their own learning preferences to the nature of what and how a manager learns and (b) to understand why experiential learning and management development must differ from traditional classroom learning; and

5. To develop an instrument that will generate thought and discussion about the process of learning, so that program content will be seen as only a part of the total learning experience.

The Model

The Learning Model for Managers (see Figure 1), which was based on these goals, has been used in industrial settings, in graduate and undergraduate courses on management and organizational behavior, and in offices in the United States and other countries. The instrument is simple to use and is designed to help the instructor or trainer explain the importance of being able to learn in many different ways, including experiential learning.

Learning comes not only through thinking or cognition, but also from experience and affect or feeling. Although some people have realized this fact for a long time, it is still "good news" for many when they discover that it is acceptable to be emotional and have feelings and that they can take pride in being able to learn from emotions and feelings. Although everyone probably has a mixture of learning preferences, a way was needed to identify a persons preferred position on a continuum from the cognitive to the affective.

The Learning Model for Managers assumes that the difference in a preference on the affective-cognitive dimension of learning is a key factor in how a person learns. This assumption is based on the idea that the affective and cognitive end points can be defined so that they correlate with a people-versus-task orientation (Blake & Mouton, 1984). Although empirical research may not show a strong correlation between a preference for the cognitive style of learning and task orientation, they seem to be closely related because of the similarity in their definitions.

This task-person and cognitive-affective correlation provides an opportunity to use this learning model for stressing the relationship of learning style and personality type to the behavior of a manager. Although managers, like other people, probably prefer learning in a particular way, it is important for them to develop the ability to learn by both thinking and feeling. The model can be used to illustrate this importance. In train-

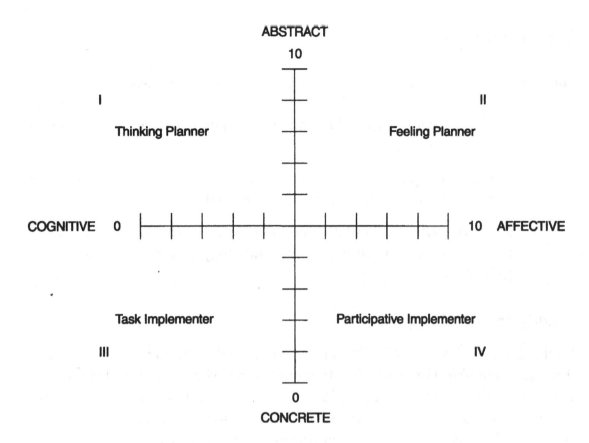

Figure 1. The Learning Model for Managers

ing managers, the trainer should thoroughly discuss this issue and show how the model correlates with the career changes the managers may expect to face.

The model's second dimension (the vertical axis) uses, as did Kolb, a concrete-abstract continuum. However, this model reverses the positions of the end points in order to place concrete (the "down-to-earth" point) on the bottom and abstract (the "in-the-air" point) on top. A preference for the concrete reflects a persons desire to come into contact with the real object, to touch it, or even to physically manipulate it. The abstract end of the continuum reflects a preference for dealing with the world in terms of thinking about it and for manipulating ideas or thoughts. The vertical axis represents the way people tend to experience life and is loosely associated with the psychology of Jung (1924). The preference for experiencing life in the concrete indicates a desire to experience through the direct senses.

The Learning Model for Managers, therefore, contains two primary axes, ranging from cognitive to affective in the horizontal dimension and from concrete to abstract in the vertical dimension. The axes divide the model into the following four domains: I, thinking planner; II, feeling planner; III, task implementer; and IV, participative implementer.

The Instrument

The Learning-Model Instrument can be used in the following ways:

1. To give feedback to individuals on their own preferred styles of learning and domains of strength;

2. To help a new group of trainees or students to learn more about one another in order to work together more effectively; and

3. To provide an overall explanation of the learning environment so that participants will gain a conceptual understanding of the experiential approach to learning.

Validity and Reliability

Establishing validity and reliability of any model and instrument of this type is difficult or impossible. However, if the face validity is positive and if the learning value is apparent, then the material should be useful when it fits the training and learning goals. The results of the instrument are not intended to label the respondents, but simply to give them feedback on their preferred styles of learning.

Administering the Instrument

Although this instrument is particularly helpful to managers and prospective managers, it is appropriate for anyone who desires to know more about his or her own preferences for learning styles. A management-development program, which was built on the model and utilized the instrument, can be summarized in the following way:

> The first session met in order to accomplish two things: (1) to allow the participants to become acquainted with at least four other participants and (2) to outline preliminary objectives for the program. During the getting-acquainted process, each person introduced one other person. Later, triads were formed to develop additional program objectives, which then became part of the program outline. The facilitator used a systems framework to explain the relationship of inputs, throughputs, and outputs. The facilitator also gave special attention to the feedback loop and discussed it in terms of the need for communication and self-control in order to make sure that the program was accomplishing its goals and that each participant was receiving what he or she needed.
>
> The next focus was on the learning model. The facilitator explained how the program activities would by necessity be heavily oriented toward experiential learning and would deal directly with the feelings and emotions that would emerge as learning took place in domains II and IV of the model.

The model and instrument were valuable in helping participants to learn something about one another, which in turn helped them in working together more effectively. After the instrument was administered, the results of the last half of the instrument were used to form groups of participants with similar scores. Each group consisted of five to seven members. Within each group, the members compared their responses and tried to determine whether or not the scores seemed valid. They also discussed the results of the first half of the instrument. Then all of the groups held a joint discussion.

Topics for such a joint discussion might include the way men are socialized to be more cognitive and women are socialized to be more affective; how background or academic interests can cause a bias; and how individuals can determine which domain they belong in if their scores place them on an axis. The discussions in both the small and large groups can help participants to be more aware of themselves, of the other participants, and of the kind of learning that will take place in the program.

This particular program was designed to place a heavy emphasis on and to give special skill-building attention to domains II and IV.

Scoring the Instrument

The scoring sheet indicates which answers receive a score of one point. The rest of the answers receive a score of zero. The total of the scores in the first half of the instrument is plotted on the vertical axis, and a horizontal line is drawn through the point. The total of the scores in the last half is plotted on the horizontal axis, and a vertical line is drawn through that point. The point of intersection of the two lines indicates the domain of the respondent.

Interpreting the Scores

The next four paragraphs give an interpretation of the four end points of the axes in the Learning Model for Managers. Following these are explanations of the four domains in the model.

Cognitive Learning

A person who scores low on the cognitive-affective axis shows a marked preference for learning through thought or other mental activity. People who intellectually grasp very quickly what they are trying to learn or who simply prefer to use controlled thought and logic will be found on the cognitive end of this axis. Rationality appeals to these individuals, as do logic and other thinking skills that are necessary for this type of learning. Although this statement is not based on hard research, it appears that a high cognitive orientation correlates with a high task orientation rather than with a people orientation.

The research about possible left-versus-right brain functioning correlates a cognitive orientation with individuals who are left-brain dominant. Therefore, the left side of the axis was deliberately assigned to the cognitive orientation to serve as an easy reminder.

Affective Learning

A person who scores high on the cognitive-affective axis shows a marked preference for learning in the affective realm. Such an individual is more comfortable with and seeks out learning from his or her emotions and feelings. These individuals desire personal interaction and seek to learn about people by experiencing them in emotional ways. This type of learner would potentially be highly people oriented. A manager with this orientation would probably seek out social interaction rather than focus exclusively on the task components of the job. In right-brain research, affective learners are said to be more intuitive, more spontaneous, and less linear. They seek out feelings and emotions rather than logic.

Concrete Life Experiencing

People with a preference for the concrete enjoy jumping in and getting their hands dirty. Handson experiences are important to them. As managers, these people want to keep busy, become directly involved, and physically approach or touch whatever they are working with. If they work with machines, they will get greasy; if they work with people, they will become involved.

Abstract Life Experiencing

People who prefer this style have no special desire to touch, but they want to keep active by thinking about the situation and relating it to similar situations. Their preferred interaction style is internal—inside their own heads.

The Four Learning Domains

A person is unlikely to be on the extreme end of either axis, and no one type of learning is "best." Any mixture of preferences simply represents a persons uniqueness. The model is useful in helping people differentiate themselves, and it offers a method for looking at the way different styles fit together. This section describes the four domains that are represented in the model.

The descriptions of these domains could be of special interest to managers, because they will help the manager understand the relationship between managerial action and learning style. A manager should be capable of learning and functioning well in all four domains, especially if he or she expects to face a variety of situations and challenges. The successful manager is likely to be the one who can operate in both a task and a people environment with the ability to see and become involved with the concrete and also use thought processes to understand what is needed. The normative assumption of the model is that a manager should learn how to learn in each of the four domains. In doing this, the manager may well build on his or her primary strengths; but the versatility and flexibility demanded in a managerial career make clear the importance of all four domains.

Domain I, the Thinking Planner. A combination of cognitive and abstract preferences constitutes domain I, where the "thinking planner" is located. This domain might well be termed the place for the planner whose job is task oriented and whose environment contains primarily things, numbers, or printouts. The bias in formal education is often toward this learning domain, and Mintzberg (1976) was critical of this bias. In this domain things are treated abstractly, and often their socioemotional elements are denied.

The domain-I learner should do well in school, should have a talent for planning, and is likely to be successful as a staff person or manager in a department that deals with large quantities of untouchable things. This domain represents an important area for management learning. Of the four domains, it seems to receive the heaviest emphasis in traditional university programs and in management-development seminars, particularly those in financial management.

Domain II, the Feeling Planner: A combination of affective and abstract preferences constitutes domain II, where the "feeling planner" is located. The managerial style associated with this domain is that of the thinker who can learn and who enjoys working with people but has limited opportunity to get close to them. This domain is important for the personnel executive or a manager with too much responsibility to interact closely with other employees.

Social-analysis skills are represented in this area. Managers in this domain should be able to think through and understand the social and emotional factors affecting a large organization.

Difficulties in this area sometimes arise when good first-line supervisors who have a natural style with people are promoted into positions that prevent them from having direct contact with others and are expected to determine without concrete experience the nature of and solutions to personnel problems.

Domain III, the Task Implementer. A combination of cognitive and concrete preferences constitutes domain III, where the "task implementer" is located. This domain includes decision makers who primarily want to understand the task and who can focus on the details and specifics of the concrete in a thoughtful manner. If these people are allowed to think about a situation, they can see the concrete issues and, after close examination, can make a well-thought-out decision. A person in this domain is often a task-focused doer. If the interpersonal skill demands are low and if the emotional climate is not a problem, this person is likely to do well.

Domain IV, the Participative Implementer. A combination of affective and concrete preferences constitutes domain IV, where the "participative implementer" is located. The manager with people skills who has the opportunity to work closely with people is found in this category. This is the place where implementers and highly skilled organization development consultants reside. This domain is for those who like to become involved and who have ability and interest in working with the emotional needs and demands of the people in an organization. This is the domain that is emphasized by most of the practical management programs, and it can be used to complement the traditional educational programs of domain I.

References

Blake, R.R., & Mouton, J.S. (1984). *Managerial grid III* (3rd ed.). Houston, TX: Gulf.

Jung, C.G. (1924). *Second impression* (H. Godwin, Trans.). New York: Harcourt Brace.

Kolb, D.A., Rubin, I.M., & McIntyre, J.M. (1974). *Organizational psychology: An experiential approach* (2nd ed.). Englewood Cliffs, NJ: Prentice-Hall.

Mintzberg, N. (1976, July-August). Planning on the left side and managing on the right. *Harvard Business Review,* pp. 49–58.

Peters, D. (1985). *Directory of human resource development instrumentation.* San Diego, CA: Pfeiffer & Company.

Pfeiffer, J.W., Heslin, R., & Jones, J.E. (1976). *Instrumentation in human relations training* (2nd ed.). San Diego, CA: Pfeiffer & Company.

Rogers, C.R. (1982). *Freedom to learn.* Columbus, OH: Charles E. Merrill.

Originally published in *The 1987 Annual Handbook for Faciliatators, Trainers, and Consultants.*

The Learning-Model Instrument[1]

Kenneth L. Murrell

Instructions: For each statement choose the response that is more nearly true for you. Place an X on the blank that corresponds to that response.

1. When meeting people, I prefer

   _____ (a) to think and speculate on what they are like.

   _____ (b) to interact directly and to ask them questions.

2. When presented with a problem, I prefer

   _____ (a) to jump right in and work on a solution.

   _____ (b) to think through and evaluate possible ways to solve the problem.

3. I enjoy sports more when

   _____ (a) I am watching a good game.

   _____ (b) I am actively participating.

4. Before taking a vacation, I prefer

   _____ (a) to rush at the last minute and give little thought beforehand to what I will do while on vacation.

   _____ (b) to plan early and daydream about how I will spend my vacation.

5. When enrolled in courses, I prefer

   _____ (a) to plan how to do my homework before actually attacking the assignment.

   _____ (b) to immediately become involved in doing the assignment.

6. When I receive information that requires action, I prefer

   _____ (a) to take action immediately.

   _____ (b) to organize the information and determine what type of action would be most appropriate.

---

[1]Copyright © 1987 by Kenneth L. Murrell. Used with permission. This instrument may be freely used for nonprofit educational/training activities. Systematic or large-scale reproduction or distribution may be done only with prior written permission from the author.

7. When presented with a number of alternatives for action, I prefer

_____ (a) to determine how the alternatives relate to one another and analyze the consequences of each.

_____ (b) to select the one that looks best and implement it.

8. When I awake every morning, I prefer

_____ (a) to expect to accomplish some worthwhile work without considering what the individual tasks may entail.

_____ (b) to plan a schedule for the tasks I expect to do that day.

9. After a full days work, I prefer

_____ (a) to reflect on what I accomplished and think of how to make time the next day for unfinished tasks.

_____ (b) to relax with some type of recreation and not think about my job.

10. After choosing the above responses, I

_____ (a) prefer to continue and complete this instrument.

_____ (b) am curious about how my responses will be interpreted and would prefer some feedback before continuing with the instrument.

11. When I learn something, I am usually

_____ (a) thinking about it.

_____ (b) right in the middle of doing it.

12. I learn best when

_____ (a) I am dealing with real-world issues.

_____ (b) concepts are clear and well organized.

13. In order to retain something I have learned, I must

_____ (a) periodically review it in my mind.

_____ (b) practice it or try to use the information.

14. In teaching others how to do something, I first

   _____ (a) demonstrate the task.

   _____ (b) explain the task.

15. My favorite way to learn to do something is by

   _____ (a) reading a book or instructions or enrolling in a class.

   _____ (b) trying to do it and learning from my mistakes.

16. When I become emotionally involved with something, I usually

   _____ (a) let my feelings take the lead and then decide what to do.

   _____ (b) control my feelings and try to analyze the situation.

17. If I were meeting jointly with several experts on a subject, I would prefer

   _____ (a) to ask each of them for his or her opinion.

   _____ (b) to interact with them and share our ideas and feelings.

18. When I am asked to relate information to a group of people, I prefer

   _____ (a) not to have an outline, but to interact with them and become involved in an extemporaneous conversation.

   _____ (b) to prepare notes and know exactly what I am going to say.

19. Experience is

   _____ (a) a guide for building theories.

   _____ (b) the best teacher.

20. People learn easier when they are

   _____ (a) doing work on the job.

   _____ (b) in a class taught by an expert.

The Learning-Model Instrument Scoring Sheet

Instructions: Transfer your responses by writing either "a" or "b" in the blank that corresponds to each item in the Learning Model Instrument.

	Abstract/Concrete		Cognitive/Affective	
	Column 1	**Column 2**	**Column 3**	**Column 4**
	1. _____	2. _____	11. _____	12. _____
	3. _____	4. _____	13. _____	14. _____
	5. _____	6. _____	15. _____	16. _____
	7. _____	8. _____	17. _____	18. _____
	9. _____	10. _____	19. _____	20. _____
Total Circles	_____	_____	_____	_____
Grand Totals	_____		_____	

Now circle every "a" in Column 1 and in Column 4. Then circle every "b" in Column 2 and in Column 3. Next, total the circles in each of the four columns. Then add the totals of Columns 1 and 2; plot this grand total on the vertical axis of the Learning Model for Managers and draw a horizontal line through the point. Now add the totals of Columns 3 and 4; plot that grand total on the horizontal axis of the model and draw a vertical line through the point. The intersection of these two lines indicates the domain of your preferred learning style.

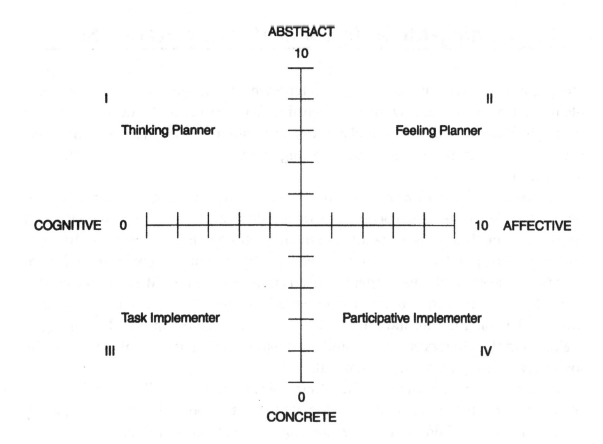

The Learning Model for Managers

The Learning–Model Instrument Interpretation Sheet

The cognitive-affective axis or continuum represents the range of ways in which people learn. Cognitive learning includes learning that is structured around either rote storing of knowledge or intellectual abilities and skills, or both. Affective learning includes learning from experience, from feelings about the experience, and from ones own emotions.

The concrete-abstract axis or continuum represents the range of ways in which people experience life. When people experience life abstractly, they detach themselves from the immediacy of the situation and theorize about it. If they experience life concretely, they respond to the situation directly with little subsequent contemplation.

The two axes divide the model into four parts or domains. Most people experience life and learn from it in all four domains but have a preference for a particular domain. Liberal-arts education has typically concentrated on abstract learning (domains I and II), whereas vocational and on-the-job training usually takes place in the lower quadrants, particularly domain III.

Occupations representative of the four styles include the following: domain I, philosopher or chief executive officer; domain II, poet or journalist; domain III, architect or engineer; and domain IV, psychologist or personnel counselor.

Managerial jobs require an ability to learn in all four domains, and a managers development depends on his or her ability to learn both cognitively and affectively. Thus, management education and development demand the opportunity for the participants to learn how to learn in each domain.

9 Time-Management Personality Profile

Debbie Seid and Kim Piker

Summary

A person's "personality" in terms of managing time and priorities can be described according to five different dimensions: attention to task, type of focus, approach to structure, style of processing, and strategy of action.

Each of these dimensions has a range of descriptors. In attention to task, people range from divergent to convergent; in type of focus, people range from detailed to global; in approach to structure, people range from tight to loose; in style of processing, people range from parallel to serial; and in strategy of action, people range from reactive to proactive.

By understanding their own strengths and areas of improvement, respondents can focus their attention on the dimensions of time management that are most problematic to themselves.

Each person has a unique "style" of organizing. Some people are naturally quite organized; others are not. Some are afraid that being too organized will stunt their creativity and spontaneity; others feel comfortable with a structured organizational system. Some people are good at doing many things at once, and some are easily distracted by outside influences.

Background and Supporting Theory

A person's "personality" in terms of managing time and priorities can be described according to five different dimensions: attention to task, type of focus, approach to structure, style of processing, and strategy of action. When people understand how they best function in terms of time management, they can develop organizational systems that work best for themselves.

Attention to Task: Divergent or Convergent

The extremes of the dimension of attention to task are "divergent" and "convergent." It is relatively easy to spot a person whose attention to task is divergent. His or her messy desk is a definite clue. When asked whether or not they are organized, most divergent people would say that they are organized. They might admit to having a messy desk, but would maintain that they know exactly where everything is.

Working with a divergent person can be a challenge for those who are convergent. Divergent people easily wander off the subject to whatever sounds interesting at the moment. This sort of subject jumping makes convergent people very nervous. Whereas convergent people draw energy from completing projects, divergent people draw energy from starting new ones.

Type of Focus: Global or Detailed

The dimension of type of focus has to do with whether a person is detail oriented or globally oriented. Detail-oriented people need facts and details about a situation in order to feel comfortable. They seek out information and verification and prefer situations that can be supported by facts and figures. Such people draw energy from seeking and organizing information.

On the other hand, globally oriented people are more drawn to "possibilities" than the facts of current reality. They enjoy thinking about the future and discussing inter-relationships. Globally oriented people often have highly tuned conceptual skills and are drawn to professions such as theater, the arts, upper management, and marketing. Although some globally oriented people also enjoy taking care of the subsequent details, most do not.

Approach to Structure: Tight or Loose

Tightly structured people like to have a system for accomplishing tasks; loosely structured people prefer to have flexibility in how they carry out tasks. For example, tightly structured people prefer that meetings start on time and follow a predesignated agenda. Loosely structured people are fine with meetings starting late and proceeding without an agenda. Tightly structured people have specific places to put specific information. Loosely structured people put information wherever is convenient at the time, resulting in many scraps of paper with valuable information scattered on their desks.

When working on a task, tightly structured people will figure out how to organize and structure what they are going to do before they begin. They will develop the approprlate system for working on the project and adjust it accordingly as the project proceeds. Loosely structured people, on the other hand, put together some system in the beginning, but as the project proceeds, they alter the system or ignore it completely.

Style of Processing: Parallel or Serial

Some people are serial processors and others are parallel processors. Parallel processors are comfortable performing more than one task at a time; serial processors prefer to focus on the task at hand.

When parallel processors have to work with serial processors, they often feel frustrated at the seemingly slow pace of progress. Parallel processors would rather keep all parts of a project in motion at the same time. In contrast, serial processors prefer to begin at the beginning and complete each step thoroughly before proceeding.

Strategy of Action: Proactive or Reactive

Reactive individuals tend to put off today what they can do tomorrow and, as a result, spend a lot of their time responding to crises or deadlines that pop up suddenly. However, some individuals will score reactive because of particular circumstances at work that are largely out of their control.

In contrast, proactive individuals take charge of the day and accomplish what they set out to do. They do not let circumstances or procrastination get in their way. They make a plan and follow it, consequently, they rarely find themselves in last-minute crisis situations.

Description of the Instrument

The Time-Management Personality Profile (TMPP) consists of forty items. The items ask participants to respond to each statement in terms of how often they engage in the behavior described. The four-point scale ranges from "almost always" (4) to "almost never" (1). Scores are translated to the five dimensions described previously. The Time-Management Personality Profile has face validity only.

Potential Uses

The Time-Management Personality Profile is versatile and can be used in a number of areas, levels, and ways in an organization. Following are some suggestions:

Use with individuals. At the individual level, the instrument can be useful to anyone who wants to understand his or her style of time management. In particular, individuals who see themselves as "disorganized" because they are not comfortable with traditional time-management techniques may find validation from this instrument. The extremes of each dimension intentionally are worded to be neutral and to allow individuals to describe themselves in neutral terms.

Use with teams. Team members typically work closely together, and individuals with different time-management styles may clash. The Time-Management Personality Profile provides a framework and offers a vocabulary for understanding individual differences and making accommodations.

Use in training. The Time-Management Personality Profile can be used in training that deals with stress management, time management, personal effectiveness, and so on.

Administration

The Time-Management Personality Profile should be administered before any lecturette on the topic of time management is offered. Having participants complete the instrument before discussing the topic will lessen their tendency to react to the items on the basis of how they expect they should behave.

Scoring

After completing the inventory, participants should be asked to transfer the number that they assigned to each item to the appropriate column on the Time-Management Personality Profile Scoring Sheet and to total the five columns. After they have computed column totals, they should be instructed to graph their results on the Time-Management Personality Profile Graph.

Interpretation

At this point, participants should be given copies of the Time-Management Personality Profile Interpretation Sheet and be asked to read it. After they have had time to read the handout, the facilitator can process the information with questions such as the following:

1. What is your reaction to the graph of your time-management personality profile? What dimensions are important to you? What do you notice about the relationships among the dimensions?

2. How does your profile compare with others? How does it compare with your perception of the "ideal" profile? What do these comparisons suggest about your time-management abilities?

3. What generalizations can you make about time-management skills? What generalizations can you make about the five dimensions and how they fit together to compose a time-management personality profile?

4. What specifically do you need to do in order to improve your time-management skills? What dimension needs attention? How can you begin that process? What is one action you can take immediately?

Summary

It is important for participants to understand that no one time-management personality profile is best. By understanding their own strengths and areas of improvement, participants can focus on the dimensions of time management that are most problematic to themselves as well as give themselves permission to enjoy their own unique approaches to time management.

Originally published in *The 1995 Annual: Volume 2, Consulting.*

Time-Management Personality Profile

Debbie Seid and Kim Piker

Instructions: Please answer each item according to how often that statement is true for you. Write your answer on the blank that precedes each item, using the following scale:

4 = Almost Always   3 = Often   2 = Sometimes   1 = Almost Never

_____   1. I have so many "to do" lists that I don't know where to begin.

_____   2. I can make decisions about minor details without needing to know how the overall plan is coming together.

_____   3. I know where I have filed most of my important papers.

_____   4. A busy environment helps me to work more efficiently.

_____   5. I find myself inundated with papers that I have to get to.

_____   6. I get distracted by the unimportant while I am in the middle of the important.

_____   7. If a party is being planned, I enjoy attending to the particulars more than I do planning the theme.

_____   8. I keep my "to-do" list handy.

_____   9. I tend to take on several tasks at one time.

_____ 10. I find myself losing sight of long-term goals when dealing with short-term crises.

_____ 11. I find myself daydreaming during meetings or discussions.

_____ 12. I am good at mapping out the steps needed to complete a project.

_____ 13. Telephone and fax numbers for my business contacts are readily accessible.

_____ 14. While working on one project, ideas about other projects come to my mind.

_____ 15. I put off making decisions until a situation becomes urgent.

_____ 16. My mind wanders when I'm working alone.

4 = Almost Always   3 = Often   2 = Sometimes   1 = Almost Never

_____ 17. In the midst of working on a project, attending to minor details as they come up helps me to keep on track.

_____ 18. I am uncomfortable when my desk is overcrowded with papers.

_____ 19. I am eager to start a new project before I even finish an existing project.

_____ 20. I prepare for things at the last minute.

_____ 21. Interruptions throughout the day affect the amount of work I am able to accomplish.

_____ 22. I am very precise in how I handle projects.

_____ 23. I keep track of all of my important deadlines.

_____ 24. When I talk on the phone during a casual conversation, I also engage in other activities (e.g., cooking, grooming, cleaning, etc.).

_____ 25. I avoid delegating work until it's absolutely necessary.

_____ 26. I have scraps of paper scattered about with bits of information on them.

_____ 27. I go home with my desk in order.

_____ 28. I keep my legal and accounting records updated and in order.

_____ 29. During a business phone conversation, I would rather look for a related file while talking than put the person on hold.

_____ 30. I find it difficult to make time for the unexpected.

_____ 31. I put off today what I can do tomorrow.

_____ 32. It is important to capture specific details of business conversations and record them verbatim.

_____ 33. I object to meetings that start late.

_____ 34. If I am trying to find a street address while driving, I would rather leave the radio on than turn it off.

_____ 35. I find myself working long hours and never catching up.

_____ 36. When I am in a meeting and someone brings up an interesting but unrelated topic, I join in the discussion about the new topic.

4 = Almost Always   3 = Often   2 = Sometimes   1 = Almost Never

_____ 37. I enjoy implementing the details of a project more than I do envisioning the end result.

_____ 38. I think that meetings that don't have an agenda are a waste of my time.

_____ 39. If I am walking around a shopping center looking for a particular store, I am comfortable chatting with a friend as I look.

_____ 40. I am disorganized because I do not have the time to get organized.

Time-Management Personality Profile Scoring Sheet

Section 1: Attention to Task

1. _____

6. _____

11. _____

16. _____

21. _____

26. _____

31. _____

36. _____

Total _____

Section 2: Type of Focus

2. _____

7. _____

12. _____

17. _____

22. _____

27. _____

32. _____

37. _____

Total _____

Section 3: Approach to Structure

3. _____

8. _____

13. _____

18. _____

23. _____

28. _____

33. _____

38. _____

Total _____

Section 4: Style of Processing

4. _____

9. _____

14. _____

19. _____

24. _____

29. _____

34. _____

39. _____

Total _____

Section 5: Strategy of Action

5. _____

10. _____

15. _____

20. _____

25. _____

30. _____

35. _____

40. _____

Total _____

Time-Management Personality Profile Graph

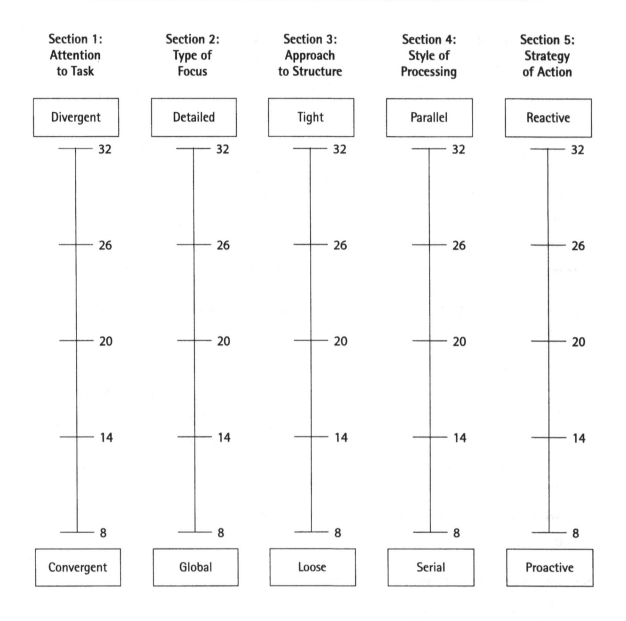

Time–Management Personality Profile
Interpretation Sheet

Attention to Task: Divergent or Convergent

The extremes of the dimension of attention to task are "divergent" and "convergent." It is relatively easy to spot a person whose attention to task is divergent. His or her messy desk is a definite clue. When asked whether or not they are organized, most divergent people would say that they are organized. They might admit to having a messy desk, but would maintain that they know exactly where everything is.

Working with a divergent person can be a challenge for those who are convergent. Divergent people easily wander off the subject to whatever sounds interesting at the moment. This sort of subject jumping makes convergent people very nervous. Whereas convergent people draw energy from completing projects, divergent people draw energy from starting new ones.

Type of Focus: Global or Detailed

The dimension of type of focus has to do with whether a person is detail oriented or globally oriented. Detail-oriented people need facts and details about a situation in order to feel comfortable. They seek out information and verification and prefer situations that can be supported by facts and figures. Such people draw energy from seeking and organizing information.

On the other hand, globally oriented people are more drawn to "possibilities" than the facts of current reality. They enjoy thinking about the future and discussing interrelationships. Globally oriented people often have highly tuned conceptual skills and are drawn to professions such as theater, the arts, upper management, and marketing. Although some globally oriented people also enjoy taking care of the subsequent details, most do not.

Approach to Structure: Tight or Loose

Tightly structured people like to have a system for accomplishing tasks; loosely structured people prefer to have flexibility in how they carry out tasks. For example, tightly structured people prefer that meetings start on time and follow a predesignated agenda. Loosely structured people are fine with meetings starting late and proceeding without an agenda. Tightly structured people have specific places to put specific information. Loosely structured people put information wherever is convenient at the time, resulting in many scraps of paper with valuable information scattered on their desks.

When working on a task, tightly structured people will figure out how to organize and structure what they are going to do before they begin. They will develop the appropriate system for working on the project and adjust it accordingly as the project proceeds. Loosely structured people, on the other hand, put together some system in the beginning, but as the project proceeds, they alter the system or ignore it completely.

Style of Processing: Parallel or Serial

Some people are serial processors and others are parallel processors. Parallel processors are comfortable performing more than one task at a time; serial processors prefer to focus on the task at hand.

When parallel processors have to work with serial processors, they often feel frustrated at the seemingly slow pace of progress. Parallel processors would rather keep all parts of a project in motion at the same time. In contrast, serial processors prefer to begin at the beginning and complete each step thoroughly before proceeding.

Strategy of Action: Proactive or Reactive

Reactive individuals tend to put off today what they can do tomorrow and, as a result, spend a lot of their time responding to crises or deadlines that pop up suddenly. However, some individuals will score reactive because of particular circumstances at work that are largely out of their control.

In contrast, proactive individuals take charge of the day and accomplish what they set out to accomplish. They do not let circumstances or procrastination get in their way. They make a plan and follow it, consequently, they rarely find themselves in last-minute crisis situations.

Summary

It is important for participants to understand that no one time-management personality profile is best. By understanding their own strengths and areas of improvement, participants can focus their attention on the dimensions of time management that are most problematic to themselves. In addition they can give themselves permission to enjoy their own unique approaches to time management.

10 The TEM Survey

George J. Petrello

Summary

The "knowledge worker," as defined by Peter Drucker (1969), is usually college educated, with expertise in some technical, professional, or administrative field. People who have freedom to control their time within their work environments are knowledge workers, in contrast to people who work on production lines, whose activities are controlled by the movement of the work along the line. Job success for knowledge workers depends largely on how effectively they use the time available to them.

Background and Supporting Theory

The literature on time management indicates that effective usage of time is greatly dependent on people's ability to pace themselves and their levels of recognizing and controlling human energy flows. Industrial psychologists have found that theories concerning "night people" and "morning people" are true for the vast majority of cases. In its simplest form, energy-level theory suggests that people realize, through self-observation, when they are at their best for physical activities such as dealing with people, presentations, and meetings and when they are at their best for mental activities such as writing, reviewing reports, and preparing budgets. If time is used for work that complements a person's energy flows, the use of time becomes more effective.

The literature indicates that effective time management also is greatly dependent on the individual's ability to process and retrieve information through a personal memory system. "Memory improvement" refers to the use of simple mechanical aids to help the person to store and retrieve information, rather than relying on the person's ability to remember in the traditional sense. Memory improvement involves careful record keeping through the use of diaries, project sheets, schedules, and so on. Thus, effective time management is linked to the individual's energy level and memory system. Research confirms that people can be taught to use their time more effectively. Sometimes the teaching does not involve communicating techniques but, rather, changing poor attitudes. Many people know or can learn what they should be doing to use their time more effectively, but they are not motivated to apply the techniques. Some people have attitudinal problems that are rooted in their environments or histories. Most people are able to change their attitudes and habits and to attain more effective use of their time.

The statements in the TEM Survey (time, energy, and memory) are derived from the author's experience in presenting time-management seminars and from the professional literature in the field. About 60 percent of these statements reflect knowledge and about 40 percent reflect attitudes. Reddin's Management Style Diagnosis Test (Reddin, 1977) was used as a model in the design of the instrument.

The author has used the TEM Survey with over three hundred knowledge workers. In posttest surveys, participants were asked if they thought that the instrument accurately described their attitudes and knowledge about time, energy, and memory. Eighty percent of the participants said that the survey was accurate; 12 percent of the participants said that they were not sure; and 8 percent of the participants said that the survey was not accurate. In almost all cases, the participants thought that the survey was an excellent way to introduce a seminar on time management.

Administration and scoring of the instrument take thirty to forty minutes. It can be used as the basis of a one- or two-hour session, or it can be used to introduce a longer seminar. It also can be used for personnel screening and as a prescriptive device.

Intsructions for Administration

After distributing copies of the TEM Survey, the facilitator should instruct the participants to read the instructions carefully, but not to read the statements until they are instructed to do so. When all participants understand the instructions, the facilitator tells them to begin and allows twenty or thirty minutes for them to complete the instrument.

When all participants have completed the instrument, the following instructions for scoring it are given:

1. Add all the "A's" in Columns 1 and 3 of the TEM Survey Answer Sheet (Step I). Insert the totals on the proper lines of Step II. Add these totals and insert this sum on the blank line for Attitude Raw Score.

2. Add all the "B's" in Columns 2 and 4 of the TEM Survey Answer Sheet (Step I). Insert the totals on the proper lines of Step III. Add these totals and insert this sum on the blank line for Knowledge Raw Score.

3. Convert the Attitude Raw Score and Knowledge Raw Score to Graph Values (Step IV) and shade in the Attitude and Knowledge Graphs that appear in Step V to the appropriate levels.

4. To find your TEM Profile, total the Raw Scores from Steps II and III and find the Range into which this total Raw Score falls. The Range indicates your potential as a Waster, User, or Achiever.

References

Bliss. E.C. (1978). *Getting things done: The ABC's of time management.* New York: Bantam.

Cooper, J.D. (1962). *How to get more done in less time.* New York: Doubleday.

Drucker, P. (1969). *The effective executive.* New York: Harper & Row.

Jay, A. (1967). *Management and Machiavelli.* London: Hodder & Stoughton.

Lakein, A. (1974). *How to get control of your time and your life.* New York: Signet.

Mackenzie, R. (1975). *The time trap.* New York: McGraw-Hill.

Raths, L.E., Harmin, M., & Simon, S.B. (1966). *Values and teaching: Working with values in the classroom.* Columbus, OH: C.E. Merrill.

Reddin, W.J. (1977). *The management style diagnosis test.* Fredericton, New Brunswick: Organizational Tests Ltd.

Originally published in *The 1983 Annual Handbook for Faciliatators, Trainers, and Consultants.*

The TEM Survey: An Assessment of Your Effectiveness in Managing Your Time, Energy, and Memory

George J. Petrello

Managers, administrators, professional practitioners, and educators are defined by Peter Drucker as "knowledge workers." These professionals are not expected to punch time clocks, nor are they expected to be clock watchers, but their use of time, energy, and memory (TEM) determines to a great extent how successful they will be in a work environment that is limited by hours, human energy, and the capacity to retain information. Many people have inefficient attitudes about time, energy, and memory management or they do not know how to become more effective users of these precious resources.

Most people can be defined as WASTERS, USERS, or ACHIEVERS in terms of their use of time, energy, or memory. The TEM Survey will help you to ascertain whether you need to improve your attitude or increase your skills in this area.

Instructions: Following are fifty sets of statements concerning attitudes or knowledge about time, energy, and memory management. Each set contains two statements, one in Column A and one in Column B. Read each set carefully, select what you believe to be the best answer, and indicate your choice on The TEM Survey Answer Sheet by writing in an "A" or a "B" in the appropriate space. Note that the items go across the answer sheet, not down. Many of the statements in the sets are unrelated. Try not to let this frustrate you in your effort to select the best of the two statements. Although some alternatives may not apply to your work environment, select the best answer as if all statements did apply.

	A	B
1.	Your time is your responsibility.	We can always control our time.
2.	Committee meetings usually are a waste of time.	Most managers could not do their jobs well without meetings.
3.	In order to better manage out time, we need to learn to set priorities.	Training people to save time is really a waste of time.
4.	Time spent waiting is unproductive but a necessary evil.	On certain days at certain times, instruct your secretary to hold all non-emergency calls so that you have a quiet time for thinking and planning.

A	B

A

5. Your time is your tool.

6. Time analysis usually is an exercise in wasting time.

7. Analyze and suggest ways to help your boss make better use of your time.

8. Prepare a weekly "to do" list in order to plan work week ahead.

9. We have two choices: to control the amount of work for which we are responsible or to expand the amount of time that we spend doing the work.

10. Have subordinates evaluate for you how wisely you use your time.

11. Prepare a job description of your work and relate it to your own use of time. Have you subordinates do the same.

12. Do not expect a secretary to be more than a typist and a file clerk.

13. We cannot always control out time because we often do work that involves other people.

14. As a participant in a meeting, you are unable to save time.

15. Outline important telephone conversations in advance.

16. Handle business in person whenever possible.

B

The individual controls time and energy; environment has little to do with it.

Your time is a company resource.

Chasing time (leg work) usually is a time saver in the long run.

As others "What can I do to help you to make better use of your time?"

Schedule recreation for weekends and evenings.

The skill of delegation is difficult, to learn.

Avoid taking notes while talking in person to others; it is threatening to them.

Delegate work, not the job of figuring out what the work is.

Telephones usually are time wasters.

Committee meetings are different from staff meetings.

Luncheon meetings are often the most productive.

Attempt to cut down on travel through the use of conference calls.

	A	**B**
17.	The telephone can be a great intruder on out time if we permit it to be.	Avoid meetings as often as possible.
18.	Do not let courtesy stand in the way of good time management.	Control your work; do not allow your work to control you.
19.	Proper training of subordinates usually is an important time saver.	Keep your appointment calendar in one central location, usually with your secretary.
20.	Have a secretary take notes after each major appointment that you have.	Ending telephone conversations is difficult for most people.
21.	Generally. "do it now" is the best philosophy in handling paperwork.	Generally, "do it now" is the best philosophy in making people or dollar decisions.
22.	Train yourself in memory techniques to rely on instant recall.	Document telephone conversations while they are in progress.
23.	Have your own special filing system.	Having subordinates present written proposals to you is unwise because it discourages creativity.
24.	Handle minor decision-making problems while waiting for airplanes or such things as the dentist.	Use your watch as time message for those who take up your time.
25.	Most people are ill-equipped to manage their time.	Leave all files to you secretary or assistant to manage. Do not waste your time on them.
26.	The larger the organization, the less actual time the chief executive will have.	Time spent truly relaxing is of no value to your career.
27.	Take as long as time permits make an important decision.	Require a secretary or assistant to schedule all your appointments.
28.	Use discretionary on-the-job time to catch up on work-related reading.	Keep the ball in the other persons court as a way of keeping the paperwork moving meaningfully.

A   **B**

29. In trying to control time, there is a clear danger that one may cut back tasks and activities too drastically.

The best advice one can give a manager or executive is to plan one work carefully and in advance, each and every day.

30. Think of work time as separate and distinct from personal time.

Interpersonel problems may be a symptom of overstaffing.

31. Require completed work from your subordinates.

Carefully plan each days schedule of activities as tightly as possible at the beginning of the day.

32. Visit with coworkers to get the job done right and quickly.

Use the telephone as a time-saving tool.

33. Try to increase your work pace from time to time.

Executives should avoid most time commitments that are nonproductive.

34. Be careful of setting deadlines for yourself and others; it can become too autocratic.

Concentrate only on one thing at a time.

35. Logging important meetings and conversations by date and title is a very effective means of memory control.

Plan routines for processing communication and be sure that those around you know them and follow them.

36. Keep meetings flexible; do not lock yourself into a specific agenda in advance.

Carry a pocket calendar and record all appointments.

37. Expect something useful to come out of every meeting.

Doing something yourself is often the best way to save time.

38. As a general rule, meetings should be 50 percent structured and 50 percent free to allow for creativity.

Inevitably, some portion of your time will be spent on activities outside your control.

39. Use a dictation machine as a memory log.

Answer or move on all correspondence within twenty-four hours.

40. Keep all short-term paperwork in neat piles on your desk.

After each important meeting, have the minutes printed and distributed.

A	**B**
41. Expect constant interruptions during your working hours.	"Know Thyself" and "Know Thy Time" are both difficult to impossible for human beings.
42. Concentrate on details. Remember, the whole is made up of many parts.	Time analysis, like financial analysis, depend on carefully documented historical data.
43. Cut off nonproductive activities as quickly as possible.	When pushing paper, handle each piece of paper only once.
44. Wise use of small portions of time, as opposed to wise of fairly large portions of time, is key to managerial effectiveness.	Select the best time of day for the type of work required.
45. Do not allow immediate time demands to deter you from long-term goals.	Discretionary time available to executives is usually much greater than we think.
46. As a general rule, catch your supervisor in a casual relaxed atmosphere to discuss important work issues.	There is always enough time for the important things.
47. On a large project, start with the easiest tasks.	Breakfast meeting and late afternoon meetings are nonproductive and should be avoided.
48. Take a memory course for the purpose of developing the skill of holding more data in your head.	On a large project, start with the most satisfactory tasks.
49. Few executives use delegation to a great extent as a time saver.	When tense, visit colleagues for a few minutes in their offices for a change of pace.
50. Committees should meet on a regular schedule.	Handle interruptions as rapidly and as thoughtfully as possible.

The TEM Survey Answer Sheet

Instructions:

1. Add all the "A's" in Columns 1 and 3 of The TEM Survey Answer Sheet (Step I). Insert the totals on the proper lines of Step II. Add these totals and insert this sum on the blank line for Attitude Raw Score.

2. Add all the "B's" in Columns 2 and 4 of The TEM Survey Answer Sheet (Step I). Insert the totals on the proper lines of Step III. Add these totals and insert this sum on the blank line for Knowledge Raw Score.

3. Convert the Attitude Raw Score and Knowledge Raw Score to Graph Values (Step IV) and shade in the Attitude and Knowledge Graphs that appear in Step V to the appropriate levels.

4. To find your TEM Profile, total the Raw Scores, from Steps II and III, and find the Range into which this total Raw Score falls. The Range indicates your potential as a Waster, User, or Achiever.

Step I

Column 1	Column 2	Column 3	Column 4
1 _____	2 _____	3 _____	4 _____
5 _____	6 _____	7 _____	8 _____
9 _____	10 _____	11 _____	12 _____
13 _____	14 _____	15 _____	16 _____
17 _____	18 _____	19 _____	20 _____
21 _____	22 _____	23 _____	21 _____
25 _____	26 _____	27 _____	28 _____
29 _____	30 _____	31 _____	32 _____
33 _____	34 _____	35 _____	36 _____
37 _____	38 _____	39 _____	40 _____
41 _____	42 _____	43 _____	44 _____
45 _____	46 _____	47 _____	48 _____
49 _____	50 _____		
A Total _____	B Total _____	A Total _____	B Total _____

Step II

_____	+	_____	=	_____
A Total Column 1		A Total Column 3		Attitude Raw Score

Step III

_____	+	_____	=	_____
B Total Column 1		B Total Column 3		Attitude Raw Score

Step IV

Raw Score:	0–5	6–10	11–15	16–20	21–25
Conversion Index	20	40	60	80	100

Step V

Attitude		Knowledge
100	Excellent	100
80	Good	80
60	Average	60
40	Below Average	40
20	Very Poor	20

Step VI

_____	+	_____	=	_____
Step II Total		Step III Total		

Your potential level of effectiveness in the management of time, energy, and memory:

Range

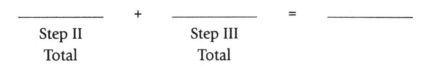

0–30	31–41	42–50
Waster	**User**	**Achiever**

11 Aptitude for Becoming a Mentor Survey

H. B. Karp

Summary

Mentoring is quickly becoming a major force for developing people within organizations. Opinions vary, however, as to what role mentoring should play, the areas it should cover, and the skills necessary to become an effective mentor. The Aptitude for Becoming a Mentor Survey (ABMS) is a twenty-item instrument that asks the respondent to assess his or her disposition toward becoming a mentor for less experienced employees of the organization. The underlying assumption of this survey is that effective mentoring, at a minimum, requires that the mentor be good at both coaching and counseling, be interpersonally competent, and possess a keen political sense.

The ABMS can be used as a diagnostic tool to allow people to gain a sense of their own proclivities toward mentoring or as part of a formal mentor training program. The author also makes the point that the desire to be a mentor is a necessary, but not the only, condition for becoming one.

Introduction

As organizations become more complex and start to use new technology, mentoring is becoming an important means of developing professional and managerial talent. Training continues to be as important to personal and professional development as it has ever been; however, in today's more complicated work environment, training alone is rarely enough. Training can be used to provide a set of skills—technical, professional, or interpersonal—for a large group of people at the same time in a consistent manner. Training is usually conducted by using a fairly uniform format with emphasis on acquiring a skill, rather than using the skill.

Because most skills are retained and/or practiced *uniquely*, a second step—development—is necessary to maximize the training, and this is where mentoring comes in. A mentor is someone with skills, experience, and perspective who has reasonable organizational influence and is willing to develop a personal working relationship with someone of lesser status in order to help that person become more effective.

Mentoring has been a recognized form of personal development for thousands of years. It was first depicted by Homer, who described Odysseus entrusting the education of his son, Telemachus, to Mentor, his chief retainer, before departing for the Trojan Wars. From that day to this, the role of the experienced guide has been revered as a means of developing the newer members of the organization.

Mentoring today takes on many aspects. It can be a single supportive encounter; an informal supportive relationship between an older, more experienced organizational member and a younger one; or a formal program sponsored and supported by an organization.

There is also a wide range of opinion regarding what types of activities comprise mentoring. Some possible activities include: training, role modeling, sponsoring, advising, coaching, counseling, guiding through organizational politics, and providing social and emotional support. The Aptitude for Becoming a Mentor Survey focuses on the last four functions: coaching, counseling, political guidance, and providing social and emotional support.

Coaching.   A coach is someone with experience in a specific area of competence whose task is to help someone else correct performance problems or find new ways to use existing skills more creatively. The main focus of coaching is task-centered, and the coach concentrates more on the protégé's cognitive abilities.

Counseling.   A counselor is typically someone with excellent interpersonal skills who assists another person in coping with personal problems and/or inappropriate behavior on the job. Counseling is people-centered, and the counselor deals with issues that are usually more emotive in nature than cognitive. Effective counselors must be able to establish empathy with the protégé, without allowing themselves to have feelings of sympathy.

Providing Political Guidance.   A political guide is an experienced and savvy organizational member who understands the system's norms and values; knows where the spheres of influence are and has access to them; and is willing to share this information with those less experienced. This is probably the most unique and helpful of all the mentoring functions. There are no training programs in "How to Be an Influential Member of the System." This can only be learned from someone who already understands the process and is willing to pass on that knowledge.

Providing Social and Emotional Support.   Mentoring calls for more than just cognitive abilities and good intentions. An effective mentor provides a place for the protégé to air partially thought-through ideas and vent feelings of anger or indecision safely. The effective mentor also provides continual encouragement as the protégé takes on new and more difficult challenges.

Description of the Survey

The Aptitude for Becoming a Mentor Survey is comprised of twenty items that measure the respondent's suitability for becoming a mentor. Each of the items deals with a skill or characteristic that is essential for effective mentoring, based on one or more of the categories described above.

Respondents rate themselves on each question using a five-point scale, then self-score the surveys to obtain a single score indicating their aptitude for becoming organizational mentors. A Rationale Sheet is provided for the facilitator to share with the respondents. The rationale for each preferred response is provided. An Interpretation Sheet is also provided that allows respondents to assess their current readiness to be a mentor by reading the implications of their particular range of scores.

There are no reliability or validity data available, as the survey is purely descriptive, rather than predictive, in nature. The survey, however, does have very high face validity in that the intention of each statement is quite clear. For that reason it is important that the facilitator state at the beginning that there are no right or wrong answers.

Administering and Scoring the Survey

The respondents answer each item by indicating their reactions to it on a five-point scale. The survey is self-scoring. Respondents simply add the numeric values of their answers together.

On all items except numbers 4, 6, 15, and 18, the items are scored from 1 through 5, from "Strongly Disagree" through "Strongly Agree." The scale is reversed on items 4, 6, 15, and 18.

Once the participants have scored their surveys, the facilitator can go over the rationale for each item by referring to the Rationale Sheet or can distribute it for later reference. The underlying assumption of the survey is that the higher one scores, the higher the probability that one has the necessary skills and outlook to become an effective mentor.

The facilitator then distributes the Interpretation Sheet and leads a discussion on the implications that can be drawn from each of the categories. This can lead to a deeper discussion of what it takes to be an effective mentor and the fact that *wanting* to be one is a necessary, but not a sufficient condition for being an effective mentor.

Originally published in *The 2000 Annual: Volume 1, Training.*

Aptitude for Becoming a Mentor Survey

H.B. Karp

Instructions: Twenty statements are listed below that pertain to effective mentoring. Please read each item carefully and circle the number on the scale that corresponds with how much you agree with the statement. Respond to each item as honestly as you can, keeping in mind that there are no right or wrong answers. When you have completed the survey, add up the numeric value of your responses and place the sum in the designated place at the end of the survey.

Please note the following scale designations:

SD = Strongly Disagree   D = Disagree   N = Neutral   A = Agree   SA = Strongly Agree

1. I am at least as people-oriented as I am task-oriented.	1 SD	2 D	3 N	4 A	5 SA
2. I see part of my job as contributing to the professional development of others.	1 SD	2 D	3 N	4 A	5 SA
3. Ordinarily, I am a good listener.	1 SD	2 D	3 N	4 A	5 SA
4. I am quick to sympathize with others' problems.	1 SA	2 A	3 N	4 D	5 SD
5. I am good at showing others better ways of doing things.	1 SD	2 D	3 N	4 A	5 SA
6. I think that political savvy is a poor substitute for professional competence.	1 SA	2 A	3 N	4 D	5 SD
7. I am good at helping other people make decisions.	1 SD	2 D	3 N	4 A	5 SA
8. I am aware of my own strengths and potential areas for growth.	1 SD	2 D	3 N	4 A	5 SA
9. I am recognized as a competent professional.	1 SD	2 D	3 N	4 A	5 SA
10. I understand how the political structure of my organization works.	1 SD	2 D	3 N	4 A	5 SA

SD = Strongly Disagree   D = Disagree   N = Neutral   A = Agree   SA = Strongly Agree

11.	I am comfortable networking with peers and those above me in the organization.	1 SD	2 D	3 N	4 A	5 SA
12.	I am good at generating alternatives.	1 SD	2 D	3 N	4 A	5 SA
13.	I am patient when working with the problems and concerns of others.	1 SD	2 D	3 N	4 A	5 SA
14.	One of my strengths is defining problems clearly.	1 SD	2 D	3 N	4 A	5 SA
15.	I have difficulty operating on the "feeling" level with other people.	1 SA	2 A	3 N	4 D	5 SD
16.	I find assisting others to be personally satisfying.	1 SD	2 D	3 N	4 A	5 SA
17.	I am held in high regard by those with whom I work and to whom I report.	1 SD	2 D	3 N	4 A	5 SA
18.	I like making decisions for other people.	1 SA	2 A	3 N	4 D	5 SD
19.	I can recognize when people need guidance or nurturing and when they need to be independent.	1 SD	2 D	3 N	4 A	5 SA
20.	I have actively sought mentors myself.	1 SD	2 D	3 N	4 A	5 SA

Total Score: _____

Aptitude for Becoming a Mentor Interpretation Sheet

There is no predetermined preferred score for this survey; however, you can get a feel for how ready you are to be mentor by reading the following interpretations of the various ranges of scores on the survey.

If You Scored Between 100 and 85

You clearly have the awareness and the confidence to be an effective mentor. You understand what it takes to support the growth of others and have a willingness to put in the necessary time and effort to do this well. You also understand and are comfortable with the role of a mentor as a political guide in the organizational "jungle."

If You Scored Between 84 and 70

You have the necessary skills and perspective to provide support for someone with less experience. You also require some growth and/or more confidence in certain areas yourself. Take the time to become clear about what it is you want to do and where your present strengths lie.

If You Scored Between 69 and 50

You have the ambition and talent to be an effective mentor in certain specific areas. It is important that you be very clear about where your talents lie and where you require some growth as well. Negotiate carefully with your protégé to decide on realistic positive outcomes from the mentoring process. When you feel less than confident or somewhat confused about what do next, discuss this with *your own mentor*.

If You Scored Between 49 and 0

Your ambition to be a mentor is exemplary and should not be ignored. To assure that the process goes well for both you and your protégé, you would do well to do some pre-work before taking on the role and responsibilities of being a mentor. If you do not have a mentor yourself, actively seek one out who can show you the ropes of mentoring. This will not only provide you with the guidance you need, but will help you to appreciate the mentoring role from the protégé's perspective. In addition, look for an opportunity to go through some formalized training to learn more about the mentoring process.

Aptitude for Becoming a Mentor Rationale Sheet

The rationale for each of the twenty items that make up the Aptitude for Becoming a Mentor Survey are given below. Although there are no right or wrong answers to the survey, some responses may indicate that one may be more or less suited for the role of a mentor. The preferred response is indicated after each item.

1. I am at least as people-oriented as I am task-oriented.   SA

    Effective mentors do put a high value on the protégé's task performance. However, it is essential that the mentor be at least as interested in the personal development of the protégé as he or she is in the protégé's successful completion of a task.

2. I see part of my job as contributing to the professional development of others.   SA

    This perspective is important for both the mentor and the organization. If the mentor sees mentoring as simply an add-on or additional burden, there is less chance of commitment. If helping to develop others is viewed as part of the job, commitment is deeper.

3. Ordinarily, I am a good listener.   SA

    The ability to listen well is the mentor's most important skill. To be able to hear and understand the protégé's concerns and problems from the protégé's perspective is the essential first step in providing any support needed.

4. I am quick to sympathize with others' problems.   SD

    On the surface, being sympathetic to a protégé's problems might seem like a positive attribute; in reality, sympathy tends to encourage protégés to take on a "victim" or "martyr" role. Empathy, on the other hand, is essential for the mentor to stay in good contact with a protégé.

5. I am good at showing others better ways of doing things.   SA

    The ability to show others better ways of doing things is comprised of two parts: (1) the capacity to see a better way of doing something and (2) the ability to explain this option clearly, concisely, and in a non-patronizing way. Effective mentoring requires not only the ability to create better solutions, but also the ability to present new options in ways that do not injure the protégé's self-esteem.

6. I think that political savvy is a poor substitute for professional
   competence.   SD

   Understanding and knowing how to work effectively within the political structure
   of the organization is one of the most important skills a mentor can pass on. Think-
   ing that political astuteness and professional competence can be separated displays
   a naiveté that would be destructive to most mentoring efforts.

7. I am good at helping other people make decisions.   SA

   Being able to assist others in making personal and professional decisions that af-
   fect their lives is an essential mentoring skill. This is quite different from actually
   making decisions for other people or assuming that you know what is best for them.
   The mentor shares his or her perspective and the protégé makes the decision.

8. I am aware of my own strengths and potential areas for growth.   SA

   Effective mentors "buy what they sell." Unless the mentor is concerned about his
   or her own growth and development, he or she will not be effective with the protégé.

9. I am recognized as a competent professional.   SA

   Acknowledging that one is a competent professional is important. Being either in-
   competent or falsely humble about one's accomplishments is a poor attribute for an
   effective mentor.

10. I understand how the political structure of my organization works. SA

    Recognizing the importance of being politically astute is the first step; understand-
    ing how the system works is the second. New protégés probably need more guid-
    ance in this area than in any other.

11. I am comfortable networking with peers and those above me in the
    organization.   SA

    Being comfortable with those on an equal or higher level is one mark of an effec-
    tive mentor. If the protégé must rely on the mentor's guidance in learning how to
    work comfortably within the system, the mentor must first be able to display that
    ability.

12. I am good at generating alternatives.   SA

    Whether the mentor is engaged in coaching or counseling, the key is to assist the
    protégé in solving problems. Generating alternatives prior to choosing a solution
    is a critical problem-solving skill.

13. I am patient when working with the problems and concerns
of others.   SA

The key to effective problem solving is having the patience to stay with the process, rather then going for the quick or easy solution. Being patient when helping a protégé with a problem not only results in a better outcome, it provides a model for the protégé to follow in the future.

14. One of my strengths is defining problems clearly.   SA

Whether the problem is personal or professional, a good mentor must stifle the impulse to go for a solution immediately. Experienced mentors understand that the more time spent analyzing the cause and nature of the problem, the easier it will be to arrive at a permanent solution.

15. I have difficulty operating on the "feeling" level with other people.   SD

Comfort with the feeling level is necessary for mentors, both in terms of providing a support base for the protégé and in acting as a counselor for specific problems.

16. I find assisting others to be personally satisfying.   SA

If the mentor-protégé relationship is to last over the long term, it must be a source of personal satisfaction for the mentor. If helping is not satisfying to the mentor, it's probably best for him or her to be available for short-term consulting, but make no attempt to establish an enduring relationship.

17. I am held in high regard by those with whom I work and to
whom I report.   SA

The more prestige the mentor has in the organization, the higher the probability that some of it will be reflected onto the protégé. Although this is not the ultimate purpose of mentoring, it does not hurt the protégé to be seen as someone who is being guided by a person of substance.

18. I like making decisions for other people.   SD

Mentors who make decisions for their protégés or who encourage protégés to follow their advice are creating an unhealthy state of dependency. Liking to make decisions for others is a control issue and hardly supports the growth of the protégé. There is nothing wrong with the mentor occasionally offering advice, so long as the protégé is encouraged to make up his or her own mind.

19. I can recognize when people need guidance or nurturing and
when they need to be independent.   SA

The long-term objective of mentoring is to help the protégé become self-supporting and independent. This is a weaning process that can happen slowly over time. It is essential for the mentor to recognize when the protégé needs the support of others and when he or she is capable of standing alone. Incidentally, the move toward protégé self-support and the eventual ending of the relationship is something that the mentor usually will be aware of long before the protégé is.

20. I have actively sought mentors myself.   SA

    This is a straightforward question. Does the mentor buy what he or she sells? A low score on this question does not preclude anyone from being an effective mentor, and it still demands an answer to the question, "If not, why not?"

12 Manager or Scientist:
An Attribute Inventory

Elizabeth N. Treher and Augustus Walker

Summary

In most technical organizations there are clear and important differences between the activity patterns, working styles, motivations, and work values of those who do scientific and technical work and those who manage them and their resources. Years of experience and hundreds of studies point to the problems often encountered when technical specialists and scientists cross the dividing line and become managers. The technical skills that served them well previously are often insufficient for managerial success and, in fact, can create significant roadblocks on the path to effective leadership and management.

The Manager or Scientist Attribute Inventory is based on twenty years of direct observation of the behavior, likes, and dislikes of successful practicing scientists and their managers. It was developed for use in supervisory and management skills workshops held for research and development groups. The inventory leads to valuable discussion and insights into managerial readiness and interests for those considering a managerial path.

Introduction

Although there is general agreement on the skills necessary for a successful manager of technical groups and specialists, tools to help individuals assess their own readiness are not readily available. We developed and have used this questionnaire in our consulting and training work in order to assist scientists and technical specialists to make the right choice and to become better managers if they move to that level. It is an empirical assessment to help technical professionals address a number of important managerial attributes, compare themselves with other technical managers, and recognize areas that may bring them potential tension and stress.

Description of the Inventory

The Manager or Scientist Attribute Inventory contains thirty paired items addressing the behaviors, attributes, motivations, and values of scientists (and other technical specialists) and managers. Participants circle items using a six-point scale and self-score their results.

Administration

This inventory can be sent to participants to complete individually before a training program or can be administered in a group setting at the time of training. Be sure to let participants know that their responses are confidential and that they will be the only ones using the data. Emphasize that there are no right or wrong answers and that no results preclude high performance as either a scientist or manager. Explain that the instrument will be helpful to the extent that their answers are as honest as possible.

Theory Behind the Inventory

Extensive research (Badawy, 1982, 1983a, 1983b; Bailey & Jensen, 1965; Boyton & Chapman, 1972; Lea & Brostrom, 1988) into differences between managers and scientists or technical workers has yielded consistent, distinct behavior patterns and preferences for these two groups. Data from the literature (Badawy, 1982, 1983a, 1983b; Boyton & Chapman, 1972) and from the authors' experience in managing technical managers and groups was distilled to produce this self-report inventory, which highlights individual preferences toward managing others and doing technical work.

You, the facilitator, must have a good grounding and understanding of the research and be able to describe the typical differences in characteristics, motivations, and behaviors of technical managers versus technical professionals. For further reading, see the list of references before the survey.

Scoring and Interpretation

To obtain a score, respondents transfer their responses to the Answer Sheet, and their numeric value is totaled by column. The following calculations are then done:

$$2M_1 + 1.5M_2 + M_3 = \text{Total Value for Managerial Attributes}$$

$$2S_1 + 1.5S_2 + S_3 = \text{Total Value for Scientist Attributes}$$

The smaller of M or S is then subtracted from the larger. The difference represents the respondent's preference for being either a manager or a scientist.

It is important to note that a strong profile for either dimension does not preclude success in the other. It does, however, indicate that there may be difficult transition issues.

Facilitating Discussion of the Inventory

It is useful to present the data on which the inventory is based after respondents fill out the inventory, but before they score it. After the discussion have the respondents predict their S and M scores relative to one another: S > M, S < M, or S = M.

Lead a discussion to review the observed and published characteristics and differences between scientists and managers. As part of that discussion, it is helpful to divide the participants into two or more small groups, each with a discussion assignment, such as listing motivators for scientists or managers, describing attributes of scientists or managers, or listing work values of scientists or managers. After these discussions, have each subgroup present its views to the total group. Such presentations are generally very consistent with published research on the topic.

Another approach is to divide the participants into four subgroups according to their scores and then assign each group the discussion questions below. Those whose scores do not place them into any of these categories can rotate and sit in on different discussions.

Group 1: Those Who Score High S and Are S. Do these results fit you? What issues might you face if you become a manager? What are likely to be your biggest challenges on becoming a manager? Do you really want to become a manager?

Group 2: Those Who Score High M and Are M. Do these results fit you? What has helped you develop management skills? Where might your views differ from those of your staff? How can you help others to develop the attributes of a good manager?

Group 3: Those Who Score High S and Are M.   Do these results fit you? What are some of your frustrations in managing technical work? What gives you the greatest satisfaction at work? How could you develop your management skills and interests further? How could you gather feedback on how you are doing as a manager?

Group 4: Those Who Score High M and Are S. Do these results fit you? What gives you the greatest satisfaction at work? How could you develop your management skills? How could you demonstrate your interest in management? Who could help you to develop into a manager? How can you combine your technical responsibilities with your management interests? What are the roadblocks, if any, to your becoming a manager.

Other Suggested Uses

This inventory has been used primarily for management and supervisory skills training. It can also be used in one-on-one coaching and in career counseling settings. It is not intended to limit or discourage individuals from becoming technical managers, but to help them better understand and prepare for potential roadblocks and sources of frustration on the road to management excellence. The inventory is also useful in helping to target areas for personal development.

Reliability and Validity

The Manager or Scientist Attribute Inventory is intended for use as an analytical tool, not a psychometric or rigorous data-gathering instrument. The inventory has shown a high level of face validity with the hundreds of technical specialists and managers who have used it.

References

Badawy, M.K. (1982). *Developing managerial skills in engineers and scientists.* New York: Van Nostrand Reinhold.

Badawy, M.K. (1983a). Managing career transitions. In *The first-level manager: Selected papers from research management.* Washington DC: Industrial Research Institute.

Badawy, M.K. (1983b). Why managers fail. In *The first-level manager: Selected papers from research management.* Washington DC: Industrial Research Institute.

Bailey, R.E., & Jensen, B.T. (1965, September/October). The troublesome transition from scientist to manager. *Personnel,* pp. 49–55.

Boyton, J.A., & Chapman, R.L. (1972). *Transformation of scientists and engineers into managers.* (NASA SP-291.) Washington DC: NASA National Academy of Science Administration.

Boyton, J.A., & Chapman, R.L. (1985). Making managers of scientists and engineers. In *The first-level manager: Selected papers from research management*. Washington DC: Industrial Research Institute.

Lea, D., & Brostrom, R. (1988, June). Managing the high-tech professional. *Personnel*, pp. 12–22.

Manners, G.E., & Steger, J.A. (1979). Implications of research on R&D manager's role to selection and training of scientists and engineers for management. *R&D Management*, 9(2), 85–91.

McBean, E.A. (1991, May/June). Analysis of teaching and course questionnaires: A case study. *Engineering Education*, pp. 431–441.

Medcof, J.W. (1985). Training technologists to become managers. *Research Management*, pp. 41–44.

Oppenheim, A.N. (1966). *Questionnaire design and attitude measurement*. New York: Basic Books.

Overton, L.M., Jr. (1969). R&D management: Turning scientists into managers. *Personnel*, 46(3), 56–63.

Pearson, A.W. (1993, January/February). Management development for scientists and engineers. *Research Technology Management*, pp. 45–48.

Walker, A.C. (1990). *Effective technical management*. Washington DC: American Chemical Society.

Originally published in *The 2000 Annual: Volume 1, Training.*

Manager or Scientist Attribute Inventory

Elizabeth N. Treher and Augustus Walker

Directions: Read each of the pairs of statements that follow. If you strongly agree with the statement on the left, circle 1. If you strongly favor the statement on the right, circle 6. If you do not strongly agree with either statement, circle the number that best represents your feelings about the two statements in general. There are no right or wrong answers. Use your own views, not those you think others might have or prefer that you have.

1. In solving nonroutine problems, the leader should provide support.

    In solving nonroutine problems, the leader should give direction and ideas.

    1   2   3   4   5   6

2. I prefer to have all the facts before making a decision.

    I am comfortable making decisions based on partial information.

    1   2   3   4   5   6

3. The organization I work for is my primary source of satisfaction and professional recognition.

    I obtain satisfaction and recognition from outside professional contacts and associations.

    1   2   3   4   5   6

4. I prefer to do many varied things and not go into any one activity too deeply.

    I prefer to focus my attention on one important thing and get to the bottom of it.

    1   2   3   4   5   6

5. I prefer to work in my own area of expertise and not become involved in projects crossing several technical disciplines.

    I enjoy working as a generalist or on interdisciplinary problems.

    1   2   3   4   5   6

6. I like to generate new information and results on problems.

    I like to see that available information is found and used effectively.

    1   2   3   4   5   6

7. Decisions should be made analytically on the basis of the facts.

    Political and human considerations should influence all decisions.

    1   2   3   4   5   6

8. I like to run things and be highly visible.

    I prefer to influence decisions quietly through my own expertise and reputation.

    1   2   3   4   5   6

9. I prefer to consider my ideas carefully and put them in writing.

    I prefer discussing my ideas with others and giving presentations.

    1   2   3   4   5   6

10. When something goes wrong, the individual responsible should take the blame.

    When something goes wrong, the manager should take the blame.

    1   2   3   4   5   6

11. I enjoy working with people from other departments and functions.

    I prefer working with people with similar backgrounds and interests.

    1   2   3   4   5   6

12. It is usually better to figure out what the real problem is rather than to take quick action.

    I have a strong sense of urgency and like to react quickly when something goes wrong.

    1   2   3   4   5   6

13. When my colleagues have arguments, I like to help resolve them.

    When my colleagues have arguments, I prefer not to become involved.

    1   2   3   4   5   6

14. People and decisions interest me more than things and ideas.

    Things and ideas interest me more than people and decisions.

    1   2   3   4   5   6

15. The most important thing is to understand and solve the problem.

    The most important thing is to meet goals and objectives.

    1   2   3   4   5   6

16. I work well under stress and with urgent schedules. Things can drift without deadlines.

   1   2   3

I work best when the pressure comes from my own interests and when schedules are realistic.

   4   5   6

17. I enjoy interpreting the business goals of the organization and deciding how technology can help achieve them.

   1   2   3

I enjoy theoretical and experimental work. In the long run it is the principal basis for growth and profit.

   4   5   6

18. I like to identify a problem and solve it myself.

   1   2   3

I like to see that problems are identified and solved as efficiently possible.

   4   5   6

19. I like to get to work early and leave late. A sense of urgency is important to the organization.

   1   2   3

I like flexibility to come and go as my work demands. Creative insights cannot always be produced by schedules and pressure.

   4   5   6

20. Generally, I study something only long enough to satisfy an immediate need.

   1   2   3

Generally, I study something thoroughly so that I can understand and use it well.

   4   5   6

21. I prefer shared accountability and interdependence.

   1   2   3

I prefer individual accountability and independent work.

   4   5   6

22. I believe that independent groups of specialists pursuing their own projects accomplish the most.

   1   2   3

I believe that integrating technical groups is essential to accomplishing the most.

   4   5   6

23. Organizational politics play a necessary role in setting goals and doing the work.

   1   2   3

Organizational politics waste time and energy and get in the way of quality, creative work.

   4   5   6

24. I sometimes ignore others'
    views in defending my position
    when I believe I am right.

    1   2   3   4   5   6

    I am flexible and willing to
    compromise my ideas for
    the organization's good.

25. A technical manager is a
    manager of people with
    technical training.

    1   2   3   4   5   6

    A technical manager is a technically
    trained person with additional
    management responsibilities.

26. I like to solve problems in
    clever and unusual ways.

    1   2   3   4   5   6

    I like to solve problems in
    familiar and established ways.

27. Understanding how things
    work is a major source of
    stimulation for me.

    1   2   3   4   5   6

    Getting things done and
    seeing practical results
    is what motivates me.

28. I enjoy helping others find
    their own answers and
    solve their own problems.

    1   2   3   4   5   6

    I prefer to answer
    questions and solve
    problems on my own.

29. To be respected, a technical
    manager should always
    know more than his or
    her subordinates.

    1   2   3   4   5   6

    To be respected, a technical
    manager must be able to
    recognize, use, and acknowledge
    subordinate strengths.

30. I like to speculate and approach
    problems from a theoretical
    and abstract point of view.

    1   2   3   4   5   6

    I like to identify the goal
    and work toward it in a
    practical and realistic way.

Manager or Scientist Attribute Inventory Scoring Key

Directions: To score the inventory, first circle the number corresponding to your answer on each question on the scoring key below. Next, add the numbers you circled in each column and enter each of the totals at the bottom of the six columns.

Use these formulas to calculate your final score:

$$M = 2M_1 + 1.5M_2 + M_3$$

$$S = 2S_1 + 1.5S_2 + S_3$$

Example: Add the numbers in each column on the manager side of the scoring sheet. Say your totals are $M_1 = 19$, $M_2 = 29$ and $M_3 = 7$. Your calculation would look like this: $M = [2(19) + 1.5(29) + 7] = 89$. Now add the numbers in each column on the scientist side of the scoring sheet. Say you have $S_1 = 6$, $S_2 = 18$, and $S_3 = 24$. Then your S calculation would look like this: $S = [2(6) + 1.5(18) + 24] = 63$.

Now subtract the smaller of M or S from the larger. The difference represents your level of preference for either the manager or the scientist attributes.

For example, if your scores had been M = 70 and S = 90, you would find an excess S of 20. See the interpretation below.

Number	Manager's Profile			Scientist's Profile		
1.	1	2	3	4	5	6
2.	6	5	4	3	2	1
3.	1	2	3	4	5	6
4.	1	2	3	4	5	6
5.	6	5	4	3	2	1
6.	6	5	4	3	2	1
7.	6	5	4	3	2	1
8.	1	2	3	4	5	6
9.	6	5	4	3	2	1
10.	6	5	4	3	2	1
11.	1	2	3	4	5	6
12.	6	5	4	3	2	1
13.	1	2	3	4	5	6
14.	1	2	3	4	5	6
15.	6	5	4	3	2	1
16.	1	2	3	4	5	6
17.	1	2	3	4	5	6

Number	Manager's Profile			Scientist's Profile		
18.	6	5	4	3	2	1
19.	1	2	3	4	5	6
20.	1	2	3	4	5	6
21.	1	2	3	4	5	6
22.	6	5	4	3	2	1
23.	1	2	3	4	5	6
24.	6	5	4	3	2	1
25.	1	2	3	4	5	6
26.	6	5	4	3	2	1
27.	6	5	4	3	2	1
28.	1	2	3	4	5	6
29.	6	5	4	3	2	1
30.	6	5	4	3	2	1

Add and
enter
the total
for each
column.

$M_1 =$ $\quad M_2 =$ $\quad M_3 =$ $\qquad\qquad S_3 =$ $\quad S_2 =$ $\quad S_1 =$

_____ _____ _____ _____ _____ _____

_____ + _____ + _____ = _____
$2M_1$ $\qquad 1.5M_2$ $\qquad M_3$ $\qquad M$

_____ + _____ + _____ = _____
$2S_1$ $\qquad 1.5S_2$ $\qquad S_3$ $\qquad S$

Interpretation

If you have a total score of M – S equal to or greater than 25, it suggests you are somewhat more comfortable with the activities and work patterns of a manager than with those of a scientist. If your S – M number is equal to or greater than 25, the reverse is true. The greater the difference, the greater the discomfort level is likely to be for someone attempting to work in the other domain. Differences of 25 or less cannot be interpreted.

Please note that even a large difference between your scores does not necessarily mean that you cannot perform well in the other domain. It does suggest that you may find it uncomfortable to do so. As a first-line technical supervisor, your work would probably continue to be highly "hands on." However, as a technical expert advances to higher levels of management, the differences become more important and apparent between those with greater technical attributes versus those with greater managerial attributes. The pressure may be very difficult for those with large differences between their S scores and their M scores.

13 Supervisory Attitudes:
The X-Y Scale[1]

Summary

This instrument is a practical way to introduce McGregor's theory to respondents, who then discuss the results and check their own understanding and supervisory attitudes.

The theory underlying this scale is explained briefly in the Supervisory Attitudes Lecturette, which follows Part II of the instrument. The intent is to use the X-Y Scale to introduce the McGregor theory by having the respondent think about his or her own style first.

Five steps can be incorporated into the use of the X-Y Scale:

1. Have trainees complete Part I of the scale.

2. Give a brief lecturette on the Theory X-Theory Y formulation.

3. Have trainees complete Part II.

4. Score Part I and illustrate how trainees locate themselves on the scale using that score.

5. Lead a discussion of the results, comparing discrepancies between self-perception and more specific data at Part I.

Originally published in *The 1972 Annual Handbook for Faciliatators, Trainers, and Consultants.*

---

[1]The X-Y Scale was adapted from an instrument developed by Robert N. Ford of AT&T for in-house training of supervisors. Ten items were taken from the longer instrument, and the selection was based on their application to a wide variety of training enterprises.

X–Y Scale: Part I

Name: _____ Group: _____

Instructions: The following sentences describe various types of behavior that a supervisor may use in relation to subordinates. Read each item carefully and decide how likely you would be to act in that manner. Do you make a great effort to do this? Do you tend to do this? Do you tend to avoid doing this? Do you make a great effort to avoid doing this?

Indicate your response by circling the appropriate number on the Supervisory Attitudes Scoring Sheet.

1. Closely supervise my subordinates in order to get better work from them.

2. Set the goals and objectives for my subordinates and sell them on the merits of my plans.

3. Set up controls to ensure that my subordinates are getting the job done.

4. Encourage my subordinates to set their own goals and objectives.

5. Make sure that my subordinates' work is planned out for them.

6. Check with my subordinates daily to see if they need any help.

7. Step in as soon as reports indicate that the job is slipping.

8. Push my people to meet schedules if necessary.

9. Have frequent meetings to keep in touch with what is going on.

10. Allow subordinates to make important decisions.

Supervisory Attitudes Scoring Sheet

	Make a Great Effort to Do This	Tend to Do This	Tend to Avoid Doing This	Make a Great Effort to Avoid This
1.	1	2	3	4
2.	1	2	3	4
3.	1	2	3	4
4.	4	3	2	1
5.	1	2	3	4
6.	1	2	3	4
7.	1	2	3	4
8.	1	2	3	4
9.	1	2	3	4
10.	4	3	2	1

Total of circled items: _____

X–Y Scale: Part II

Instructions: Read the descriptions of the two theories of leadership below. Think about your own attitudes toward subordinates and locate on the scale below where you think you are in reference to these sets of assumptions.

Theory X Assumptions

1. The average human being has an inherent dislike of work and will avoid it if he or she can.

2. Because of this human characteristic of dislike for work, most people must be coerced, controlled, directed, and threatened with punishment to get them to put forth adequate effort toward the achievement of organizational objectives.

3. The average human being prefers to be directed, wishes to avoid responsibility, has relatively little ambition, and wants security above all.

Theory Y Assumptions

1. The expenditure of physical and mental effort in work is as natural as play or rest.

2. External control and threats of punishment are not the only means of coaxing effort toward organizational objectives. Human beings will exercise self-direction and self-control for objectives to which they are committed.

3. Commitment to objectives is a function of the rewards associated with their achievement.

4. The average human being learns under proper conditions not only to accept but also to seek responsibility.

5. The capacity to exercise a high degree of imagination, ingenuity, and creativity in the solution of organizational problems is widely—not narrowly—distributed in the population.

6. Under the conditions of modern industrial life, the intellectual potential of the average human being is only partially utilized.

Indicate on the scale below where you would classify your own basic attitudes toward your subordinates in terms of McGregor's Theory X and Theory Y.

Theory X   10   20   30   40   Theory Y

How does your placement compare with the total of the items you circled on the Supervisory Attitudes Scoring Sheet?

Supervisory Attitudes Lecturette[2]

Douglas McGregor (1957, 1966) linked a psychological view of human motivation to a theory of management, originating the terms "Theory X" and "Theory Y." For McGregor, Theory X assumptions considered the average person to be lazy and to avoid work, necessitating that workers be controlled and led. In contrast, Theory Y assumptions viewed workers as responsible and eager to be involved in their work. McGregor believed that the role of management was to set up a framework so that workers could meet their own goals by investing effort in the organization's goals.

McGregor's approach was based on the motivation theory of Abraham Maslow (1943). Maslow's hierarchy of human needs can be depicted as a pyramid, with survival needs as the bottom layer and with security, social, esteem, and self-development needs as successive layers (see Figure 1). Before one of these needs can be met, its underlying needs must first be fulfilled, at least to some extent. Therefore, if the workers' survival and security needs are met, work that fulfills their higher needs can enable them to direct their efforts toward organizational as well as individual goals.

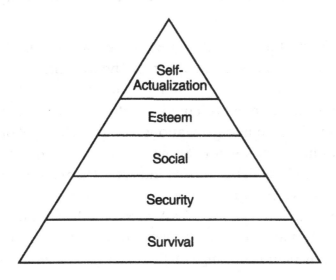

Figure 1. Maslow's Hierarchy of Human Needs

This approach is predicated on managers' diagnosing individual workers' needs and offering opportunities to meet those needs. However, although specific individual needs span a great range, the basic categories of need are few in number. In addition, involving workers in delineating their own needs, goals, and potential rewards makes the task of creating appropriate organizational conditions more feasible.

---

[2] Based on Marshall Sashkin, "An Overview of Ten Management and Organizational Theorists," in J.E. Jones & J.W. Pfeiffer (Eds.), *The 1981 Annual*, pp. 206-221. San Francisco: Pfeiffer, 1981.

McGregor stated:

> There are big differences in the kinds of opportunities that can be provided for people to obtain need satisfaction. It is relatively easy to provide means (chiefly in the form of money) for need satisfaction-at least until the supply is exhausted. You cannot, however, provide people with a sense of achievement, or with knowledge, or with prestige. You can provide *opportunities* for them to obtain these satisfactions through efforts directed toward organizational goals. What is even more important, *the supply of such opportunities*—unlike the supply of money—*is unlimited.* (1966, pp. 44–45)

Jacoby and Terborg (1986), in their "Managerial Philosophies Scale," make the following observations about Theory X and Theory Y behaviors:

> Berelson and Steiner, in their classic book, *Human Behavior* (New York: Harcourt Brace), list 1,045 findings from scientific studies of human behavior . . . . Strong support is advanced by Berelson and Steiner for McGregor's Theory Y as a simple restatement of the characteristics shown by scientific research to be typical for the "average" person in our culture. Thus, the probability is .68, or greater than 2 to 1, that people encountered by managers will possess characteristics and, under proper conditions, display traits consistent with Theory Y expectations. (p. 4)

Since McGregor's introduction of the terms, organizations have shown a shift from an obvious Theory X orientation to an apparent Theory Y orientation. Berelson and Steiner's conclusion that 68 percent of employees hold Theory Y beliefs supports the idea that a Theory Y management orientation will be appropriate most of the time for most employees. The shift in organizations toward a Theory Y orientation has resulted in an interesting phenomenon. Some managers have developed the rhetoric of Theory Y while exhibiting behavior that indicates Theory X assumptions. As a result, these managers give an illusion of a Theory Y orientation that is in fact a disguised Theory X orientation. The mixed X-Y messages that result can create distrust and ineffectiveness. Managers can build trust and contribute to improved organizational effectiveness by demonstrating consistency between what they say and what they do.

References

Jacoby, J., & Terborg, J.R. (1986). *Managerial philosophies scale.* The Woodlands, TX: Teleometrics International.

McGregor, D.M. (1957). The human side of enterprise. *The Management Review, 46*(11), 26.

McGregor, D.M. (1966). A philosophy of management. In W.G. Bennis & E.H. Schein (Eds.), with the collaboration of C. McGregor, *Leadership and motivation: Essays of Douglas McGregor.* Cambridge, MA: MIT. Press.

Part 2
Present Performance

Assessments in the previous section looked at the values, fears, attitudes, and personality traits that lie behind management behavior. The ones in this section paint a picture of the behavior itself. Some are self-scoring. Others allow subordinates, peers, and higher-level managers to provide individuals with feedback about how they are perceived by others—and the effects of those perceptions on the job performance of everyone involved.

The insights harvested by these instruments not only isolate areas in which an individual needs to improve but provide a powerful incentive to make those improvements. You can *say* you want to lead a team whose members trust each other and pull together for the good of the organization, but do your actions support that goal or undermine it? How effectively do you communicate with your followers, or with people in other units, or with those from different cultural backgrounds?

Information like that is worth its weight in gold in management development initiatives. It also can help the organization determine who should be given a management role in the first place. One assessment in this section, "Supervisor Selection," is designed to do precisely that. Some others could be used for the same purpose.

Here are thumbnail descriptions of the eleven instruments in Section 2.

- Leading Workplace Collaboration: A Literature-Based Model and Self-Assessment Inventory—Managers rate themselves or are rated by others on their ability to foster collaboration and promote unity in work groups.

- The Leadership Dimensions Survey—Subordinates or peers rate a manager's leadership ability on four dimensions.

- Role Efficacy Scale—Measures the perceived degree of autonomy, fulfillment, and effectiveness that managers experience in their current job roles.

- The Communication Climate Inventory—Measures behaviors of individual managers and supervisors that affect the level of honesty and openness in the work groups they oversee.

- Cross-Cultural Interactive Preference Profile—Examines both individual preferences and the ability to communicate effectively with people whose cultural conditioning differs from one's own.

- The High-Performance Factors Inventory: Assessing Work-Group Management and Practices—A working group and its leader are assessed on twenty-five factors that correlate with high performance.

- Organization Behavior Describer Survey (OBDS)—Can be used to assess communication behaviors of a boss, a subordinate, a peer, or oneself.

- Cornerstones: A Measure of Trust in Work Relationships—Rates the level of trust between individuals in the same work group or organization.

- Supervisor Selection: The Supervisory Assessment Instrument—Allows managers to rate the skills and aptitude of candidates for supervisory positions.

- Simulations: Pre- and Post-Evaluations of Performance—Pre- and post-assessments designed for use in conjunction with in-basket exercises and other management-training simulations.

- Organizational Role Stress—Managers or executives concerned that they are approaching "burnout" analyze factors contributing to their stress.

14 Leading Workplace Collaboration:
A Literature-Based Model and Self-Assessment Inventory

Doug Leigh

Summary

Leader-managers influence their subordinates' performance each day they enter their workplaces. But how are they to improve collaboration among those they supervise? What attributes should they seek to develop? At least six patterns emerge from relevant management and organizational behavior literature regarding how leader-managers build unity through collaboration: teaming, motivating subordinates, career counseling, communicating with subordinates, professional relationships, and issues related to morale and quality of work life. This article describes the literature basis for these characteristics and applies this to a self-assessment instrument that calibrates leader-managers' success in fostering collaboration within their organizations.

Effective leader-managers understand that their duty is twofold. First, they are entrusted with the accomplishment of organizational objectives. Through these performances, they enable their organizations to deliver useful results to internal and external stakeholders alike. However, the second charge of the leader-managers rarely appears on their job descriptions: the development of unity among those subordinates whose work they oversee. Without this, even the most well-planned undertakings are likely to yield less than optimal results. Even in the rare instances in which objectives do happen to be accomplished despite a work environment unfavorable to effective collaboration, those results are often achieved at a much slower pace, require costly rework, and do little to increase employees' morale. The breakneck speed of today's organizations, coupled with the quality expectations of customers and service recipients, make such allowances unacceptable.

Customers and other stakeholders vote with their feet—if they don't receive that which they were promised, they'll find it elsewhere. By developing the six characteristics described below, leader-managers can increase their ability to deliver useful organizational results through fostering increased collaboration among their subordinates.

Characteristic 1: Teaming

The first characteristic of effective leader-managers is the ability to form and maintain teams to achieve organizational objectives. Hersey and Blanchard (1982) suggest that tasks should be delegated to followers at the highest "maturity" (or readiness) level, when they are both able and willing to carry out the job at hand. Thus, it is important that teams be formed only when appropriate. When teams are formed, organizational politics often require that leader-managers "go to bat" for subordinates to secure resources necessary for their success (Bolman & Deal, 1997). Fostering active participation in teams has been found to have the capacity to simultaneously increase both productivity and morale (Levine & Tyson, 1990). However, promoting participation in and of itself will not necessarily yield desired results unless leader-managers trust subordinates to work independently. Similarly, while performance feedback is critical to team success, the feedback subordinates receive must not be too general, but be specific to the tasks to be accomplished (Kluger & DeNisi, 1998). Last, effective leader-managers must also grant subordinates the authority to carry out the tasks assigned to them (Bennis & Nanus, 1985). Zander and Zander (2000) liken this act of empowerment to that of the symphony conductor whose own power comes from bringing out the power of other musicians.

Characteristic 2: Motivating Subordinates

The second essential characteristic of the leader-manager is motivating subordinates' to make useful contributions toward departmental objectives. Of the multitude of approaches to motivation, perhaps the most promising means by which to influence goal-directed behavior is through managing subordinates' expectations of successful goal accomplishment as well as the perceived value of those goals (Weiner, 1992). To this end, the first job of motivating subordinates is to inform them of the purpose of tasks assigned to them (Bridges, 1991). Second, leader-managers must ensure that subordinates perceive the accomplishment of organizational goals as being valuable and worthwhile.

Characteristic 3: Career Counseling

Building collaboration in the workplace requires leader-managers to counsel subordinates on matters of performance and professional development. Bolman and Deal (1997) point out that very often change initiatives require collateral investments in training and education. Thus, subordinates should receive career counseling regarding educational opportunities that are relevant to both current and future jobs required of them. In addition, career counseling provides leader-managers an opening to align the results achieved within their departments to accomplishments benefiting the organization and it's external clients, including society (Leigh, 2003). Argyris and Schön (1996) describe this practice as consistent with a model of interpersonal dynamics that is characterized by leader-managers openly expressing their own perspectives on organizational goals, while seeking to understand and learn from the perspectives of subordinates. Last, if subordinates are to learn and improve from their undertakings, their supervisors must also monitor their performance following career counseling. Such evaluation serves to help subordinates redefine past practices, break from the status quo, and establish new beliefs regarding the organization (Rallis, 1980).

Characteristic 4: Communicating with Subordinates

Associated with the issue of counseling is the fourth characteristic of leader-managers: communicating effectively with subordinates. Organizational communications serve not only to send and receive information, but also to give meaning to messages (Goldhaber, 1993). A prerequisite for communication, then, is that leader-managers openly and confidently engage in professional dialogue with their subordinates. A second aspect of communications involves ensuring that verbal directions provided to subordinates regarding tasks are not misunderstood, thus creating the necessity for rework. In addition to giving performance feedback, an open communicator not only accepts subordinates' observations regarding operations, but also actively solicits and makes informed decisions about the appropriate action to be taken on the basis of such feedback. Leader-managers must also take care to ensure that verbal communications are not contradicted by "body language" or other nonverbal forms of communication (Knapp & Hall, 1997). Last, Kanter (1983) points out that promoting change often begins with gaining the buy-in of one's supervisors. Because of this, leader-managers should not only maintain effective communications with subordinates, but also be skillful at communicating up their organizational reporting structures as well.

Characteristic 5: Professional Relationships

Building professional relationships is the fifth characteristic of effective leader-managers. That communication within an organization can travel up, down, or across an organizational hierarchy is not a new idea (see Shannon & Weaver, 1949). Leader-managers are obliged to develop linkages through networking not only up the organizational hierarchy, but also among peers, key stakeholders, and outside information brokers. Internally, mentoring relationships are critical for the development of subordinates' skills (Galbraith & Cohen, 1995). However, in an examination of faculty mentoring behaviors, Blackwell (1990) warns of the tendency to choose protégés only from like ethnic and gender backgrounds. In the interest of capitalizing on the strengths of a diverse workforce, leader-managers in business could also stand to benefit from developing mentoring relationships with those from marginalized or underrepresented groups. Similarly, while overt forms of racism and sexism are less common in today's organizations, leader-managers should take care to prevent inappropriate discriminatory practices between subordinates in the workplace.

Characteristic 6: Improving Morale and Quality of Work Life

The final characteristic of leader-managers who foster collaboration in the workplace involves improving morale and maintaining positive perceptions of the quality of life at work. Faltering morale among subordinates can lead to missed work days, which can result in productivity problems and even a rise in medical and disability claims (Bridges, 1991). In extreme cases, subordinates may even request transfers or quit due to dissatisfaction with their work center. Clearly, then, leader-managers should ensure that morale problems are addressed quickly and appropriately.

Description and Administration of the Instrument

The Workplace Collaboration Inventory is designed to provide a personal assessment of a leader-manager's competencies regarding six patterns of unity-building through collaboration: teaming, motivating subordinates, career counseling, communicating with subordinates, professional relationships, and issues related to morale and quality of work life. Developed as a self-assessment tool, the Inventory solicits individual reflections regarding one's skills and abilities as they currently exist, as well as how they should ideally be. The inventory should be completed individually, in one sitting, and will likely not take more than 20 minutes to complete.

Scoring the Instrument

The Workplace Collaboration Inventory is not intended to provide an overall score, but rather suggest gaps between "What is" and "What should be" according to six related characteristics of effective collaboration. To score each of these scales, simply input the values from the survey in the scoring tables and make the necessary calculations. First total down within each column, then subtract the total "What is" score from the total "What should be" score for each scale, finally dividing the score by the number of items in the scale. It is possible to have negative total scores within each scale: scale totals can range from +6 to −6. Note that while "What is" appears on the left of the instrument and "What should be" on the right, *this sequence is reversed in the scoring sheet* to facilitate tabulation of results.

Interpreting the Results

While there are no absolutes regarding the interpretation of scores on the Workplace Collaboration Inventory, some general guidelines can be suggested. Overall scores of 3 or lower on any scale indicate that a particular behavior may be insufficient on the part of the leader-manager. In such cases, it may be important to examine which items are contributing most to the discrepancy and work to resolve the misalignment. On the other hand, overall scores that are negative suggest that the leader-manager may be dedicating too much time and effort to a particular behavior, perhaps at the expense of other important activities. Again, individual items should be analyzed to identify possible extreme cases that are skewing the totals. In any case, individual "What is" items scored as 1, 2, or 3 may be seen as requiring the most immediate attention, as they typically indicate a relative inattention of a particular behavior.

Suggested Uses

The results of this assessment can be useful both as a tool for individual growth and as one of the components used in performance evaluations of leader-managers. In addition to providing a self-assessment of one's collaboration skills, asking subordinates and supervisors about their perceptions of the leader-manager's competencies can also provide useful information. Alternative approaches to the inventory include asking subordinates to complete the instrument *about their leader-managers* (replacing "I" with "My supervisor" and conjugating verbs in the third person), or using variants of the instrument in a multi-rater or 360-degree evaluation.

References

Argyris, C., & Schön, D. (1996). *Organizational learning II: Theory, method and practice.* Reading: MA: Addison-Wesley.

Bennis, W.G., & Nanus, B. (1985). *Leaders: Strategies for taking charge.* New York: Harper-Collins.

Blackwell, J.E. (1990). Operationalizing faculty diversity. *AAHE Bulletin, 42* (10), 8–9.

Bolman, L.G., & Deal, T.E. (1997). *Reframing organizations: Artistry, choice, and leadership.* San Francisco: Jossey-Bass.

Bridges, W. (1991). *Managing transitions: Making the most of change.* Reading, MA: Addison Wesley.

Galbraith, M.W., & Cohen, N.H. (1995). *Mentoring: New strategies and challenges.* San Francisco: Jossey-Bass.

Goldhaber, G.M. (1993). *Organizational communication.* Madison, WI: Brown & Benchmark.

Hersey, P., & Blanchard, K. (1982). *Management of organizational behavior: Utilizing human resources* (4th ed.). Englewood Cliffs, NJ: Prentice-Hall.

Kanter, R.M. (1983). *The change masters: Innovations for productivity in the American corporation.* New York: Simon & Schuster.

Kluger, A., & DeNisi, A., (1998). Feedback interventions: Toward the understanding of a double-edged sword. *Current Directions in Psychological Science, 7*(3), pp. 67–72.

Knapp, M.L., & Hall, J.A. (1997). *Nonverbal communications in human interaction.* Fort Worth, TX: Harcourt Brace.

Leigh, D. (2003). How can I become a more effective leader-manager? In M. Silberman (Ed.), *The 2003 training and performance sourcebook.* Princeton, NJ: Active Training.

Levine, D., & Tyson, L. (1990). Participation, productivity, and the firm's environment." In A. Blinder (Ed.), *Paying for productivity: A look at the evidence.* Washington, DC: Brookings Institution.

Rallis, S. (1980). *Different views on knowledge use by practitioners.* Unpublished paper, Graduate School of Education, Harvard University.

Shannon, C.E., & Weaver, W. (1949). *The mathematical theory of communication.* Urbana, IL: University of Illinois Press.

Weiner, B. (1992). *Human motivation: Metaphors, theories, and research.* Newbury Park, CA: Sage.

Zander, R.S., & Zander, B. (2000). *The art of possibility.* Boston, MA: Harvard Business School Press.

Originally published in *The 2004 Pfeiffer Annual: Volume 1, Training.*

Workplace Collaboration Inventory

Doug Leigh

Instructions: Please consider each of the following statements and provide *two responses* to each question:

| What Is | | | | | | | | | | | | What Should Be | | | | | |

Completely Agree	Strongly Agree	Agree	Disagree	Strongly Disagree	Completely Disagree	What Is	What Should Be	Completely Agree	Strongly Agree	Agree	Disagree	Strongly Disagree	Completely Disagree
						"What Is" describes how you see yourself *currently* functioning.	"What Should Be" describes how you think you *should be* functioning.						
1	2	3	4	5	6	1. I form teams only when my subordinates are both able and willing to carry out the task at hand.		1	2	3	4	5	6
1	2	3	4	5	6	2. I make sure that my teams receive the resources required to be successful.		1	2	3	4	5	6
1	2	3	4	5	6	3. I encourage active participation of all team members.		1	2	3	4	5	6
1	2	3	4	5	6	4. I trust my subordinates not to take unfair advantage of the participative systems that I design.		1	2	3	4	5	6
1	2	3	4	5	6	5. Teams that I form receive task-specific feedback from me.		1	2	3	4	5	6
1	2	3	4	5	6	6. I allow my subordinates the authority to accomplish objectives using the means that they know to be most effective.		1	2	3	4	5	6
1	2	3	4	5	6	7. I inform subordinates about the purpose of tasks assigned to them.		1	2	3	4	5	6

What Is   **What Should Be**

						What Is	What Should Be						
Completely Agree	Strongly Agree	Agree	Disagree	Strongly Disagree	Completely Disagree	"What Is" describes how you see yourself *currently* functioning.	"What Should Be" describes how you think you *should be* functioning.	Completely Agree	Strongly Agree	Agree	Disagree	Strongly Disagree	Completely Disagree

1	2	3	4	5	6	8.	My subordinates perceive the accomplishment of tasks as valuable.	1	2	3	4	5	6
1	2	3	4	5	6	9.	I counsel subordinates on issues of career advancement and educational opportunities, both before and after performance evaluations.	1	2	3	4	5	6
1	2	3	4	5	6	10.	My subordinates and I mutually set goals during counseling.	1	2	3	4	5	6
1	2	3	4	5	6	11.	After counseling them, I monitor progress to give subordinates useful feedback.	1	2	3	4	5	6
1	2	3	4	5	6	12.	I openly communicate with my subordinates.	1	2	3	4	5	6
1	2	3	4	5	6	13.	I prevent rework by providing clear and understandable verbal directions.	1	2	3	4	5	6
1	2	3	4	5	6	14.	I take appropriate actions based on feedback from others.	1	2	3	4	5	6
1	2	3	4	5	6	15.	I ensure that there are no discrepancies between my verbal and nonverbal communications.	1	2	3	4	5	6
1	2	3	4	5	6	16.	I report effectively up the organizational hierarchy.	1	2	3	4	5	6
1	2	3	4	5	6	17.	I develop and maintain professional networks.	1	2	3	4	5	6

What Is

What Should Be

Completely Agree	Strongly Agree	Agree	Disagree	Strongly Disagree	Completely Disagree		What Is	What Should Be			Completely Agree	Strongly Agree	Agree	Disagree	Strongly Disagree	Completely Disagree
							"What Is" describes how you see yourself *currently* functioning.	"What Should Be" describes how you think you *should be* functioning.								
1	2	3	4	5	6	18.	I mentor subordinates of demographic backgrounds different from my own.				1	2	3	4	5	6
1	2	3	4	5	6	19.	I do not tolerate discriminatory behaviors between my subordinates.				1	2	3	4	5	6
1	2	3	4	5	6	20.	Morale problems do not lead to absenteeism among my subordinates.				1	2	3	4	5	6
1	2	3	4	5	6	21.	My subordinates do not request transfers due to dissatisfaction with our department.				1	2	3	4	5	6
1	2	3	4	5	6	22.	I address morale problems quickly and appropriately.				1	2	3	4	5	6

Workplace Collaboration Inventory Scoring Sheet

Teaming

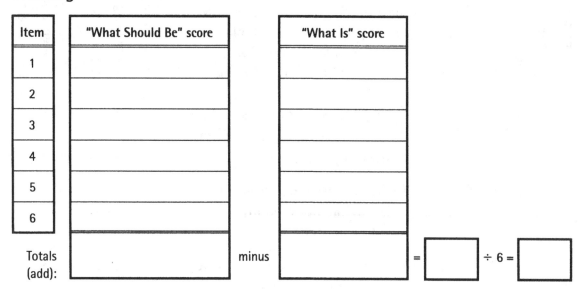

Item	"What Should Be" score
1	
2	
3	
4	
5	
6	
Totals (add):	

"What Is" score

minus   =   ÷ 6 =

Motivating Subordinates

Item	"What Should Be" score
7	
8	
Totals (add):	

"What Is" score

minus   =   ÷ 2 =

Career Counseling

Item	"What Should Be" score
9	
10	
11	
Totals (add):	

"What Is" score

minus   =   ÷ 3 =

Communicating with Subordinates

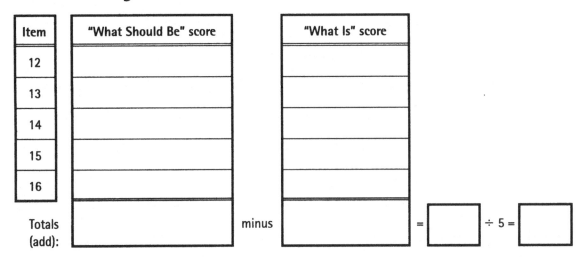

Item	"What Should Be" score		"What Is" score
12			
13			
14			
15			
16			
Totals (add):		minus	

= [ ] ÷ 5 = [ ]

Professional Relationships

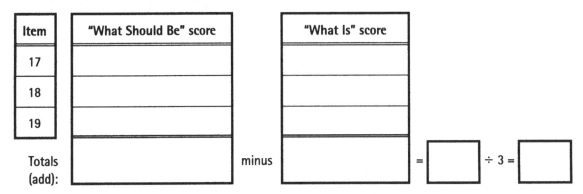

Item	"What Should Be" score		"What Is" score
17			
18			
19			
Totals (add):		minus	

= [ ] ÷ 3 = [ ]

Improving Morale and Quality of Work Life

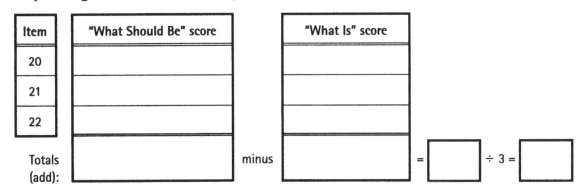

Item	"What Should Be" score		"What Is" score
20			
21			
22			
Totals (add):		minus	

= [ ] ÷ 3 = [ ]

15 The Leadership Dimensions Survey

Gerald V. Miller

Summary

The Leadership Dimensions Survey is a tool to assist those on the odyssey of leadership. The survey is based on four leadership competencies: profound knowledge, profound strategy, purposeful direction, and purposeful behaviors. These four competencies, when paired on a grid, yield four leadership dimensions or "virtues": constancy of purpose, congruity of activity, competency of outcome, and compatibility of values. The four competencies, as measured by the Leadership Dimensions Survey, allow for the generation and sustenance of trust between leader and follower, which forms the basis for a work environment that is both productive and able to adapt to and thrive in a changing and complex business world.

The Leadership Dimensions Survey can be used for self-discovery, leadership development, coaching in human dimensions of leadership, and other leadership applications.

Reframing Leadership

In a world of unceasing change, downsizing, reinventing, reengineering, business process redesign, customer focus, and high-performance teams, the business leader of today must balance the tremendous demands of managing that change and complexity with work output and productivity. Those leaders who operate on the 19th Century model of bureaucracy, a model based on words and actions, of control and order, are not going to pass muster in the next millennium.

Successful business leaders have mastered a new set of knowledge, skills, and attitudes with which to face the challenges of corporate reality—in effect, a completely new form of leadership. This form of leadership is observable and learnable. Given the opportunity to learn, receive feedback, and practice, those who desire to lead and improve their ability to lead can do so.

Leadership Competencies and Dimensions

Today's leaders must think in terms of a leadership system, seeing a framework of patterns and interrelationships. Unfortunately, we usually focus on isolated parts instead of seeing the whole system of leadership, and then we wonder why our efforts at solving problems or perpetuating successes fail.

It is especially important to see the world of leadership as a whole system as it continues to grow more complex. Complexity can overwhelm and undermine our efforts if we do not have a model or a system to guide our efforts. A model helps us see the patterns that lie behind events and details, which can simplify the art of leadership.

The leadership systems model is based on four interrelated competencies:

- Profound knowledge,

- Profound strategy,

- Purposeful direction, and

- Purposeful behaviors.

These competencies can be visualized on an interconnecting axis, as shown in Figure 1.

The word "profound" connotes something deep-seated. To be profound is to go beyond the surface, beneath the veneer issues to what is the true essence of something. It requires an intellectual depth and insight. Perhaps you can remember a time when you were conversing with someone who said something profound. It took the conversation to a new depth.

Profound knowledge is a necessary competency that ensures a basis of information, experience, expertise, and data. To possess profound knowledge is to possess something beyond mere perceptions.

Profound strategy indicates a well-thought-out plan or course of action that goes beyond the status quo. It is the insightful art of development of the exceptional blueprint or scheme.

To be "purposeful" is to be, literally, full of purpose. To be purposeful is to be meaningful. It is acting with thoughtful intention, not out of convenience. It requires resolution and determination. When one is purposeful, one has an aim or goal, a reason for behaving in a particular manner.

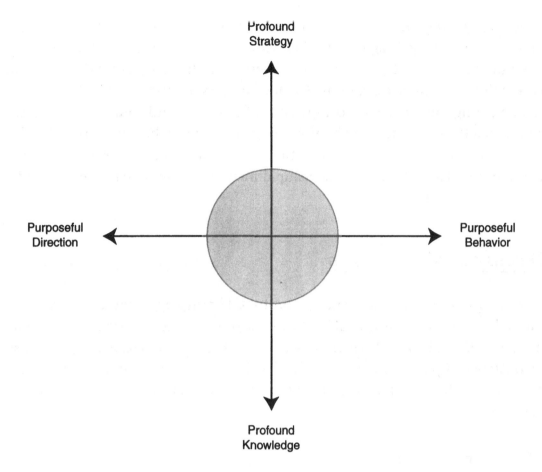

Figure 1. Competencies Axis

Purposeful direction implies that there is a vision, goal, and mission that will result in a desired future state uniquely different from the present state.

Purposeful behavior indicates that the leader's behaviors are, in fact, meaningful and are, on some level, inextricably attached to a vision or goal. The behaviors provide a role model for the values and skills needed to achieve a desired state.

The Role of Trust in Leadership

Leadership is not just about leaders; it is also about followers. Successful leadership depends far more on the followers' perception of the leader than on any other factor. It is a reciprocal process, occurring between people. Followers, not the leader, determine when someone possesses the qualities of leadership.

People would rather follow, and confer leadership on, individuals they can count on—even when they disagree with their viewpoints—rather than people they agree with but who shift positions frequently. Everything effective leaders do is congruent with their values, their viewpoints. The four leadership dimensions of constancy of purpose, congruity of activity, competency of outcome, and compatibility of values are realized through consistent behavior over time. This behavior is the basis of trust for followers who buy into the vision, the shared goals, and objectives and then confer leadership. Each of the four leadership dimensions takes time to generate and sustain. The result is trust.

Dimensions of Leadership

When we put the four competencies—profound knowledge, profound strategy, profound direction, and purposeful behavior—together, we form a grid with four quadrants, as seen in Figure 2. Each of these quadrants represents a leadership dimension: I: Constancy of purpose, II: Congruity of activity, III: Competency of outcome, and IV: Compatibility of values. It is these four dimensions that can be used to measure leadership proficiency.

I. Constancy of Purpose

Constancy of purpose is steadfastness, continued unwavering focus on the vision, "keeping one's eye on the prize." Purposeful direction and profound strategy make up this dimension of leadership, allowing for the development of basic trust between leader and follower, derived from a meaningfully communicated vision and strategy.

Trust requires repeated interactions between leaders and followers and begins with vision. In nurturing an environment in which people are aware of the vision, of what is important and why it is critical, the leader creates meaning. With meaning comes trust.

Meaning also emerges from concepts, words endowed with relevance and purpose. Words are powerful. The leader, therefore, must have a "talk" to nurture the vision-oriented environment. The leader must consistently state and restate the vision in a meaningful, purposeful way that encourages people to enroll for the duration. The vision must inspire. It must articulate passion. Speaking with passion, leaders light fires under others. When the leader is a "wet match," there are no sparks to ignite passion in others and the vision is set inside. It is the role of the leader to ensure that people know and buy in to the vision.

The leader helps define the vision (purposeful direction) and "talks the talk," laying the foundation for the development of trust between the leader and the followers.

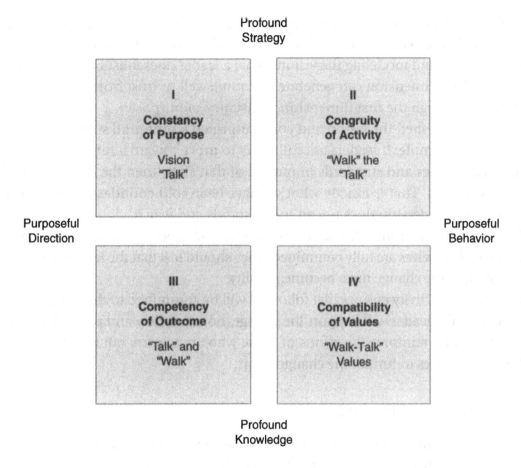

Figure 2. Dimensions of Leadership

The fulfillment of the vision, by definition, implies a change from the state in which we are to the state in which we want to be. This understanding on the part of the leader is the result of a well-thought-out plan and a course of action that goes beyond the status quo, the insightful art of developing the exceptional blueprint or scheme, the profound strategy.

Constancy of purpose occurs when followers believe that the leader has clear and specific reasons for initiating a change; has a clear and specific outcome in mind; understands the resources necessary to put changes into effect; understands the scope and organizational impact of a change; and understands the human impact of the change.

II. Congruity of Activity

Congruity of activity is the ability to match words and deeds, that is, to "practice what one preaches." Profound strategy and purposeful behaviors make up this dimension of leadership, promulgating the further development of trust between leader and follower and moving the organization and its people toward realization of the vision.

Saying one thing and doing another is perhaps the surest way to destroy trust. People are deeply concerned with congruity of word and deed. Congruity of activity is walking the talk and modeling the vision. What a leader does must be congruent with the vision. This dimension can generate a groundswell of trust from the foundation established through the first dimension, constancy of purpose.

Having established the vision and communicated a profound strategy, the leader must lead by example. If leaders ask followers to move toward a future state and observe certain values and standards in pursuit of that state, then the leaders must live by the same rules. That is exactly what we have been told countless times by exemplary leaders. Leadership does not sit in the stands and watch.

In order to fully commit themselves to the change process, members must believe that leaders themselves are fully committed. They should feel that the leaders are strongly convinced that the change must become a reality.

Congruity of activity ensures that followers will be committed to the change process. It shows that the leader will support the change, both publicly and privately; monitor change activities; reinforce the efforts of those who are to carry out the change effort; and make sacrifices to further the change effort.

III. Competency of Outcome

Competency of outcome is expressed in what one says, that is, "I've been there and I've done that." It occurs when a leader has profound knowledge and purposeful direction.

Dimensions I and II show how a leader must have a "talk" and a "walk"—constancy of purpose and congruity of activity. The next, dimension—competency of outcome—demands a "talk" and a "walk" backed up by substantive and demonstrable experience. This is leadership competence. To buy into leaders' visions, people must trust that leaders know what they are talking about and what they are doing. To instill trust, a leader must be seen as capable and effective. If people doubt the leader's abilities, they are unlikely to enlist in the change effort and pursue the vision.

Leadership competence does not necessarily refer to a leader's technical ability. Rather, people look for competency in the following areas:

- Systems thinking,

- Human side of management,

- Communication and interpersonal relationships,

- Giving and receiving feedback,

- Understanding and responding to needs of individual team members,

- One-on-one consultation (problems and individual needs),

- Team building and group dynamics,

- Employing informal power to influence team behavior and desired outcomes,

- Linking individuals, groups, and projects together across the organization, and

- Training and coaching in operational, administrative, and managerial functions.

Competency of outcome solidifies the trust developed thus far, setting the stage for the fourth dimension, compatibility of values.

IV. Compatibility of Values

Compatibility of values is the integration of what one believes, says, and does with the organizational value system, that is, "evidence of trust begets trust." It occurs when a leader has profound knowledge and purposeful behavior.

Compatibility of values manifests itself in interdependence, the necessarily shared value for effective leadership. Leaders must value and protect interdependence, rather than creating a climate of independence, dependence, or codependence. When held and employed unilaterally, interdependence creates a work environment of the highest efficiency, effectiveness, and professional and personal satisfaction.

Interdependence calls for coactive (synergistic) behaviors, consistent with the highest good of all concerned. Too often leaders encourage pure independence. Especially in the workplace, people must be interdependent. In the workplace, independence translates as adolescent, self-centered behavior. It is the role of the leader to believe in, value, and demonstrate the importance of interdependence. Figure 3 illustrates the developmental nature of interdependence.

The leader promotes an interdependent climate for team members and does not interfere unless it becomes necessary. The team members are trusted and given freedom (empowered and enabled) to plan their own ways of doing their work (the how) in accord with the leader's vision (the what and why). They are expected to solve problems and to ask for guidance only when it is needed. By providing freedom of work, encouraging initiative, and supporting experimentation and teamwork, leaders also help to satisfy the followers' needs for belonging, affection, and security.

Summary

Although both management and leadership are necessary to the success of any effort in today's business world, change, complexity, and continued demands for productivity and efficiency require a greater emphasis on leading. The specific knowledge, behaviors,

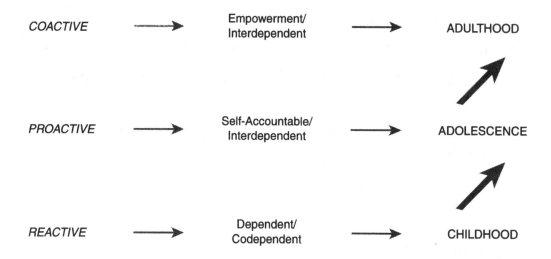

Figure 3. The Development of Interdependence

and skills that exceptional leaders have in common, all operating under the umbrella of human systems thinking, have been identified. They are embodied in the four dimensions of leadership: constancy of purpose, congruity of activity, competency of outcome, and compatibility of values.

Proper leadership empowers and enables the individuals and teams that constitute an organization. Good leaders make team members feel that they are at the very heart of things. Followers feel that they, interdependently, make a difference to the success of the organization. This sense of empowerment can lead to increased productivity and efficiency, keys to maintaining success in a changing business world.

The Instrument

The Leadership Dimensions Survey is designed to assess the leadership skills of aspiring, potential, or present leaders on four dimensions. The survey consists of a thirty-two-item questionnaire, a scoring sheet, an interpretation sheet that covers results on each of the four dimensions, and a Leadership Dimensions Map on which one can chart the results of his or her survey. In addition, a sample letter for participants to send to respondents and an action planning sheet are included here.

The survey is designed to be completed by five of the leader's peers, supervisors, or subordinates (the "respondents"). Each question presents a statement about the leader. Respondents are asked to mark whether they strongly agree, are inclined to agree, are inclined to disagree, or strongly disagree with the statement as it applies to the leader.

Validity and Reliability

No validity or reliability data are available on the Leadership Dimensions Survey. However, the instrument has face validity, as its purpose is to make participants more aware of their leadership behaviors through this feedback process.

Administration

The following process is suggested for facilitating a workshop on leadership with several participants. At least a week prior to working with the leaders, give each of them five copies of the Leadership Dimensions Survey and copies of the Leadership Dimensions Letter to Participants. Tell them to write letters on their own stationery similar to the sample letter to respondents, attach letters to the survey, and give them to five peers, supervisors, or subordinates, who are to follow the instructions to complete it and return it in a sealed envelope anonymously either to the leader or to you, the facilitator. (*Note:* Be sure to specify whether you are to receive the surveys or whether the leaders will collect them. An advantage of collecting them yourself is that they are less likely to be forgotten on the day of the workshop.) Anonymity allows for more candid responses. If the surveys are returned in time, they may be scored prior to the workshop, but it is important for leaders to do their own interpretation and mapping.

Scoring

The questionnaires can be scored either before or during the workshop. Both the Leadership Dimensions Scoring Sheet and Leadership Dimensions Interpretation Sheet sort the thirty-two statements by leadership dimension.

Hand out the completed Leadership Dimensions Scoring Sheets (or ask the leaders to score their own during the session) to the appropriate leader along with blank copies of the Leadership Dimensions Interpretation Sheet. If they are scoring their own surveys, tell the leaders to transfer the scores they received for each question to the A, B, C, D, and E columns on the Scoring Sheet. Each column represents one respondent. Be sure that they total the scores *horizontally* and divide by the number of responses to determine their average scores for each question, then write their scores in the "average" column. Next, tell leaders to add the averages *vertically* to obtain a total score for each dimension.

When they have finished filling out the Scoring Sheet, hand out the Leadership Dimensions Map and tell the leaders to plot their four totals in the appropriate quadrants. Draw a sample on the flip chart to show them how to map their leadership dimensions. Next, hand out Leadership Dimensions Interpretation Sheets to all leaders and ask them to study their scores. Discuss the meaning of various combinations of scores and have people share their maps and thoughts in small groups or in pairs. After everyone knows what his or her results say, hand out copies of the Leadership Dimensions Action Planning Sheet and ask leaders to make action plans to improve their leadership dimensions in the future. Ask everyone to share as appropriate.

The scoring, mapping, and interpretation of the Leadership Dimensions Survey usually requires thirty minutes to an hour to complete. The discussion phase and action planning will take another hour.

Potential Uses of the Instrument

The Leadership Dimensions Survey is designed as a self-discovery and feedback tool. It has the following potential uses:

- As part of leadership training wherein participants have the survey completed by supervisors, peers, and subordinates prior to the training event. During the leadership training, the results can be discussed as the foundation for the workshop.

- As a coaching tool to be administered by the supervisor of someone who wishes to improve his or her leadership skills. The coach can review the results of the survey with the learner.

- As an assessment tool for future leaders. The results can form the basis of an individual leadership development plan.

- As a process intervention tool for consultants working with leaders. The results can show contributions the leaders make to the organization, point out potential pitfalls they have, and lead to suggestions for improvement and development.

- As a basis for discussion throughout an organization about the relationship between present and desired leadership styles.

- As a format for any organization that wishes to assess its readiness to implement a more effective style of leadership.

References

Bennis, W., & Nanus, B. (1986). *Leaders: The strategies for taking charge.* New York: Harper & Row.

Forkas, C.M,. & DeBacker, P. (1996). *Maximum leadership.* New York: Holt.

Hesselbein, F., Goldsmith, M., & Beckhard, R. (Eds.). (1996). *The leader of the future.* San Francisco, CA: Jossey-Bass.

Kotler, J.P. (1996). *Leading change.* Boston, MA: Harvard Business School Press.

Levine, S.P., & Crom, M.A. (1993). *The leader in you: How to win friends, influence people and succeed in a changing world.* New York: Dale Carnegie.

O'Toole, J. (1995). *Leading change: Overcoming the ideology of comfort and the tyranny of custom.* San Francisco, CA: Jossey-Bass.

Senge, P.M. (1990). *The fifth discipline.* New York: Currency Doubleday.

Originally published in *The 1999 Annual: Volume 1, Training.*

Leadership Dimensions Survey Letter to Participants

To the Participant:

The Leadership Dimensions Survey is designed to assess your leadership skills on four dimensions by providing you with feedback about how others view the leadership practices you use.

Attached are five copies of the Leadership Dimensions Survey. Write your name on each as the person who is being evaluated. Distribute copies of the questionnaire to any five people (peers, subordinates, and/or supervisors) whom you believe know you well enough to comment on what you would do (and do not do) as a leader. *Please distribute all five, as this increases the reliability and validity of the results.*

Ask each respondent to complete the questionnaire anonymously and return it to you (or to the facilitator of your leadership training group) in a sealed envelope. A sample of a letter you can give to respondents explaining the purpose of the survey is shown below.

Sample Letter to Respondents Completing the Leadership Dimensions Survey

Dear Respondent:

Attached is one copy of the Leadership Dimensions Survey. I would appreciate it if you could fill out the survey about my own behavior as a leader. The purpose of this survey is to assist me in understanding my own behavior and the impact of that behavior on others in a work setting.

Your honest responses will help me to assess my leadership qualities. Please rate each behavior following the instructions at the top of the survey.

Do not write your name on the survey form. It is designed to be completed anonymously. Please return the completed survey in a sealed envelope marked to my attention [or to the facilitator].

Thank you for your time and honest feedback.

Sincerely,
[your name]

Leadership Dimensions Survey

Gerald V. Miller

Person Being Assessed: _____

Instructions: Think of the person who gave this survey to you to complete, named above. To what extent do the following thirty-two statements apply to this person? For each statement, circle the response that best applies, using the following scale.

Strongly Agree = 3   Inclined to Agree = 2   Inclined to Disagree = 1   Strongly Disagree = 0

This person:

1.	Can describe the kind of future that he or she would like to create.	3	2	1	0
2.	Has behavior that is congruent with his or her leadership philosophy.	3	2	1	0
3.	Is aware of new developments in our field.	3	2	1	0
4.	Is consistently an ethical and upstanding leader.	3	2	1	0
5.	Can give a clear, specific outcome that would result from change.	3	2	1	0
6.	Supports projects and changes, both publicly and privately.	3	2	1	0
7.	Has experienced what he or she is talking about and knows what he or she is doing.	3	2	1	0
8.	Practices principles of self-accountability.	3	2	1	0
9.	Appeals to others to join in the vision of the future.	3	2	1	0
10.	Is consistent in practicing what he or she preaches.	3	2	1	0
11.	Seeks out challenging opportunities that test and stretch the organization's skills and abilities.	3	2	1	0
12.	Encourages team members to be interdependent and empowered team members.	3	2	1	0
13.	Has clear and specific reasons for initiating change.	3	2	1	0

Strongly Agree = 3   Inclined to Agree = 2   Inclined to Disagree = 1   Strongly Disagree = 0

14.	Monitors projects and change activities with clear goals, plans, and established milestones.	3	2	1	0
15.	Is consistently well-prepared for any project or change effort contingency.	3	2	1	0
16.	Is sincere when asking for others' suggestions and opinions.	3	2	1	0
17.	Clearly communicates a hopeful and inspiring outlook for the future of the organization.	3	2	1	0
18.	Reinforces and rewards the efforts of those who carry out projects and change efforts.	3	2	1	0
19.	Typically can provide team members with a thorough understanding of any project or change effort.	3	2	1	0
20.	Creates an atmosphere of mutual trust during projects and change efforts.	3	2	1	0
21.	Understands the resources necessary to put change into effect.	3	2	1	0
22.	Experiments and takes risks with new approaches, regardless of the chance of failure.	3	2	1	0
23.	Is capable and effective in both technical and leadership abilities.	3	2	1	0
24.	Makes a concerted effort to tell the organization about the good work done by the team.	3	2	1	0
25.	Shows others how their interests can be realized by joining a common vision.	3	2	1	0
26.	Makes personal sacrifices in order to complete projects and to further change efforts.	3	2	1	0
27.	Is competent in understanding how all the interacting parts of our organization come together.	3	2	1	0
28.	Can always be believed about what he or she is saying.	3	2	1	0

Strongly Agree = 3   Inclined to Agree = 2   Inclined to Disagree = 1   Strongly Disagree = 0

29. Understands the scope of proposed changes
    and the impact of change on people and the
    organization.   3   2   1   0

30. Practices innovative leadership that fosters a sense
    of ownership in others.   3   2   1   0

31. Challenges the status quo regarding the way things
    are done.   3   2   1   0

32. Typically establishes open, trusting work
    relationships.   3   2   1   0

Leadership Dimensions Scoring Sheet

Instructions: This scoring sheet is divided into four sections, each representing one dimension of leadership: constancy of purpose, congruity of activity, competency of outcome, or compatibility of values. Transfer the scores given to you by each respondent to the appropriate blanks below. Remember that items are not in numerical order, but are divided by quadrant. Each letter, A through E, represents a different respondent.

After you have filled in the scores for each question, add them horizontally and divide by the number of responses you received to determine your average score. Write your average scores for each question in the blank provided. Next add the eight average scores for each section and write the number in the blank marked "total."

I. Constancy of Purpose: Profound Strategy and Purposeful Direction

	Respondents					
	A	B	C	D	E	Average
1. Can describe the kind of future that he or she would like to create.	__	__	__	__	__	_____
5. Can give a clear, specific outcome that would result from change.	__	__	__	__	__	_____
9. Appeals to others to join in the vision of the future.	__	__	__	__	__	_____
13. Has clear and specific reasons for initiating change.	__	__	__	__	__	_____
17. Clearly communicates a hopeful and inspiring outlook for the future of the organization.	__	__	__	__	__	_____
21. Understands the resources necessary to put change into effect.	__	__	__	__	__	_____
25. Shows others how their interests can be realized by joining a common vision.	__	__	__	__	__	_____
29. Understands the scope of proposed changes and the impact of change on people and the organization.	__	__	__	__	__	_____

Total _____

II. Congruity of Activity: Profound Strategy and Purposeful Behavior

	A	B	C	D	E	Average
			Respondents			
2. Has behavior that is congruent with his or her leadership philosophy.	—	—	—	—	—	———
6. Supports projects and changes, both publicly and privately.	—	—	—	—	—	———
10. Is consistent in practicing what he or she preaches.	—	—	—	—	—	———
14. Monitors projects and change activities with clear goals, plans, and established milestones.	—	—	—	—	—	———
18. Reinforces and rewards the efforts of those who carry out projects and change efforts.	—	—	—	—	—	———
22. Experiments and takes risks with new approaches, regardless of the chance of failure.	—	—	—	—	—	———
26. Makes personal sacrifices in order to complete projects and to further change efforts.	—	—	—	—	—	———
30. Practices innovative leadership that fosters a sense of ownership in others.	—	—	—	—	—	———

Total ———

III. Competency of Outcome: Profound Knowledge and Purposeful Direction

	A	B	C	D	E	Average
			Respondents			
3. Is aware of new developments in our field.	—	—	—	—	—	———
7. Has experienced what he or she is talking about and knows what he or she is doing.	—	—	—	—	—	———

	Respondents					
	A	B	C	D	E	Average
11. Seeks out challenging opportunities that test and stretch the organization's skills and abilities.	___	___	___	___	___	_____
15. Is consistently well-prepared for any project or change effort contingency.	___	___	___	___	___	_____
19. Typically can provide team members with a thorough understanding of any project or change effort.	___	___	___	___	___	_____
23. Is capable and effective in both technical and leadership abilities.	___	___	___	___	___	_____
27. Is competent in understanding how all the interacting parts of our organization come together.	___	___	___	___	___	_____
31. Challenges the status quo regarding the way things are done.	___	___	___	___	___	_____
					Total	_____

IV. Compatibility of Values: Profound Knowledge and Purposeful Behavior

	Respondents					
	A	B	C	D	E	Average
4. Is consistently an ethical and upstanding leader.	___	___	___	___	___	_____
8. Practices principles of self-accountability.	___	___	___	___	___	_____
12. Encourages team members to be interdependent and empowered team members.	___	___	___	___	___	_____
16. Is sincere when asking for others' suggestions and opinions.	___	___	___	___	___	_____

	Respondents					
	A	B	C	D	E	Average
20. Creates an atmosphere of mutual trust during projects and change efforts.	—	—	—	—	—	———
24. Makes a concerted effort to tell the organization about the good work done by the team.	—	—	—	—	—	———
28. Can always be believed about what he or she is saying.	—	—	—	—	—	———
32. Typically establishes open, trusting work relationships.	—	—	—	—	—	———
					Total	———

Leadership Dimensions Map

Instructions: Plot your scores for each quadrant. For example, if you received a score of 19 for Quadrant I, Constancy of Purpose, mark the score on both the Profound Strategy and Purposeful Direction lines. Then draw a rule perpendicular to each line and make an X where the two lines meet in the quadrant. Do the same for your scores in each of the other quadrants as shown in the example.

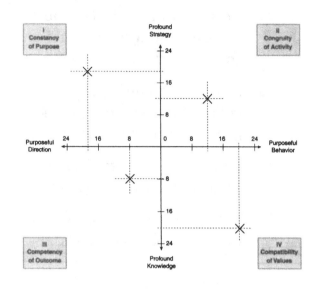

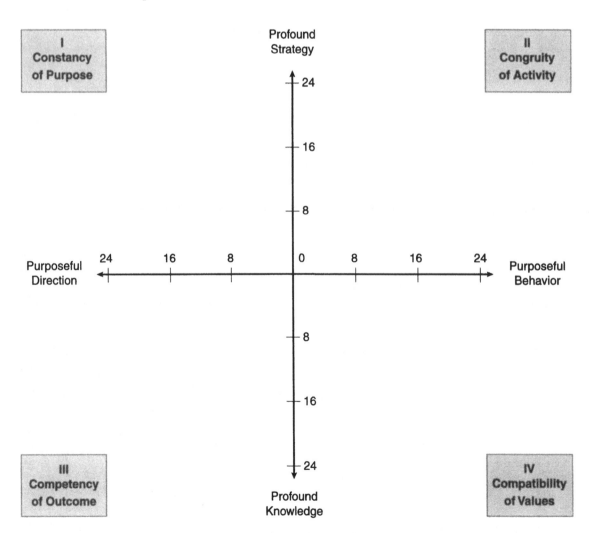

Leadership Dimensions Interpretation Sheet

Instructions: The most crucial step for learning is to answer the questions, "So what?" and "Now what?" Now that you have completed your Leadership Dimensions Scoring Sheet, you will want to interpret what the scores have to say and take action to improve your leadership skills. Utilizing what you have learned about how you behave in real-world leadership situations, you can make plans for your professional development.

The Leadership Dimensions Survey is interpreted on an item-by-item basis, as well as by comparison of total category scores. You will be able to determine the following information from your scores.

Individual Item Scores

Average scores for *individual items* of 2.0 and above reflect strengths, that is, respondents are telling you that they observe your use of this practice.

Average scores for items of 1.7 to 1.9 are questionable, that is, the total itself provides insufficient information on which to draw a conclusion. You must, instead, look at the spread of scores to determine whether the average score reflects a strength or a weakness. For example, you may receive a score of 1.8 because four people were "inclined to agree" about that item and one person was "inclined to disagree." This would not reflect a weakness. However, if you receive one "strongly agree," one "inclined to agree," and two "inclined to disagree," you may need to improve on that item.

Average scores of 1.6 or lower reflect weaknesses.

Category Scores

For each dimension, look at the total score (sum of all averages). Use the following scale to determine your skill level:

  0 to 9 = Skills Need Significant Improvement

  10 to 19 = Skills Are Adequate, But Could Be Improved

  20 to 24 = Excellent Employment of the Skills

This will help you to apply what you have learned about yourself. For best results, focus on dimensions on which you scored between 10 and 19 (areas for improvement) and between 0 and 9 (areas requiring concerted effort).

Also address individual questions on which your average score was 1.6 or lower, which reflects a weakness, and between 1.7 and 1.9, which reflects a "wait and see" attitude on the part of the respondents.

What can you do to make improvements in each of the quadrants? Read all of the suggestions that follow the interpretation of your scores and then complete the Leadership Dimensions Action Planning Sheet.

Constancy of Purpose

Low (0 to 9) scores in this quadrant indicate that the following areas require improvement:

- Being able to describe the future toward which you are leading your team;

- Formulating clear, specific reasons and outcomes before initiating changes;

- Showing others how their interests can be realized by achieving a common vision and purpose and inspiring them to join you; and

- Showing your understanding of proposed changes and the impact they will have on people and the organization.

Suggestions for Improvement

- Take a course in public speaking or presentation skills.

- Read a book about motivating others and practice what you have learned.

- Develop your interpersonal skills in the areas of opening up and sharing your vision, purpose, and concerns with others.

Congruity of Activity

Low (0 to 9) scores in this quadrant indicate that the following areas require improvement:

- Backing up what you have said, both publicly and privately;

- Monitoring and reinforcing any project or change efforts;

- Fostering a sense of ownership in your team;

- Personally sacrificing to further any project or change; and

- Practicing innovative leadership.

Suggestions for Improvement

- Initiate third-party shadowing, for example, ask a trusted advisor to spend extensive time with you to observe your behavior and provide feedback to you.

- Begin daily "journaling" to note any behaviors that might lead others to believe that you are saying one thing and doing another.

Competency of Outcome

Low (0 to 9) scores in this quadrant indicate that the following areas require improvement:

- Keeping abreast of and ahead of any new developments in your field of expertise;

- Balancing your leadership skills with top-notch technical skills;

- Challenging the status quo and finding new ways of doing work; and

- Rolling up your sleeves and doing the actual work along with your team members.

Suggestions for Improvement

- Obtain just-in-time, experiential training that provides you with actual work skills.

- Request to be mentored by a trusted expert practitioner, someone who has a reputation for excellent application skills.

Compatibility of Values

Low (0 to 9) scores in this quadrant indicate that the following areas require improvement:

- Being responsible and accountable;

- Creating an atmosphere of mutual trust through open and direct communication;

- Communicating your personal and the organization's ethical standards of operation and values; and

- Encouraging team members to be empowered and interdependent.

Suggestions for Improvement

- Attend experiential business ethics training with emphasis on job satisfaction, cooperation, achievement, creativity, tolerance, dignity and respect, truth, honor, and loyalty.

- With the aid of a trusted consultant, conduct a values clarification activity with your team.

Leadership Dimensions Action Planning Sheet

Summary

The quadrant in which I scored the lowest was _____.

   List the questions on which you scored 1.6 or lower and 1.7 to 1.9 below. These indicate areas for improvement.

Statements in the other three quadrants for which I scored 1.6 or lower include:

Planning

1. As a result of this survey I have learned:

2. The cost of not making changes would be:

3. In order to improve my leadership I must:

    Continue doing:

    Start doing:

Stop doing:

4. My sources for help include:

    Mentors:

    Training:

    Readings and resources:

    Other:

5. To ensure success I will:

6. I will know I have been successful when:

7. I will improve by taking the following actions:

Action	Start Date	Complete By

16 Role Efficacy Scale

Udai Pareek

Summary

The performance of people working in an organization depends on their own potential effectiveness, their technical competence, their managerial skills and experience, and the design of the roles they perform in the organization. It is the integration of individuals and their roles that ensures their effectiveness in the organization. Unless people have the requisite knowledge, technical competence, and skills required for their roles, they cannot be effective. But if the role does not allow a person to use his or her competence, and if the individual constantly feels frustrated in the role, effectiveness is likely to be low. The closer that role taking (responding to the expectations of various other people) moves to role making (taking the initiative in designing the role creatively so that the expectations of others as well as of the role occupant are integrated), the more the role is likely to be effective. This potential effectiveness can be called efficacy. Role efficacy can be seen as the psychological factor underlying role effectiveness.

Dimensions of Role Efficacy

Role efficacy has ten dimensions, and the more these dimensions are present in a role, the higher the efficacy of that role is likely to be.

1. Centrality vs. Peripherality

   The dimension of centrality measures the role occupant's perception of the significance of his or her role. The more central that people feel their roles are in the organization, the higher will be their role efficacy. For example, "I am a production manager, and my role is very important."

2. Integration vs. Distance

Integration between the self and the role contributes to role efficacy, and self-role distance diminishes efficacy. "I am able to use my knowledge very well here."

3. Proactivity vs. Reactivity

When a role occupant takes initiative and does something independently, that person is exhibiting *pro*active behavior. On the other hand, if he or she merely responds to what others expect, the behavior is *re*active. For example, "I prepare the budget for discussion" versus "I prepare the budget according to the guidance given by my boss."

4. Creativity vs. Routinism

When role occupants perceive that they do something new or unique in their roles, their efficacy is high. The perception that they do only routine tasks lowers role efficacy.

5. Linkage vs. Isolation

Interrole linkage contributes to role efficacy. If role occupants perceive interdependence with others, their efficacy will be high. Isolation of the role reduces efficacy. Example of linkage: "I work in close liaison with the production manager."

6. Helping vs. Hostility

One important aspect of efficacy is the individual's perception that he or she gives and receives help. A perception of hostility decreases efficacy. "Whenever I have a problem, others help me," instead of "People here are indifferent to others."

7. Superordination vs. Deprivation

One dimension of role efficacy is the perception that the role occupant contributes to some "larger" entity. Example: "What I do is likely to benefit other organizations also."

8. Influence vs. Powerlessness

Role occupants' feeling that they are able to exercise influence in their roles increases their role efficacy. The influence may be in terms of decision making, implementation, advice, or problem solving. "My advice on industrial relations is accepted by top management." "I am able to influence the general policy of marketing."

9. Growth vs. Stagnation

   When a role occupant has opportunities—and perceives them as such—to develop in his or her role through learning new things, role efficacy is likely to be high. Similarly, if the individual perceives his or her role as lacking in opportunities for growth, role efficacy will be low.

10. Confrontation vs. Avoidance

    When problems arise, either they can be confronted and attempts made to find solutions for them, or they can be avoided. Confronting problems to find solutions contributes to efficacy, and avoidance reduces efficacy. An example of confrontation: "If a subordinate brings a problem to me, I help to work out the solution." "I dislike being bothered with interpersonal conflict" is a statement indicating avoidance.

Using the Data Generated

Measurement of role efficacy is not done for its own sake; it should lead to a program of improvement in efficacy. Because factors concerned both with the individual (the role occupant) and with the design of the role contribute to efficacy, two approaches can be adopted for increasing role efficacy.

Role Redefinition

After the dimensions in which role efficacy is low have been diagnosed, the problem can be approached from the perspective of the role. The diagnosis may show that some dimensions are missing from the role and may suggest various ways of building in those missing dimensions. For example, if centrality is missing from the role, ways can be worked out to enrich the role. However, there are no standard solutions to build various dimensions into the role; the solutions will differ from situation to situation. In redefining roles, various ways of developing the missing dimensions can be prepared first by individuals involved in the situation (the role occupant and significant persons who work with him or her). Then these individual suggestions can be discussed in detail to discover to what extent they are feasible and likely to increase role efficacy.

Action Planning

It is equally important to work on role efficacy from the point of view of the role occupant. Role efficacy may be low because the role occupant is not able to perceive certain dimensions in the role, or the individual may not be able to use his or her own power to build those dimensions into the role. Counseling and coaching may be necessary. For example, if the person perceives that linkages with other roles are weak, he or she can be worked with to build stronger linkages with other roles. Or if the individual feels that his or her role does not provide opportunities to learn new things and grow, the person can be helped to perceive other dimensions of the role. The purpose of action planning is to help the individual take necessary steps without waiting for redesign of the role.

Uses of the Role Efficacy Scale

The Role Efficacy Scale is useful in a number of different situations. It can be used for role clarification in team building, for coaching key managers, for problem identification within a work team, and for training managers and supervisors about the concept of role efficacy.

Originally published in *The 1980 Annual Handbook for Faciliatators, Trainers, and Consultants.*

Role Efficacy Scale

Udai Pareek

Your name: _____   Your role: _____

Instructions: In each of the following sets of three statements, check the one (a, b, or c) that most accurately describes your own experience in your organizational role. You must choose only one statement in each set.

1. ____ a. My role is very important in this organization; I feel central here.

   ____ b. I am doing useful and fairly important work.

   ____ c. Very little importance is given to my role in this organization; I feel peripheral here.

2. ____ a. My training and expertise are not fully utilized in my present role.

   ____ b. My training and knowledge are not used in my present role.

   ____ c. I am able to use my knowledge and training very well here.

3. ____ a. I have little freedom in my role; I am only an errand runner.

   ____ b. I operate according to the directions given to me.

   ____ c. I can take initiative and act on my own in my role.

4. ____ a. I am doing usual, routine work in my role.

   ____ b. In my role I am able to use my creativity and do something new.

   ____ c. I have no time for creative work in my role.

5. ____ a. No one in the organization responds to my ideas and suggestions.

   ____ b. I work in close collaboration with some other colleagues.

   ____ c. I am alone and have almost no one to consult in my role.

6. ____ a. When I need some help, none is available.

   ____ b. Whenever I have a problem, others help me.

   ____ c. I get very hostile responses when I ask for help.

7. _____ a. I regret that I do not have the opportunity to contribute to society in my role.

   _____ b. What I am doing in my role is likely to help other organizations or society.

   _____ c. I have the opportunity to have some effect on the larger society in my role.

8. _____ a. I contribute to some decisions.

   _____ b. I have no power here.

   _____ c. My advice is accepted by my seniors.

9. _____ a. Some of what I do contributes to my learning.

   _____ b. I am slowly forgetting all that I learned (my professional knowledge).

   _____ c. I have tremendous opportunities for professional growth in my role.

10. _____ a. I dislike being bothered with problems.

   _____ b. When a subordinate brings a problem to me, I help to find a solution.

   _____ c. I refer the problem to my boss or to some other person.

11. _____ a. I feel quite central in the organization.

   _____ b. I think I am doing fairly important work.

   _____ c. I feel I am peripheral in this organization.

12. _____ a. I do not enjoy my role.

   _____ b. I enjoy my role very much.

   _____ c. I enjoy some parts of my role and not others.

13. _____ a. I have little freedom in my role.

   _____ b. I have a great deal of freedom in my role.

   _____ c. I have enough freedom in my role.

14. ____ a. I do a good job according to a schedule already decided.

____ b. I am able to be innovative in my role.

____ c. I have no opportunity to be innovative and do something creative.

15. ____ a. Others in the organization see my role as significant to their work.

____ b. I am a member of a task force or a committee.

____ c. I do not work in any committees.

16. ____ a. Hostility rather than cooperation is evident here.

____ b. I experience enough mutual help here.

____ c. People operate more in isolation here.

17. ____ a. I am able to contribute to the company in my role.

____ b. I am able to serve the larger parts of the society in my role.

____ c. I wish I could do some useful work in my role.

18. ____ a. I am able to influence relevant decisions.

____ b. I am sometimes consulted on important matters.

____ c. I cannot make any independent decisions.

19. ____ a. I learn a great deal in my role.

____ b. I learn a few new things in my role.

____ c. I am involved in routine or unrelated activities and have learned nothing in my role.

20. ____ a. When people bring problems to me, I tend to ask them to work them out themselves.

____ b. I dislike being bothered with interpersonal conflict.

____ c. I enjoy solving problems related to my work.

Role Efficacy Scoring and Interpretation Sheet

Instructions: Circle the number corresponding to your response to each of the twenty items. Total these numbers and enter this sum in the box just below the key. Then compute your Role Efficacy Index according to the formula given.

Dimension	Item	a	b	c	Item	a	b	c
Centrality	1.	+2	+1	−1	11.	+2	+1	−1
Integration	2.	+1	−1	+2	12.	−1	+2	+1
Proactivity	3.	−1	+1	+2	13.	−1	+2	+1
Creativity	4.	+1	+2	−1	14.	+1	+2	−1
Interrole Linkage	5.	−1	+2	+1	15.	+2	+1	−1
Helping Relationship	6.	+1	+2	−1	16.	−1	+2	+1
Superordination	7.	−1	+2	+1	17.	+1	+2	−1
Influence	8.	+1	−1	+2	18.	+2	+1	−1
Growth	9.	+1	−1	+2	19.	+2	+1	−1
Confrontation	10.	−1	+2	+1	20.	+1	−1	+2

Your total

Role Efficacy

$$\frac{\text{Total score} + 20}{60} \times 100 =$$

Example: $\dfrac{36 + 20}{60} \times 100 = 93\%$

Interpretation

Note that the scale (–1, +1, +2) allows a maximum score of +40 and a minimum score of –20. Your Role Efficacy Index represents a percentage of your potential effectiveness in your organizational role. A high percentage indicates that you perceive that in your role you have a great deal of opportunity to be effective.

The ten dimensions of role efficacy are each measured by two items. Look at each dimension to determine in what areas you perceive yourself as having less than what you think you need to be effective. Look for pairs of items for which you have low scores and compare these dimensions. You may want to discuss your findings with your colleagues and your supervisor.

17 Exploring Supportive and Defensive Communication Climates
The Communication Climate Inventory
James I. Costigan and Martha A. Schmeidler

Summary

The communication climate in any organization is a key determinant of its effectiveness. Organizations with supportive environments encourage worker participation, free and open exchange of information, and constructive conflict resolution. In organizations with defensive climates, employees keep things to themselves, make only guarded statements, and suffer from reduced morale. This instrument can help with the diagnosis and correction of non-productive organizational climates.

Gibb (1961) identified six characteristics of a "supportive environment" and six characteristics of a "defensive one." Gibb affirmed that employees are influenced by the communication climate in the organization. He characterized a supportive climate as one having description, problem orientation, spontaneity, empathy, equality, and provisionalism and a defensive climate as having evaluation, control, strategy, neutrality, superiority, and certainty. These items are paired opposites. Capsule definitions of the terms follow:

Exploring

Characteristics of a Defensive Climate

Evaluation—The supervisor is critical and judgmental and will not accept explanations from subordinates.

Control—The supervisor consistently directs in an authoritarian manner and attempts to change other people.

Strategy—The supervisor manipulates subordinates and often misinterprets or twists and distorts what is said.

Neutrality—The supervisor offers minimal personal support for and remains aloof from employees' personal problems and conflicts.

Superiority—The supervisor reminds employees who is in charge, closely oversees the work, and makes employees feel inadequate.

Certainty—The supervisor is dogmatic and unwilling to admit mistakes.

Characteristics of a Supportive Climate

Descriptive—The supervisor's communications are clear, describe situations fairly, and present his or her perceptions without implying the need for change.

Problem Orientation—The supervisor defines problems rather than giving solutions, is open to discussion about mutual problems, and does not insist on employee agreement.

Spontaneity—The supervisor's communications are free of hidden motives and honest. Ideas can be expressed freely.

Empathy—The supervisor attempts to understand and listen to employee problems and respects employee feelings and values.

Equality—The supervisor does not try to make employees feel inferior, does not use status to control situations, and respects the positions of others.

Provisionalism—The supervisor allows flexibility, experimentation, and creativity.

Description of the Instrument

The Communication Climate Inventory uses the twelve factors described above as a means of assessing the communication climate within work groups in an organization. Thirty-six questions are presented in a Likert response format. The odd-numbered questions describe a defensive atmosphere, and the even-numbered questions describe a supportive environment. The following chart shows which questions are linked to which characteristic.

Defensive Climate

Questions 1, 3, 5—Evaluation
Questions 7, 9, 11—Control
Questions 13, 15, 17—Strategy

Supportive Climate

Questions 2, 4, 6—Provisionalism
Questions 8, 10, 12—Empathy
Questions 14, 16, 18—Equality

Defensive Climate   **Supportive Climate**

Questions 19, 21, 23—Neutrality   Questions 20, 22, 24—Spontaneity
Questions 25, 27, 29—Superiority   Questions 26, 28, 30—Problem Orientation
Questions 31, 33, 35—Certainty   Questions 32, 34, 36—Description

Guidelines for Interpretation

The Communication Climate Inventory is designed so that the lower the score, the greater the extent to which either climate exists in an organization. However, low defensive scores will probably be an indication that supportive scores are high and vice versa, simply because both climates would not exist together in an organization, although scores will vary according to the supervisor being evaluated.

If the communication climate of an organization appears to be supportive and nondefensive, then probably no changes need to be made. However, if the communication climate is defensive and nonsupportive, an intervention is called for to improve the climate. Structured experiences that develop interpersonal communication skills are useful for this purpose. Overall ratings can be gleaned by having each department plot its scores on the scale at the bottom of the scoring sheet and then looking at any trouble spots.

Scoring the Instrument

If a person agrees or strongly agrees (a score of 1 or 2) with the statements measuring a specific characteristic, that factor is important in the person's work environment. If the person scores the statement as a 4 or 5 (disagree or strongly disagree), it indicates that the characteristic being measured is not part of the person's work environment. A score of 3 indicates uncertainty or that the characteristic occurs infrequently in the environment.

The total of the scores from the odd-numbered questions indicates the degree to which the work environment is defensive, and the total of the scores from the even-numbered questions indicates the degree to which the work environment is supportive. For each individual characteristic, then, a total score of 3 to 6 indicates agreement or strong agreement on either the defensive or supportive scales, a total of 12 to 15 indicates disagreement or strong disagreement, and a total of 7 to 11 indicates a neutral or uncertain attitude.

The lowest possible overall climate score is 18 on either the defensive or supportive scales, which means that the respondent strongly agreed with all questions. The highest possible overall score is 90, which means that the respondent strongly disagreed with all questions. Both extremes are highly improbable.

If more than one person fills out the questionnaire, obtaining the mean score for each item is the most convenient method of scoring the inventory. Summing the means for the questions in each category provides the overall score for the type of climate (defensive or supportive), and comparing those two scores provides a rough estimate of the general organizational climate. The following scales can be used to provide a way of checking the communication climate.

Defensive Scale	**Supportive Scale**
Defensive, 18–40	Supportive, 18–40
Defensive to Neutral, 41–55	Supportive to Neutral, 41–55
Neutral to Supportive, 56–69	Neutral to Defensive, 56–69
Supportive, 70–90	Defensive, 70–90

In administering the inventory, it is important to be specific about which communication climate (which supervisor's communication) is being surveyed.

Uses of the Instrument

The Communication Climate Inventory can be used to measure the organization's total communication environment or the climate of individual work areas. The scores from this inventory can be used to plan needed changes in the communication environment or to indicate which practices should be encouraged.

Organizational consultants can use the inventory to determine whether the communication environment is causing problems. Educators can use it to help students understand the characteristics of supportive and defensive climates. Supervisors can use it to assess how their subordinates feel about their handling of communications in the work environments.

References

Combs, G.W. (1981). Defensive and supportive communication. In J.E. Jones & J.W. Pfeiffer (Eds.), *The 1981 annual*. San Francisco: Pfeiffer.

Gibb, J.R. (1961). Defensive and supportive communication. *Journal of Communications, 11*, 141–148.

Originally published in *The 1984 Annual Handbook for Faciliatators, Trainers, and Consultants.*

Communication Climate Inventory

James I. Costigan and Martha A. Schmeidler

Instructions: The statements below relate to how your supervisor and you communicate on the job. There are no right or wrong answers. Respond honestly to the statements, using the following scale:

1 = Strongly Agree   2 = Agree   3 = Uncertain   4 =Disagree   5 = Strongly Disagree

_____   1. My supervisor criticizes my work without allowing me to explain.

_____   2. My supervisor allows me as much creativity as possible in my job.

_____   3. My supervisor always judges the actions of his or her subordinates.

_____   4. My supervisor allows flexibility on the job.

_____   5. My supervisor criticizes my work in the presence of others.

_____   6. My supervisor is willing to try new ideas and to accept other points of view.

_____   7. My supervisor believes that he or she must control how I do my work.

_____   8. My supervisor understands the problems that I encounter in my job.

_____   9. My supervisor is always trying to change other people's attitudes and behaviors to suit his or her own.

_____   10. My supervisor respects my feelings and values.

_____   11. My supervisor always needs to be in charge of the situation.

_____   12. My supervisor listens to my problems with interest.

_____   13. My supervisor tries to manipulate subordinates to get what he or she wants or to make himself or herself look good.

_____   14. My supervisor does not try to make me feel inferior.

_____   15. I have to be careful when talking to my supervisor so that I will not be misinterpreted.

_____   16. My supervisor participates in meetings with employees without projecting his or her higher status or power.

1 = Strongly Agree   2 = Agree   3 = Uncertain   4 =Disagree   5 = Strongly Disagree

_____ 17. I seldom say what really is on my mind, because it might be twisted and distorted by my supervisor.

_____ 18. My supervisor treats me with respect.

_____ 19. My supervisor seldom becomes involved in employee conflicts.

_____ 20. My supervisor does not have hidden motives in dealing with me.

_____ 21. My supervisor is not interested in employee problems.

_____ 22. I feel that I can be honest and straightforward with my supervisor.

_____ 23. My supervisor rarely offers moral support during a personal crisis.

_____ 24. I feel that I can express my opinions and ideas honestly to my supervisor.

_____ 25. My supervisor tries to make me feel inadequate.

_____ 26. My supervisor defines problems so that they can be understood but does not insist that his or her subordinates agree.

_____ 27. My supervisor makes it clear that he or she is in charge.

_____ 28. I feel free to talk to my supervisor.

_____ 29. My supervisor believes that if a job is to be done right, he or she must oversee it or do it.

_____ 30. My supervisor defines problems and makes his or her subordinates aware of them.

_____ 31. My supervisor cannot admit that he or she makes mistakes.

_____ 32. My supervisor tries to describe situations fairly without labeling them as good or bad.

_____ 33. My supervisor is dogmatic; it is useless for me to voice an opposing point of view.

_____ 34. My supervisor presents his or her feelings and perceptions without implying that a similar response is expected from me.

_____ 35. My supervisor thinks that he or she is always right.

_____ 36. My supervisor attempts to explain situations clearly and without personal bias.

Communication Climate Inventory Scoring and Interpretation Sheet

Instructions: Place the numbers that you assigned to each statement in the appropriate blanks. Now add them together to determine a subtotal for each climate description. Place the subtotals in the proper blanks and add your scores. Place an X on the graph to indicate what your perception is of your organization or department's communication climate. Some descriptions of the terms follow. You may wish to discuss with others their own perceptions and interpretations.

Part I: Defensive Scores

Evaluation

Question 1 _____

Question 3 _____

Question 5 _____

Subtotal _____

Neutrality

Question 19 _____

Question 21 _____

Question 23 _____

Subtotal _____

Control

Question 7 _____

Question 9 _____

Question 11 _____

Subtotal _____

Superiority

Question 25 _____

Question 27 _____

Question 29 _____

Subtotal _____

Strategy

Question 13 _____

Question 15 _____

Question 17 _____

Subtotal _____

Certainty

Question 31 _____

Question 33 _____

Question 35 _____

Subtotal _____

Subtotals for Defensive Scores

Evaluation _____

Control _____

Strategy _____

Neutrality _____

Superiority _____

Certainty _____

Total _____

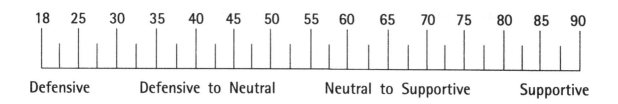

| 18 | 25 | 30 | 35 | 40 | 45 | 50 | 55 | 60 | 65 | 70 | 75 | 80 | 85 | 90 |

Defensive   Defensive to Neutral   Neutral to Supportive   Supportive

Part II: Supportive Scores

Provisionalism

Question 2 _____

Question 4 _____

Question 6 _____

Subtotal _____

Spontaneity

Question 20 _____

Question 22 _____

Question 24 _____

Subtotal _____

Empathy

Question 8 _____

Question 10 _____

Question 12 _____

Subtotal _____

Problem Orientation

Question 26 _____

Question 28 _____

Question 30 _____

Subtotal _____

Equality	**Description**
Question 14 _____	Question 32 _____
Question 16 _____	Question 34 _____
Question 18 _____	Question 36 _____
Subtotal _____	**Subtotal** _____

Subtotals for Supprtive Scores

Provisionalism _____

Empathy _____

Equality _____

Spontaneity _____

Problem Orientation _____

Description _____

Total _____

```
18   25   30   35   40   45   50   55   60   65   70   75   80   85   90
 |    |    |    |    |    |    |    |    |    |    |    |    |    |    |
```

Defensive   Defensive to Neutral   Neutral to Supportive   Supportive

18 Cross-Cultural Interactive Preference Profile

Morris Graham and Dwight Miller

Summary

Many people encounter problems interacting in environments that are culturally different from their own. Everyone has preferences regarding interpersonal interactions, and these may vary from culture to culture as well as from individual to individual.

One important dimension of culture is *context*, which ranges from *high context*, (collectivism) to *low context* (individualism). The Cross-Cultural Interactive Preference (CCIP) Profile measures an individual's preferences for level of context as well as his or her ability to interact effectively across contexts. This profile comprises the following factors: socialization of information, socialization of people, spatial orientation, and time orientation. As a result of understanding his or her own preferences, a person can become more aware of the role that context plays in individual and group interactions.

Most people do not do really well when interacting in an environment that is foreign to their own or with people of cultural preferences different from their own. This is particularly true within cross-cultural or cross-functional groups. Preferences regarding interpersonal interactions, group interactions, and information may vary from one culture to another, just as they also vary from one individual to another, regardless of cultural origin. People's interactive preferences need to be understood in order to facilitate productive group work. Such understanding can help to reduce potential interpersonal conflicts and can increase group effectiveness.

In cross-cultural or cross-functional group settings, what we can learn about ourselves through others is as important as what we can learn about others and their cultures. The ways in which we feel, think, and behave can be checked in terms of how others perceive and interact with us. Things take on new meanings in the context of other cultural orientations. Moreover, things that we may consider to be uniquely individual about our "selves" are actually shaped by our culture, which determines, to a large extent, how we respond in different situations.

The Cross-Cultural Interactive Preference Profile (CCIP Profile) identifies how the respondents would prefer to interact in group activities or in situations in which more than one cultural orientation is involved.

Definitions of Terms

Understanding any subject area requires a basic working vocabulary. In the cross-cultural field, this vocabulary has grown with the advance of research. However, only the essential terms are defined here, for the purpose of interpreting the CCIP Profile.

Assimilate: To become absorbed into the cultural traditions of another ethnic population or group.

Context: The information that surrounds an event and is inextricably bound up with the meaning of the event. The elements that combine to produce a given meaning— events and context—vary in proportion from culture to culture. The cultures of the world can be compared on a scale from low context to high context (Hall & Hall, 1990).

Cross-Cultural Activities: Activities that involve more than one cultural set, viewpoint, or environment. Such activities deal with an individual's personal and cultural self-awareness, other-awareness, intercultural communication barriers, and interaction skills (Brislin, 1990).

Culture: A collection of many beliefs, values, perspectives, behaviors, activities, institutions, and learned patterns of communication largely shared in common by a group of people.

High-Context Message: Communication in which the vast majority of the information is either internalized in the individual or the physical context of the situation. Very little is in the explicit transmission or coding of the message (Hall, 1977; Hall & Hall, 1990).

Judgment: The process of forming conclusions about what has been perceived by an individual.

Low-Context Message: Communication in which the mass of information is in the explicit coding of the message and not resident within the individuals involved or within the situation or context (Hall, 1977).

Microculture: A subculture or new culture formed by the interaction of two or more major cultures such as business organizations, nations, or persons. A formulation of beliefs, behaviors, values, characteristics, patterns of communication, etc., shared by a specific group of people, that originates from diverse, major cultural groupings (Fontaine, 1989).

Multicultural Individual: An individual who has assimilated understanding, precepts, knowledge, and characteristics of more than his or her own native culture by experiencing microcultural activities of cross-cultural groups. Adler (1986) notes that members of multicultural groups should recognize and integrate all the cultures represented.

Multiculturalism: Situations in which people from more than one culture (and frequently more than one country) interact regularly, thus forming a number of perspectives, approaches, and—in the case of businesses—business methods (Adler, 1986).

Personality: The result of conditioning by culture; the total of the individual's characteristic reactions to his or her environment.

Predisposition: The condition of being inclined beforehand or having a susceptibility to act or react in a particular way.

Conceptual Background:
Low-Context and High-Context Orientations

Theorists have identified a major dimension of cultural variability, called "context" (Chinese Culture Connection, 1987; Hall, 1977; Hall & Hall, 1990; Hofstede, 1984; Kluckhohn & Strodtbeck, 1961; Marsella, DeVos, & Hsu, 1985; Triandis, 1988). The two basic dimensions of are low context (individualism) and high context (collectivism).

Low-Context Cultures (Individualism)

Low-context, or "individualistic," people and cultures place emphasis on individualism and individual goals, facts, the management of time, nonverbal communication, privacy, and compartmentalization.

The cultural norms associated with low context, which dominate most North American and Northern European societies, are essentially task-oriented, focusing on data to provide the answers to living well. Progress is measured in tangibles. Goals are action-oriented and geared to produce short-term material profits. The driving force of a low-context culture is work, which is the usual context in which a person is honored. Societies are structured to honor individuals who succeed financially. Emotions are suspect and considered inappropriate in most social and work settings.

Low-context people are highly individualistic, assertive, directive, dominating, results-oriented, independent, strong-willed, competitive, quick to make decisions, impatient, time-conscious, solution-oriented, control-seeking, well-organized, and self-contained. The individual has a high need to be recognized for his or her performance.

Individualistic social skills include meeting people quickly, putting them at ease, finding topics of conversation that others can discuss readily, being interesting so that the others will have memories of the interaction six months later, and so forth. These skills are useful, as they allow people to obtain information from others, central to the pursuit of individual goals (Brislin, 1993).

In a group setting, low-context individuals need less time to develop new, progressive programs that can be changed easily and quickly. However, these individuals can create less cohesion and stability in the group. Also, they are less committed to group agreements or planned actions.

In low-context cultures, when there is a conflict between an individual's goals and those of a valued group (i.e., co-workers), consideration of the individual's goals is of major importance. Individualists report (Brislin, 1993) that they would feel stifled if they were surrounded by others. There would be too many people whose opinions would have to be considered before an individualist could act in the pursuit of his or her goals. Individualists find that clearing their plans with others interferes too much with their desire "to do their own thing."

High-Context Cultures (Collectivism)

High-context, or "collectivistic," individuals and cultures place emphasis on relationships, group goals, the process and surrounding circumstances, time as natural progression, verbal communication, communal space, and interrelationships.

High-context cultural norms are primarily group-oriented, i.e., honoring the relationships of their cultural group before that of an "out-group," such as a university, company, or country. Family and community ties are strong; feelings and emotions are valued and encouraged to be expressed; religious and spiritual beliefs are deep.

In a high-context culture, behavior is viewed in a complex way. People look beyond the obvious to note nuances in meaning, nonverbal communication cues, and the status of others in context. In general, Asian cultural orientations are high context.

Personal characteristics include being indirect, highly affiliative, team-oriented, systematic, steady, quiet, patient, loyal, dependable, informal, servicing, sharing, slow in making decisions, respectful, and good listeners. A longer amount of time is needed for individuals to become acquainted with and trusting of one another; after that, communication is fast. The culture is rooted in the past; it is a slow-to-change, highly stable, unified group.

Collectivists feel comfortable with the constant psychological presence of a group. Important collective social attributes are loyalty to the group, cooperation, contributing to the group without the expectation of immediate reciprocity, and public modesty about one's abilities (Triandis, 1988). People are more likely to downplay their own goals in favor of the goals of the valued group. Individuals are more committed to group agreements and planned actions.

Contextual Factors

The factors or dimensions of context are time and space (Hall, 1977; Hall & Hall, 1990). These factors can be considered across all cultures; they are not specific to one culture or another or have meaning in and of themselves. Hall notes the importance of these factors as information is disseminated and acted on.

Hall uses the terms "monochronic" and "polychronic" to describe the individual orientations to time. In monochronic time, one pays attention to and does only one thing at a time. Events, functions, people, communication, and information flow are compartmentalized. In monochronic cultures, people are governed by time and work and they communicate in a linear fashion. In polychronic time, many things may happen or receive attention at the same time. In polychronic cultures, there is great involvement with people and events. People take precedence over time and schedules, and there is an emphasis on completing human transactions.

Monochronic cultures are basically low-context cultures that control and restrict information flow and communication. Polychronic cultures are basically high-context cultures in which information flows freely among all participants. Because the information is available to all, one is expected to use intuition and to understand automatically.

The purpose of meetings and communication in low-context cultures is to pass and/or determine information in order to evaluate and make decisions. In high-context cultures, the purpose of meetings is to reach consensus about what is already known. The two processes are mutually exclusive in that in the low context, meaning is derived primarily from the coding of the messages. In the high context, the individuals already have the information or message within them. Hall and Hall (1990, p. 19) strongly emphasize the fact that "one must always be contexted to the local time systems" when working across cultures.

Spatial changes influence and often give definition to communications and human interaction even to the extent of overriding the spoken word. Spatial cues are perceived by all of the senses. Some cultures may attune more to the auditory, some to kinesthetic, others to visual, and so on. Each individual is surrounded by invisible boundaries of personal space or territories. These often communicate ownership or power when linked to physical location. With low-context monochronic societies and individuals, personal space is private, controlled, and often large. In contrast, in high-context polychronic societies or individuals, space is often shared with subordinates and centralized or shared in an information network. Time and space are often closely linked in that access to individuals is often dictated by both location and timing. An individual's availability is often determined by how well he or she is screened or separated from others.

Context and Communication

In his book, *Beyond Culture,* Hall (1977) identifies the critical need for individuals to transcend cultural barriers. He challenges us to " . . . recognize and accept the multiple hidden dimensions of unconscious culture . . . " (p. 2), because each culture has its own hidden or unconscious dimensions. In analyzing communication factors, Hall notes that it is impossible to know the meaning of a communication without knowing the context. Barker (1968) established that as the ecology or environment changed, so did people's responses.

With regard to context in relation to meaning, Hall (1977) states that context will largely determine the message that a person receives. Hall defines the collectivistic, high-context (HC) message or communication as one in which the vast majority of the information is either internalized in the individual or in the physical context of the situation. Very little is in the explicit transmission or coding of the message. With the individualistic, low-context (LC) message, the mass of information is in the explicit coding of the message, not within the individual or the situation (context).

Individuals perform the critically important function of correcting for distortions or omissions in the messages they receive. The key to being effective in communicating across cultures is in knowing the degree of information—context—that must be supplied and in the correct reading of another individual's verbal and nonverbal behavior. The context—the information surrounding an event that gives it meaning—varies from culture to culture and is often the determining factor in whether or not individuals from different cultures will communicate effectively, reach understanding, and make decisions. The integration of both verbal message and context is the basis of effective communication (Hall, 1977; Hall & Hall, 1990).

The Profile

High versus low context, individualism versus collectivism, and the factors of time and space are not the only dimensions by which culture can be analyzed. However, they are ways in which a determination can be made as to how to communicate and work with individuals, regardless of their cultural orientations. Although many comparisons of major ethnic and national groups have been made based on contextual needs and decision-making processes, few, if any, have been developed to measure individual responses. The Cross-Cultural Interactive Preference Profile (CCIP Profile) was developed to reveal an individual's preferences in terms of contextual needs and socialization in interactive, group-decision-making processes so that effective communication, facilitation, and training designs could be established.

Development

The profile items were developed from a review of the literature and were given to seven experts who had extensive knowledge and experience in cross-cultural environmental learning and group interaction. A conceptual review was completed first. To establish content validity on revisions, a Delphi panel was asked to review each of the profile items for appropriateness and inclusion. This panel was selected on the basis of working experience in highly cross-cultural learning environments and experience in designing either assessment tools or training materials that had been applied in that environment. Panel members also had worked as consultants or employees in business and industry. They reviewed items based on appropriateness to the culturally defined categories, readability, comprehension, and the exclusion of culturally charged contextual items. Individual reviews and further revisions continued until at least 75 percent of panel members agreed on each of the forty-eight retained items.

The profile was pilot tested with a culturally mixed group of university students, and feedback was solicited about the profile through focus groups and an interview process. Particular attention was paid to comprehensibility of the language. Minor adjustments were made before administering the CCIP Profile to 512 freshmen and sophomore students (247 males and 265 females) at Brigham Young University-Hawaii, where fifty cultural orientations were represented. Approximately 20 percent of the students were from the mainland United States and other (predominantly European) Western cultural mixes, 25 percent were from Hawaii, 25 percent were from the South Pacific, 25 percent were from the Asian-rim countries, and the remainder were from other parts of the world. It was observed that most foreign students, after their arrival on campus, would develop and retain socialization patterns that maintained close ties to their own cultural groups through culture-based clubs and organizations. Thus, the majority of the students surveyed were close to their native orientations.

The CCIP Profile is intended for use with individuals who are involved in cross-cultural activities that result in the development of knowledge and skills. The profile is designed to foster awareness of, and sensitivity to, contextual orientation that affect interactive behavior in culturally diverse groups.

Validity

The content validity of the profile was assured through the implementation of the literature review, the iterative Delphi panel, and interviews during the pilot-testing stages.

Construct validity was determined by assessing the relationship of test items with cultural groups through the use of factor analysis and multi-discriminant analysis. The profile employs a Likert scale, which resulted in a single factor or construct when factor analysis was applied. Factor loadings were above a level of .45. To assure validity, more than ten respondents per item were utilized. Item analysis utilizing two-tail probability showed ap-value .001 on all items.

Overall validity was based on the strength of the factor-1 loadings and the significance levels of the individual items. However, it is noted that there are some weaknesses to be dealt with through a continued analysis with additional populations.

Reliability

There are no current tests or standards with which to compare the results of the profile administration. A coefficient of internal consistency was determined utilizing a single-test administration. Cronbach's Coefficient Alpha was used to test reliability, as the profile relies on a nondichotomous, six-level Likert scale to circumvent a neutral or nonresponse, and a method of rational equivalence could not be used. Reliability coefficients (alphas) were: .49 in seven of the eight factor groupings, with the eighth at .34.

Suggested Use

The CCIP Profile can be used in various aspects of group decision making, cross-cultural conflict resolution, training and development, and team development in diverse work and educational settings. It is particularly useful as a clarification tool with newly organized groups or teams. Facilitators can be assured that finding out about one's own and others' preferences is a releasing experience, not a restricting one, as may be feared. Finding out about cultural preferences frees group members to recognize their own natural predispositions and to respect and learn how to effectively interact with the differences in the group with a minimum of conflict. Groups can become less polar or fragmented and more multi-culturally sensitive and unified in their interactions.

References

Adler, N.J. (1986). In D.A. Ricks (Ed.), *International dimensions of organizational behavior* (The Kent International Business Series). Boston, MA: Kent Publishing.

Barker, R.G. (1968). *Ecological psychology.* Stanford, CA: Stanford University Press.

Brislin, R. (1993). *Understanding culture's influence on behavior.* Fort Worth, TX: Harcourt Brace College.

Brislin, R.W. (Ed.). (1990). *Applied cross-cultural psychology* (Cross-Cultural Research and Methodology Series No. 14). Newbury Park, CA: Sage.

Chinese Culture Connection. (1987). Chinese values and the search for culture-free dimensions of culture. *Journal of Cross-Cultural Psychology, 18,* 143–164.

Fontaine, G. (1989). *Managing international assignments.* Englewood Cliffs, NJ: Prentice Hall.

Hall, E.T. (1977). *Beyond culture.* Garden City, NY: Anchor Press/Doubleday.

Hall, E.T., & Hall, M.R. (1990). *Understanding cultural differences*. Yarmouth, ME: Intercultural Press.

Hofstede, G. (1984). *Culture's consequences: International differences in work-related values*. Newbury Park, CA: Sage.

Kluckhohn, F., & Strodtbeck, F. (1961). *Variations in value orientations*. New York: Row, Peterson.

Marsella, A.J., DeVos, G., & Hsu, F.L.K (Eds.). (1985). *Culture and self: Asian and Western perspectives*. New York: Tavistock.

Triandis, H.C. (1988). Collectivism vs. individualism: A reconceptualization of a basic concept in cross-cultural psychology. In G. Verma & C. Bagley (Eds.), *Cross-cultural studies of personality, attitudes and cognition* (pp. 60–95). London: Macmillan.

Triandis, H.C. (1990). Cross-cultural studies of individualism-collectivism. In J. Berman (Ed.), *Nebraska Symposium on Motivation 1989* (Vol. 35, pp. 41–53). Lincoln, NE: University of Nebraska Press.

Originally published in *The 1995 Annual: Volume 1, Training.*

Cross-Cultural Interactive Preferences Profile

Morris Graham and Dwight Miller

There are no right or wrong answers on this questionnaire. The answers will be useful only if you respond honestly and candidly. By doing this, you will help us to better understand the ways in which you prefer to interact within a group where there is more than one culture represented.

Instructions: The following items describe how you might interact within a work or problem-solving group. Respond to each item by filling in the circle that best describes your preference, that is, how strongly you agree or disagree with the statement. This should take about fifteen minutes.

Example:

You would mark your questionnaire

(SD) (D) (MD) (MA) (A) ●

If you strongly agreed with this statement:

↓

It's O.K. for new situations or ideas to be presented to the group for a decision even if some details are not included.

You would mark your questionnaire

(SD) ● (MD) (MA) (A) (SA)

If you disagreed with this statement:

↓

I would let members do their own work the way they think best.

SD = Strongly Disagree   MA = Mildly Agree   A = Agree
D = Disagree   MD = Mildly Disagree   SA = Strongly Agree

(SD) (D) (MA) (MD) (A) (SA)   1. I need the leader of the group to explain the details before I can make a decision.

(SD) (D) (MA) (MD) (A) (SA)   2. I work best when we share information and then reach consensus as a group.

SD = Strongly Disagree   **MA = Mildly Agree**   **A = Agree**
D = Disagree   **MD = Mildly Disagree**   **SA = Strongly Agree**

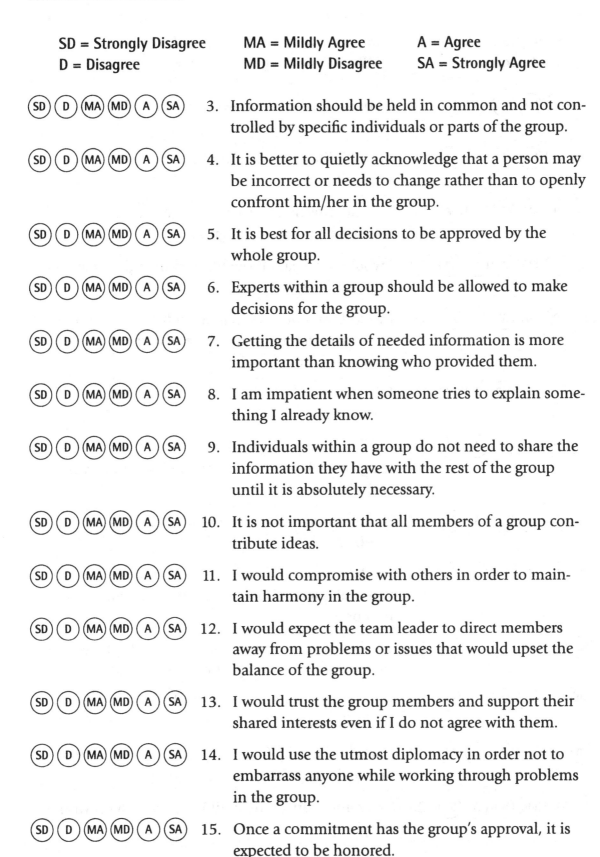

(SD) (D) (MA) (MD) (A) (SA)   3. Information should be held in common and not controlled by specific individuals or parts of the group.

(SD) (D) (MA) (MD) (A) (SA)   4. It is better to quietly acknowledge that a person may be incorrect or needs to change rather than to openly confront him/her in the group.

(SD) (D) (MA) (MD) (A) (SA)   5. It is best for all decisions to be approved by the whole group.

(SD) (D) (MA) (MD) (A) (SA)   6. Experts within a group should be allowed to make decisions for the group.

(SD) (D) (MA) (MD) (A) (SA)   7. Getting the details of needed information is more important than knowing who provided them.

(SD) (D) (MA) (MD) (A) (SA)   8. I am impatient when someone tries to explain something I already know.

(SD) (D) (MA) (MD) (A) (SA)   9. Individuals within a group do not need to share the information they have with the rest of the group until it is absolutely necessary.

(SD) (D) (MA) (MD) (A) (SA)   10. It is not important that all members of a group contribute ideas.

(SD) (D) (MA) (MD) (A) (SA)   11. I would compromise with others in order to maintain harmony in the group.

(SD) (D) (MA) (MD) (A) (SA)   12. I would expect the team leader to direct members away from problems or issues that would upset the balance of the group.

(SD) (D) (MA) (MD) (A) (SA)   13. I would trust the group members and support their shared interests even if I do not agree with them.

(SD) (D) (MA) (MD) (A) (SA)   14. I would use the utmost diplomacy in order not to embarrass anyone while working through problems in the group.

(SD) (D) (MA) (MD) (A) (SA)   15. Once a commitment has the group's approval, it is expected to be honored.

SD = Strongly Disagree   **MA = Mildly Agree**   **A = Agree**
D = Disagree   **MD = Mildly Disagree**   **SA = Strongly Agree**

(SD) (D) (MA) (MD) (A) (SA)   16. I would decide on my own what should be done and how it should be done.

(SD) (D) (MA) (MD) (A) (SA)   17. I would direct others toward getting results as soon as possible.

(SD) (D) (MA) (MD) (A) (SA)   18. I would directly confront problems or conflicts between individuals in the group.

(SD) (D) (MA) (MD) (A) (SA)   19. I would say what I thought, even though it may hurt others' feelings.

(SD) (D) (MA) (MD) (A) (SA)   20. I would want outstanding individual performers in group activities rewarded more than those who did not contribute as much.

(SD) (D) (MA) (MD) (A) (SA)   21. I don't like doing work on my own or being separate from the group.

(SD) (D) (MA) (MD) (A) (SA)   22. I feel uncomfortable when there are individuals in the group who remain distant and don't interact with the group.

(SD) (D) (MA) (MD) (A) (SA)   23. In a group meeting, it is important that we stay close together.

(SD) (D) (MA) (MD) (A) (SA)   24. It is best to have the leader in a centralized location where all members of the group can interact with him or her.

(SD) (D) (MA) (MD) (A) (SA)   25. The best way to work in a group is to stay together in the same room until agreement is reached.

(SD) (D) (MA) (MD) (A) (SA)   26. I don't want to be interrupted when I'm working on or thinking about a problem.

(SD) (D) (MA) (MD) (A) (SA)   27. I need to be away from the group in order to think and make a decision.

(SD) (D) (MA) (MD) (A) (SA)   28. I prefer to work alone until I am ready to get with the group.

SD = Strongly Disagree   MA = Mildly Agree   A = Agree
D = Disagree   MD = Mildly Disagree   SA = Strongly Agree

(SD) (D) (MA) (MD) (A) (SA) 29. The leader of a group or organization needs to be separate but where I can go to him or her when I need to.

(SD) (D) (MA) (MD) (A) (SA) 30. When working in a group, I prefer to work with individuals who think as I do.

(SD) (D) (MA) (MD) (A) (SA) 31. I would desire lots of time and flexibility to accommodate the different personalities in the group.

(SD) (D) (MA) (MD) (A) (SA) 32. If there were disagreement in the group, I would be patient while others worked through and resolved conflicts before proceeding.

(SD) (D) (MA) (MD) (A) (SA) 33. It is more important to take the time needed to develop or share ideas before making a decision than it is to meet deadlines.

(SD) (D) (MA) (MD) (A) (SA) 34. It is O.K. to stop a group discussion and take a break whenever needed.

(SD) (D) (MA) (MD) (A) (SA) 35. Plans should always be open to change.

(SD) (D) (MA) (MD) (A) (SA) 36. A group should not stop working or discussing until a solution is found or a decision is made.

(SD) (D) (MA) (MD) (A) (SA) 37. I would not tolerate postponements.

(SD) (D) (MA) (MD) (A) (SA) 38. It is very important that a schedule be maintained.

(SD) (D) (MA) (MD) (A) (SA) 39. The group should deal with only one thing at a time until a decision is made.

(SD) (D) (MA) (MD) (A) (SA) 40. When the group has finished its work, it is best to move on and form new relationships.

CCIP Profile Scoring Sheet

Instructions: Convert each rating that you gave to a profile item to a number, as shown, and place that number in the appropriate spaces on this sheet.

SD = 0   D = 1   MD = 2   MA = 3   A = 4   SA = 5

Place the *total scores* in the appropriate boxes on the following sheet.

Factor	Subscores			
Socialization of Information	**Item — Highly Shared Flow**		**Item — Controlled Flow**	
	1. _____		6. _____	
	2. _____		7. _____	
	3. _____		8. _____	
	4. _____		9. _____	
	5. _____		10. _____	
	Total _____		Total _____	
Socialization of People	**Item — Collectivist**		**Item — Individualist**	
	11. _____		16. _____	
	12. _____		17. _____	
	13. _____		18. _____	
	14. _____		19. _____	
	15. _____		20. _____	
	Total _____		Total _____	
Spatial Orientation	**Item — Shared/Central**		**Item — Personalized**	
	21. _____		26. _____	
	22. _____		27. _____	
	23. _____		28. _____	
	24. _____		29. _____	
	25. _____		30. _____	
	Total _____		Total _____	
Time Orientation	**Item — Polychronic**		**Item — Monochronic**	
	31. _____		36. _____	
	32. _____		37. _____	
	33. _____		38. _____	
	34. _____		39. _____	
	35. _____		40. _____	
	Total _____		Total _____	

CCIP Profile Interpretation Graph

Instructions:

1. Place the total scores from the CCIP Profile Scoring Sheet in the Factor boxes above.

2. Sum each row across to determine the Factor Score. Sum each column down to determine the Context Score.

3. Plot the "contextual level scores" on the graph, with the high-context score on the left axis and the low-context score on the right axis. Draw a line between the two plotted points.

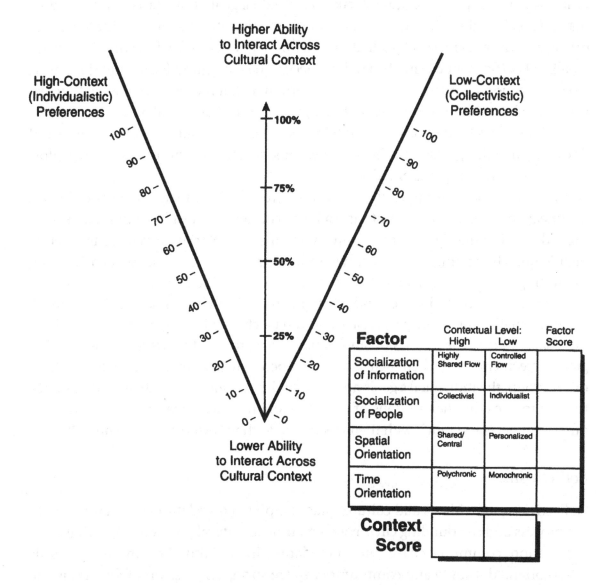

Factor	Contextual Level: High	Low	Factor Score
Socialization of Information	Highly Shared Flow	Controlled Flow	
Socialization of People	Collectivist	Individualist	
Spatial Orientation	Shared/ Central	Personalized	
Time Orientation	Polychronic	Monochronic	
Context Score			

CCIP Profile Interpretation Sheet

Background

As individuals develop within their cultures and in interactions with others, they form preferences about various aspects of interpersonal interactions. Many of these preferences have been identified in terms of what is called "context." Two basic contexts are "individualistic" and "collectivistic." The context in which one is interacting affects how one relates to others, communicates, interprets information, and so on.

Individualistic

Individualistic people and cultures focus on individual goals, tasks, facts, solutions, time management, and privacy. Individualists are assertive, directive, controlling, results-oriented, independent, strong-willed, competitive, quick to make decisions, impatient, organized, self-contained, and have a high need to be recognized for their performance. Goals are action-oriented to produce short-term material profits, and financial success is esteemed. Emotions are considered inappropriate in most social and work settings.

Individualists tend to have a monochronic time focus. One pays attention to and does only one thing at a time. Events, functions, people, communication, and information flow are compartmentalized.

Individualistic communication is "low context," which means that interactions are linear and specific and do not carry a lot of cultural "context" within them. Meaning is derived primarily from the coding of the message. Social skills include meeting people quickly, finding topics of conversation that others can discuss readily, being interesting so that the others will have memories of the interaction six months later, and obtaining information from others in pursuit of individual goals (Brislin, 1993).

Individualists' plans are progressive and can be changed quickly. However, such individuals can create less cohesion and stability in a group. They are less committed to group agreements, and when there is a conflict between an individual's goals and those of the group, the individual's goals are of major importance. Individualists do not like to have to consider the opinions of others before they act. Clearing their plans with others interferes too much with their desire "to do their own thing" (Brislin, 1993).

Collectivistic

Collectivistic individuals and cultures place emphasis on relationships, group goals, the process and surrounding circumstances, time as natural progression, verbal communication, communal space, and interrelationships. Cultural norms are primarily group oriented. Family and community ties are strong; expression of feelings is valued and encouraged; religious and spiritual beliefs are deep. These mutual under-standings and beliefs supply the "high context" of this orientation.

In such a culture, behavior is viewed in a complex way. People look beyond the obvious to note nuances in meaning, nonverbal communication cues, and the status of others in the context of a shared history and understanding. Thus, language need not be as specific; relationships are part of the message. Because the information is available to all, one is expected to use intuition and to understand automatically.

Personal characteristics include being: indirect, affiliative, informal, team-oriented, loyal, systematic, quiet, patient, dependable, cooperative, sharing, slow in making de-cisions, respectful, a good listener, contributing to the group without the expectation of immediate reciprocity, and public modesty about one's abilities (Triandis, 1990). A longer amount of time is needed for individuals to become acquainted with and trusting of one another; after that, communication is fast. The culture is rooted in the past; it is slow-to-change, highly stable, unified.

People are more likely to downplay their own goals in favor of the goals of the group, and individuals are more committed to group agreements.

Collectivists tend to have a polychronic time focus. Many things may happen or receive attention at the same time. There is great involvement with people and events. People take precedence over time and schedules, and there is an emphasis on com-pleting human transactions.

Hall (1977) notes that it is impossible to know the meaning of a communication without knowing the context. Context largely determines what one pays attention to or does not pay attention to. The information surrounding an event that gives it mean-ing varies from culture to culture. The key to being effective in communicating across cultures is in knowing the degree of information—context—that must be supplied and in the correct reading of another individual's verbal and nonverbal behavior.

Individual Application

People who score high on one side of the CCIP Profile Interpretation Graph and low on the opposite side (a steeply sloped profile) may interact well with those who have profiles similar to theirs, but not with others.

People whose scores are relatively high on both sides of the graph (a flat profile) probably have little difficulty in interacting within groups in which there are vary-ing levels of contextual requirements. These people are better able to move between situations and/or groups with ease, to be more flexible and adaptable in interpreta-tion and decision-making situations, and to be more responsive in learning and de-cision making. The higher the flat profile, the greater the flexibility.

The factor scores represent relative levels in each of the factor preference areas. Where flexibility and adaptability problems exist, low scores may indicate which orientation or requirement may be responsible. Sub scores will indicate the dominance of the characteristic. The differences between sub scores indicate level of flexibility for a characteristic (higher differences represent higher flexibility). In general, low scores represent a potential difficulty in interacting across contextual boundaries.

Note: Language, religion, philosophical, and other communication or social barriers are not included in this profile.

References

Brislin, R. (1993). *Understanding culture's influence on behavior.* Fort Worth, TX: Harcourt Brace College.

Hall, E.T. (1977). *Beyond culture.* Garden City, NY: Anchor Press/Doubleday.

Triandis, H.C. (1990). Cross-cultural studies of individualism-collectivism. In J. Berman (Ed.), *Nebraska Symposium on Motivation 1989* (Vol. 35, pp. 41–53). Lincoln, NE: University of Nebraska Press.

19 The High-Performance Factors Inventory:
Assessing Work-Group Management and Practices[1]

Robert P. Crosby

Summary

Twenty-five factors have been identified that are necessary for the creation of an empowered and high-performing organization. The High-Performance Factors Inventory can be used to assess group and/or its manager in terms of these factors and to identify areas in which further development is needed. Research has shown that when these factors are attended to, productivity, quality, and employee satisfaction are high.

In this article, the twenty-five factors are explained, and a four-step plan is presented for working through the inventory and planning action steps based on the results.

Empowerment in organizations is a balance of management authority and employee influence. It is also helping people to channel the power they already have toward qualitative and productive ends. Unfortunately, many managers flip from being too authoritarian to being too permissive and back again. Finding the appropriate balance is difficult.

The creation of an empowered and high-performing organization is dependent on many factors; twenty-five that impact performance have been identified through the use of data resulting from the author's instrument, the *People Performance Profile*. When these factors are attended to, productivity and quality are high, absenteeism is

[1]Adapted from the book, *Walking the Empowerment Tightrope* by Robert P. Crosby, © 1992, published by Organization Design and Development, Inc., King of Prussia, PA.

low, accidents are reduced, and employees are more likely both to enjoy and be motivated in their work environment.

The twenty-five high-performance factors are influenced by the manager of the work team or leader of the group. In teams without any management or leadership, the use of consensus is overly time consuming and often is controlled by the most rigid or resistant group members. Authoritarian management often is associated with pinpointing what is wrong and blaming. Permissive management often is associated with avoidance of responsibility and chaos. The balanced management approach is focused on "making it work."

The leader must have enough authority to create a participative culture and a loyalty that motivates followers. The opportunity to do productive work in a humane organization, with clarity of direction, is the most powerful motivating and esteem-enhancing force known. It also leads to bottom-line results.

High-Performance Factors

The twenty-five high-performance factors are as follows.

1. Sponsorship

The most critical factor in the success or failure of a plan or change project is the presence or absence of clear sponsorship from all managers and supervisors whose employees are involved in or affected by the plan or change. Sponsorship must be cascaded so that all are aligned. When such alignment is missing, employees receive conflicting messages. Lack of clarity about sponsorship is a primary cause of mistrust and dysfunction. Clarity reduces ambiguity and increases the possibility of success. This includes clarity about both direction and implementation. The fundamental principle is that one can only sponsor direct reports. Therefore, alignment down and across the organization is critical.

2. Openness

When autocratic managers refer to "troublemakers," they often are referring to people who bring up problems, ask questions, or make suggestions. Effective managers create an open climate in which information flows overtly rather than covertly. This involves "practicing what you preach," welcoming open—rather than underground—resistance, and listening actively so that people know that their messages have been heard and they have a chance to clarify any misperceptions. When the manager and group members have been trained in communication, arguments and blaming are reduced, and productivity increases.

3. Influence

Everyone should understand that the manager's or group leader's role is necessary. Likewise, the group members have roles. The manager makes certain decisions and puts certain systems in place. Group members must ensure that they have clarity about their jobs, about who decides what, and about how they are doing. All need to have the ability to get commitments from others, information they need to do their jobs, and materials or other resources they need to do their jobs. All need to have the ability to impact productivity and quality issues and to influence decisions that affect them, such as work space and environmental factors, procedures and processes, equipment, measurements of work, schedules, compensation, and openness about what is and what is not working.

4. Distinguish Between Decision Making and Influence

The group leader and the group members must understand the different decision-making and influence styles and know which ones they employ. Lack of clarity about decision making and influence is a dominant cause of mistrust and low productivity. It is also important to know who makes which decisions. In different circumstances, the leader may make a unilateral decision, describe the problem and ask for recommendations from group members before deciding, accept a majority decision from the group, ask for a consensus decision, or delegate the decision. What the leader should not do is make a decision and then pretend to solicit input. In each case, the type of decision should be made clear.

5. Decisions Are Made

Taking too much time to make a decision is as bad as not taking enough time or not making a decision at all. A person with a high need for accuracy often postpones decisions, always seeking more information. A person with a high relationship orientation may postpone decisions while striving for agreement or consensus. On the other hand, a hard-charging person could make a decision without understanding its impact. It is important to understand one's decision-making style and *manage* it productively. Group members also can help one another and their manager by "calling" one another on decision-making problems when needed.

6. Implementation

Many organizations and managers announce plans or changes and then act as if a magic wand had been waved and the plans or changes were immediately in effect. In fact, implementation is the most critical step. If the people affected by the plan or change are to buy into it, they must be involved in the planning of both the plan or change and the implementation strategy. As with other factors, clarity is essential in all aspects of the implementation.

7. Input Needs

Input is what is received into the unit. Throughput is what happens to that material, information, order, etc., as it moves through the unit—the work flow and processes. Output is what goes to the internal or external customer. Building relationships with suppliers can improve the quality and timeliness of input. More timely notification of needs and better adherence to procedures about paperwork can help the suppliers achieve this.

8. Throughput

Continuous improvement of throughput processes is essential. Initially, survey feedback is a useful tool if there is a lot of data to be gathered regarding manager/employee relations, role clarity, accountability, intergroup issues, and other dimensions related to group effectiveness. Often, other groups and the relationships with them need to be considered, and the groups' processes may need to be aligned. Creating models of each process, developing flow charts, and clarifying individual tasks and perceptions are useful in the development of efficient throughput. Measurement of results is critical. Then continual review of processes with the goals of updating and improving helps to keep things productive, keep quality up, and ensure safety.

9. Output

Obtaining feedback on output is the best way to track quality and customer satisfaction. Developing a feedback form may be problematic if the persons involved have different perceptions of their jobs, so creating clarity and alignment again is essential. The feedback form can contain yes/no questions, multiple choice questions, scaled responses, and/or open-ended questions (these are more difficult to score, but a wider range of information can be obtained). If the feedback reveals problems, the manager and group engage in identifying the actual problem, identifying possible solutions, analyzing solutions and possible results, and developing a plan for action.

10. Meetings

Most meetings can be improved. Deciding on the purpose of each meeting; asking whether the purpose can be served better by means of telephone calls, memos, or electronic mail; and determining who actually needs to attend and who does not can help to keep meetings from becoming time wasters. An agenda should be developed for each meeting, with estimated times, and all key agenda items should be addressed. Discussions that can be conducted with smaller groups should be assigned to another time. All commitments and action items should be recorded, with the "who," "what," and "by when" specified. All members should feel empowered to comment on process, such as when the meeting strays from the topic. Finally, each meeting should be reviewed briefly with the aim of continually improving the process.

11. Creativity

A climate for creativity is built when people are thanked for contributing ideas, whether one agrees with them or not. Brainstorming is a good way to introduce the creative process. Looking for the kernel in wild ideas often yields productive applications. If the group members are assured of the manager's support, they will learn to keep contributing, even when some of their ideas are not accepted or implemented.

12. Job Clarity

Confusion about priorities is a common cause of lack of job clarity. Confusion between the understood job assignment and what one is asked to do and assignments or requests from multiple sources are other causes. If other people are unclear about a person's role, they may ask that person to do things outside of the person's understood role. The manager should clarify his or her expectations of each member's role, and members should clarify their expectations of one another. Duplication of effort can be eliminated, and gaps can be filled.

13. Person–Task Fit

Organizations function best when their members can do what they do well and enjoy doing. Of course, some routine, uninspiring tasks need to be done, but it is often possible to adjust tasks in order to achieve a better person-task fit. The manager and group members can discuss the possibilities for shifting work around or doing it differently. Team planning also can lead to trading of tasks and cross-training so that people can support one another better.

14. Authority

A recurring problem in organizations is that people have responsibility for tasks but not the authority to carry them out. Authority may mean being able to enlist help or attain resources. This is experienced by managers as well as others. If this problem can be solved without bringing it to the attention of higher levels, so much the better. If not, it is important to identify the sponsors of the tasks and enlist their aid.

15. Resource Availability

Resources include people, information, time, materials, equipment, and repairs. Availability of resources is a system issue and demands a system response. To tackle this issue, both workers and decision makers must be involved. It may require an ad hoc team effort, with membership from all parts of the organization and a skilled facilitator. Dialogue must be kept open between key decision makers and the problem solvers, and the effort may take some time. Nevertheless, the effort is required, as lack of resources cannot be solved at the work-group level although it greatly impairs productivity at that level.

16. Team Measurements

Many aspects of input, throughput, and output are measurable. The idea of continuous improvement is based on measurement to chart progress. Choosing what is to be measured is a shared activity, and it must be remembered that measurement is aimed at improvement, not at assigning blame. If measurement devices are kept simple, they will not impede the usual work flow.

Productivity measurements may include increases in numbers of items produced or processed, profit, accuracy, new clients, etc. They also may include reductions in time, absenteeism, costs, returns, incorrect shipments, and so on.

17. Big-Picture Perspective

Most people work better when they understand the "big picture" related to a task and their role in it. When group members understand the manager's and the group's goals, risks, and market opportunities, they are better able to participate in creating success. It is important that the group leader answer questions and realize that different people may want different information. Keeping group members informed of changes in the marketplace, the organization, and the competition helps them to understand why they are doing what they are doing.

18. Training

"Just in time" training is based on the idea that training loses its effectiveness if it does not immediately precede application. For example, computer training at an outside facility is largely forgotten if the workers do not immediately begin to use what they have learned on computers in the workplace. Implementing continuous improvement and measurement practices will help to pinpoint training needs, which should be met as soon as possible so that inefficient practices do not become part of work habits.

19. Priorities

Lack of clear priorities is a common complaint in organizations, although it may be expressed as "I have too much work" or "I have too many bosses." Many people find it difficult to say no or to draw boundaries. Thus, they feel stressed and victimized. It is important that the manager take responsibility for setting priorities or determining exactly how they are set. Clear job descriptions and task expectations help. Often, a lead member of the team may be assigned responsibility for keeping track of priorities. Task priorities should be related to each member of the team at least once each week.

20. By-When's

When people leave a meeting, it should be clear who will do what and by when it will be done. "I'll get around to it" is not a commitment. Each meeting should begin with a review of the commitments made at the previous meeting. The right to ask for a "by-when" must go up and down and laterally across the organization. Whoever has responsibility for a task must be empowered to remind others of their commitments when breakdowns occur.

21. Follow Through

Making a good decision is not the same as taking action. Too often, assumed action does not take place. People do things to which they are committed. If someone says, "I'll try . . .," it is an indication of low commitment, whereas "I will . . ." is an indication of dedication to achieving results. In addition to obtaining "by-when's," it is important to obtain acceptance of responsibility for achievement. When people give their word, others need to be able to count on it so that actions can happen in a predictable way. People also need to know that if they have overcommitted, they can go to the manager or the group and rectify the situation. When a group norm of following through on commitments has been established, schedules are met, budgets are accurate, and a new energy flow is created.

22. Single-Point Accountability

It is important that someone be accountable for the satisfactory completion of each task. This person can keep track of schedules, resources, and people, and spot small problems or delays before they become major ones. This person is a catalyst of the task. Accountability is a particular problem in a matrixed organization. Matrices create holes through which fingers can be pointed and people can escape from accountability. When two or more groups share a task, it is important that managers agree among themselves about where accountability for each segment will lie. Each manager then communicates this to his or her employees.[2]

23. Reinforcement

A fundamental principle of psychology is that people repeat behaviors that they are rewarded for. Too often, people in organizations only hear about what they have done wrong. Managers can reward employees by giving them a chance to work with people, projects, or equipment they are interested in; by sponsoring their attendance at training events and conferences; by providing relief from repetitive tasks; and by saying "thank you" privately and publicly in a timely manner. Organizations can introduce motivational profit-sharing programs and can celebrate achievement by inviting employees to dinners and cake breaks and by handing out free passes to movies or other events. Timely recognition that states specifically what performance is being recognized will reinforce that achievement.

24. Reprimands

If managers' expectations are made clear, and employees have clarity about their roles and responsibilities, reprimands are not needed as often and are not as much of a surprise when they occur. When reprimands are stated in general and judgmental ways, they are destructive. In order for them to be constructive, certain preconditions must be met: job assignments and expectations must be clear, positive reinforcement must occur when things are done right, and there must be a climate of openness in the organization. Then reprimands must be given privately, not publicly; they must be specific about which behaviors are unacceptable; and the timing of the reprimand must be close to the event that required it. After making a reprimand, the manager should make it clear what behaviors should replace the undesirable ones and should assure the employee of his or her value to the group.

25. Work Relationships

Most conflict at work is not interpersonal but is caused by poor sponsorship, unclear roles and priorities, and confused authority and decision making. However, people often assign blame for these things to others and complain about the person rather than attempting to solve the problem. In this triangle, the person being complained about has no chance to defend himself or herself or to solve the problem. A norm of

---

[2] Crosby's book, *Solving the Cross-Work Puzzle* (Seattle, WA: LIOS Publishing, 1994) is about these issues.

speaking directly to the person involved can help to nip many work-group problems in the bud. If the issue is severe, a third party or skilled facilitator may be asked to moderate the conversation. If work-group members are focused on problem solving rather than on blaming, interpersonal issues are resolved more easily.

Many of the factors discussed here are organizational system problems rather than individual problems. It is important to remember the formula used by Kurt Lewin: Behavior is a function of the person and the environment.

Uses of the Instrument

The High-Performance Factors Inventory can be used by members of a group or team to assess the group's functioning. It also can be used by the manager of a team or by a team leader to assess his or her management influence. The respondent(s) then should follow the steps outlined below to generate an improvement plan and follow through for the group.

Administration of the Instrument

Step One: Appraising the Group

The facilitator can begin by stating the purpose of the instrument without divulging its content to the point that respondents attempt to give the "right" answers. Each respondent is given a pencil and a copy of the High-Performance Factors Inventory and reviews the instructions on the inventory.

Step Two: Reviewing the Results

When the respondents have completed the inventory, copies of the High-Performance Factors Scoring and Interpretation Sheet are distributed to them. They add up the scores they gave the items on the inventory and read the feedback for their totals.

Step Three: Developing an Improvement Plan

The respondents are asked to review the items for which their scores were lower than they would wish and to think about some specific ways to improve them. The facilitator then posts the list of the twenty-five High-Performance Factors and explains each factor, in turn. Respondents may be asked to reveal their ideas for improving their scores for that factor, while the facilitator records all suggestions on newsprint.

The facilitator suggests that the respondents list actions that they would want from others and also list what they intend to do to improve those factors rated low. The principle is as follows:

> You are your words and your actions. If your words are "probably," "I hope," "if I can," "I'll try," "I don't know when," "it wasn't my fault," and "nobody told me," you will create a pattern of not achieving, of blaming, and of finding excuses. If your words are "here's what I expect," "how can I support you?," "when do you need this?," "I'll complete it by (when)," and "here's when I need this from you," you will create a pattern of achieving. You must not only meet your commitments, you must provide others with the resources and support they need to make their commitments. You can begin to recast accountability and support in your organization. You create by initiating your own behavior.

The respondents and supervisor agree on specific actions and record who will do what and by when.

Step Four: Involving Work-Group Members in Follow Through

The next step, which should be taken within approximately a month, is to meet again and review the agreements. Members and managers can score each agreement on a "1" to "10" scale ("1" is low and "10" is high) and discuss their results. Some will score high, and some will score low. There will be successes and breakdowns. Celebrate the successes and fix the breakdowns.

Originally published in *The 1996 Annual: Volume 2, Consulting.*

High Performance Factors Inventory[3]

Robert P. Crosby

Instructions: For each item that follows, circle the number on the continuum that best represents your work group.

1. Sponsorship

   The supervisor firmly supports his/her direct reports, providing direction, resources, clarity, and enthusiasm to guarantee success.

Almost Always				Almost Never
5	4	3	2	1

2. Openness

   Data flows accurately so that problems are identified. Disagreements are viewed as opportunities for dialogue and are dealt with directly.

Almost Always				Almost Never
5	4	3	2	1

3. Influence

   Employees have input and influence on factors that impact their work life, i.e., suggesting solutions, often seeing suggestions being acted on, and getting feedback when suggestions are rejected.

Almost Always				Almost Never
5	4	3	2	1

4. Distinguish Between Decision Making and Influence

   Managers are clear about the distinction between "who is deciding" versus "who is influencing" and communicate that.

Almost Always				Almost Never
5	4	3	2	1

---

[3]Reprinted from the book, *Walking the Empowerment Tightrope* by Robert P. Crosby, © 1992, published by Organization Design and Development, Inc., King of Prussia, PA.

5. Decisions Are Made

Decisions are made in an expedient amount of time; it does not take forever to get a decision made.

Almost Always				Almost Never
5	4	3	2	1

6. Implementation

Once decisions are made, they are effectively implemented in a timely way.

Almost Always				Almost Never
5	4	3	2	1

7. Input Needs

We get on time and with quality what we need from outside or inside suppliers, such as materials, maintenance support, information, equipment, and/or commitments to service.

Almost Always				Almost Never
5	4	3	2	1

8. Throughput

Once input is received, we are organized in the best possible way to produce quality output in a timely manner with clear and efficient processes. Our equipment is up-to-date and effectively used.

Almost Always				Almost Never
5	4	3	2	1

9. Output

We give to others what they need and provide excellent service, on time and with quality. This includes internal customers (within the organization) and external customers.

Almost Always				Almost Never
5	4	3	2	1

10. Meetings

Our meetings are effective. Time is not wasted. Appropriate people attend. Participation is shared. When needed, we solve issues, and decisions are made.

Almost Always				Almost Never
5	4	3	2	1

11. Creativity

New ideas for improving work processes, communication, product development, etc., are encouraged. It is easy in our climate to suggest or try something new.

Almost Always				Almost Never
5	4	3	2	1

12. Job Clarity

I know exactly what I am to do. My boss' expectations are clear. My job does not unnecessarily duplicate someone else's job.

Almost Always				Almost Never
5	4	3	2	1

13. Person-Task Fit

The right people are doing the right tasks. My skills and the skills of others are being used effectively here.

Almost Always				Almost Never
5	4	3	2	1

14. Authority

People have the authority to do what they are expected to do. They typically do not have to be persuaded or manipulated to act in the absence of higher authority.

Almost Always				Almost Never
5	4	3	2	1

15. Resource Availability

We are able to get the resources we need to do our jobs well. These include information, equipment, materials, and maintenance.

Almost Always				Almost Never
5	4	3	2	1

16. Team Measurements

We have measurements that help us regularly track key factors related to our input, throughput, and output so that we can monitor and quickly solve identified problems and issues.

Almost Always				Almost Never
5	4	3	2	1

17. Big-Picture Perspective

We know the larger picture, i.e., where our organization is headed, how world and national economic and competitive factors affect us, and how we are doing. On everyday tasks we know why we are doing what we are doing.

Almost Always				Almost Never
5	4	3	2	1

18. Training

Members of our work team are well-trained technically as well as in teamwork and communication skills.

Almost Always				Almost Never
5	4	3	2	1

19. Priorities

No time is wasted wondering which task is more important. Priorities are consistently clear.

Almost Always				Almost Never
5	4	3	2	1

20. By-When's

    Whenever a decision is made, someone clarifies who will do what and by when. Also, by-when's are not only *given* to bosses but *received* from them as well.

Almost Always				Almost Never
5	4	3	2	1

21. Follow Through

    Commitments are effectively tracked, i.e., reviewed at subsequent meetings or tracked by computer. Missed commitments are discussed and recommitted or are reassigned to someone else.

Almost Always				Almost Never
5	4	3	2	1

22. Single-Point Accountability

    There is one person accountable for each task. Even on a matrixed group across departments, one person holds the single-point accountability rather than the group.

Almost Always				Almost Never
5	4	3	2	1

23. Reinforcement

    People are appreciated for work well done. Expressions of thanks are clear enough so that the receivers know precisely what they did that was liked.

Almost Always				Almost Never
5	4	3	2	1

24. Reprimands

    When our supervisor is unhappy with our work, he/she tells us as soon as possible, privately. The reprimand is clear and very specific about the unappreciated work or action but not accusatory, judgmental, or vindictive.

Almost Always				Almost Never
5	4	3	2	1

25. Work Relationships

Work relationships are maintained. When two or more people disagree, the issue is dealt with directly and effectively rather than avoided or escalated.

Almost Always				Almost Never
5	4	3	2	1

High Performance Factors Scoring and Interpretation Sheet[4]

Instructions: Total the numbers that you circled for each of the items on the High-Performance Factors Inventory and write the total here:

107 and Over: Outstanding

Congratulations, your group is among the rare, high-performing groups. The chances are that your leader and group members are open, nondefensive, and problem-solving people who balance caring with clarity about expectations.

95 to 106: Excellent

Your group is in the top tenth of those studied. You are doing very well and could easily reach a higher goal.

77 to 94: Good

Many groups score in this range. Applying the insights from your discussions about group performance can boost your scores. Achieving a higher level of performance is within reach.

76 and Below: Needs Improvement

The majority of groups score in this range. Opportunities abound. To make improvements, your group may need some coaching. The lower your score, the greater the need to seek skilled, outside help from someone who can see the high-performance factors either happening or not happening. A skilled consultant also notices when intentions do not match behaviors within the group and can help the members to learn more effective ways of interacting and working.

---

[4] Reprinted from the book, *Walking the Empowerment Tightrope* by Robert P. Crosby, © 1992, published by Organization Design and Development, Inc., King of Prussia, PA.

Conclusions

In addition, you may want to consult with two or three other groups that have scores for the twenty-five factors. Share your scores and support one another by making suggestions in areas where you have high scores and others have lower scores. If you are the group's manager or leader, you may want to consult with other managers or leaders whose groups have completed the inventory.

Answering the following questions can help you to prepare for looking at how to improve your group's functioning:

- What is the mission of the group? If it is part of a larger organization, what is the organization's stated mission? What is the group's "piece of the pie"?

- What values are important to the group members? To the group collectively? Are these in line with the organization's stated values? Do the organization's values impact its day-to-day activities or are they simply slogans?

- What are the group's business objectives? What do the members want to achieve in the next twelve months?

- Who supports and has ownership of the objectives? The group leader or manager? The members? A higher manager?

- Are the mission, values, and business objectives known and integrated in the daily work life? Do group members know what they can do to impact these? Do they know their "piece of the pie"?

- Are organizational progress reports regularly made available to all group members?

- Are you (as the group's leader or manager) able to state the group's specific business objectives and values? Can you state what is expected from group members to achieve these?

20 Organization Behavior Describer Survey (OBDS)

Roger Harrison and Barry Oshry

Summary

The Organization Behavior Describer Survey (OBDS) was developed to assess the behavior of line and staff managers and administrators in group and interpersonal situations arising during the course of work. It can be used as a self-evaluation form or to obtain descriptions of behavior from others.

The OBDS originally was developed deductively from Argyris's (1962) theory of interpersonal behavior in organizations. Argyris postulates two kinds of administrative competence: rational-technical competence and interpersonal competence. Rational-technical competence is the ability to meet intellectual-knowledge and technical-skill requirements of the job; interpersonal competence is the individual's willingness and ability to deal directly and openly with the emotional aspects of interpersonal relationships in the organization.

Argyris's theory is similar to other two-factor theories of organizational behavior, notably Fleishman's Initiating Structure and Consideration, Blake's Managerial Grid, and McGregor's Theory X and Theory Y. Another Fleishman instrument, the Supervisory Behavior Questionnaire, was already available for assessing supervisory behavior on the dimensions of Initiating Structure and Consideration. It focused on supervisor-subordinate relationships and was primarily designed for the first-line level of supervision. In contrast, the OBDS was designed to produce a more general measure of interpersonal behavior, not only downward in the organization but laterally and upward as well.

In the first attempt to construct the instrument, twenty items were deductively composed—ten representing rational—technical aspects of interpersonal behavior and ten describing interpersonal competence as defined by Argyris. These items were factor analyzed, using 321 descriptions of managers in a technical manufacturing firm at middle levels of responsibility. Instead of the two expected factors, three important dimensions emerged from the analysis: rational-technical competence (24 percent of the variance), interpersonal competence (22 percent of the variance), and emotional expressiveness (11 percent of the variance).

These results indicated that the expressive and receptive aspects of interpersonal competence were not seen by respondents as closely related to each other. Being open to the ideas and feelings of others was seen as quite different from being open in expression of one's feelings. This seemed an important finding, because it identified another factor beyond the two usually considered important in organizational behavior and because it implied that aspects of interpersonal behavior that trainers and organizational consultants have carelessly tended to think of together may be quite separate processes.

Correlations were calculated between the three scales of the OBDS and the rating on Fleishman's *Supervisory Behavior Questionnaire.* As expected, the interpersonal competence scale showed moderately high correlations (median = .62) with Fleishman's Consideration Scale. Both the rational-technical and emotional expressiveness scales of the OBDS were moderately correlated with Fleishman's Initiating Structure Scale (median _ .47). The emotional expressiveness scale showed negligible correlations with Fleishman's Consideration Scale and lower correlations with the OBDS interpersonal competence scale than with the rational-technical scale. This provided further evidence that the receptive and expressive aspects of interpersonal behavior may be seen quite differently.

Based on these preliminary results, development of the OBDS was carried out. A thirty-six-item questionnaire was constructed, and the descriptions by 189 subordinates of middle managers attending human relations training workshops were factor analyzed. An essentially similar factorial structure was obtained. This was tested by further factor analysis of descriptions of middle managers by fellow participants in a human relations training laboratory (T-group). In this artificial and specialized interaction situation, similar factors were found to those obtained from on-the-job descriptions. The resulting scales are presented here for use in studies of organizational behavior, evaluation of training, and the analysis of interpersonal behavior in groups.

In the current version of the OBDS, four scales are used. These are not altogether independent factorially. The basic factor structure is still three dimensional. However, the items in each of the four scales cluster rather neatly together and have a unity of connotation that argues for separate scoring. The median interscale correlations and reliability estimates of these scales are given in Table 1.

Interscale correlations are based on twelve samples (median N = 51), including:

1. Descriptions by fellow members of managers participating in a T-group laboratory;

2. Descriptions of industrial managers by self, supervisor, subordinate, and peer;

3. Descriptions of managers in an applied-research organization by the categories of describers in (2); and

4. Descriptions of YMCA executives by the categories of describers in (2).

Table 1. Median Interscale Correlations and Reliability Estimates of OBDS Scales

Scale	Rational-Technical Competence	Verbal Dominance	Consideration	Emotional Expressiveness
Rational-Technical Competence	.73 (pre-post)[1] .83 (split half)[2]	.69	.36	−.03
Verbal Dominance		.71 (pre-post) .84 (split half)	.23	.13
Consideration			.70 (pre-post) .92 (split half)	−.29
Emotional Expressiveness				.70 (pre-post) .89 (split half)

[1]Pre-post correlations are with intervening training experience and are based on eleven samples (median N=49).
[2]Speaman-Brown split-half reliabilities are based on four samples (median N=80).

Inspection of Table 1 shows reasonable independence of the scales, with the exception of verbal dominance and rational-technical competence, which are closely related. It is interesting to note the low negative correlation between consideration and emotional expressiveness in view of the attempts by practitioners of laboratory training to encourage increases in behavior on both dimensions. There is, in fact, a consistent tendency in our research for managers who rank high on emotional expressiveness to be seen in generally negative ways by their associates.

The reliabilities reported in Table 1 are adequate, especially considering the shortness of the scales. The pre-test correlations are also evidence of considerable stability, considering that they are based on pre-test time differences averaging two months and that they encompass an intervening human relations training experience designed to produce change along the dimensions measured by the OBDS.

With an instrument measuring behavior through descriptions, it is important to consider not only intra-describer reliability but also to assess inter-describer reliability: the degree of agreement among observers of the same individual's behavior. Accordingly, correlations were calculated between descriptions of the same person by self, supervisor, and subordinate. The findings, presented in Table 2, are based on the same populations as the figures in Table 1.

Table 2. Median Inter-Describer Correlations, OBDS Scales

| Scale | Correlations Based on Different Roles (13 Samples) | | Correlations Based on Same Roles (Subordinate) (2 Samples) | |
	Median r	Range	r	N
Rational-Technical Competence	.14	−.03 to .27	.39 .24	70 28
Verbal Dominance	.20	−.05 to .47	.28 .40	61 22
Consideration	.14	−.07 to .40	.15 .45	69 26
Emotional Expressiveness	.30	.09 to .56	.50 .56	66 29

Note: Median N = 53; range of N's: 15 to 66.

These findings are not very encouraging if one hopes to obtain a composite measure from several describers of an individual's interpersonal style in his or her organizational setting. When compared with the respectable intra-describer reliabilities, these figures are small indeed.

The inclusion of self-subordinate and self-supervisor correlations in this determination may be questioned on the grounds that self-descriptions are more subject to distortion than are descriptions by associates. There is, however, no indication from the distribution of correlations that this is the case. Roughly the same range of relationships was found in those correlations involving self-descriptions as in those based on observations by subordinate and supervisor. The data suggest, rather, that there is in fact considerable inconsistency in personal style, depending on some combination of the perceptual idiosyncracies of the observer and the behavior-determining role relationships between the observer and the individual described. From the data in Table 2, it can be seen that correlations between descriptions by two subordinates of the same supervisor are, on all scales, higher than the median of correlations based on different roles. This suggests that some of the unreliability between raters is indeed due to role relationships that influence interpersonal style. However, even within the same role, the inter-rater correlations leave a great deal to be desired.

It also is of interest that the correlations tend to be higher for verbal dominance and emotional expressiveness than they do for rational-technical competence and consideration. The items in the latter two scales require a higher degree of inference and refer less directly to observable behavior than do the items in the verbal-dominance and emotional-expressiveness scales. The more inference we require from the describer, of course, the more we can expect his or her judgment to be affected by his or her own psychological processes. For this reason the "best" scale should be one that is based most heavily on concrete descriptions of observable behavior.

In this connection it is interesting to compare Fleishman's Supervisory Behavior Questionnaire with the OBDS. In the study in which the OBDS was first developed, we also obtained descriptions on Fleishman's instrument from self, supervisor, peer, and subordinate (N = 50). The median inter-rater correlations were .39 for initiating structure and .16 for consideration. Thus, the OBDS and the *Supervisory Behavior Questionnaire* compare favorably in inter-rater reliability on the consideration dimension, but Fleishman's instrument has a better showing on initiating structure than the OBDS has on verbal dominance, the closest OBDS scale in content.

The rather high mean scores on the OBDS suggest that the responses could be designed to produce a greater spread of scores. For example:

4 = Always

3 = Most of the time

2 = Often

1 = Occasionally

0 = Seldom

References

Argyris, C. (1962). *Interpersonal competence and organizational effectiveness.* New York: John Wiley & Sons.

Blake, R.R., & Mouton, J.S. (1964). *The managerial grid.* Houston, TX: Gulf.

Fleishman, E.A. (date unknown). *Initiating structure and consideration.*

Fleishman, E.A. (date unknown). *Supervisory behavior questionnaire.*

McGregor, D.M. (1960). *The human side of enterprise.* New York: McGraw-Hill.

Originally published in *The 1976 Annual Handbook for Faciliatators, Trainers, and Consultants.*

Organization Behavior Describer Survey (OBDS)

Roger Harrison and Barry Oshry

Instructions: Listed below are twenty-five descriptions of ways that people behave in staff and problem-solving meetings. Choose an actual person in your organization and select the alternative in each item that comes closest to describing that person's behavior at work. Select a number using the five-point scale given below and write in the number in the first blank. Write only one alternative for each item. Keep in mind that you are limiting yourself to a description of how this person behaves only in *meetings* and *work-oriented situations or conversations*.

The person I am describing is: (check one)

_____ Myself

_____ My superior

_____ My subordinate

_____ Someone who works at the same level as I

_____ Other (specify) _____

I have known this person for approximately _____ years.

I spend about _____ hours per month with this person in *meetings* and/or *work-oriented situations or conversations*.

4 = Always   3 = Most of the time   2 = Often   1 = Occasionally   0 = Seldom

_____ _____   1. He/She tries to understand the feelings (anger, impatience, rejection) expressed by others in the group.

_____ _____   2. He/She shows intelligence.

_____ _____   3. He/She sympathizes with others when they have difficulties.

_____ _____   4. He/She expresses ideas clearly and concisely.

_____ _____   5. He/She expresses his/her own feelings, e. g., when he/she is ignored, angry, impatient.

_____ _____   6. He/She is tolerant and accepting of other people's feelings.

_____ _____   7. He/She thinks quickly.

4 = Always   3 = Most of the time   2 = Often   1 = Occasionally   0 = Seldom

_____ _____   8. He/She is angry or upset when things do not go his/her way.

_____ _____   9. He/She is persuasive, a "seller of ideas."

_____ _____   10. You can tell quickly when he/she likes or dislikes what others do or say.

_____ _____   11. He/She listens and tries to use the ideas raised by others in the group.

_____ _____   12. He/She demonstrates high technical or professional competence. He/She "knows his/her stuff."

_____ _____   13. He/She is warm and friendly with those who work with him/her.

_____ _____   14. He/She is able to attract the attention of others.

_____ _____   15. His/Her feelings are transparent; he/she does not have a "poker face."

_____ _____   16. He/She comes up with good ideas.

_____ _____   17. He/She encourages others to express their ideas before he/she acts.

_____ _____   18. He/She tries to help when others become angry or upset.

_____ _____   19. He/She tries out new ideas.

_____ _____   20. He/She is competitive; he/she likes to win and hates to lose.

_____ _____   21. He/She presents his/her ideas convincingly.

_____ _____   22. If others in the group become angry or upset, he/she listens with understanding.

_____ _____   23. He/She offers effective solutions to problems.

_____ _____   24. He/She tends to be emotional.

_____ _____   25. When he/she talks, others listen.

Totals [   ] R-TC   [   ] VD   [   ] EE   [   ] C

OBDS Scoring and Interpretation Sheet

Scoring instructions:

1. Go back over your responses to the twenty-five items on the Organization Behavior Describer Survey and assign a number value to each of your responses, using the scale below:

    4 = Always   3 = Most of the time   2 = Often
    1 = Occasionally   0 = Seldom

2. In the second blank in front of each item, write one of the following codes:

Items	Code
2, 7, 12, 16, 19, 23	R-TC
4, 9, 14, 20, 21, 25	VD
5, 8, 10, 15, 24	EE
1, 3, 6, 11, 13, 17, 18, 22	C

3. Sum the scores of the items for each code and enter them in the four boxes at the end of the instrument.

Interpretation: Your profile of scores describes a person's behavior according to the following four major dimensions.

R-TC: Rational-Technical Competence.   This is the degree to which the person behaves intelligently and quickly, demonstrates competence, has good ideas, tries out new ideas, and offers effective solutions to problems.

VD: Verbal Dominance.   This score reflects your assessment of the degree to which the person tends to behave competitively, persuasively, and in an attention-getting manner; presents ideas convincingly; commands attention; and expresses ideas clearly and concisely.

EE: Emotional Expressiveness.   This is the degree to which the person becomes emotional (e.g., acts angry or upset when things do not go his or her way), expresses his or her own feelings and emotions, and expresses how he or she feels about what other people say.

C: Consideration.   This score reflects the degree to which the person listens and responds to the ideas raised by others, encourages others to express their ideas, tries to understand the feelings expressed by others, tries to help when others become angry or upset, listens empathically, and is warm and friendly with those who work with him or her.

Because the four scales do not have an equal number of items, you can make them comparable by utilizing the following procedure:

1. Copy your four total scores below.

2. Divide each score by the appropriate number below and enter the result in the boxes.

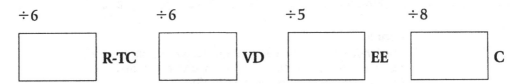

These scores can be plotted on the following diagram and compared with the norms.

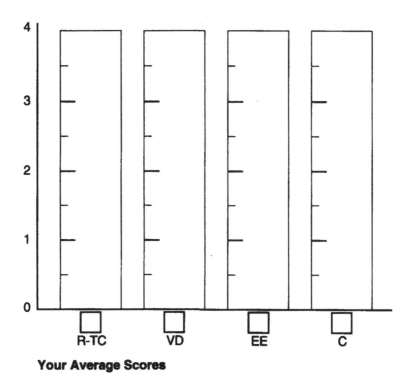

Your Average Scores

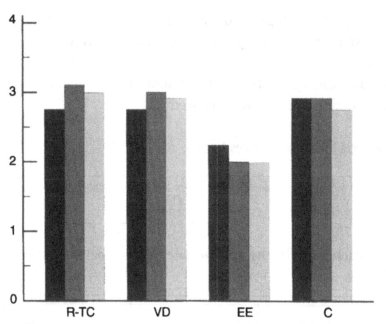

Norms

Combined norms of human relations laboratory participants, research and development managers, and YMCA managers (groups virtually identical on the OBDS)

Self N = 214

Subordinate N = 365

Superior N = 201

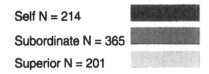

21 Cornerstones:
A Measure of Trust in Work Relationships
Amy M. Birtel, Valerie C. Nellen, and Susan B. Wilkes

Summary

Trust between co-workers in the workplace has been demonstrated to be a key component of effective management, organizational commitment, and job satisfaction. The Cornerstones Trust Survey can be used to assess the level of trust between individuals in organizational life and in work relationships. It measures three dimensions of trust: *competence* (the person's perceived ability to do the work), *credibility* (the person's consistency and predictability), and *care* (the other person's valuing of the respondent's needs and concerns).

Respondents answer fifteen questions regarding their level of trust for an identified colleague. Composite scores are obtained on the three dimensions. Instructions are included for using this instrument as a basis for personal feedback and action planning.

Introduction

The Cornerstones Trust Survey is designed to assist the professional in assessing the level of interpersonal trust among respondents who work together. The reasons for wanting to measure interpersonal trust are many and are supported by research emphasizing the importance of trust between individuals in the workplace. McAllister (1995) suggests that it is especially important for managers to be able to build trust with employees, as much of their work function involves acting as a conduit between people and/or systems. Mishra and Morrissey's (1990) study of employee/employer relationships found six main advantages for an organization when workers trusted their leaders: improved communication; greater predictability, dependability, and confidence; a reduction in employee turnover; openness and willingness to listen and accept criticism non-defensively;

repeat business; and a reduction of friction between employees. Posner and Kouzes (1988), two highly regarded scholars of leadership, cite research in which the degree to which employees trusted their management directly affected their organizational commitment, job satisfaction, role clarity, and perceptions of organizational effectiveness. It thus seems evident that the ability to inspire interpersonal trust is an invaluable asset in the workplace and that evaluating it and finding ways to improve it are important in today's organizations.

There is a great deal of research on the situational antecedents of trust, and many of the findings are similar or related. For purposes of this instrument, many of the researchers' suggested antecedents were subsumed into three major categories: *competence, credibility,* and *care.* A similar grouping is seen in the work of Mayer, Davis, and Schoorman (1995). *Competence* refers to the ability of the individual in question to perform the task or activity on which the assessment of trust is being based. For example, if a person is thinking about allowing a doctor to perform heart surgery on him or her, the person must trust in the doctor's skill as a cardiac surgeon. In the same way, an employee must trust his or her co-worker or manager to carry out assigned duties in a highly effective way. *Credibility* is defined as a measure of the individual's consistency across situations. For example, one person's trust in another is strongly influenced by the degree to which that person's word matches his or her deeds, as well as by the predictability of the person's behaviors based on previous behaviors or statements. Finally, the construct of *care* provides an assessment of how much the individual in question has demonstrated a willingness to value the needs and concerns of the person who is thinking about trusting him or her. People are more likely to trust others if they have evidence to suggest that the others will consider their interests when taking actions that may affect them, especially important in employer/employee relationships.

Description of the Instrument

The Cornerstones Trust Survey is a self-scoring instrument with fifteen items, five on each of the three dimensions described above. Respondents use a seven-point Likert scale to rate the trust they hold in an identified colleague, co-worker, or supervisor. The instrument takes approximately five minutes to complete.

Respondents can calculate their own scores on this survey, using the Cornerstones Trust Survey Self-Scoring Sheet. After scores have been tabulated, they are plotted onto a grid provided on the scoring sheet. There are a number of potential uses for the results, described in the "Using the Results" section.

Administering the Survey

Explain to respondents that they will complete a brief survey to determine the level of trust they feel for an identified colleague. If the results will not be shared with the other person, assure the respondents that they do not need to write the person's name on the survey and that you will not be "sharing" their results with others or requiring them to do so. In this case, mention that some people do find it helpful to use the survey simply as a way to get in touch with their own feelings about another.

If the survey *is* being used as a feedback tool, remind them to be especially conscientious, as they will be sharing their answers with the persons they rated. Remind them that the purpose of the instrument is not only to help them learn about trust and its component parts but to provide feedback to their colleagues in order to improve their working relationships.

Distribute copies of the survey. Instruct participants to think of only one colleague and to use the full range of responses from 1 to 7 when answering each of the questions about that particular colleague. (It is possible to use this survey in a team-building workshop, in which case a small work group fills out surveys on each of their co-workers and their manager and then spends time sharing with one another one-to-one and in a facilitated group discussion.)

After respondents have finished filling out the survey, but prior to scoring it, give a brief explanation about the importance of interpersonal trust in the workplace. Explain the three components of trust that have been identified in the research and distribute a copy of the Cornerstones Trust Survey Handout to each respondent.

Explain that it is important for colleagues to build trust in order to work together effectively and to maximize job satisfaction and organizational commitment. Show the participants the key components of trust, as seen on the diagram on the handout; then read through the handout with them. *Competence* refers to the ability of the individual in question to perform the task or activity on which the assessment of trust is being based. For example, if a person is thinking about allowing a doctor to perform heart surgery on him or her, the person must trust in the doctor's skill as a cardiac surgeon. In the same way, an employee must trust his or her co-worker or manager to carry out assigned duties in a highly effective way. *Credibility* is defined as a measure of the individual's consistency across situations. For example, one person's trust in another is strongly influenced by the degree to which that person's word matches his or her deeds, as well as by the predictability of the person's behaviors based on previous behaviors or statements. Finally, the construct of *care* provides an assessment of how much the individual in question has demonstrated a willingness to value the needs and concerns of the person who is thinking about trusting him or her. People are more likely to trust others if they have evidence to suggest that the others will consider their interests when taking actions that may affect them, especially important in employer/employee relationships.

Scoring the Survey

Hand out copies of the Cornerstones Trust Survey Self-Scoring Sheet. Instruct respondents to transfer their answers to the scoring sheet and to follow the instructions for calculating their scores. Offer assistance to any participants who may need help.

Once respondents have scored their surveys, have them plot their scores to create a visual representation of the levels of trust experienced on the three dimensions using the diagram on the second page of the scoring sheet. The center of the triangle represents 0 and each point of the triangle represents a score of 35 on that dimension. After participants have plotted their scores, tell them to connect the three points to create a "trust triangle" that can be used as a basis for discussion, if desired. If the survey is being used as the focus of a team-building session, repeat the process for each member of the team before continuing.

Interpreting the Results

Next, help the respondents interpret their results. Draw a sample triangle on a piece of flip-chart paper with scores of 10, 23, and 15 on care, competence, and credibility, respectively. Note how, in this case, the respondent feels that the person is skilled, but the respondent is not confident that the individual being rated cares about him or her personally or would be truthful under all circumstances. On the other hand, if the scores were high on care, high on credibility, and low on competence, the interpretation might be that the respondent thinks the person is open, honest, and can be trusted, but that he or she needs to improve his or her overall competence in doing the work. Finally, tell respondents that the overall size of the triangle can be interpreted as a measure of general trust, with a small but balanced triangle suggesting that improving trust on all three dimensions might be useful. Suggest that examining individual items to detect particular areas of strength or weakness in their level of trust for the other person can also be beneficial. They should mark items that they want to discuss one-on-one.

Using the Results

Following are a number of ways that the Cornerstones Trust Survey can be used.

1.   The survey can be included as an activity in a workshop module on trust, leadership, or team building. The focus would be on understanding the compo-

nents of trust and on learning more about the implications of levels of trust in work relationships. Additional discussion topics might include ways of building trust in work relationships.

2. The survey can provide a basis for intervention in dyads offering one another one-on-one feedback. Participants can provide feedback to one another in pairs, using their survey results. In some cases, it may be useful for this discussion to be facilitated by a skilled consultant. In preparation for giving one another feedback, the participants may want to review specific items with particularly high or low scores. As with any form of feedback, remind participants to provide examples and to focus on actual behavior rather than on personal characteristics or on supposition about another's motives.

3. The survey can be employed in 360-degree feedback sessions by aggregating a number of respondents' scores for one individual and providing the scores to that person with accompanying qualitative feedback.

4. The survey may be adopted on a team or organization-wide basis to assess general levels of trust within the organization by compiling a number of individual results.

In all of these cases, an action plan should be created to assist the individual(s) to apply what each has learned. Generally speaking, an action plan would include goals, specific action steps leading to the achievement of the goals, and a time frame for accomplishing each step.

Psychometric Properties of the Instrument

Demographics of the Sample

In order to test reliability of the instrument, 118 employees from a variety of organizations completed the Cornerstones Trust Survey. Of those completing the survey, 69.8 percent were female and 30.2 percent were male. The large majority of the respondents were working adults, 88.7 percent of whom were twenty-six or older (61.7 percent were thirty-six or older). Racial breakdowns were as follows: 82.8 percent Caucasian, 9.5 percent African-American, 3.4 percent Asian-American, 3.4 percent Latino, and .9 percent "other."

Reliability

Internal consistency for the overall scale and each of the three subscales was calculated using Cronbach's alpha for the full sample of 118 participants. The internal consistency score for the overall scale of fifteen items was very high, with an alpha of .96. Alpha coefficients for the subscales of competence, caring, and credibility were .95, .92, and .92, respectively.

Validity

Validity of the instrument as a measure of trust in a work relationship was assessed by examining the relationship between scores on the scales and a separate item about trust. The item was "This is a person I trust." Correlations between the item and the scales are noted in Table 1. All correlations were significant at the $p < .01$ level.

Table 1. Correlations for General Item

	General Trust Item
Competence Score	.617
Care Score	.860
Credibility Score	.853

References

Mayer, R.C., Davis, J.H., & Schoorman, F.D. (1995). An integrative model of organizational trust. *Academy of Management Review, 20*(3), 709–734.

McAllister, D.J. (1995). Affect- and cognition-based trust as foundations for interpersonal cooperation in organization. *Academy of Management Journal, 38*(1), 24–59.

Mishra, J., & Morrisey, M.A. (1990). Trust in employee/employer relationships: A survey of West Michigan managers. *Public Personnel Management, 19*(4), 443–486.

Posner, B., & Kouzes, J. (1988). Relating leadership and credibility. *Psychological Reports, 63*(2), 527–530.

Originally published in *The 2002 Annual: Volume 2, Consulting.*

Cornerstones Trust Survey

Amy M. Birtel, Valerie C. Nellen, and Susan B. Wilkes

Instructions: Think of the individual for whom you are filling out this survey and, using the seven-point scale below, respond to the following with only that person in mind. Circle the numbers that correspond to your level of agreement. If you will be sharing your feedback with this person, write his or her name at the top of the page.

1 = Very Strongly Disagree   3 = Disagree   5 = Agree   7 = Very
2 = Strongly Disagree   4 = Neutral   6 = Strongly Agree   Strongly Agree

This is a person . . .

1. who effectively completes the tasks
    on which he or she works.   1   2   3   4   5   6   7

2. who tells me the truth.   1   2   3   4   5   6   7

3. who considers my needs and interests
    when making decisions that impact me.   1   2   3   4   5   6   7

4. to whom I would delegate important
    tasks, if I had the opportunity.   1   2   3   4   5   6   7

5. who keeps confidential any information
    that he or she has promised not to share.   1   2   3   4   5   6   7

6. who does things to help me out when
    I need help.   1   2   3   4   5   6   7

7. who demonstrates an appropriate level
    of skill in completing tasks.   1   2   3   4   5   6   7

8. who honors his or her commitments.   1   2   3   4   5   6   7

9. who demonstrates concern for my
    well-being.   1   2   3   4   5   6   7

10. who produces work that is useful to
    others.   1   2   3   4   5   6   7

11. who is honest about his or her own
    ability to get things done.   1   2   3   4   5   6   7

| 1 = Very Strongly Disagree | 3 = Disagree | 5 = Agree | 7 = Very |
| 2 = Strongly Disagree | 4 = Neutral | 6 = Strongly Agree | Strongly Agree |

12. who has expectations of me that challenge me, but who provides the support I need to live up to those expectations.   1   2   3   4   5   6   7

13. who demonstrates competence in his or her work.   1   2   3   4   5   6   7

14. who makes statements that are credible.   1   2   3   4   5   6   7

15. who knows some personal details of my life outside of work because I've felt comfortable sharing that information.   1   2   3   4   5   6   7

Cornerstones Trust Survey Self-Scoring Sheet

Instructions: Transfer your responses for each question to this page. Add the numbers in each column to obtain a total score for each dimension of trust.

1. _____	2. _____	3. _____
4. _____	5. _____	6. _____
7. _____	8. _____	9. _____
10. _____	11. _____	12. _____
13. _____	14. _____	15. _____
Totals: _____	_____	_____
Competence	Credibility	Care

What Your Scores Mean

29 through 35: You have a great deal of trust in this individual on this dimension.

20 through 28: You have a reasonable amount of trust in this individual on this dimension, but would like to feel more comfortable trusting the individual.

11 through 19: You are somewhat wary of this individual on this dimension, and your relationship would likely benefit from increased trust.

5 through 10: You have very little trust in this individual on this dimension, and it is imperative that this be improved in order for you to work well together.

Now plot your scores on the following diagram, with the middle of the triangle representing a score of 0 and each end point representing a score of 35 on the dimension identified. Finally, connect the plotted points to create a "trust triangle" representing your overall level of trust in the identified individual.

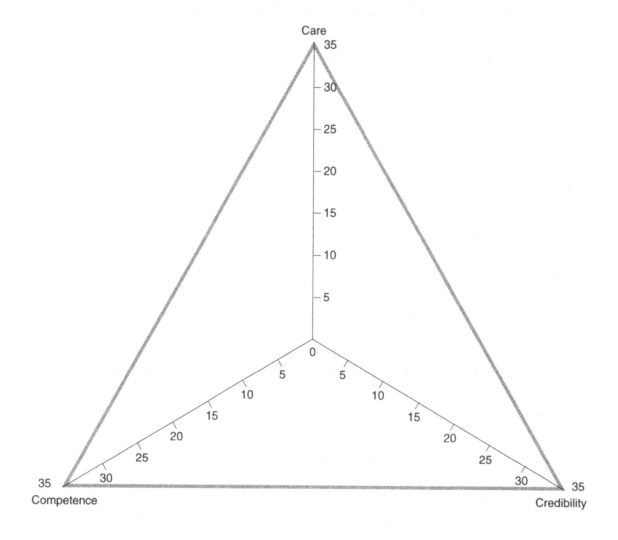

Cornerstones Trust Survey Handout

Competence refers to the ability of the individual in question to perform the task or activity on which the assessment of trust is being based. For example, if a person is thinking about allowing a doctor to perform heart surgery on him or her, the person must trust in the doctor's skill as a cardiac surgeon. In the same way, an employee must trust his or her co-worker or manager to carry out assigned duties in a highly effective way.

Credibility is defined as a measure of the individual's consistency across situations. For example, one person's trust in another is strongly influenced by the degree to which that person's word matches his or her deeds, as well as by the predictability of the person's behaviors based on previous behaviors or statements.

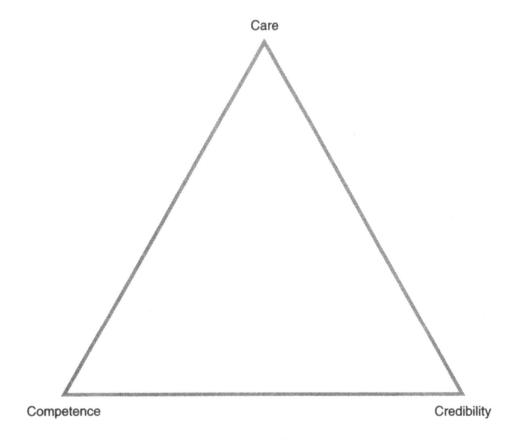

Finally, the construct of *care* provides an assessment of how much the individual in question has demonstrated a willingness to value the needs and concerns of the person who is thinking about trusting him or her. People are more likely to trust others if they have evidence to suggest that the other will consider their interests when taking actions that may affect them, especially important in employer/employee relationships.

22 Supervisor Selection:
The Supervisory Assessment Instrument
Philip Benham

Summary

In too many cases, senior managers look back at their decisions to promote others to management with regret. Many managers are not competent and contaminate their organizations with uninspired leadership and inefficient administration. This instrument addresses a major cause of poor performance by managers: the criteria used to promote people into managerial positions in the first place.

The Supervisory Assessment Instrument (SAI) assesses three competencies essential to managerial performance: technical skills, interpersonal skills, and conceptual skills. Assessors rate prospects for supervisory positions on twenty items, measuring observed proficiency in each skill area. The results indicate a prospect's readiness to assume a supervisory position.

In addition to assessing a prospect's readiness, the instrument can be used to determine training and development needs for prospective managers. It can also be used in orientation programs to explain performance expectations of supervisors. Finally, the instrument can be used to design a performance appraisal system appropriate to managerial work.

Advancing from a nonsupervisory position to supervisor is often a difficult transition. The conventional wisdom that the best predictor of future success is past success is useless in this situation. Past success in nonsupervisory positions has important but limited value in predicting how well someone will perform as a supervisor. Managerial work is different from nonmanagerial work (Heisler & Benham, 1992; Katz, 1974; McCall, Lombardo, & Morrison, 1988; Mintzberg, 1972).

Nonsupervisory work is largely technical in nature. It requires proficiency with tools and equipment and in performing task procedures with consistent accuracy. To a lesser extent, nonsupervisory work requires interpersonal skills—the ability to work effectively with others as a co-worker. Conceptual skills—the ability to reason in the abstract and envision the larger context in which one's job is performed—also play a role in nonsupervisory work.

On the other hand, supervisory work requires a more astute understanding of human behavior and a much higher level of proficiency in interpersonal skills. The competencies in this area range from effective listening to providing constructive feedback on performance. Maintaining one's composure with difficult people while confronting them candidly on matters that may require discipline are part of the interpersonal skill set required. Avoiding unpleasant people whose behavior is disrupting the work team or production crew and detracting from work quality is not an option for an effective supervisor.

Supervisory work also requires a growing awareness of and proficiency in conceptual thinking—the ability to analyze unstructured situations and to interpret information needed for effective decision making. Complexity and ambiguity, in other words, define much of the nature of managerial work and many of the demands made of managers. Anyone who has conducted annual performance review feedback sessions with employees who differ in talents and personalities understands this point well.

To increase our confidence in selecting the best prospects for supervision, we need to use criteria that provide better measures of the demands of supervisory work. The Supervisory Assessment Instrument provides relevant criteria to make these measurements.

Description of the Instrument

The Supervisory Assessment Instrument is designed to be used by experienced supervisors and upper level managers to assess the readiness of employees to become supervisors. The twenty items in the SAI provide measures on the three competencies—technical, interpersonal, and conceptual skills—that are essential for effective supervisory performance. Each item is scored on a four-point scale indicating the extent or frequency with which the skill is observed.

Validity

The items in the instrument are derived from research and from practical applications in several organizations. Construct validity, therefore, is quite high. Statistical assessments of content validity and of predictive validity have not been made; however, the instrument is intended to be an action research tool rather than a rigorous model intended for empirical research and theory building.

Administration of the Instrument

Total time required to administer, score, and interpret the SAI is approximately fifteen minutes per prospect or individual being evaluated.

Each rater will need one copy of the SAI per person being evaluated. The instrument is self-scoring, and it contains all the information required to score and interpret it. Suggest that raters may wish to obtain more information from the sources listed in the references. For more in-depth discussion, see Katz (1974). Katz notes that managers rely increasingly on human (relational) and conceptual skills to perform effectively. Conversely, technical skills—proficiency with tools, equipment, and operating procedures—play a diminishing role as one progresses through the ranks of management. Katz believes that management selection methods, therefore, should rely more on relational and conceptual skills than on technical skills if they are to be valid predictors of future success.

For a more comprehensive discussion of management, the work by Kotter (1982) is very instructive. Kotter concludes that effective managers are able to set agendas, that is, know what has to be done and why, and form networks, that is, establish relationships capable of providing valuable and timely information to carry out agendas. Reasoning and interpersonal skills, therefore, are key to success in situations that are often ambiguous and more complex than those encountered in nonmanagerial work.

Finally, the work by Gardner (1990) provides an excellent discussion of the attributes of leadership important to managerial success. Gardner emphasizes the role that values play in defining effective leadership. If a management prospect does not believe that people respond favorably to managers who care about their potential to grow and develop, that prospect will probably discount people's ability to contribute and to improve. In turn, these prospects will most likely neglect their interpersonal skills and fail to appreciate the role these skills play in their performance as managers.

Introduce the Session

Note that "Past is not always prologue" when it comes to selecting first-time managers. The skills that make a good functional specialist or technician are not the skills that make a good supervisor. Say that the SAI will provide a set of selection criteria that can improve greatly the accuracy of selection decisions for first-time supervisors.

Fill Out the SAI

Give participants copies of the instrument and ask them to complete it by thinking of one of their subordinates as a prospect for becoming a supervisor and to rate this person using the SAI. After everyone has finished, ask them to total the scores for the candidates they have rated and to fill out their recommendations, then lay the instrument aside.

Summarize the Katz Model

Present a brief summary of the Technical-Interpersonal-Conceptual Skill Model introduced by Katz (1974) and elaborated on in the introductory section above. The model classifies performance skills into three categories: *technical*, emphasizing proficiency with tools, equipment, and procedures; *human or relational*, emphasizing proficiency as a listener and speaker in gaining the respect and support of others; and *conceptual*, emphasizing abstract reasoning skills such as the ability to clarify an ambiguous situation and then map out an effective course of action. The model also notes that supervisors must rely more on their relational and conceptual skills than they did previously in non-supervisory positions. Explain that as managers progress to higher levels of authority and responsibility, moreover, they should increase their use of conceptual skills and decrease their use of technical skills to meet the changing need for abstract reasoning skills in these higher level positions. Draw the model below on a flip chart.

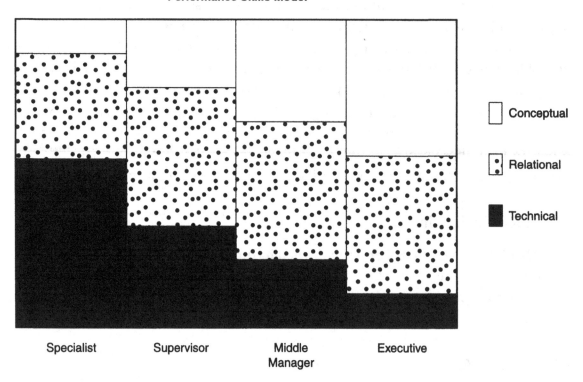

Performance Skills Model

Specialist   Supervisor   Middle Manager   Executive

Conceptual

Relational

Technical

Ask for Reactions

Encourage participants to share their reactions to the model and to the instrument and the value they will have in coaching and counseling, as well as in selecting prospects to become supervisors in the future. Give everyone copies of the Guidelines for Interpreting the SAI and go through it with participants. Answer any questions they may have about the instrument and the results they have obtained, helping them to understand their results and to make employee-development plans, if appropriate.

References

Gardner, J.W. (1990). *On leadership*. New York: The Free Press.

Heisler, W.J., & Benham, P.O. (1992). The challenge of management development in North America in the 1990s. *The Journal of Management Development, 11*(2), 16–31.

Katz, R.L. (1974). The skills of an effective administrator. *Harvard Business Review, 52*(5), 90–102.

Kotter, J.P. (1982). *The general managers*. New York: The Free Press.

McCall, M.W., Lombardo, M.M., & Morrison, A.M. (1988). *The lessons of experience: How successful executives develop on the job*. Lexington, MA: Lexington.

Mintzberg, H. (1973). *The nature of managerial work*. New York: Harper & Row.

Originally published in *The 1999 Annual: Volume 1, Training.*

Supervisory Assessment Instrument

Philip Benham

Part I: Information About Prospect

Name of Supervisory Prospect: _____

Current Position (Title): _____

Department/Group/Section: _____

Previous Assignments and Years of Experience:

(Assignments)	**(Years of Experience)**
1. _____	_____
2. _____	_____
3. _____	_____

Part II: Assessment of Prospect

Directions: Using the rating scale below, place an X in the appropriate column by each numbered item to indicate the *consistency* with which the person you are rating exhibits the behavior.

Rating Scale SA = Strongly Agree A = Agree D = Disagree SD = Strongly Disagree	SA	A	D	SD
Technical Competence				
1. Interprets instructions accurately.				
2. Follows task procedures correctly.				
3. Verifies the accuracy and completeness of assigned tasks; rarely has work returned because of errors/mistakes.				
4. Uses required tools and/or equipment correctly, i.e., follows proper start-up, shut-down and/or operating procedures.				

Rating Scale **SA** = Strongly Agree **A** = Agree **D** = Disagree **SD** = Strongly Disagree	SA	A	D	SD
5. Follows administrative procedures correctly, i.e., follows proper safety, security, routing and/or documentation procedures.				
6. Writes clearly and accurately; rarely has to explain the content of written work orally.				
7. Learns new technology applications correctly.				
Interpersonal Competence				
8. Maintains composure with difficult people and in difficult situations.				
9. Gives credit to others for their accomplishments and efforts.				
10. Seeks the opinions of others and incorporates their concerns into plans and actions.				
11. Speaks clearly and confidently to others.				
12. Obtains the willing support of others for tasks requiring cooperation and teamwork.				
13. Listens respectfully to others in order to understand their positions or concerns.				
14. Disagrees with others without being rude or offensive.				
Conceptual Competence				
15. Sets appropriate priorities for work assignments.				
16. Understands the job's contribution to organizational goals.				
17. Shows the importance of continuous learning by taking the initiative to improve current skills and to learn new skills.				
18. Takes the initiative to determine a course of action when assignments are unclear or ill-defined.				

Rating Scale
SA = Strongly Agree
  A = Agree
  D = Disagree
SD = Strongly Disagree
	SA	A	D	SD

19. In handling job-related problems, demonstrates an awareness of the long-term implications of a course of action, i.e., avoids quick fixes or expedient solutions that may later prove to be inadequate.				
20. Shows the importance of networking as a means of learning about issues and trends outside the company by becoming involved in professional and community organizations.				
Determining Total Score				
Step 1: Total the Xs marked in each column:	___	___	___	___
Step 2: Multiply numbers in Step 1 by:	×4	×3	×2	×1
Step 3: Add column totals:	+	+	+	
Step 4: Add four column totals for aggregate score:	= [ ]			

Now use the same scoring system to determine the total score under each scale: Technical Competence, Interpersonal Competence, and Conceptual Competence.

Do Not Recommend if:

- Candidate excludes self from consideration.

- Candidate scores below:

    21 on Technical Competency Scale

    18 on Interpersonal Competency Scale

    14 on Conceptual Competency Scale

Recommend if:

- Candidate's aggregate score is between 53 and 60 points (Long-Term Prospect)

- Candidate's aggregate score is between 61 and 70 points (Intermediate-Term Prospect)

- Candidate's aggregate score is between 71 and 80 points (Near-Term Prospect)

Developmental Needs

- Long-Term Prospect: Needs Skills Training in:

- Intermediate-Term Prospect: Needs Skills Training in:

- Near-Term Prospect: Needs Skills Training in:

- Evaluator's Signature: _____

    Date: _____

Guidelines for Interpreting the SAI

Key Terms

Rater: The participant completing the SAI on a prospect.

Prospect: The subordinate being evaluated by the participant using the SAI.

Prospect Not Recommended

1. *Prospect Excludes Self.* Identify the reason and note whether it is circumstantial or attitudinal in nature. *Circumstantial* refers to temporary situations of a personal nature that make the timing inconvenient for the prospect. Prospects who exclude themselves for circumstantial reasons should be reconsidered for supervisory opportunities at a later time. *Attitudinal* refers to a prospect's unwillingness to become a supervisor. Some people object to the increased complexity and ambiguity of supervisory work. The discomfort caused by the complexity and ambiguity is so unsettling that it preempts any attraction that increased pay and status accompanying a promotion may have. Prospects who exclude themselves for attitudinal reasons should probably be removed from the prospect list. Unless the attitude is caused by misinformation about what is expected in a supervisory role, the person probably will not succeed as a supervisor.

2. *Prospect's Ratings Are Too Low.* If the prospect fails to obtain the minimum score in one or more competencies, note the nature and severity of the difficulty. For example, did the prospect fail in one competency or in all three? Did the prospect miss the minimum score by only one or two points? Assess the likelihood that the prospect will receive a passing score after completing remedial training and some on-the-job coaching. If the likelihood is low, the prospect should be removed from the list. If the likelihood is high, however, use the data profile from the SAI to develop a plan for remedial work. As the employee responds to the training and coaching, showing improvement in the competencies targeted for development, consider reclassifying the person as a prospect.

Prospect Recommended

1. *Long-Term Prospect.* Generally, long-term prospects (those scoring between 53 and 60 points on the SAI) need additional training and exposure to certain performance situations before they will be strong candidates for promotion to supervisor. Normally, the time required to make the improvements will be twelve to eighteen months. Long-term prospects usually need improvement in interpersonal and conceptual skills.

2. *Intermediate-Term Prospect.* Generally, intermediate-term prospects (those scoring between 61 and 70 points on the SAI) need training in just a few skills before they will be strong candidates for promotion to supervisor. Normally, the time required to make the improvements will be six to twelve months. Intermediate-term prospects usually need improvement in their interpersonal skills.

3. *Near-Term Prospect.* Generally, near-term prospects (those scoring between 71 and 80 points on the SAI) require coaching on a limited range of techniques before being nominated for promotion to supervisor. Normally, the time required to make the improvements will be one to six months. Near-term prospects usually need improvement in coaching and counseling techniques, especially those needed to implement the organization's performance appraisal system.

Developmental Needs

Although training that is experiential in nature, such as role playing, is very helpful in developing skills targeted by the SAI, selected job assignments are powerful learning opportunities that often go unrecognized by managers (see McCall, Lombardo, & Morrison for an extensive discussion of this issue). For confirmed supervisory prospects, a task force assignment can be quite helpful in developing interpersonal and conceptual skills. Consider the following example:

> An interdepartmental systems conversion task force is being formed to assure that information processing needs throughout the organization are identified and integrated into a plan that is both comprehensive in scope and compatible in design. Your department must nominate someone to serve on the task force. Terry, one of your near-term prospects for supervisor, could well serve the needs of the department with technical expertise and administrative insight. You recognize, however, that the task force is also an opportunity to develop Terry's conceptual skills.
>
> Terry shows great promise for success as a supervisor. Terry needs some exposure to situations, however, that provide insight to how the organization functions as a whole. Terry also needs to experience differences of opinion that stem largely from different types of jobs and job demands. The task force assignment will provide the experience Terry needs to develop these conceptual insights as well as some skill in building consensus among people with different perspectives on matters of common interest. You nominate Terry, citing the reasons just mentioned.

Other Benefits of the SAI

In addition to providing a valid means for determining readiness levels among prospects for promotion to supervision, the SAI can help with the following:

1. *Compliance with EEO/AA Legislation and Guidelines.* The SAI provides a means for showing consistent treatment of employees in selection decisions. It also identifies specific needs for development and it provides a time frame for completing a developmental plan. This documentation can help avoid unexplained variances between protected and unprotected classes, as defined in the law, in promotion rates to supervision.

2. *Compliance with Americans with Disabilities Act.* The SAI provides a substantial start in compiling a list of "essential functions" required of a supervisor. Knowing these essential functions will help organizations comply with the ADA in screening prospects who are considered to be disabled. The SAI will also help identify when "reasonable accommodations" can be made for well-qualified prospects who may require an accommodation to perform the job of supervisor satisfactorily.

3. *Retention of Promising Employees.* The SAI can generate interest in the development and advancement of an organization's most promising employees. Often this interest can make the difference in keeping an employee who may resign to take a position elsewhere.

4. *Performance Appraisal.* The SAI provides a way to use job-related behavior as a basis for evaluating supervisory performance. It also provides consistency between criteria used to select people for supervisory positions and criteria used subsequently to evaluate actual job performance. This consistency will help reinforce the importance of these behaviors to both the managers making the evaluations and the supervisors being evaluated.

Reference

McCall, M.W., Lombardo, M.M., & Morrison, A.M. (1988). *The lessons of experience: How successful executives develop on the job.* Lexington, MA: Lexington.

23 Simulations:

Pre- and Post-Evaluations of Performance

Ira J. Morrow

Summary

Large-scale behavioral simulations are frequently used in management education and in training and development programs. However, these simulations generally do not include a way to provide quantitative or qualitative feedback to participants, thus limiting the potential for learning from them. The three evaluation instruments presented here are a way for participants to receive feedback from peers and to do self-assessment immediately before and after a simulation. Ways to use these instruments to help participants reflect on their performance, learn how they are perceived by others, develop insight about themselves, and obtain the information needed to improve their managerial performance are discussed.

Ever since the development of "Looking Glass" by the Center for Creative Leadership in Greensboro, North Carolina, in 1983, the use of large-scale behavioral simulations to enhance the realism and value of management training, development, and education programs has become common. Such simulations provide the means for introducing participants to the complexity and ambiguity of organizational life and decision making and to the value of teamwork, cooperation, coordination, and communication. Opportunities are generally provided for experimenting with new behaviors and for demonstrating and enhancing leadership skills, the ability to influence others, and problem-solving skills, all of which are critically important in today's business world.

Experience with various large-scale behavioral simulations suggests that their potential value is enhanced not only by a comprehensive debriefing session led by an experienced facilitator, but by providing participants with opportunities to evaluate the effectiveness of their own performance and the performance of their peers during the simulation. Such feedback allows participants to more fully capitalize on the learning potential of the simulation and provides the basis for subsequent efforts to alter or improve performance. It is in this regard, however, that most large-scale behavioral simulations are lacking. That is, the materials that are supplied to users generally do not include adequate feedback mechanisms.

The three instruments presented here provide a way to obtain self and peer feedback. Suggestions for discussion of the results are provided that will result in self-reflection and greater insight on one's own behavior.

These instruments are not designed to be used with any particular large-scale behavioral simulation product, but can be adapted for use with any simulation package used for management development.

Description of the Instruments

Pre-Simulation Self-Assessment (Instrument 1)

The Pre-Simulation Self-Assessment consists of twenty-nine items with a five-point response scale ranging from 1 (very dissatisfied) to 5 (very satisfied). One item asks participants how satisfied they think they will be with their overall performance, and another asks them to predict their satisfaction with others' overall performance. Specific behavioral dimensions related to effectiveness as a manager are addressed, including goal setting, time management, stress management, ability to delegate, decision making, problem solving, creativity, motivation, the ability to motivate others, sensitivity to others, listening, assertiveness, diplomacy, ability to win others' trust and to trust others, self-disclosure, negotiation, team contribution, conflict management, consensus building, ability to change, communication, influencing, leadership, use of power, energy level, and ability to work hard. The instrument concludes with three open-ended items that ask participants which of their skills they believe will help them the most, which they are most concerned about needing during the simulation, and how they think their performance is likely to change over time.

Theory Behind Instrument 1

The twenty-nine items reflect issues that frequently come up in management and leadership training and development programs due to their relationship to managerial performance. Not surprisingly, such issues are usually embedded within large-scale behavioral simulations and may be emphasized by particular consultants and trainers. Moreover, as one would expect, such issues are frequently discussed in skills-oriented management books, such as Whetten and Cameron (2002).

Administration of Instrument 1

It is suggested that a general description of the simulation and its training or developmental objectives be given, as well as a brief overview of the simulated company/situation and its structure/tasks. Generally in a simulation, an annual report describing the history, structure, and performance of the company is distributed to participants, and they are likely to receive an organizational chart as well. In most such simulations, participants are assigned to fill specific positions. This can be done in several ways, including self-nomination, assignment through discussion and consensus agreement by teams or groups, or appointment by the facilitator. Prior to receiving in-baskets of written memoranda, letters, and reports custom-designed for their assigned positions, all participants may receive a pre-work package of general information, memos, and reports about the company. In any case, at some point during this introduction, orientation, and familiarization process, participants will develop increasingly informed impressions of what the simulation is about and the demands it might make on them. They will also start to feel how well they are likely to perform during the simulation. These feelings will range from the extremely pessimistic to the extremely optimistic. The Pre-Simulation Evaluation gives respondents an outlet for their feelings and perceptions along specific behavioral and skill dimensions.

This instrument should be completed by participants after they have received their general orientation to the program, been assigned to teams, seen an organizational chart, and been appointed to or have selected a specific position, but before receiving their individualized in-baskets of materials. Participants should be told in advance whether this instrument and subsequent assessment instruments will be collected and seen by the instructor, facilitator, or assigned observers or whether only they will see and keep the completed instrument. In any case, the advantages of frank and honest self-reporting on all assessment instruments should be stressed. Encourage as much honesty as possible by giving complete control, use of, and access to assessment instruments to the participants themselves. You may choose to collect the instruments, and certainly a case can be made for this approach as well. One factor that should weigh in the decision of "to collect or not to collect" is whether the simulation is being used primarily for individual or team skill development or for assessment. Familiarize respondents with the instrument by walking them through it. The Pre-Simulation Self-Assessment instrument should take approximately 10 or 15 minutes to complete.

The Scoring Process for Instrument 1

The scoring of this instrument is direct in that the score for each rating item is simply what was given by the respondent without any conversion of the scores. A total score and an average score can be calculated for the twenty-nine rated items.

Further ways to use the scores on this instrument are discussed in conjunction with scoring of the Post-Simulation Evaluation instrument below.

Post-Simulation Evaluation (Instrument 2)

The Post-Simulation Evaluation includes the same twenty-nine items and five-point response scale used for the Pre-Simulation Evaluation (Instrument 1) described above. The intention is to allow for the comparison of pre- and post-scores on an item-by-item basis. The major distinction between the two instruments is that, whereas the Pre-Simulation Self-Assessment asks participants, "Based on what you have heard about this simulation. how satisfied do you think you will be with the following," the Post-Simulation Evaluation asks, "Based on what you have experienced during this simulation, how satisfied are you with the following." Another distinction between the two instruments is in the open-ended questions section, which is more comprehensive and probing for the Post-Simulation Evaluation, as participants now know their behaviors and performance. The open-ended questions for Instrument 2 ask participants about the skills that helped them the most while working through the simulation and which skills, if improved, would enhance their performance. Other areas addressed include how their behavior changed over time during the simulation, their views on who contributed the most to the effectiveness of their team and how, lessons they learned from observing others during the simulation, and how they would rank themselves compared to the way they feel that others would rank them in terms of their overall contribution to the team. In addition, participants are asked to comment on who they helped the most and who helped them the most during the simulation, which simulation event or achievement they are most proud of, and what they would do differently if they could repeat the simulation. Finally, participants are given an opportunity to reflect on what they learned about themselves and about management and leadership from the simulation.

Theory Behind Instrument 2

Since the twenty-nine rated items are the same here as for the first instrument, the same logic and theoretical rationale for their use applies. The issue that is likely to come up when using this instrument is the theoretical rationale for having respondents rate the same items again. Simply highlight the difference between forming expectations of one's performance based on performance in similar experiences or on rumors, hearsay, and emotions, on the one hand, and looking back and reflecting in a more informed manner on one's performance after the performance has taken place. The theoretical rationale for gathering data pre-simulation and post-simulation is similar to the rationale for action research, where there is a pre-measurement, an intervention, and then post-measurement.

Here, however, the participant's skills may have been enhanced from pre- to post-measurement by participating in the simulation, which is the rationale for its use as a training and development tool. Thus, you are providing the measurement tools to compare how participants feel they will perform before the simulation begins and how they think that they did perform now that the simulation has ended. This in turn relates to how we form expectations, the accuracy of our expectations, and our self-insight, issues that are discussed further below.

Administration of Instrument 2

At the conclusion of the interactive phase of a large-scale behavioral simulation, a number of closing activities are likely to take place. Often, some participants, including but not limited to the participant who holds the most senior position in the simulation, are asked to prepare a presentation to the rest of the simulated company (the other participants) about the state of the organization. Generally, all simulation-related activities following these presentations are designed to help debrief participants, to provide opportunities for venting, and to discuss the events of the simulation and the simulated organization's performance. In addition, it is useful to allow participants to reflect in a more formalized and structured fashion on how they feel they performed as individuals. Instrument 2 is designed for this purpose.

Facilitators should walk participants through the instrument, point out similarities to and differences from the Pre-Simulation Self-Assessment, encourage frank and honest responses, and discuss who—if anyone besides the respondent—will see this information. Completion of this instrument should take approximately 15 to 20 minutes.

Scoring Process for Instruments 1 and 2

Actively encourage participants to take the time and effort needed to make comparisons between their pre- and post-scores. They can calculate an overall summary and an average score for the entire set of items and compare these figures. They can also examine scores on an item-by-item basis for the purpose of identifying particular skill areas where their scores increased, decreased, or remained the same.

Encourage respondents to look for patterns that emerge in particular areas or skill domains in which their self-perceptions improved or deteriorated and to try to account for the specific events or behaviors in the simulation that may explain differences in scores. This could logically lead to a discussion of the importance of self-knowledge, self-insight, and of having a realistic self-image.

Stress the importance of individuals becoming more knowledgeable about how they confront and deal with different situations, including those that are intentionally complex and ambiguous. Discuss how their expectations should increasingly become more in line with actual outcomes.

Post–Simulation Peer Assessment (Instrument 3)

The Post-Simulation Peer Assessment contains an open-ended section that asks for a listing of effective and ineffective behaviors observed, suggested developmental needs, and specific developmental recommendations or actions to be taken. It also includes twenty-eight items with the same five-point rating scale used in the prior two instruments. The stem statement for these items reads: "Based on what I observed of your behavior in the simulation, I would rate your performance as follows." These items correspond to the items and skill areas measured in the previous instruments, with the exception of one item. The last section of the instrument contains four additional open-ended questions asking respondents to indicate the skills that helped the participant being rated the most during the simulation, how the participant's behavior changed over time, when the participant was at his or her best, and which other participant the participant being rated helped the most.

Theory Behind Instrument 3

One of the most important and beneficial aspects of the use of large-scale behavioral simulations is their emphasis on social interaction and working with others. Clearly, in light of the duration and intensity of these experiences, participants generally have extensive opportunities to form perceptions of others and how they perform.

Besides providing participants with a structured format for reflecting on their own performance, it can be equally or more rewarding to provide a structured and formalized means for receiving both quantitative and qualitative feedback from peers. The importance of feedback from others about one's own performance is of course widely recognized in the management literature (Luthans, 1998; Whetten & Cameron, 2002). Aside from simply allowing participants to receive quantitative behavioral feedback from others, a relatively rare and valuable event in and of itself, the Post-Simulation Peer Assessment enables participants to compare their self-perceptions with the perceptions of others. The importance of this process is emphasized by Haney (1992), who states: "The handicap of inaccurate self-knowledge and the unwillingness to construct a more realistic self-image seem to be very widespread. In thirty-five years of organizational research and consulting, I have known scores if not hundreds . . . who seemed to have all the requisites for continued success . . . but they had one vital failing—they did not know themselves. The image they held of themselves was pitifully out of phase with that which they were projecting to others. To successfully discharge the responsibilities of a challenging, people-oriented position requires the possession of a more-than-ordinarily-realistic self-image—an exceptionally realistic self-image."

Thus, all three of the instruments provided here may be thought of as tools for enabling participants in large-scale behavioral simulations to develop a more realistic self-image.

Administration of Instrument 3

This instrument is designed to be given to a particular participant, but it is completed anonymously to encourage frank feedback. Working with the organizational chart, the facilitator may provide general guidance as to which individuals should be providing feedback to whom. The facilitator can also gather the completed forms solely for the purpose of sorting them by recipient for subsequent delivery to that person. The facilitator can keep track of who has not received adequate feedback in order to encourage those who worked with that person to give it. Depending on the number of participants in the simulation, the facilitator can indicate a minimum number of peer feedback forms that each individual should receive. Obviously, the more feedback the better, but since time is always a constraint, a minimum of three forms for each participant is a good target.

Interpreting Scores for Instrument 3

There is an obvious value in providing participants with written quantitative and qualitative feedback from peers whom they worked closely with during the simulation. It gives participants something concrete to leave the simulation with, to file away, and to refer back to on occasion as a way to check their progress in developing or enhancing their management skills and performance in the future.

It should be stressed to participants that the feedback they have received reflects the way they are perceived by others—specific to their actions during the simulation. Perceptions do not constitute reality, and in fact, in complex organizations reality is often ambiguous, not totally known, and largely socially constructed. However, for better or worse, perceptions do matter, and they can determine our career success or failure. Advise participants to look for patterns that emerge as they digest the peer feedback they have received and to give less weight to discrepant or idiosyncratic feedback and more to convergent or consistent feedback.

Other Suggested Uses for Instruments 2 and 3

A less obvious, but potentially striking use of the Post-Simulation Peer Assessment is to provide the additional data needed to make comparisons between peer post-simulation ratings and the self post-simulation ratings. Average scores for all the peer item ratings can be calculated and compared to the average for all the self item ratings. Peer feedback item-by-item average scores can be calculated as well and compared to individual item scores. When there is close agreement between self and average peer ratings in an area, that is, when one's self-perception is consistent with the way others perceive one, it suggests the presence of a more realistic self-image.

However, to the extent that one's self-ratings are inconsistent with peer feedback, one's self-image as to performance in the simulation was not in line with reality. In this case, questions of accuracy are largely irrelevant, since reality is socially constructed. Unfortunately, although others' perceptions may be off the mark, they nevertheless matter. More important questions to consider are the direction of the discrepancy. The pattern of overly inflated self-ratings and less flattering peer ratings suggests that either a person is overestimating his or her performance in terms of its impact on others or that, for some reason, his or her potential strengths are not being picked up on by others. The question then is whether this is a pattern that emerges in other settings as well. If this is the case, there may be value in learning to adjust one's self-image to be more consistent with the views of others or in changing one's performance so that one's self-perceived strengths become more obvious to others. When the pattern is one of weak self-ratings, but more glowing peer ratings, the participant may be underestimating his or her performance in terms of its impact on others and may be prone to self-doubt. The question in this case is whether or not this is a pattern that emerges in other settings as well and what the reasons and implications for the future might be. There could well be an argument in favor of learning to adjust one's self-image upward to be more in step with the perceptions of others.

Summary

In summary, the three assessment instruments described here may be used in conjunction with large-scale behavioral simulations that are frequently found in management development programs. Instrument scores can be retained for long-term analysis and reflection by participants, providing the information that participants may need to capitalize fully on the great learning potential inherent in the use of simulations, to develop a more realistic self-image, or to modify skills and behavior in order to be more effective in the managerial roles and assignments that await them in the future.

Reliability and Validity of the Instruments

The three instruments discussed here are designed to stimulate personal reflection on one's skills and performance as exhibited in a single developmental episode, namely in a large-scale behavioral simulation. They are not meant to measure more enduring or general qualities possessed by the person or exhibited in other settings. As such they constitute a training and development tool that may be used in conjunction with large-scale simulations.

The items have face validity in that they address the management and leadership skill issues discussed in the literature and generally embedded in such simulations. There is no implication that any of these instruments measures a single construct, so neither inter-item reliability nor construct validity pertain. In fact, a strong case can be made that scores should differ widely on different items in that they refer to different skills. Test-retest reliability is also not relevant in this case, in that we would expect scores to change with each participation in a different simulation and with interactions with different sets of peers in these simulations.

References

Haney, W.V. (1992). *Communication and interpersonal relations* (6th ed.). Homewood, IL: Richard D. Irwin.

Luthans, F. (1998). *Organizational behavior* (8th ed.). New York: McGraw-Hill.

Whetten, D.A., & Cameron, K.S. (2002). *Developing management skills* (5th ed.). Upper Saddle River, NJ: Prentice Hall.

Originally published in *The 2004 Pfeiffer Annual: Volume 2, Consulting.*

Pre-Simulation Self-Assessment (Instrument 1)

Ira J. Morrow

Instructions: Based on what you have heard about the simulation we are about to do, predict the level of satisfaction you will have later with the behavior you will exhibit during the simulation, using the following scale:

1 = Very Dissatisfied   **3 = Neither Satisfied nor Dissatisfied**   **5 = Very Satisfied**
2 = Somewhat Dissatisfied   **4 = Somewhat Satisfied**

1a. How satisfied do you think you will be with *your* overall performance?	1	2	3	4	5
2a. How satisfied do you think you will be with *others'* overall performance?	1	2	3	4	5

How satisfied do you think you will be with each of the following:

3a. Your ability to set clear, realistic, demanding goals.	1	2	3	4	5
4a. Your ability to manage your time effectively.	1	2	3	4	5
5a. Your ability to handle stress.	1	2	3	4	5
6a. Your ability to delegate work to others.	1	2	3	4	5
7a. Your ability to make effective decisions.	1	2	3	4	5
8a. Your ability to solve problems.	1	2	3	4	5
9a. Your ability to think of creative ideas.	1	2	3	4	5
10a. Your own level of motivation.	1	2	3	4	5
11a. Your ability to motivate others.	1	2	3	4	5
12a. Your ability to interact with others in a sensitive manner.	1	2	3	4	5
13a. Your ability to listen to others.	1	2	3	4	5
14a. Your ability to be assertive.	1	2	3	4	5
15a. Your ability to treat others in a diplomatic manner.	1	2	3	4	5

1 = Very Dissatisfied   3 = Neither Satisfied nor Dissatisfied   5 = Very Satisfied
2 = Somewhat Dissatisfied   4 = Somewhat Satisfied

16a.	Your ability to gain the trust of others.	1	2	3	4	5
17a.	Your willingness to trust others.	1	2	3	4	5
18a.	Your willingness to disclose information about yourself to others.	1	2	3	4	5
19a.	Your ability to negotiate effectively.	1	2	3	4	5
20a.	Your ability to contribute to the team.	1	2	3	4	5
21a.	Your ability to manage conflict.	1	2	3	4	5
22a.	Your ability to build a consensus.	1	2	3	4	5
23a.	Your willingness to change when necessary.	1	2	3	4	5
24a.	Your ability to communicate with others.	1	2	3	4	5
25a.	Your ability to persuade/influence others.	1	2	3	4	5
26a.	Your ability to lead others.	1	2	3	4	5
27a.	Your ability to use power effectively.	1	2	3	4	5
28a.	Your energy level.	1	2	3	4	5
29a.	Your ability to work hard.	1	2	3	4	5

Now add up the scores you gave yourself and put the total here: _____

Next average your scores by dividing the total by 29.
Put your average score, carried to two decimal places, here: _____

Open-Ended Questions

- Which of your skills or abilities do you think will help you the most during this simulation? Why?

- Which of your skills or abilities are you most concerned about in this simulation? Why?

- As the simulation takes place, what changes in your behavior are likely to be exhibited over time? Why do you think this?

Notes/Comments:

Post-Simulation Evaluation (Instrument 2)

Ira J. Morrow

Instructions: Based on what you experienced while participating in this simulation, rate your level of satisfaction with your performance by answering the following questions. Circle the appropriate answers based on the following scale:

1 = Very Dissatisfied **3 = Neither Satisfied nor Dissatisfied** **5 = Very Satisfied**
2 = Somewhat Dissatisfied **4 = Somewhat Satisfied**

1b.	How satisfied were you with *your* overall performance?	1	2	3	4	5
2b.	How satisfied were you with *others'* overall performance?	1	2	3	4	5

How satisfied were you with the following:

3b.	Your ability to set clear, realistic, demanding goals.	1	2	3	4	5
4b.	Your ability to manage your time effectively.	1	2	3	4	5
5b.	Your ability to handle stress.	1	2	3	4	5
6b.	Your ability to delegate work to others.	1	2	3	4	5
7b.	Your ability to make effective decisions.	1	2	3	4	5
8b.	Your ability to solve problems.	1	2	3	4	5
9b.	Your ability to think of creative ideas.	1	2	3	4	5
10b.	Your own level of motivation.	1	2	3	4	5
11b.	Your ability to motivate others.	1	2	3	4	5
12b.	Your ability to interact with others in a sensitive manner.	1	2	3	4	5
13b.	Your ability to listen to others.	1	2	3	4	5
14b.	Your ability to be assertive.	1	2	3	4	5
15b.	Your ability to treat others in a diplomatic manner.	1	2	3	4	5

1 = Very Dissatisfied   3 = Neither Satisfied nor Dissatisfied   5 = Very Satisfied

2 = Somewhat Dissatisfied   4 = Somewhat Satisfied

16b.	Your ability to gain the trust of others.	1	2	3	4	5
17b.	Your willingness to trust others.	1	2	3	4	5
18b.	Your willingness to disclose information about yourself to others.	1	2	3	4	5
19b.	Your ability to negotiate effectively.	1	2	3	4	5
20b.	Your ability to contribute to the team.	1	2	3	4	5
21b.	Your ability to manage conflict.	1	2	3	4	5
22b.	Your ability to build a consensus.	1	2	3	4	5
23b.	Your willingness to change when necessary.	1	2	3	4	5
24b.	Your ability to communicate with others.	1	2	3	4	5
25b.	Your ability to persuade/influence others.	1	2	3	4	5
26b.	Your ability to lead others.	1	2	3	4	5
27b.	Your ability to use power effectively.	1	2	3	4	5
28b.	Your energy level.	1	2	3	4	5
29b.	Your ability to work hard.	1	2	3	4	5

Add your selections together to arrive at a total and write it here: _____

Obtain an average score by dividing the total score above by 29 and carrying it to two decimal places. Write the answer here: _____

Open-Ended Questions

- Which of your skills or abilities do you think helped you the most during this simulation? Why?

- Which of your skills or abilities do you particularly have to improve in order to enhance your performance in a simulation of this sort? Why?

- As the simulation took place, what changes in your behavior did you exhibit over time? Why?

- What observations can you make about the performance of others in general?

- In your opinion, which individuals contributed the most to the effectiveness of the team? In what ways did they contribute?

- What lessons did you learn from observing others' behavior during this simulation?

- Where would you rank yourself in terms of your overall contribution to your team? Place an X in the Self-Ranking column below to indicate your belief.

- How do you think your team members would rank you? Place an X in the Peer Ranking column below to indicate your estimate.

	Self-Ranking	Peer's Ranking
Top 10 percent		
Top quartile		
Top half		
Bottom half		
Bottom 10 percent		

Explain Your Rankings

- Which people helped you the most? In what ways did they help?

- Which people did you help the most? In what ways did you help?

- What achievement or event are you proudest of when you look back at your performance in this simulation? Why?

- What would you do differently, if you could? Why?

- What did you learn about yourself from this simulation?

- What did you learn about management from this simulation?

Notes/Comments:

Post–Simulation Peer Assessment (Instrument 3)

Ira J. Morrow

Instructions: Write in the name of the person you are providing feedback for below.

To: _____

Effective Behaviors I Observed

1.

2.

3.

4.

5.

Ineffective Behaviors I Observed

1.

2.

3.

4.

Developmental Needs I Saw

1.

2.

3.

4.

Developmental Recommendations/Actions

1.

2.

3.

4.

Based on what I observed of your behavior during the simulation, I had the following reactions to your performance:

1 = Very Dissatisfied   3 = Neither Satisfied nor Dissatisfied   5 = Very Satisfied
2 = Somewhat Dissatisfied   4 = Somewhat Satisfied

1c.	Your overall performance.	1	2	3	4	5
2c.	Your ability to set clear, realistic, demanding goals.	1	2	3	4	5
3c.	Your ability to manage your time effectively.	1	2	3	4	5
4c.	Your ability to handle stress.	1	2	3	4	5

1 = Very Dissatisfied   3 = Neither Satisfied nor Dissatisfied   5 = Very Satisfied
2 = Somewhat Dissatisfied   4 = Somewhat Satisfied

5c.	Your ability to delegate work to others.	1	2	3	4	5
6c.	Your ability to make effective decisions.	1	2	3	4	5
7c.	Your ability to solve problems.	1	2	3	4	5
8c.	Your ability to think of creative ideas.	1	2	3	4	5
9c.	Your own level of motivation.	1	2	3	4	5
10c.	Your ability to motivate others.	1	2	3	4	5
11c.	Your ability to interact with others in a sensitive manner.	1	2	3	4	5
12c.	Your ability to listen to others.	1	2	3	4	5
13c.	Your ability to be assertive.	1	2	3	4	5
14c.	Your ability to treat others in a diplomatic manner.	1	2	3	4	5
15c.	Your ability to gain the trust of others.	1	2	3	4	5
16c.	Your willingness to trust others.	1	2	3	4	5
17c.	Your willingness to disclose information about yourself to others.	1	2	3	4	5
18c.	Your ability to negotiate effectively.	1	2	3	4	5
19c.	Your ability to contribute to the team.	1	2	3	4	5
20c.	Your ability to manage conflict.	1	2	3	4	5
21c.	Your ability to build a consensus.	1	2	3	4	5
22c.	Your willingness to change when necessary.	1	2	3	4	5
23c.	Your ability to communicate to others.	1	2	3	4	5
24c.	Your ability to persuade/influence others.	1	2	3	4	5
25c.	Your ability to lead others.	1	2	3	4	5
26c.	Your ability to use power effectively.	1	2	3	4	5
27c.	Your energy level.	1	2	3	4	5
28c.	Your ability to work hard.	1	2	3	4	5

Open-Ended Questions

- The skills or abilities that helped you the most in this simulation were:

- The skills or abilities that helped you the least in this simulation were:

- As the simulation continued, I noticed that your behavior changed in the following ways:

- I noticed that you were at your best when:

- I noticed that you were especially helpful to:

General Comments:

24 Organizational Role Stress

Udai Pareek

Summary

Executive burnout is often the end result of stress experienced, but not properly coped with, by an executive. Burnout symptoms include exhaustion, irritation, ineffectiveness, inaction, discounting of self and others, and problems of bad health and drug use. On the other hand, stress properly coped with can lead to feelings of challenge, high job satisfaction, creativity, effectiveness, better adjustment to work and life, improved efficiency, career growth, and happiness. It is useful to look at the factors that contribute to the burnout of executives, and one of the most significant is role stress.

The Concept of Role

The concept of "role" is key to understanding how any individual functions in any system. It is through his or her role that an individual interacts with and is integrated into a system (Pareek, 1976). Role has been defined in several ways. Here, it is defined as any position one holds in an organization as defined by the expectations various significant persons, including oneself, have for that position (Pareek, 1976). "Function" is defined as the set of interrelated expectations from a role. As here defined, sales manager is a role, while developing the sales force and customer contacts are functions.

Some conflict is always present because the very nature of role has built-in potential for conflict or stress. The main characteristic of role conflict is the incompatibility of some variables related to the role. Buck (1972) defines "job pressure" as the resultant psychological state of the individual who perceives that (1) conflicting forces and incompatible commitments exist in connection with work, (2) at least one of the forces is coming from outside, and (3) the forces recur or are stable over time.

Kahn, Wolfe, Quinn, Snoek, and Rosenthal (1964) were the first to draw attention to organizational stress in general and role stress in particular. As suggested by Katz and Kahn (1966), an organization can be defined as a system of roles. Kahn and his associates used three categories (role ambiguity, role conflict, and role overload) to define role stress. This classification has been used by many other researchers. However, because each role is also a system of functions, from the point of view of individuals, two aspects of their roles are most important: role set, the role system within the organization of which roles are a part and by which individual roles are defined, and role space, the roles people occupy and perform.

Because the concept of role is inextricably linked with expectations, the organizational context is especially important. For example, authoritarian organizational structure and control systems are potent sources of stress because they breed dependency, afford little scope for initiative and creativity, and channel behaviors along narrowly defined paths. Many variables are involved, including oneself, the other roles in the organization, the expectations held by those in other roles, and one's own expectations.

Using This Instrument

Many classification systems have been used to describe role conflict and role stress. The Organizational Role Stress Scale was developed as one way to categorize role stress in terms of role space and role set. The instrument measures role-space conflict in terms of interrole distance (IRD), role stagnation (RS), role-expectations conflict (REC), personal inadequacy (PI) and self/role conflict (S/RC). Role-set conflict is measured in terms of role erosion (RE), role overload (RO), role isolation (RIs), role ambiguity (RA), and resource inadequacy (RIn). Definitions of these terms have been developed as follows:

Role-Space Conflicts

Interrole Distance. Conflicts may exist between two roles a person attempts to play. For example, executives often face conflicts between their organizational roles and their family roles. These may be incompatible and are quite frequently a source of conflict in a society in which people increasingly occupy multiple roles in various organizations and groups.

Role Stagnation. People "grow into" the roles they occupy in an organization. As they advance, their roles change and there is always a need to take on a new role for personal challenge. The problem is especially acute when a person has occupied a role for a long time and may feel secure and, therefore, hesitate to take on a new challenge. At middle age, and usually at middle-management levels, careers become more problematic, and many executives find their progress slowed, if not actually stopped. Job opportunities are fewer, those jobs that are available take longer to master, and old knowledge and methods become obsolete. Levinson (1973) and Constandse (1972) depict these managers as suffering fear and disappointment in silent isolation.

Role-Expectations Conflict. Because individuals develop expectations as a result of their socialization and identification with significant others, there is usually some incompatibility between a person's own expectations of a role and the expectations of others. For example, a professor may feel that the demands of teaching and of doing research are incompatible, whether they are or not. Others in the organization also are very likely have expectations of the person filling the role that conflict with the person's own.

Personal Inadequacy. If an individual has sacrificed his or her own interests, preferences, and values for the job, it may be because of fears of being inadequate otherwise to fill the role. The fear of demotion or obsolescence is especially strong for those who have reached a career ceiling, and most people will suffer some erosion of status before they retire. The company tends to sense an employee's feelings of inadequacy and often hesitates to promote because of it. McMurray (1973) describes what he calls "the executive neurosis": the overpromoted manager who is grossly overworked just in order to keep the job and, at the same time, hide a sense of insecurity and feelings of personal inadequacy.

Self/Role Conflict. Conflict often develops between people's self-concepts and their expectations of themselves in their job roles. For example, an introverted person may have trouble in the role of salesperson. It is also fairly common for people to experience conflict between the way they treat others in everyday life and the way they are required to treat others in their organizational roles, where maintaining distance from others may be necessary. Such conflicts are very common.

Role-Set Conflicts

Role Erosion. Employees often feel that some functions important to their roles are being performed by someone in another role. Role erosion is likely to be experienced in an organization that is redefining roles and creating new roles. As much stress is experienced by people with not enough to do or not enough responsibility for a task as by those with too much to do. People do not enjoy feeling underutilized.

Role Overload. On the other hand, when the role occupant feels that there are too many expectations, stress exists from "role overload" (Kahn et al., 1964). Kahn and Quinn (1970) suggested some conditions under which role overload is likely to occur: in the absence of role integration; in the absence of role power; when large variations exist in expected output; and when duties cannot be delegated. Marshall and Cooper

(1979) categorized overload into "quantitative" and "qualitative." Quantitative refers to having too much to do, and qualitative refers to work that is too difficult. A number of studies have shown (Breslow & Buell, 1960; French & Caplan, 1970; Margolis, Kroes, & Quinn, 1974; Miller, 1969; and Russek & Zohman, 1958) that quantitative overload is significantly related to a number of symptoms of stress: alcohol abuse, absenteeism, low motivation, lowered self-esteem, and many physical ailments. Some evidence also shows that (for some occupations) qualitative overload is a significant source of stress and of lowered self-esteem (French, Tupper, & Mueller, 1965). French and Caplan (1973) summarize the research by suggesting that both qualitative and quantitative overload produce at least nine different symptoms of psychological and physical strain: job dissatisfaction, job tension, lowered self-esteem, paranoia, embarrassment, high cholesterol levels, rapid heart rate, and increased smoking.

Role Isolation. Role occupants tend to feel that those occupying other roles are either psychologically near or at a distance. The main criterion of perceived role-role distance is frequency and ease of interaction. When linkages are strong, the role-role distance is seen as low. In the absence of strong linkage, the role distance can be measured in terms of the gap between the desired and the existing linkages. Both Kahn et al. (1964) and French and Caplan (1970) came to the conclusion that mistrust of persons one worked with was positively related to high role ambiguity and to low job satisfaction.

Role Ambiguity. When people are not clear about the expectations others have of them in their roles, whether due to poor feedback or poor understanding, they experience role ambiguity. Kahn and Quinn (1970) suggested that role ambiguity may be in relation to activities, responsibilities, personal style, and norms. They suggest that it was created by the actual expectations held for the role occupant by others, the expectations of the role occupant, and the expectations the role occupant receives and interprets in the light of prior information and experience. According to Kahn and Quinn, four kinds of roles are most likely to experience ambiguity: roles new to the organization, roles in expanding or contracting organizations, roles in organizations exposed to frequent changes in demand, and roles concerned with process.

Kahn et al. (1964) found that people who suffered from role ambiguity experienced low job satisfaction, high job-related tension, a sense of futility, and low self-confidence. Kahn (1973) distinguished two components of role ambiguity: present ambiguity and future-prospect ambiguity.

Resource Inadequacy. Resource inadequacy refers to people's feeling that they do not have adequate resources to perform their roles effectively, whether through lack of supplies, personnel, information in the system, or historical data, or through lack of knowledge, education, or experience on their own.

The author's surveys using this instrument have shown that senior managers experience role stress in the following order: role isolation, self/role conflict, role erosion, and interrole distance and that middle managers tend to experience more role stagnation (for more details, see Pareek, 1982).

Reliability and Validity

Retest-reliability coefficients were calculated for a group of about five hundred managers after an interval of eight weeks. These ranged from .37 to .73 for the various role stresses. All were significant at the .001 level. Therefore, the Organizational Role Stress Scale would appear to be reliable for training purposes.

Some evidence of validity is provided by the measure of consistency of an instrument. Each item was correlated with the total score on the instrument for the approximately five-hundred respondents. All but two correlations were significant at the .001 level: one at .002 and another at .008. The results show high internal consistency for the scale. Mean and standard-deviation values of the items also were analyzed. The lowest mean value was 2.42 and the highest was 4.66. The two items that had low correlation with the total had high mean values.

The responses also were factor analyzed, which produced exactly ten factors, corresponding to the ten role stresses, explaining 99.9 percent variance.

Scoring the Instrument

The instrument has an accompanying scoring sheet. The responses are ratings from a five-point Likert scale that indicates how descriptive a particular statement is for the respondent. The role-stress scale-score range is from a minimum of 5 to a maximum of 25. The total score ranges from 50 to 250. The columns are to be totaled to yield scale scores, and the columns are summed to yield a total score.

References

Breslow, L., & Buell, P. (1960). Mortality from coronary heart disease and physical activity of work in California. *Journal of Chronic Diseases, 11*, 617–626.

Buck, V.E. (1972). *Working under pressure.* London: Staples Press.

Constandse, W.J. (1972). Mid-40s man: A neglected personnel problem. *Personnel Journal, 51*(2), 129–133.

French, J.R.P., Jr., & Caplan, R.D. (1970). Psychosocial factors in coronary heart disease. *Industrial Medicine, 39*, 383–397.

French, J.R.P., Jr., & Caplan, R.D. (1973). Organizational stress and individual strain. In A.J. Marrow (Ed.), *The failure of success.* New York: AMACOM.

French. J.R.P., Jr., Tupper, C.J., & Mueller, E.I. (1965). *Workload of university professors.* Unpublished research report. Ann Arbor, MI: University of Michigan.

Kahn, R.L. (1973). Conflict, ambiguity and overload: Three elements in job stress. *Occupational Mental Health, 3,* 1.

Kahn, R.L., & Quinn, R.P. (1970). Role stress: A framework for analysis. In A. McLean (Ed.), *Mental health and work organizations.* Chicago, IL: Rand McNally.

Kahn, R.L., Wolfe, D.M., Quinn, R.P., Snoek, J.D., & Rosenthal, R.A. (1964). *Organizational stress: Studies in role conflict and ambiguity.* New York: John Wiley & Sons.

Katz, D., & Kahn, R.L. (1966). *The social psychology of organizations.* New York: John Wiley & Sons.

Levinson, H. (1973). Problems that worry our executives. In A.J. Marrow (Ed.), *The failure of success.* New York: AMACOM.

Margolis, B.L., Kroes, W.H., & Quinn, R.P. (1974). Job stress: An unlisted occupational hazard. *Journal of Occupational Medicine, 16*(1), 654–661.

Marshall, J., & Cooper, C.L. (1979). *Executive under pressure: A psychological study.* London: Macmillan Press.

McMurray, R.N. (1973). The executive neurosis. In R.L. Noland (Ed.). *Industrial mental health and employee counselling.* New York: Behavioural Publications.

Miller. J.G. (1969). Information input overload and psychopathology. *American Journal of Psychiatry, 8,* 116.

Pareek, U. (1976). Interrole exploration. In J.W. Pfeiffer & J.E. Jones (Eds.), *The 1976 annual.* San Francisco: Pfeiffer.

Pareek, U. (1982). *Role stress scales manual.* Ahmedabad, India: Navin Publications.

Russek. H.I., & Zohman, B.L. (1958). Relative significance of heredity, diet, and occupational stress in coronary heart disease of young adults. *American Journal of Medical Sciences, 235,* 266–275.

Originally published in *The 1983 Annual Handbook for Faciliatators, Trainers, and Consultants.*

Organizational Role Stress Scale

Udai Pareek

Name: _____   Title: _____

Date: _____   Organization: _____

Instructions: People have different perceptions of their work roles. Some statements describing such perceptions are listed below. Read each statement and decide how often you have the thought expressed in the statement in relation to your role in your organization. Circle the number on the scale that indicates your perception of your organizational role.

If you find that none of the categories given adequately indicates your opinion, use the one that is closest to your perception.

1 = Never or scarcely ever see things this way
2 = Occasionally (a few times) see things this way
3 = Sometimes see things this way
4 = Frequently see things this way
5 = Very frequently or always see things this way

1.	My role tends to interfere with my family life.	1	2	3	4	5
2.	I am afraid that I am not learning enough in my present role to prepare myself for higher responsibility.	1	2	3	4	5
3.	I am not able to satisfy the conflicting demands of various people who are over me in the organization.	1	2	3	4	5
4.	My role recently has been reduced in importance.	1	2	3	4	5
5.	My work load is too heavy.	1	2	3	4	5
6.	Other role occupants do not give enough attention and time to my role.	1	2	3	4	5
7.	I do not have adequate knowledge to handle the responsibilities in my role.	1	2	3	4	5
8.	I have to do things in my role that are against my better judgment.	1	2	3	4	5

1 = **Never or scarcely ever see things this way**
2 = **Occasionally (a few times) see things this way**
3 = **Sometimes see things this way**
4 = **Frequently see things this way**
5 = **Very frequently or always see things this way**

9.	I am not clear about the scope and responsibilities of my role (job).	1	2	3	4	5
10.	I do not receive the information that is needed to carry out the responsibilities assigned to me.	1	2	3	4	5
11.	My role does not allow me to spend enough time with my family.	1	2	3	4	5
12.	I am too preoccupied with my present role responsibilities to be able to prepare for taking on greater responsibilities.	1	2	3	4	5
13.	I am not able to satisfy the conflicting demands of the various people at my peer level and of my subordinates.	1	2	3	4	5
14.	Many of the functions that should be part of my role have been assigned to other roles.	1	2	3	4	5
15.	The amount of work that I have to do interferes with the quality I want to maintain.	1	2	3	4	5
16.	There is not enough interaction between my role and other roles.	1	2	3	4	5
17.	I wish I had more skills to handle the responsibilities of my role.	1	2	3	4	5
18.	I am not able to use my training and expertise in my role.	1	2	3	4	5
19.	I do not know what the people with whom I work expect of me.	1	2	3	4	5
20.	I do not have access to enough resources to be effective in my role.	1	2	3	4	5

1 = Never or scarcely ever see things this way
2 = Occasionally (a few times) see things this way
3 = Sometimes see things this way
4 = Frequently see things this way
5 = Very frequently or always see things this way

21. I have various other interests (social, religious, etc.,) that are neglected because I do not have the time to attend to them.   1   2   3   4   5

22. I do not have the time or opportunities to prepare myself for the future challenges of my role.   1   2   3   4   5

23. I am not able to satisfy the demands of clients and others because they conflict with one another.   1   2   3   4   5

24. I would like to take more responsibility than I have at present.   1   2   3   4   5

25. I have been given too much responsibility.   1   2   3   4   5

26. I wish there were more consultation between my role and other roles.   1   2   3   4   5

27. I have not had pertinent training for my role.   1   2   3   4   5

28. The responsibilities I have are not related to my interests.   1   2   3   4   5

29. Several aspects of my role are vague and unclear.   1   2   3   4   5

30. I do not have enough people to work with me in my role.   1   2   3   4   5

31. My organizational responsibilities interfere with my nonwork roles.   1   2   3   4   5

32. There is very little room for personal growth in my role.   1   2   3   4   5

33. The expectations of my seniors conflict with those of my subordinates.   1   2   3   4   5

34. I can do much more than what I have been assigned.   1   2   3   4   5

35. There is a need to reduce some parts of my role.   1   2   3   4   5

1 = Never or scarcely ever see things this way
2 = Occasionally (a few times) see things this way
3 = Sometimes see things this way
4 = Frequently see things this way
5 = Very frequently or always see things this way

36. There is no evidence of involvement of several roles (including my role) in joint problem solving or collaboration in planning action.   1   2   3   4   5

37. I wish that I had prepared myself well for my role.   1   2   3   4   5

38. If I had full freedom to define my role, I would be doing some things differently from the ways I do them now.   1   2   3   4   5

39. My role has not been defined clearly and in detail.   1   2   3   4   5

40. I am worried that I lack the necessary resources needed in my role.   1   2   3   4   5

41. My family and friends complain that I do not spend time with them because of the heavy demands of my work role.   1   2   3   4   5

42. I feel stagnant in my role.   1   2   3   4   5

43. I am bothered with the contradictory expectations that different people have of my role.   1   2   3   4   5

44. I wish that I would be given more challenging tasks to do.   1   2   3   4   5

45. I feel overburdened in my role.   1   2   3   4   5

46. Even when I take initiative for discussions or help, there is not much response from other roles.   1   2   3   4   5

47. I feel inadequate for my present job role.   1   2   3   4   5

48. I experience conflict between my values and what I have to do in my job role.   1   2   3   4   5

49. I am not clear about what the priorities are in my role.   1   2   3   4   5

50. I wish that I had more financial resources for the work assigned to me.   1   2   3   4   5

Organization Role Stress Scale Scoring Sheet

Instructions: Enter your scores from the Organizational Role Stress Scale in the spaces provided below.

1. _____	2. _____	3. _____	4. _____	5. _____
11. _____	12. _____	13 _____	14. _____	15. _____
21. _____	22. _____	23. _____	24. _____	25. _____
31. _____	32. _____	33. _____	34. _____	35. _____
41. _____	42. _____	43. _____	44. _____	45. _____

TOTALS

_____	_____	_____	_____	_____
IRD: Inter-Role Distance	RS: Role Stagnation	REC: Role-Expectations Conflict	RE: Role Erosion	RO: Role Overload

6. _____	7. _____	8. _____	9. _____	10. _____
16. _____	17. _____	18. _____	19. _____	20. _____
26. _____	27. _____	28. _____	29. _____	30. _____
36. _____	37. _____	38. _____	39. _____	40. _____
46. _____	47. _____	48. _____	49. _____	50. _____

TOTALS

_____	_____	_____	_____	_____
RIs: Role Isolation	PI: Personal Inadequacy	S/RC: Self/Role Conflict	RA: Role Ambiguity	RIn: Resource Inadequacy

GRAND TOTAL _____

Definitions

IRD   *Interrole Distance*: conflict between one's organizational role and other roles, e.g., between travel on the job and spending time with one's family.

RS   *Role Stagnation*: a feeling of stagnation and lack of growth in the job because of few opportunities for learning and growth.

REC   *Role-Expectations Conflict*: conflicting demands placed on one from others in the organization, e.g., producing excellent work but finishing under severe time restraints.

RE   *Role Erosion*: a decrease in one's level of responsibility or a feeling of not being fully utilized.

RO   *Role Overload*: too much to do and too many responsibilities to do everything well.

RIs   *Role Isolation*: feelings of being isolated from channels of information and not being part of what is happening.

PI   *Personal Inadequacy*: lack of knowledge, skill, or preparation to be effective in a particular role.

S/RC   *Self/Role Conflict*: a conflict between one's personal values or interests and one's job requirements.

RA   *Role Ambiguity*: unclear feedback from others about one's responsibilities and performance.

RIn   *Resource Inadequacy*: lack of resources or information necessary to perform well in a role.

Section 3
Managing the Organization

The attitudes and behaviors that managers bring to work each day are heavily influenced by the nature of the organization for which they work. CEOs may insist that they want managers to become more innovative or to build more cohesive teams or to instill more loyalty in the troops, but experienced trainers and consultants have learned the hard way that it's no use teaching people how to pursue such goals if the organization's real values, policies, or systems won't allow them to do it.

Under the heading "Managing the Organization," we have grouped instruments that serve at least one of three main purposes.

1. Several of the assessments measure climate factors that influence or determine the way managers will actually behave regardless of what official pronouncements (or training programs) may encourage them to do. Examples include The Organizational Climate Questionnaire and The Innovation Capability Audit. These instruments also could be useful in organization development efforts or in "action learning" programs in which managers build skills by investigating and tackling actual organizational change initiatives.

2. A few of the assessments are intended precisely for that latter purpose—to study and clarify specific organizational problems that require attention. Examples: The Problem-Analysis Questionnaire and Why Don't They Do What I Want?

3. Two instruments focus on the skills and aptitudes of individuals, but within the context of a particular organizational climate or development initiative. In Mentoring Skills Assessment, a prospective mentor and protégé work out their expectations for the relationship. In The Organizational I-Boundary Inventory, managers assess the political workings of their organization with an eye toward learning how to operate more effectively within their present environment.

Here are brief descriptions of the thirteen assessments.

- Problem-Analysis Questionnaire—Using an actual problem in the organization, analyze factors that may be preventing you, your subordinates, other managers, or the organization itself from resolving the situation.

- The Organizational Health Survey—Executives and others rate the organization's practices and its competitive standing on seven dimensions, from strategic marketplace position to employee-performance management.

- The Organizational Climate Questionnaire (OCQ)—Rates the organization on fourteen climate factors determined or heavily influenced by management practices.

- Strategic Leadership Styles Instrument—Identifies both the leadership styles currently prevailing in an organization and the styles that individual managers would like to adopt.

- Conflict Management Climate Index—Takes an organization's temperature with respect to the way power is used, feelings are expressed, and disagreements are handled.

- Why Don't They Do What I Want? Understanding Employee Motivation—Managers analyze performance problems with regard to particular workplace initiatives by examining the likely effects on various stakeholders.

- Motivational Analysis of Organizations—Climate (MAO-C)—Analyzes six underlying factors that determine the values and fears motivating the prevailing behavior in an organization.

- The Organizational Readiness Inventory (ORI): Diagnosing Your Organization's Ability to Adapt to the Future—Managers and others rate the organization's systems and practices in seven key dimensions.

- The Organizational I-Boundary Inventory: A Model for Decision Making—Managers measure and develop their savvy in company politics.

- Innovation Capability Audit—Managers assess their organization's willingness and capacity to change and innovate.

- Organizational Norms Opinionnaire—Managers rate the organization's climate and practices with regard to their effect on employees' effectiveness and job satisfaction.

- Mentoring Skills Assessment—An instrument to be used by a prospective mentor and protégé to clarify expectations before the start of a formal mentoring relationship.

- Organizational Type Inventory—Measures how managers and others perceive the working climate established by the CEO and senior executives.

25 Problem–Analysis Questionnaire

Barry Oshry and Roger Harrison

Summary

This instrument was designed to ferret out two types of problems in organizations: rational-technical and openness within the organization, in others, and in oneself.

Research indicates that those factors that sustain problem situations in organizations can be categorized into two types: rational-technical failures and failures in openness. Further, these two types of failures can be found in three areas: in others, in the organization, and in oneself.

	Others		Organization		Self	
Item	Rational-Technical	Closed	Rational-Technical	Closed	Rational-Technical	Closed

Rational–Technical Failures

In the area of *others*, rational-technical failures include lack of initiative, unwillingness to devote sufficient time and effort to the problem, inadequate ideas, and a tendency not to confront issues.

In the *organization*, this type of failure includes excessive demands, insufficient time to complete tasks, refusal to consider the problem important, and inadequate guidance or assistance.

For *self*, rational-technical failures consist of inadequate initiative, inadequate planning, poor communication, unrevealed desires and objectives, and unclear analysis of the problem.

Failures in Openness

In *others,* failures in openness can be seen when people are resentful of outside suggestions or attempts to help, unwilling to cooperate, unwilling to adjust to the realities of the situation, resistant to changing their ways, not sensitive to the effects of their actions on others, difficult to approach, and unwilling to listen to others' viewpoints.

Failures in openness in the *organization occur* when the organization becomes inflexible, has old-fashioned or outdated ideas, resists suggestions, is unwilling to adapt to the demands of new situations, or resists experimentation.

Examples of failures in openness that relate to the *self* occur when a person is difficult to approach, is insensitive to others' needs and goals, resists others' suggestions, expects too much of others, is competitive, is not objective, is resistant to change, and is unwilling to understand the other person's point of view.

The Problem-Analysis Questionnaire

This questionnaire has the following purposes:

1. It is intended to help the respondent analyze the reasons for the problem he or she has identified.

2. It offers an instrument to be used to survey and analyze a commonly agreed-on problem.

3. It functions as a tool to evaluate the effects of training.

Preliminary research results indicate an order of expected responses, ranging from high to low:

Others/Rational-Technical

Others/Closed

Organization/Rational-Technical

Organization/Closed

Self/Rational-Technical

Self/Closed

In other words, people tend to blame others most for problems, then the organization, and only lastly themselves.

However, it also seems apparent that human relations training effects a shift toward higher Self scores, indicating more ownership of one's behavior and its effects, and toward lower Organization and Others scores, a result that suggests that as individuals take more responsibility for their problems, they tend to blame outside influences less.

———————

Originally published in *The 1975 Annual Handbook for Faciliatators, Trainers, and Consultants.*

Problems-Analysis Questionnaire

Barry Oshry and Roger Harrison

This questionnaire asks you to consider in detail a meaningful human relations problem with which you are confronted in your work. The problem that you select should meet the following criteria:

a. *You* are directly involved in the situation.

b. The problem is presently *unresolved*.

c. You are *dissatisfied* with the situation and would like to change it.

d. The situation is *interpersonal*, involving your relationship with some other person or persons.

e. The problem is *important* to you.

Some typical work problems follow:

- A manager is dissatisfied with the quality of a subordinate's work and with that person's apparently negative attitude.

- A chief engineer thinks that the plant superintendent is not effective in resolving a persistent conflict between the engineering and manufacturing departments.

- A staff specialist believes that his or her services are being resisted or not adequately used by the administration.

- A subordinate has been unable to convince his or her superior that certain policy changes are needed.

- A marketing manager thinks that the staff is overly competitive, more interested in destroying one another than in collaborating.

To give this questionnaire maximal value, first select the *most critical interpersonal problem* confronting you at work. Then consider each of the following forty-eight possible factors. Indicate the degree to which you think each has contributed to the problem by writing in front of each item the number corresponding to your feelings about the importance of this causative factor.

1. It is *totally unimportant* in creating or maintaining this problem.

2. It is *relatively unimportant* in creating or maintaining this problem.

3. It is *moderately important* in creating or maintaining this problem.

4. It is *important* in creating or maintaining this problem.

5. It is *very important* in creating or maintaining this problem.

In the questionnaire the term "others" or "the other persons" means those with whom you are directly involved in the problem. The term "organization" means aspects of the work situation other than "the other persons" directly involved. The "organization" includes policies and procedures, structure, and decisions of groups and persons not directly involved in the problem.

_____ 1. I have not let the others know just where I stand on this problem.

_____ 2. The organization demands too much of me to be able to handle this problem adequately.

_____ 3. I have been relatively difficult to approach.

_____ 4. There is a great deal of organizational bureaucracy.

_____ 5. The other persons are resentful of any outside suggestions or attempts to help.

_____ 6. The other persons have not planned adequately.

_____ 7. I have not taken as much initiative as I should have to remedy this situation.

_____ 8. The organization does not allow me enough time to handle this problem adequately.

_____ 9. I have been insensitive to the needs and goals of the others.

_____ 10. The organization has become inflexible.

_____ 11. The other persons directly involved in the problem are unwilling to cooperate.

_____ 12. The other persons are lacking in initiative.

_____ 13. I have tended to let the problem slide rather than attack it directly.

_____ 14. The organization is lax in taking corrective action.

_____ 15. I have tended to resist suggestions from others.

_____ 16. Organizational policies have not changed sufficiently with the times to handle this type of problem.

_____ 17. The other persons are unwilling to adjust to the realities of the situation.

_____ 18. The other persons do not carry their share of the load.

_____ 19. I have not planned adequately to meet this situation.

_____ 20. Organizational policies and procedures are not adequate guides for dealing with this situation.

_____ 21. I have tended to expect the other persons to go my way more than is reasonable.

_____ 22. The organization resists suggestions aimed at producing change.

_____ 23. The other persons overestimate their own abilities.

_____ 24. The other persons are unwilling to devote enough time and effort to solve this problem.

_____ 25. I have not been clear in communicating my own position to the other persons.

_____ 26. The organization does not consider this type of problem sufficiently important to provide the means for solving it.

_____ 27. I have been competitive, thus hindering the solution of the problem.

_____ 28. The organization is unwilling to adjust to the demands created by new situations.

_____ 29. The other persons resist changing their ways of doing things.

_____ 30. The other persons have not suggested ideas to solve this problem, or their suggestions have been inadequate.

_____ 31. I have tended to keep my own desires and objectives hidden.

_____ 32. The organization does not offer help on this type of problem.

_____ 33. Because of my own interests, I have been unable to look at the problem objectively.

_____ 34. The organization resists attempts to experiment with new ways of solving problems.

_____ 35. The other persons are not sensitive to the effect of their actions.

_____ 36. The other persons are not willing to devote the money or other resources needed to solve this problem.

_____ 37. I have not experimented with new ways of handling the situation.

_____ 38. The organization does not provide adequate resources for dealing with this kind of problem.

_____ 39. I have resisted changing my usual patterns of action.

_____ 40. It is difficult to get some favorable action from authorities in the organization.

_____ 41. The other persons are unwilling to listen to others' points of view.

_____ 42. The other persons do not give a high priority to solving this problem.

_____ 43. I have not adequately analyzed the situation.

_____ 44. The situation is not receiving sufficient guidance from authorities in the organization.

_____ 45. I have been unwilling to make an effort to understand the other persons' viewpoints.

_____ 46. Policies and procedures of the organization do not permit the changes needed to deal with this problem.

_____ 47. The other persons have been difficult to approach.

_____ 48. The other persons have let the problem slide.

Problem–Analysis Questionnaire Scoring Sheet

Instructions: Transfer your responses to the forty-eight questionnaire items to the appropriate spaces that follow and sum each of the six columns.

	Others		Organization		Self	
Item	Rational-Technical	Closed	Rational-Technical	Closed	Rational-Technical	Closed
1.					_____	
2.			_____			
3.						_____
4.				_____		
5.		_____				
6.	_____					
7.					_____	
8.			_____			
9.						_____
10.				_____		
11.		_____				
12.	_____					
13.					_____	
14.			_____			
15.						_____
16.				_____		
17.		_____				
18.	_____					
19.					_____	
20.			_____			
21.						_____
22.				_____		

	Others		Organization		Self	
Item	Rational-Technical	Closed	Rational-Technical	Closed	Rational-Technical	Closed
23.	_____	_____				
24.	___ _____					
25.					___ _____	
26.			_____ _____			
27.						_____
28.				_____		
29.		_____				
30.	___ _____					
31.					_____	
32.			_____ _____			
33.						_____
34.				_____		
35.		_____				
36.	___ _____					
37.					_____	
38.			_____ _____			
39.						_____
40.				_____		
41.		_____				
42.	___ _____					
43.					_____	
44.			____ _____			
45.						_____
46.				_____		
47.		_____				
48.	___ _____					

	Others		Organization		Self	
	Rational-Technical	Closed	Rational-Technical	Closed	Rational-Technical	Closed
Raw Scores						
Average Importance Scores*						

*Divide each raw score by 8.

Problem–Analysis Questionnaire Profile Sheet

Instructions:

1. In the boxes below the graph, copy your average importance scores from the Scoring Sheet.

2. Shade in the bar above each score to the level indicated by that score.

3. Compare your profile with those depicted below.

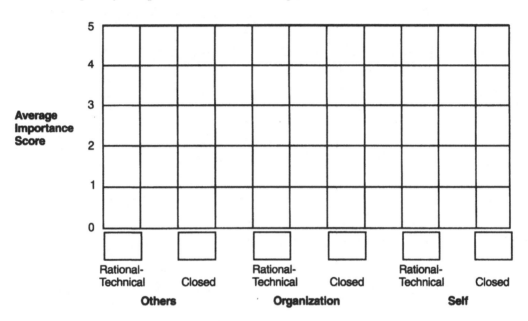

NORMATIVE DATA

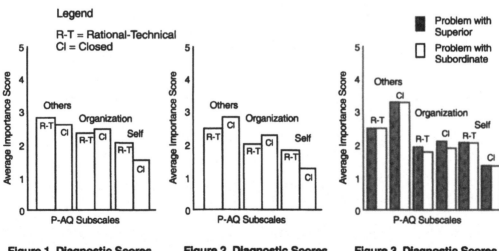

Figure 1. Diagnostic Scores for 167 Managers in Manufacturing Organizations

Figure 2. Diagnostic Scores for 87 Civil Service Middle Managers

Figure 3. Diagnostic Scores for 50 Managers in Manufacturing Organizations

26 The Organizational–Health Survey

Will Phillips

Summary

The Organizational-Health Survey (Short Form) and The Organizational-Health Survey (Long Form) both measure an organization's health along these seven dimensions. The short form consists of seven scales along which participants are asked to position the organization. Although this placement is highly individual, strong agreement exists within the same level in an organization. Scoring of the instrument is done subjectively by the participants. The long form consists of forty-five questions.

Dimensions of Organizational Health

In examining organizational health, certain key questions should be addressed in seven dimensions:

1. *Strategic position.* Strategic position is a measure of how well the organization is situated in relation to its external world. A well-positioned organization supplies a growing market; high barriers prevent competitors from entering the market; supplies are plentiful; and there are no threats of changes in legislation, economy, technology, or social climate. How well has the organization designed itself to respond to its market in the current external environment? Is the external environment helping or hindering?

2. *Purpose.* A well-defined purpose directs all of the organization's resources and energy toward achieving a goal. Purpose focuses on meeting the needs of five entities: the customers, the business (cash, profit, and growth), the owners, the employees, and the community. A healthy organizational purpose is clear, and everyone in the organization agrees to it. The most successful purposes add meaning to each individual's work by integrating the organization's purpose with the individual's purpose. How well is the organization focused on its direction, and how well do the key people and employees understand and adhere to the direction and priorities?

3. *Alignment.* A well-aligned organization is very powerful and efficient. It does not waste human energy. The organization's purpose is used to align, evaluate, and refocus every other organizational decision. How well do the organization's strategic support factors (such as culture, plans, structure, systems, and incentives) actually support the purpose of the organization?

4. *Stretching versus coasting.* People stretch when four conditions exist: they are challenged; they feel that they can make a difference in the outcome; they are rewarded rather than punished for stretching; and they are trusted. Is the organization challenging itself and its people? Is there too much challenge (causing strain), too little challenge (resulting in coasting), or just the right amount for maximum productivity?

5. *Control versus responsiveness.* An organization that is over controlled will not allow for flexibility, change, and creativity. What is the balance between control and responsiveness in the organization? A well-controlled organization is rarely surprised. A responsive organization is able to innovate and adapt to changes quickly.

6. *Growth versus profit.* When an organization is in a fast-growth mode, there is a high likelihood that growth may become its downfall. On the other hand, an organization that is spinning off very high amounts of cash and is not growing will also undermine itself. What is the balance between these two goals? Is there enough profit to sustain growth? Is there enough growth to challenge people and to provide opportunities for individual growth?

7. *Individual versus organization.* Every successful organization must find an appropriate balance between serving the needs of the individuals and the needs of the organization. One measure of an organization's focus on individual needs is its ability to attract, develop, and keep talented people. When organizations do not respond to individual needs for challenge, promotion, and increased income, those individuals move or transfer, and the organization loses. What is the balance needed for the organization to meet its own goals and needs along with the goals and needs of individuals in the organization?

The Instruments

Questions are asked relating to each of the seven dimensions of organizational health. Scoring is objective; participants can score their own instruments, or the facilitator can do all the scoring.

The short form of the instrument saves time in administration and scoring. However, a lecturette on the seven dimensions must be presented before using the instrument. The short form is especially useful in companies with a history of open and honest communication. Perhaps the best use of the short form is as a discussion starter and agenda builder for management groups.

The long form does not require a lecturette on the seven dimensions. In fact, if a lecturette is given, it should follow the administration of the instrument in order to avoid biased responses. Long forms can be administered individually in advance and scored before a group meeting.

Although no controlled research compares the two forms, experience shows the short form will yield a diagnosis that essentially matches that of the long form. The latter does hold certain advantages, including (1) more depth, (2) more specific input for use in action planning, and (3) more power for eliciting results that motivate organizations to change constructively.

Purpose of the Instruments

These instruments address the following purposes:

1. To provide a structure through which an organization can broadly assess its current health and its potential for future success;

2. To provide diagnostic output that can be used to build an action plan for organizational improvement;

3. To encourage consultants and managers to use a broader range of data in understanding and evaluating an organization's health;

4. To provide a tool to motivate and energize key organizational members to engage in constructive change; and

5. To define more clearly the goal of organizational and individual development efforts in an organization.

Validity and Reliability

The instruments and the seven dimensions of organizational health have been presented to approximately three hundred company presidents in one-half to one-day sessions. They have also been used for in-depth workshops with the top-management teams of approximately two dozen organizations. In each case the dimensions and the results of the instruments found a high degree of acceptance.

Agreement on ratings among members of an organization is quite uniform (less than 10-percent variation) when the organization is characterized as having open and honest communication. When this is not the norm, variation may go up to 30 percent on some items. Most variations occur between levels in an organization; that is, the president usually scores the organization as healthier on all dimensions than does the next level of managers. Lowest-level scores come from the lowest hierarchical level. The more unhealthy the organization, the more dramatic the differences between levels.

Whom to Survey

Regardless of how well the executive director, president, or CEO knows an organization, that person has a strong tendency to see the organization as he or she wants it to be rather than as it is. Additional opinions should be sought from others, such as members of the management team, employees, customers, board members, and vendors.

One of the more effective and efficient ways of getting valuable opinions on the health of the organization is to administer the instruments with members of some or all of these groups plus the CEO in a single meeting. Interaction between the members will lead to more depth, more learning, and eventually more commitment and energy for making improvements and changes in the organization's health.

Certain dangers must be considered before bringing a group of people together to do this, including the following:

- The process will not work if the norm in the organization is not to speak openly and frankly.

- Without adequate structure and appropriate control, the process can degenerate into a gripe session, which is nonproductive.

- It is possible to generate too much data and to be locked into a state of paralysis by overanalysis.

When the survey is used in an organization with a closed culture where communication is guarded and criticism is not accepted well, a good deal of time must be devoted to discussing results. The benefits of team diagnosing can be gained and dangers avoided if a competent outside facilitator with experience in diagnosis conducts the session. The facilitator must have established clear expectations with the CEO, division manager, owner, and others about how the closed culture will be opened before leading a team discussion on the results.

Interpretation of Scores

In interpreting scores, it is important to realize that all of the dimensions share a dynamic relationship with one another. Increasing one often decreases another. The skill is to balance them correctly. A discussion of the results should not be sidetracked to the instruments and their accuracy. The best use of the instruments is to open discussions among key people and launch an improvement process.

The following statements offer an overview of how scores on the instruments can be interpreted.

- High strategic position scores are a cause for celebration. However, medium and low scores need quick attention; if not corrected, they will make little difference in how well the organization is managed internally, but future failure is likely. Strategic planning and management are the recommended treatments, in an effort to unfreeze and reorient the organization's focus.

- High purpose scores reflect a very proactive organization. When purpose scores are medium or low, inefficiency and frustration begin to build. Strategic planning and strategic management are the key treatments to improving the organization's purpose. Thorough communication of the purpose throughout the organization then must follow.

- Once the purpose is clear, focused, and agreed on, the rest of the organization can be aligned. Long-term improvements in culture, structure, systems, or incentives depend on a clear purpose to provide healthy guidelines for design.

- When purpose and alignment scores are high, the organization will naturally be stretched. In addition, stretch can be facilitated by a management team skilled in delegation, listening, performance appraisal, and holding people accountable.

- Low control scores are often a precursor to going out of control, particularly in cash management, hiring, acquisitions, or legal suits. Immediate short-term controls should be instituted to provide time to build effective control systems. These systems should also be aligned with the organization's desired purpose, culture, structure, and systems.

- High control and low flexibility scores indicate great barriers to making any significant changes in the organization. The key treatment in this case is in-depth unfreezing of the organization so that a new culture can be designed and commitment to changes can be made with integrity. A long-term follow-up system will be needed to ensure results. Well-led strategic planning can be the vehicle for this unfreezing, but it requires significant participation by key people in a cathartic diagnosis and planning activity.

- Lack of balance in growth and profit may lead to immediate problems. This is especially true when growth exceeds the organization's ability to generate cash, train qualified people, and make good decisions. Rapid growth often creates a sense of invincibility, which is a sure precursor to problems. Treatment consists of recognizing the dangers of growth; having the humility to accept the need to change; and taking specific actions to increase control and build good foundations for growth in the areas of strategy, money, and people. Revitalization of growth must be initiated by a commitment from the top plus in-depth strategic planning.

- High-profit/low-growth organizations have severe problems, but the impact is long term. An organization with low growth will not attract and keep high performers because they see little future for personal growth. Such an organization tends to be managed by good stewards at best and bureaucrats at worst.

- In most cases, organizations pay more attention to organizational needs than to those of individuals. Low ratings on the organizational area are best treated by a clear and agreed-on purpose with an increase in the control areas. Low individual scores may be superficially treated with an increase in personnel or human resource management activities. More significant changes usually require an accompanying change in the culture.

Summary

These two instruments are the result of extensive work with company presidents and their executive teams. They were developed to help executives and managers to understand better the purpose of organizational and individual development efforts. The instruments are based on a model of organization health that centers around seven essential dimensions. These seven dimensions seek to maximize strategic position, purpose, and alignment, while balancing stretching and coasting; control and responsiveness; growth and profit; and needs of the individual and the organization.

Either of the instruments may be used any time that management is willing to spend a half a day or more to gain better insight about the organization, its current health, and its potential for future success. The impact of either instrument is significantly enhanced if the top management team is also fully involved.

Although the instruments should not be overused with the same people, they are very useful on an annual basis for comparisons and as measures of progress. One practical and effective use of the instruments is as structure for all or part of an organizational retreat. In most cases, a two-day retreat is spent first learning about the dimensions and rating them and then assessing what should be done about changing them in the organization. The output of the session is an agreed-on action plan detailing who will do what by when over the next year to make changes in the seven dimensions.

The Short Form

Administration

The following steps are suggested for administering the short form:

1. Deliver a lecturette on the seven dimensions of organizational health, using the questions posed earlier in this article as guides.

2. Have participants rate the organization on the seven dimensions using a scale of one to ten, indicating the organization's present position on each continuum with an "X."

3. Have participants draw arrows to indicate any trends of movement to the right or left along the continua.

4. Have participants draw circles to indicate where they believe the organization should be on the continua in order to be healthy.

Using the Data from the Short Form

Information obtained from more than one person can be summarized on a blank form. A simple mathematical average can hide valuable information; therefore, it is more useful to plot each X, circle, and arrow on a master short form. A different color for each person may add clarity. As an alternative presentation, the short form can be drawn on a flip chart or overhead transparency; each participant then publicly expresses his or her data. Each type of information (X's, circles, and arrows) can be discussed separately. The facilitator might use the following procedure:

1. Decide whether or not the master score summary accurately represents the organization. If not, discuss and agree on changes to the summary.

2. Select the two or three dimensions that would be most beneficial to improve.

3. Identify specifics of these dimensions. Avoid involved discussions of what is or is not true, or what is and is not improvable.

4. Design tasks to address improvement in these dimensions.

5. Assign people and deadlines.

6. Decide how to monitor progress.

The Long Form

Administration

Suggestions for administering the long form include the following:

1. Select participants as outlined in "Whom To Survey."

2. Schedule a meeting of one-half to one and one-half days so that the participants can interpret the data and build an action plan.

3. Have the participants complete the long form.

4. Decide if the facilitator will score the instruments or if the participants will score their own.

5. Combine the individual score summaries before the meeting and prepare a master score summary.

Using the Data from the Long Form

Begin the meeting with the lecturette or an expanded presentation based on the material in this article. Lead a discussion that focuses on the following:

1. Decide whether or not the master score summary accurately represents the organization. If not, discuss and agree on changes to the summary.

2. Select the two or three dimensions that would be most beneficial to improve.

3. Identify specifics of these dimensions. Avoid involved discussions of what is or is not true, or what is and is not improvable.

4. Design tasks to address these areas.

5. Assign people and deadlines.

6. Decide how to monitor progress.

———

Originally published in *The 1989 Annual: Developing Human Resources.*

The Organizational-Health Survey (Short Form)

Will Phillips

Name: _____

Instructions: The following items were chosen to assess seven major dimensions of organizational functioning. Taken together they will give an overall indication of the state of health of the organization. Respond to each question to the best of your experience even though you may not have complete background knowledge.

Rate the organization on each of the following seven dimensions using a scale of one to ten, indicating the organization's position on each continuum with an "X." Next, draw arrows to indicate any trends of movement to the right or to the left along the continua. Finally, draw circles to indicate where you believe the organization should be in order to be healthy.

1. Strong Strategic Position   Weak

   10 – – 9 – – 8 – – 7 – – 6 – – 5 – – 4 – – 3 – – 2 – – 1

2. Purposeful   Unfocused

   10 – – 9 – – 8 – – 7 – – 6 – – 5 – – 4 – – 3 – – 2 – – 1

3. Aligned   Unaligned

   10 – – 9 – – 8 – – 7 – – 6 – – 5 – – 4 – – 3 – – 2 – – 1

4. Strained   Stretched   Coasting

   10 – – 9 – – 8 – – 7 – – 6 – – 5 – – 4 – – 3 – – 2 – – 1

5. Control   Flexibility
   Continuity   Change
   Stability   Creativity

   10 – – 9 – – 8 – – 7 – – 6 – – 5 – – 4 – – 3 – – 2 – – 1

6. Profit   Growth

   10 – – 9 – – 8 – – 7 – – 6 – – 5 – – 4 – – 3 – – 2 – – 1

7. Individual   Organizational
   Needs Met   Needs Met

   10 – – 9 – – 8 – – 7 – – 6 – – 5 – – 4 – – 3 – – 2 – – 1

The Organizational–Health Survey (Long Form)

Will Phillips

Name: _____

Instructions: The items starting on the next page were chosen to assess the major dimensions of organizational functioning (represented in the instrument by sections SP, P, A, S, C, F, PR, G, I, and O). Taken together they will give an overall indication of the state of health of the organization. Respond to each question to the best of your experience even though you may not have complete background knowledge.

Circle the response following each question that corresponds to one of the following:

SA = Strongly Agree

A = Inclined to Agree

U = Unsure

D = Disagree

SD = Strongly Disagree

Respond to all forty-five items first; then go back through the instrument and complete the scoring for each section.

Section SP

SA = Strongly Agree		U = Unsure	D = Disagree
A = Inclined to Agree			SD = Strongly Disagree

1. Our market is growing.   SA   A   U   D   SD

2. There is a steady demand for our products/services.   SA   A   U   D   SD

3. In the eyes of our customers, we are clearly distinguished from our competitors.   SA   A   U   D   SD

4. It is very difficult and/or costly to enter our line of business.   SA   A   U   D   SD

5. We are not overly dependent on suppliers of materials, information, or labor.   SA   A   U   D   SD

6. We are not overly dependent on a small number of customers.   SA   A   U   D   SD

7. There are no products or services that are likely to replace ours in the near future.   SA   A   U   D   SD

8. There are few threats to our organization from changes in technology, laws, demog-raphy, the economy, or social attitudes.   SA   A   U   D   SD

SP Scoring

	SA	A	U	D	SD
Number of circles in each column:	___	___	___	___	___
Multiply column total by the weighting factor shown:	×10	×8	×0	×−10	×−20
Compute the total: =	___	+___	+___	+___	+___

= [   ]

SP Total

Section P

SA = Strongly Agree			D = Disagree	
A = Inclined to Agree		U = Unsure	SD = Strongly Disagree	

		SA	A	U	D	SD
9.	I clearly understand the direction in which our organization is heading.	SA	A	U	D	SD
10.	We listen to our customers.	SA	A	U	D	SD
11.	I know how my work contributes to the overall organization.	SA	A	U	D	SD
12.	I am proud of our company.	SA	A	U	D	SD
13.	We have clear priorities.	SA	A	U	D	SD

P Scoring

	SA	A	U	D	SD
Number of circles in each column:	___	___	___	___	___
Multiply column total by the weighting factor shown:	×16	×13	×0	×–15	×–30
Compute the total: =	___	+___	+___	+___	+___

= ☐

P Total

Section A

SA = Strongly Agree	**U = Unsure**	**D = Disagree**		
A = Inclined to Agree		**SD = Strongly Disagree**		

14. We have a strong sense of teamwork and cooperation. SA   A   U   D   SD

15. The people who work here trust and respect one another. SA   A   U   D   SD

16. The way our jobs are divided is clear and makes sense. SA   A   U   D   SD

17. I get accurate and timely information that helps me do my job. SA   A   U   D   SD

18. Our resources (people, money, time, equipment, and so on) are focused to produce the best results. SA   A   U   D   SD

19. There are incentives to encourage us to do what is important. SA   A   U   D   SD

A Scoring

	SA	A	U	D	SD
Number of circles in each column:	___	___	___	___	___
Multiply column total by the weighting factor shown:	×13	×12	×0	×−10	×−20
Compute the total: =	___	+___	+___	+___	+___

= [   ]

A Total

Section S

SA = Strongly Agree	**U = Unsure**	**D = Disagree**
A = Inclined to Agree		**SD = Strongly Disagree**

20. The work I do is very challenging. SA   A   U   D   SD

21. The people I work with try to do their best. SA   A   U   D   SD

22. We are not overworked or overstressed. SA   A   U   D   SD

23. We are not spread too thin. SA   A   U   D   SD

S Scoring

	SA	A	U	D	SD
Number of circles in each column:	____	____	____	____	____
Multiply column total by the weighting factor shown:	×20	×15	×0	×–15	×–20
Compute the total: =	____	+____	+____	+____	+____

= [   ]

S Total

Section C

SA = Strongly Agree		D = Disagree	
A = Inclined to Agree	U = Unsure	SD = Strongly Disagree	

24. Our actual sales, cost, or profit figures rarely surprise us.

   SA   A   U   D   SD

25. We are in compliance with all laws and with agreements we have made.

   SA   A   U   D   SD

26. We have accurate, useful, and timely reports on key performance areas.

   SA   A   U   D   SD

27. We regularly measure customer satisfaction.

   SA   A   U   D   SD

28. We regularly measure employee satisfaction.

   SA   A   U   D   SD

C Scoring

	SA	A	U	D	SD
Number of circles in each column:	___	___	___	___	___
Multiply column total by the weighting factor shown:	$\times 16$	$\times 13$	$\times 0$	$\times -15$	$\times -30$
Compute the total: =	___	+___	+___	+___	+___

= [   ]

C Total

Section F

SA = Strongly Agree			
A = Inclined to Agree	U = Unsure	D = Disagree	
		SD = Strongly Disagree	

29. We respond to changes in the outside world that may affect our organization. SA A U D SD

30. We regularly seek and use ideas and comments from our customers. SA A U D SD

31. Everyone is encouraged to think of ways of doing things better. SA A U D SD

32. We regularly fine-tune or make improvements in how we do things in all departments. SA A U D SD

33. We have a high readiness to make changes if needed. SA A U D SD

F Scoring

	SA	A	U	D	SD
Number of circles in each column:	___	___	___	___	___
Multiply column total by the weighting factor shown:	×16	×13	×0	×−15	×−30
Compute the total: =	___	+___	+___	+___	+___

= [   ]

F Total

Section PR

SA = Strongly Agree		**D = Disagree**	
A = Inclined to Agree	**U = Unsure**	**SD = Strongly Disagree**	

34. We produce enough profit to regularly invest it in people, our facility, or im-proving our products and services. SA A U D SD

35. We have an ample gross margin that does not erode during pro-duction or delivery. SA A U D SD

36. We have ample cash available. SA A U D SD

PR Scoring

	SA	A	U	D	SD
Number of circles in each column:	____	____	____	____	____
Multiply column total by the weighting factor shown:	×27	×22	×0	×–30	×–50
Compute the total: =	____ +	____ +	____ +	____ +	____

= [   ]

PR Total

Section G

SA = Strongly Agree		U = Unsure	D = Disagree		
A = Inclined to Agree			SD = Strongly Disagree		

37. Our market share is growing significantly.	SA	A	U	D	SD
38. Our sales are increasing at over 5 percent per year.	SA	A	U	D	SD
39. We are not growing too fast.	SA	A	U	D	SD

G Scoring

	SA	A	U	D	SD
Number of circles in each column:	____	____	____	____	____
Multiply column total by the weighting factor shown:	×27	×22	×0	×–30	×–50
Compute the total: =	____	+____	+____	+____	+____

$$= \boxed{}$$

G Total

Section I

SA = Strongly Agree	**U = Unsure**	**D = Disagree**	
A = Inclined to Agree		**SD = Strongly Disagree**	

40. There is a real opportunity for employees to grow and develop here.   SA   A   U   D   SD

41. We have little undesired.   SA   A   U   D   SD

42. The organization cares for its employees.   SA   A   U   D   SD

I Scoring

	SA	A	U	D	SD
Number of circles in each column:	___	___	___	___	___
Multiply column total by the weighting factor shown:	×27	×22	×0	×−30	×−50
Compute the total: =	___	+___	+___	+___	+___

$$= \boxed{}$$

I Total

Section O

SA = Strongly Agree		**D = Disagree**	
A = Inclined to Agree	**U = Unsure**	**SD = Strongly Disagree**	

43. People are held accountable for their performance.   SA   A   U   D   SD

44. People will give a lot to help our organization.   SA   A   U   D   SD

45. Our organization demands a lot from everyone.   SA   A   U   D   SD

O Scoring

	SA	A	U	D	SD
Number of circles in each column:	___	___	___	___	___
Multiply column total by the weighting factor shown:	×27	×22	×0	×–30	×–50
Compute the total: =	___	+___	+___	+___	+___

= [   ]

O Total

The Organizational–Health Survey
Scoring and Interpretation Sheet

Instructions: Transfer the score from each section of the long form to this score summary.

1. SP = Strategic Position Score   _____

2. P = Purpose Score   _____

3. A = Alignment Score   _____

4. S = Stretch Score   _____

5. C = Control Score   _____

       F = Flexibility Score   _____

6. PR = Profit Score   _____

       G = Growth Score   _____

7. I = Individual Score   _____

       O = Organization Score   _____

Transfer the scores to the following graph by indicating the score on the vertical line. For dimension 5, plot the control score on the left of line 5 and plot the flexibility score on the right-hand side. Plot the scores for 6 and 7 in the same manner.

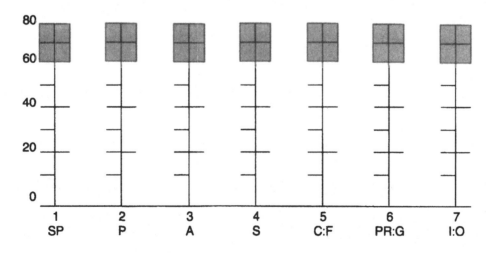

Interpretation

Scores that fall in the shaded area (60–80) indicate health. Other scores indicate "not sick" if it feels good or "sick" if it feels bad. In many organizations, the employees will score less than 60 yet not feel as if anything is wrong with the organization. This is exactly what "not sick" feels like. Weightings for the scores are quite harsh.

"Disagree" and "Strongly Disagree" responses will drop scores significantly. This is intentional in order to surface areas that "feel good" now but can lead to disaster in the future (for example the well-performing organization that depends 100 percent on a single customer). If the stretch score is below 60, individual questions should be examined to determine if there is too much or too little tension.

27 The Organizational Climate Questionnaire (OCQ)

Adrian Furnham and Leonard D. Goodstein

Summary

Although several organizational climate instruments are available, few have the formal psychometric characteristics necessary for practical use and few have been standardized on a broad international population. This 108-item questionnaire, which contains a seven-point Likert-type scale, has been developed on the basis of extensive pilot testing. Fourteen different climate dimensions are tapped by the instrument: role clarity, respect, communication, reward system, career development, planning and decision making, innovation, relationships, teamwork and support, quality of service, conflict management, commitment and morale, training and learning, and direction.

The instrument provides two scores for each of the fourteen dimensions: *agreement* (employee satisfaction with how things are done) and *importance* (the degree to which respondents believe that the item is a significant aspect of the way in which work is performed in the organization). These two scores provide a fourfold table of action steps: (1) *ignore*—low agreement and low importance—areas unworthy of further consideration; (2) *consider*—high agreement and low importance—unimportant things done well (often misguided efforts that could be reduced); (3) *celebrate*—agreement and importance both high—management should celebrate the fact that these things are being done well; and (4) *fix*—low agreement and high importance—things that need prompt attention.

Organizational climate is a topic of increasing interest in the management literature. The initial interest in organizational climate usually is attributed to Kurt Lewin (1951) and his field theory of motivation. Managers became more aware of the importance of organizational climate through the work of George Litwin and his colleagues (Litwin

& Stringer, 1968; Tagiuri & Litwin, 1968) and of Forehand and Von Gilmer (1964) and James and Jones (1964). The topic remains one of considerable theoretical and practical interest (Jackofsky & Slocum, 1988; Kozlowski & Doherty, 1989; La Follette, 1975; Payne, 1990; Qualls & Puto, 1989; Schneider, Brief, & Guzzo, 1996).

Organizational climate is defined as a psychological state strongly affected by organizational conditions, such as systems, structures, and managerial behavior. Organizational climate is a perception of how things are in the organizational environment, which is composed of a variety of elements or dimensions. As Tagiuri and Litwin point out (1968), there is no universal set of dimensions or properties for organizational climate. Rather, one must describe climate along different dimensions, depending on the kind of organization involved and which particular behaviors are studied. Tagiuri and Litwin consider climate to be a molar, synthetic, and changeable construct. Organizational climate is relatively malleable; changes in systems, structures, and managerial behavior impact the climate, while enduring group values and norms tend to stabilize the climate.

Although organizational climate is shaped by a variety of organizational factors, climate itself impacts both individual and group performance. Litwin and Stringer (1968) empirically demonstrate how different organizational climates impacted both individual and organizational performance in a variety of research settings. Schneider, Brief, and Guzzo (1996) provide similar evidence that organizational climate directly affects organizational change efforts.

Organizational climate can be understood as a moderator variable, serving as an indirect link between job satisfaction and productivity. Caused by organizational structures, systems, and managerial behavior, climate directly affects job satisfaction which, in turn, impacts both individual and organizational productivity.

Organizational culture refers to the relatively enduring set of values and norms that underlie a social system. An organization's culture provides a "meaning system" that provides members of a culture a way to attribute meaning and value to the endless variety of events that occur, both within and outside the organization. Climate is the more transitory of the two; changes in culture take time and considerable effort and typically must be preceded by systematic and consistent changes in the climate of the organization. Burke and Litwin (1989) provide a useful model of how climate and culture interact both with each other and with a myriad of other organizational variables.

A number of measures of organizational climate exist, including the trail-blazing instrument of Litwin and Stringer (1968), a fifty-item questionnaire that taps nine dimensions: structure, responsibility, reward, risk, warmth, support, standards, conflict, and identity. Other instruments include the Organization Description Questionnaire (House & Rizzo, 1972); the Survey of Organizations (SOO) (Taylor & Bowers, 1972); the Business Organization Climate Index (Payne & Pheysey, 1971), which is based on

Stern's (1967) Organizational Climate Index (developed to describe university climates); and many others. Two limitations that all these instruments share are poor internal reliability and weak validation data—inadequate psychometrics. Applied-research needs required the development of a new instrument, presented here, the Organizational Climate Questionnaire (OCQ).

Several considerations were paramount in developing the OCQ. First, the instrument should be comprehensive—covering all the salient dimensions of climate—but not overlong or redundant. Second, the instrument should be highly reliable, showing strong internal consistency. Third, the instrument should be valid, that is, have clear evidence that it does measure organizational climate. Four, the instrument should travel well, so that it can be used in different organizations and different cultures, permitting comparisons of the same or different companies internationally. Fifth, it should ask respondents to state the degree of importance of each element of the culture. This is not a feature of the preexisting instruments, which only tap the degree to which respondents agree or disagree that specific elements of organizational climate are present in their organization. Having a rating of importance, as well as agreement, is a way of assessing the validity of the questionnaire; items that measure climate should be regarded by respondents as of more than passing interest.

The OCQ is comprehensive and can be used as a before-and-after measure to evaluate the effectiveness of organizational change programs. Although the OCQ collects personal views and beliefs, these inevitably reflect the organizational structures and systems that affect them. As Payne (1990) points out, climate measures inevitably involve structural issues because "social structures are designed to produce certain patterns of behavior and belief" (p. 79). In recognition of this concern, items on the OCQ are phrased to minimize this problem. Nevertheless, users of the OCQ and other such instruments must keep this important issue in mind.

Development of the Questionnaire

A review of the organizational climate literature in both academic and applied publications led to the identification of a number of dimensions. Items tapping each of these dimensions were written. These items were then reviewed by several directors of human resources in a large number of both large and small organizations as well as by a number of management consultants and teachers of organizational behavior and management. On the basis of this feedback, many changes were made: some dimensions were added, others were removed, and still others were collapsed or subdivided. In the end, fourteen dimensions remained, with a total of 108 questions.

Field Testing

The final questionnaire was field tested on two samples, both employees of an American-owned international airline. High levels of reliability (internal consistency) were obtained as was evidence of validity.

The first sample consisted of 204 British subjects, 110 males and 94 females, performing a variety of jobs from secretarial to engineering. They ranged in age from their early twenties to their middle fifties; 43 held managerial positions, and 161 were nonmanagers. Length of service varied from new hire to over seventeen years, averaging twelve-plus years. These clearly were people who had experienced the organizational climate.

The second sample consisted of 345 employees, 177 males and 168 females, working in seven different European countries where the airline had operations. These employees, all of whom were fully fluent in English, held the same range of positions as those in the first sample, with a similar age range. There were 67 managers and 244 nonmanagers. The length of service of the employees in the second sample did not differ significantly from that of the first.

Copies of the questionnaire, with postage-paid envelopes, were distributed to all employees, with a request that they be returned to the consultants for analysis. Despite the guarantee of anonymity, the response rate varied as a function of organizational segment and country, ranging from 40 percent to 80 percent. All employees were provided with extensive group feedback about two months after the surveys were conducted.

The OCQ asks respondents to read each item carefully and to decide how much they agree with the statement, using a seven-point Likert rating scale ranging from "strongly agree" (7) to "strongly disagree" (1). After rating all 108 items, respondents are asked to reread each and then rate it on its importance to the success of the organization, again using a seven-point Likert scale ranging from "essential" (7) to "quite unimportant" (1). In the field tests, the instructions generated no questions, suggesting that they are self-explanatory.

Reliability

Cronbach Alpha coefficients—a measure of internal consistency—were calculated for each of the fourteen OCQ dimensions, separately for the two samples and for the "agreement" and "importance" ratings. For the British sample, the Alphas for the agreement ratings ranged from .60 to .86, with a mean of .77; for the European sample, the Alphas ranged from .63 to .85, with a mean of .78. For both samples, the lowest Alphas were for dimension I, teamwork and support, suggesting some caution in interpreting this dimension. For the importance ratings, the Alphas ranged from .70 to .88, with a mean of .78 for the British sample, and from .73 to .87, with a mean of .81, for the European sample. These results offer strong support for the internal consistency of both scales, with the possible exception of the agreement with dimension I, teamwork and support. Interestingly, the Alphas for the agreement and importance scales are virtually identical. Overall, these data indicate that the OCQ improves the reliability of climate measures, as the data represent a significant improvement over those reported for the other instruments.

Interrelation Among Measures

Because previous work has indicated that the dimensions of climate are correlated with one another, a number of inter-correlational matrices were calculated. As expected, most of the correlations were low and positive, ranging from .22 to .70, with an average of .51. This suggests that, although organizational climate has a common core, the fourteen dimensions are indeed rather distinct. Some dimensions, e.g., L, commitment and morale, significantly correlated with virtually all other dimensions (.34 to .69); the opposite is true for other dimensions, e.g., H, client relationships (.19 to .50).

It is important to note that the correlations between ratings of agreement and importance for the fourteen dimensions are quite low, ranging from -.08 to .24, with an average of .06. These results strongly suggest that respondents are quite able to understand the distinction between agreement and importance and to make independent ratings of the these two critical aspects of organizational climate.

Demographic Differences

Both the agreement and importance scores for each of the fourteen dimensions were compared with a variety of demographic variables, including gender, age, seniority, country, department, and job function. An inspection of the data led to three conclusions. First, there were no differences in importance ratings as a function of sex, age, or seniority, which indicates strong consensus about the relative importance of climate dimensions. Second, there were some statistically significant differences in agreement ratings as a function of gender, and there were some for age; however, they were few in number, and no clear patterns were discernable. (For gender, there were four differences found in the British sample and four in the European sample, but none of them were the same; for age, there were five differences for the British and two for the Europeans, with no overlap.) Third, the differences with seniority were systematic, substantial, and very similar for the two samples. The more senior the employee, the higher the rating they gave all fourteen of the climate dimensions. Clearly, the more senior the employee, the better the climate appears. The data do not allow an answer to the question of whether the more satisfied employees tend to stay or whether remaining on the job leads to greater satisfaction with the climate. Longitudinal research on this issue is necessary.

Validity

The validity of the OCQ was dealt with in two ways. First, the introduction of the importance ratings meant that it was possible to examine the average importance rating on the fourteen dimensions for the two samples. The mean on each of these dimensions exceeded 5.0 (on a seven-point scale) for both samples, indicating that, overall, the respondents believed the dimensions to be important. Since the correlations between the importance and agreement dimensions were negligible, importance was independent of how the respondents perceived the climate of the company.

Second, a set of statistical analyses (ANOVA) were computed between the various scores on the OCQ and the obtained demographic data. These analyses revealed negligible differences as a function of gender, age, job site, job function, and nationality, but striking differences as a function of seniority. These data strongly suggest that the employees had a shared perception of the organizational climate of the company, regardless of where they worked, both within and between countries, or what they did on the job. The one difference that was found, that seniority led to more positive ratings, was both predictable and expected (Jackofsky & Slocum, 1988). These two sets of findings provide strong preliminary evidence for the validity of the OCQ.

Using the OCQ

The OCQ should be duplicated and distributed to participants with a cover letter explaining how and why the instrument will be used. Anonymity should be assured, and the completed questionnaires should be returned to a neutral, external party.

The completed questionnaires should be tabulated so that mean scores are developed for agreement and importance on each of the 108 items. Results with the two samples described above suggest that average agreement scores of 4.0 or above can be considered high, and scores of 2.5 and below can be considered low. Average scores of 5.0 or above on importance can be considered high, and importance scores of 2.0 and below can be considered low. Users, however, should inspect their own array of scores to determine what are the appropriate cutting scores that differentiate the upper and lower quartile of each distribution of scores.

Once the items that yield high and low scores have been determined, the actual item numbers should be entered into the matrix that appears below:

	Importance	
Ratings	Low	High
Performance — High	Consider	Celebrate
Low	Ignore	Fix

The process identifies four different courses of action for the identified items, depending on where they fall in the matrix:

Fix: These are the items that are high in importance but for which performance is low. It is these items that warrant the most prompt attention, particularly those that have very low performance coupled with very high importance ratings.

Ignore: These are the items that involve behaviors that are neither very present nor very important. These items are of little importance to the organization. Efforts to change them are unlikely to pay off and are not worthy of attention.

Consider: These are items for which performance is high (i.e., positive) but of low importance. Employees see that certain things are being done well but are not very important. These behaviors need to be considered, as they may represent misguided efforts. Reducing attention to these may give management the time and resources to concentrate on those items that need to be fixed.

Celebrate: Where both performance and importance are high, management can celebrate that important issues are receiving the attention they deserve. It is important that these behaviors be maintained while the organization attempts to fix the problem areas.

It is also possible to use this process to subdivide the data for the total organization and to study the climate in different functions, locations, and departments. Further, summary scores can be developed for each of the fourteen dimensions. These scores can provide an overall picture of the organizational climate. The OCQ provides a valuable diagnostic tool for organizations to study how organizational climate is experienced and to develop action plans to fix what needs to be fixed.

References

Burke, W.W., & Litwin, G.L. (1989). A causal model of organizational performance. In J.W. Pfeiffer (Ed.), *The 1989 annual.* San Francisco: Pfeiffer.

Forehand, G., & Von Gilmer, B. (1964). Environmental variations in studies of organizational behavior. *Psychological Bulletin, 62,* 362–381.

House, R., & Rizzo, J. (1972). Toward a measure of organizational practices: Scale development and validation. *Journal of Applied Psychology, 56,* 388–396.

Jackofsky, E., & Slocum, J. (1988). A longitudinal study of climate. *Journal of Organizational Behavior, 9*, 319–334.

James, L., & Jones, A. (1974). Organizational climate: A review of theory and research. *Psychological Bulletin, 72*, 1096–1112.

Kozlowski, S., & Doherty, M. (1989). Integration of climate and leadership: Examination of a neglected topic. *Journal of Applied Psychology, 74*, 546–553.

La Follette, W. (1975). How is the climate in your organization? *Personnel Journal, 6*, 376–379.

Lewin, K. (1951). *Field theory in the social sciences.* New York: Harper.

Litwin, G.L., & Stringer, R. (1968). *Motivation and organizational climate.* Cambridge, MA: Harvard University Press.

Payne, R. (1990). Madness in our method: A comment on Jackofsky and Slocum's "A longitudinal study of climate." *Journal of Organizational Behavior, 11*, 77–80.

Payne, R., & Pheysey, D. (1971). C.G. Stern's organizational climate index. *Organizational Behavior and Human Performance, 18*, 45–62.

Qualls, W., & Puto, C. (1989). Organizational climate and decision framing. *Journal of Marketing Research, 26*, 179–192.

Schneider, B., Brief, A., & Guzzo, R. (1996). Creating a climate and culture for sustainable organizational change. *Organizational Dynamics, 24*(4), 7–19.

Stern, C.G. (1967). *People in context.* Syracuse, NY: Syracuse University Press.

Tagiuri, R., & Litwin, G.L. (Eds.). (1968). *Organizational climate: Explorations of a concept.* Cambridge, MA: Harvard University Press.

Taylor, J., & Bowers, D. (1972). *Survey of organizations: A machine-scored standardized questionnaire instrument.* Ann Arbor, MI: University of Michigan.

Originally published in *The 1997 Annual: Volume 2, Consulting.*

The Organizational Climate Questionnaire (OCQ)

Adrian Furnham and Leonard D. Goodstein

Instructions: Read each item carefully. Then rate how much you *agree* with each item, using the seven-point scale immediately below, recording your rating in the space provided to the left of the item.

- 7 = Strongly agree
- 6 = Agree
- 5 = Slightly agree
- 4 = Neither agree or disagree
- 3 = Slightly disagree
- 2 = Disagree
- 1 = Strongly disagree

After you have rated your agreement with each of the 108 items, then rate each item on *how important you think it is to your organization's success,* using the seven-point scale immediately below, using the space provided to the right of each item.

- 7 = Essential
- 6 = Important
- 5 = Somewhat important
- 4 = Neither important or unimportant
- 3 = Somewhat unimportant
- 2 = Unimportant
- 1 = Quite unimportant

Agreement Rating		Importance Rating
	A. Role Clarity	
_____	1. I have clear goals and objectives for my job.	_____
_____	2. I am clear about my priorities at work.	_____
_____	3. I know what my responsibilities are.	_____
_____	4. I know exactly what is expected of me.	_____
_____	5. I know what most people in the company do.	_____
_____	6. Work in the company makes the best use of people's experience.	_____

Agreement Rating			**Importance Rating**
_____	7.	I know what most people around me do.	_____
_____	8.	I know what most departments do.	_____
_____	9.	The company has good quality workers.	_____

B. Respect

_____	10.	I feel valued by my colleagues in the department.	_____
_____	11.	I value my colleagues in the department.	_____
_____	12.	I feel valued by my colleagues in the company as a whole.	_____
_____	13.	I value my colleagues in the company as a whole.	_____
_____	14.	My department respects other departments.	_____
_____	15.	My department is respected by other departments.	_____

C. Communication

_____	16.	I receive all the information I need to carry out my work.	_____
_____	17.	People in this company do not spend too much time on nonessentials.	_____
_____	18.	I am kept adequately informed about significant issues in the company as a whole.	_____
_____	19.	I am kept appropriately informed by the grapevine and other informal means.	_____
_____	20.	My department works well with other departments.	_____
_____	21.	My department receives all the information it needs to carry out its function well.	_____
_____	22.	My department is kept adequately informed about significant issues in the company as a whole.	_____
_____	23.	I understand clearly how I can contribute to the general goals of the company.	_____

Agreement Rating		Importance Rating

_____ 24. I have adequate opportunities to express my views in my department. _____

_____ 25. My colleagues are generally eager to discuss work matters with me. _____

_____ 26. In general, communication is effective in this company. _____

_____ 27. I work effectively because other employees communicate regularly with me. _____

D. Reward System

_____ 28. Good work is recognized appropriately. _____

_____ 29. I think my boss is too tolerant of poor performers. _____

_____ 30. Work that is not of the highest importance is dealt with appropriately. _____

_____ 31. In general, people are adequately rewarded in this company. _____

_____ 32. In my opinion, the company's pay scale is competitive with similar companies. _____

_____ 33. I receive an appropriate salary. _____

_____ 34. I receive appropriate benefits. _____

_____ 35. There is an appropriate difference between the pay awarded to good and bad performers. _____

_____ 36. I feel a strong sense of job satisfaction. _____

_____ 37. Virtually everyone in the company receives an appropriate salary. _____

E. Career Development

_____ 38. My work is regularly reviewed with my development in mind. _____

_____ 39. I understand how the appraisal system works. _____

Agreement Rating			Importance Rating
_____	40.	There is an adequate means of appraising my performance.	_____
_____	41.	I can develop my career within the company.	_____
_____	42.	I have an opportunity to see my appraisal report and discuss it with my supervisor.	_____
_____	43.	In general, there is an adequate system for career development in the company.	_____
_____	44.	There is the opportunity to work for this company until I retire.	_____
_____	45.	People are promoted fairly in this company.	_____
_____	46.	My current job makes full use of my talents.	_____
_____	47.	Career development is taken seriously in the company.	_____

F. Planning and Decision Making

Agreement Rating			Importance Rating
_____	48.	The work of departments is well-coordinated.	_____
_____	49.	People here rarely start new projects without deciding in advance how they will proceed.	_____
_____	50.	In general, planning is carried out appropriately in the company.	_____
_____	51.	I am allowed to participate sufficiently in significant decisions that affect my work.	_____
_____	52.	I am delegated work and authority appropriate to my expertise.	_____
_____	53.	I am made responsible only for those things I can influence.	_____
_____	54.	My supervisor likes me to consult him/her before take action.	_____
_____	55.	I have confidence in the process by which important decisions are made in the company.	_____

Agreement Rating			Importance Rating
_____	56.	I'm kept well enough informed for me to make decisions well.	_____
_____	57.	I feel that I have the right amount of authority over my subordinates.	_____
_____	58.	In general, delegation, responsibility, and decision making are all handled well in this company.	_____

G. Innovation

_____	59.	I am encouraged to be innovative in my work.	_____
_____	60.	My department is encouraged to innovate.	_____
_____	61.	The company plans adequately for the future.	_____
_____	62.	The company responds promptly to new commercial and technical innovations.	_____
_____	63.	Work methods here are quickly changed to meet new conditions.	_____

H. Relationships

_____	64.	Workers' needs are well met by this company.	_____
_____	65.	The needs of women and minority employees are greatly respected here.	_____
_____	66.	Virtually everybody in the company is aware of people's special needs.	_____
_____	67.	This company is flexible in order to meet people's needs.	_____
_____	68.	The ways in which women and minority employees are treated in this company is likely to attract other women and minority workers.	_____

I. Teamwork and Support

_____	69.	My department collaborates well with other departments.	_____

Agreement Rating		**Importance Rating**

_____ 70. By and large, people in my group pull their weight. _____

_____ 71. I am rarely put under undue work pressure by my colleagues. _____

_____ 72. People here generally support each other well. _____

_____ 73. I usually do not have to put in long hours to complete my work. _____

_____ 74. I do not feel that the pressure of work is excessive. _____

_____ 75. Work rarely piles up faster than I can complete it. _____

_____ 76. There is rarely too much work and too little time. _____

_____ 77. In general, this is a caring and cooperative organization. _____

J. Quality of Service

_____ 78. When it comes to the provision of our services, we do the best. _____

_____ 79. We are proud of the quality of service our company provides. _____

_____ 80. We are proud of the quality of service in our department. _____

_____ 81. This company has quality standards that are higher than those of its competitors. _____

K. Conflict Management

_____ 82. Conflicts are constructively/positively resolved in this company. _____

_____ 83. We are generally encouraged to resolve our conflicts quickly rather than let them simmer. _____

_____ 84. There are helpful ways of preventing conflicts from getting out of hand in the company. _____

_____ 85. There is little conflict between departments. _____

_____ 86. In general, conflict is managed well here. _____

Agreement Rating		Importance Rating
	L. Commitment and Morale	
_____	87. Motivation is kept at high levels in the company.	_____
_____	88. Morale is high in most departments.	_____
_____	89. Morale is high in my department.	_____
_____	90. My personal morale is high.	_____
_____	91. The commitment of the staff is high in this company.	_____
_____	92. The company solves the vast majority of its important problems.	_____
_____	93. I am proud to be part of this company.	_____
_____	94. I feel that I am a valued member of the company.	_____
_____	95. In general, people are strongly committed to the company.	_____
	M. Training and Learning	
_____	96. Most departments review their work on a regular basis.	_____
_____	97. There are appropriate orientation procedures in this company.	_____
_____	98. I have received the training I need to do a good job.	_____
_____	99. Most of us in this company are committed to helping one another learn from our work.	_____
_____	100. In general, this company learns as much as is practically possible from its activities.	_____
_____	101. The training I receive is of high quality.	_____
_____	102. I get the training I need to further develop my skills.	_____

Agreement   **Importance**
Rating   **Rating**

N. Direction

_____ 103. The future of this company has been well communicated to all employees.   _____

_____ 104. We all feel part of the company.   _____

_____ 105. I am clear about the part I can play in helping this company achieve its goals.   _____

_____ 106. The future objectives of the company are consistent with my personal objectives.   _____

_____ 107. The future of this company is bright.   _____

_____ 108. The vast majority of the employees share a clear understanding of where the company is going and what it is trying to achieve.   _____

The Organizational Climate
Questionnaire (OCQ) Profile Sheet

Instructions: Tabulate the mean (average) agreement score on each of the 108 items for all the completed questionnaires. Then calculate the mean (average) importance score for each of the 108 items. In general, mean agreement scores of 4.0 or above can be considered *high,* and mean agreement scores of 2.5 or below can be considered *low.* Mean importance scores of 5.0 or above can be considered *high,* and mean importance scores of 2.0 or below can be considered *low.* Users, however, should inspect their own array of scores and determine what are appropriate cutting scores that differentiate the upper (high) and lower (low) quartile of each distribution of scores.

Once the items that yielded high and low scores have been determined, the item numbers should be entered into the matrix that follows:

		Importance	
	Ratings	Low	High
Performance	High		
	Low		

The process identifies four different courses of action for the identified items, depending on where they fall in the matrix:

Fix (lower right): These are the items that are high in importance but for which there is agreement that performance is low. These items warrant the most prompt attention, particularly those that are very low in performance (agreement) and very high in importance.

Ignore (lower left): These are the items that are not being well done but also are not very important. They should be ignored. Efforts to change them are unlikely to pay off and are not worthy of attention.

Consider (upper left): These are the items for which performance (agreement) is high but they are perceived as being of low importance. Employees see these things as being done well but as not very important. These things should be considered, in that they may represent misguided efforts on the part of the organization, thus reducing the time and resources available for those items that do need to be fixed.

Celebrate (upper right): When both performance (agreement) and importance are high, management can celebrate that important issues are receiving the attention they deserve. It is important that these behaviors be maintained as the organization focuses on fixing the problem areas.

28 Strategic Leadership Styles Instrument[1]

Gaylord Reagan

Summary

Leadership styles are not static. They can be changed to serve the needs of an individual, group, or organization. A small investment of time and energy to identify and then to consider the significance of a strategic leadership style can return big dividends. Productive individuals, groups, and organizations that willingly make this investment and accept responsibility for shaping their own futures refuse to go on "doing what comes naturally."

The Instrument

Theoretical Framework

Consultant Lawrence M. Miller (1989) writes:

> All living things . . . exhibit patterns or cycles of development, moving from periods of vitality and growth, to periods of decay and disintegration. The pattern of business growth and decline—and the behavior of leaders—follows this same course. . . . It is natural for leaders in every stage to rely on responses they find most comfortable and to fail when they do not adopt innovative responses . . . . [The history] of corporations demonstrates this relationship, between the behavior of leaders and the cycle of growth and decline. (p. 1)

Based on this observation, Miller constructs "a theory of corporate life cycles," which explains the natural stages of evolution experienced by organizations and the people

---

[1]This instrument is based on *Barbarians to Bureaucrats: Corporate Life Cycle Strategies—Lessons from the Rise and Fall of Civilizations* by Lawrence M. Miller (1989). New York: Crain Publishers, Inc.

who lead them as they confront day-to-day challenges. Miller also identifies a series of leadership styles that dominate each of the six stages of organizational life.

In designing the Strategic Leadership Styles Instrument, the author separated Miller's Builder and Explorer styles, added the Synergist style, and sequenced the resulting styles as follows:

1. *Prophet:* A visionary who creates breakthroughs and has the human energy to pursue them. The Prophet adheres to a set of values and has high standards. In pursuing goals, the Prophet tends to rely on the support of a small circle of true believers.

2. *Barbarian:* A conqueror who commands the organization and pursues rapid growth. The Barbarian takes the Prophet's vision and begins implementing it in a direct, pragmatic, action-oriented, and forceful manner. Adherents of this style are self-confident and personally involved, and they demand complete loyalty from others.

3. *Builder:* A developer of structures required for successful organizational growth. Builders increase the efficiency of the Barbarian's early efforts. They focus on expansion, quantity, quality, and diversification, and they initiate the shift from command to collaboration.

4. *Explorer:* A developer of skills required for successful organizational growth. Explorers increase the efficiency of the Barbarian's early efforts. They focus on expansion, quantity, quality, diversification, and competition.

5. *Synergist:* A leader who helps the organization successfully balance expansion and the structures required to sustain that growth.

6. *Administrator:* An integrator of systems and structures to help organizations successfully shift their focus from expansion to safe and routine operation. The Administrator stresses perfecting financial and management practices but does not become involved with production operations.

7. *Bureaucrat:* An imposer of tight controls. Unlike the Prophet, the Bureaucrat has no interest in creativity; and unlike the Barbarian, no interest in growth. To improve performance the Bureaucrat relies on strategic planning, cost cutting, and acquiring (not inventing) new products or services.

8. *Aristocrat:* An alienated inheritor of others' results. Aristocrats do no work and produce only organizational disintegration. They also tend to be autocratic. They communicate poorly, tolerate warfare among internal fiefdoms, seek to acquire symbols of power, and avoid making decisions.

Reliability and Validity

The Strategic Leadership Styles Instrument is designed to be used as an action-research tool rather than as a rigorous data-gathering instrument. Applied in this manner, the instrument has demonstrated a high level of face validity when administered to groups ranging from executive managers to nonmanagement personnel.

Administration

The following suggestions will be helpful to the facilitator who administers the instrument:

1. Before respondents complete the instrument, discuss briefly the concept of organizational life cycles. Miller (1989) describes a process whereby all living things, including organizations, move through a series of developmental cycles. These cycles begin with vitality and growth but can end with decay and disintegration. Miller's model also describes the challenges confronted by leaders as their organizations pass through these cycles. Miller contends that by breaking this cyclical pattern, leaders can help their organizations grow and develop.

2. Distribute copies of the Strategic Leadership Styles Instrument and read the instructions aloud as the respondents follow.

3. Instruct the respondents to read all eight phrases in a group before assigning ranking numbers. Make sure they understand that assigning "8" indicates that the phrase most accurately describes the respondent's behavior or beliefs and that "1" indicates the least accurate phrase. Respondents should select their "8" phrases first, then their "1" phrases, then assign the intermediate rankings ("2" through "7") to the remaining phrases.

4. Ask respondents to wait to score the instrument until everyone has completed the rankings.

Scoring

Each respondent should be given a copy of the Strategic Leadership Styles Instrument Scoring Sheet. Each respondent should complete the scoring sheet by transferring the ranking numbers from the instrument to the corresponding blanks on the scoring sheet. Then the five numbers in each category should be totaled. Respondents should then proceed to their scoring grids. Each respondent circles the appropriate score below each of the eight styles. A line should then be drawn on the grid to connect the circled numbers.

Interpretation and Processing

The percentiles on the left side of the scoring grid offer respondents a means for assessing the strength of their relative preferences for the eight styles. The descriptors across the bottom of the grid help respondents assess the impact of their styles on their organizations; that is, they indicate whether their preferred styles fall into the command, collaboration, or disintegration area or some combination of those areas. Respondents should try to determine how their preferences match the current and future needs of their organizations.

It is sometimes useful for the facilitator to prepare a large copy of the scoring grid on newsprint. In this case, the facilitator polls the individual respondents and posts their individual scores for each of the eight styles, drawing a line to connect each individual's scores. The various patterns can form the basis for a discussion. It may also be useful to compute average scores for each of the eight styles and provide the respondents with group norms.

The facilitator distributes the Strategic Leadership Styles Interpretation Sheet, which gives brief descriptions of the eight leadership styles. It also offers suggestions to respondents whose supervisors exemplify the different styles and to supervisors whose employees demonstrate preferences for the various styles.

The facilitator divides the respondents into small groups (four or five members in each group). If intact work groups are present, they should constitute the small groups. The Strategic Leadership Styles Instrument Discussion Guide is distributed, and the facilitator instructs the groups to use the guide to stimulate discussion and then to prepare individual action plans.

Uses of the Instrument

The Strategic Leadership Styles Instrument is designed to accomplish the following objectives:

1. To help individual respondents to examine their relative preferences for strategic leadership styles associated with Miller's developmental cycles;

2. To help respondents to differentiate the impact of the eight leadership styles on their organizations;

3. To facilitate discussion among members of intact work groups about their collective style pattern;

4. To initiate discussions about the appropriateness of individual or group leadership style preferences within the context of an organization's short- and long-term viability; and

5. To stimulate planning designed to increase individual and group use of appropriate leadership styles.

References

Clifford, D.K, Jr. (1985). *The winning performance: How America's high-growth midsize companies succeed.* New York: Bantam.

Collins, E.G.C. (Ed.). (1983). *Executive success: Making it in management.* New York: John Wiley & Sons.

Hickman, C.R., & Silva, M.A. (1984). *Creating excellence: Managing corporate culture, strategy, and change in the new age.* New York: New American Library.

Kilmann, R.H. (1989). *Managing beyond the quick fix: A completely integrated program for creating and maintaining organizational success.* San Francisco: Jossey-Bass.

Kouzes, J.M., & Posner, B.Z. (1989). *The leadership challenge: How to get extraordinary things done in organizations.* San Francisco: Jossey-Bass.

Maccoby, M. (1988). *Why work: Leading the new generation.* New York: Simon & Schuster.

Manz, C.C., & Sims, H.P., Jr. (1989). *Super leadership: Leading others to lead themselves.* Englewood Cliffs, NJ: Prentice-Hall.

Miller, L.M. (1989). *Barbarians to bureaucrats: Corporate life cycle strategies-lessons from the rise and fall of civilizations.* New York: Clarkson N. Potter.

Steers, R.M. (1977). *Organizational effectiveness: A behavioral view.* Santa Monica, CA: Goodyear.

Tichy, N.M., & Devanna, M.A. (1986). *The transformational leader.* New York: John Wiley & Sons.

Waterman, R.H., Jr. (1987). *The renewal factor: How the best get and keep the competitive edge.* New York: Bantam.

Originally published in *The 1993 Annual: Developing Human Resources.*

Strategic Leadership Styles Instrument

Gaylord Reagan

Instructions: Within each of the five groups of statements (Group A through Group E), read all eight statements; then write the number "8" in the space preceding the statement that most accurately describes you, your behavior, or your beliefs with regard to your organization. Next write the number "1" in the space preceding the statement that least accurately describes you or your behavior or beliefs. Finally, use the numbers "2" through "7" to indicate the best intermediate rankings for the remaining statements. Then proceed to the next group and repeat the process. Rank all statements (leave none blank), and use each ranking number only once within each group of statements.

Group A

_____ 1. My ideas are long range and visionary.

_____ 2. My top priority is survival, and my mission is clear and urgent.

_____ 3. I enjoy actually making products or delivering services.

_____ 4. I am a convincing and enthusiastic communicator.

_____ 5. I seek to balance opposing forces.

_____ 6. Thus far, my career has taken place mainly in staff areas rather than production areas.

_____ 7. In meetings, my remarks review what has already happened.

_____ 8. I have not personally developed a new product or service in a long time.

Group B

_____ 9. I am willing to make sacrifices to see my ideas realized.

_____ 10. I do not like analyzing numbers and trends prior to acting.

_____ 11. I like measuring the results of my work.

_____ 12. Sometimes I feel as though I work for my customers or clients rather than for this organization.

_____ 13. I openly discuss the philosophy and values behind my decisions.

_____ 14. I consider myself to be an expert at procedures, processes, and systems.

_____ 15. I do not see my job as including the development of new products or services.

_____ 16. I concentrate on strategic planning rather than actually producing products or services.

Group C

_____ 17. I tend to withdraw for long periods to think about ideas.

_____ 18. I am in charge and am very comfortable making decisions.

_____ 19. I make decisions quickly, take action, and see the results.

_____ 20. I like to keep score and am competitive by nature.

_____ 21. I am hard on performance but soft on people.

_____ 22. Order, consistency, and smooth operations are high priorities for me.

_____ 23. Views of the organization are more important than those of its customers.

_____ 24. A person in my position has a right to enjoy exclusive perks.

Group D

_____ 25. Other people see me as being a bit different.

_____ 26. Other people say I am authoritarian and do not consult them on decisions.

_____ 27. I am not a visionary and do not devote a lot of time to dreaming.

_____ 28. I believe this organization should place a greater emphasis on expansion.

_____ 29. I stress teamwork and constant improvement of products and services.

_____ 30. I focus more on the present than on the future.

_____ 31. I believe that tighter controls will solve many of the organization's problems.

_____ 32. Only I and a few others really understand the organization's strategy.

Group E

_____ 33. I am neither well organized nor overly interested in details.

_____ 34. I am action oriented and do not like careful planning.

_____ 35. I do not like wasting time doing things through committees.

_____ 36. I feel that the organization gets bogged down in paperwork.

_____ 37. I believe in the value of organizational flexibility.

_____ 38. I place heavy emphasis on control and discipline.

_____ 39. I spend more time with staff personnel than production personnel.

_____ 40. Many times I cannot trust people to do what is right.

Strategic Leadership Styles Instrument Scoring Sheet

Instructions: Transfer the number you assigned to each statement in the Strategic Leadership Styles Instrument to the corresponding blank on this sheet. Then add the numbers under each category and write the total in the blank provided.

1. **Prophet Category:**

   Statement 1.   _____

   Statement 9.   _____

   Statement 17.   _____

   Statement 25.   _____

   Statement 33.   _____

   Total =   _____

This is your *Prophet* score. Prophets are visionaries who create breakthroughs and the human energy needed to propel organizations forward.

2. **Barbarian Category:**

   Statement 2.   _____

   Statement 10.   _____

   Statement 18.   _____

   Statement 26.   _____

   Statement 34.   _____

   Total =   _____

This is your *Barbarian* score. Barbarians are leaders who thrive on crisis and conquest, who command organizations during periods of rapid change.

3. **Builder Category:**

   Statement 3.   _____

   Statement 11.   _____

   Statement 19.   _____

Statement 27.   _____

Statement 35.   _____

Total =   _____

This is your *Builder* score. Builders are developers of the specialized structures required for successful change and growth. They initiate the shift from command to collaboration.

4. **Explorer Category:**

Statement 4.   _____

Statement 12.   _____

Statement 20.   _____

Statement 28.   _____

Statement 36.   _____

Total =   _____

This is your *Explorer* score. Explorers are developers of the specialized skills required for successful change and growth. They complete the shift from command to collaboration.

5. **Synergist Category:**

Statement 5.   _____

Statement 13.   _____

Statement 21.   _____

Statement 29.   _____

Statement 37.   _____

Total =   _____

This is your *Synergist* score. Synergists are leaders who maintain a balance and continue the forward motion of a growing and complex organization by unifying and appreciating the diverse contributions of Prophets, Barbarians, Builders, Explorers, and Administrators.

6. **Administrator Category:**

Statement 6. _____

Statement 14. _____

Statement 22. _____

Statement 30. _____

Statement 38. _____

Total = _____

This is your *Administrator* score. Administrators create integrating systems and structures, and they shift the organization's focus from expansion toward security.

7. **Bureaucrat Category:**

Statement 7. _____

Statement 15. _____

Statement 23. _____

Statement 31. _____

Statement 39. _____

Total = _____

This is your *Bureaucrat* score. Bureaucrats impose tight controls that inhibit the creativity of Prophets and the risk-taking habits of Barbarians.

8. **Aristocrat Category:**

Statement 8. _____

Statement 16. _____

Statement 24. _____

Statement 32. _____

Statement 40. _____

Total = _____

This is your *Aristocrat* score. Aristocrats are those who inherit success and are alienated from those who do the actual work. They often cause rebellion and disintegration.

Strategic Leadership Styles Instrument Scoring Grid

Instructions: On the grid below, circle your scores for each of the eight leadership styles shown at the top. Then connect the circles with a line to form a graph of your comparative style preferences.

Prophet	Barbarian	Builder	Explorer	Synergist	Administrator	Bureaucrat	Aristocrat
40	40	40	40	40	40	40	40
39	39	39	39	39	39	39	39
38	38	38	38	38	38	38	38
37	37	37	37	37	37	37	37
36	36	36	36	36	36	36	36
35	35	35	35	35	35	35	35
34	34	34	34	34	34	34	34
33	33	33	33	33	33	33	33
32	32	32	32	32	32	32	32
31	31	31	31	31	31	31	31
30	30	30	30	30	30	30	30
29	29	29	29	29	29	29	29
28	28	28	28	28	28	28	28
27	27	27	27	27	27	27	27
26	26	26	26	26	26	26	26
25	25	25	25	25	25	25	25
24	24	24	24	24	24	24	24
23	23	23	23	23	23	23	23
22	22	22	22	22	22	22	22
21	21	21	21	21	21	21	21
20	20	20	20	20	20	20	20
19	19	19	19	19	19	19	19
18	18	18	18	18	18	18	18
17	17	17	17	17	17	17	17
16	16	16	16	16	16	16	16
15	15	15	15	15	15	15	15
14	14	14	14	14	14	14	14
13	13	13	13	13	13	13	13
12	12	12	12	12	12	12	12
11	11	11	11	11	11	11	11
10	10	10	10	10	10	10	10
9	9	9	9	9	9	9	9
8	8	8	8	8	8	8	8
7	7	7	7	7	7	7	7
6	6	6	6	6	6	6	6

└─ Command ─┘   └─────── Collaboration ───────┘   └─ Disintegration ─┘

Strategic Leadership Styles
Instrument Interpretation Sheet

This interpretation sheet gives a brief description of the eight strategic leadership styles. Now that you have determined which leadership style or styles you generally use, you should be able to recognize the styles used by others in your organization. Under each description listed below, you will find some suggestions about how to work with both managers and subordinates who exhibit that style. You may find it useful to share the suggestions under your own leadership style with your manager and your subordinates.

1. *Prophets* are at their best when organizations are getting started or are entering a period of major restructuring and renewal. Prophets hold—and engender in others—a strong belief in new products and services. They have high standards and do not believe in the abilities of people outside their own small group. They make decisions by themselves; and although they may listen to others, they are not likely to make effective use of participative decision making. They tend to have many ideas that can confuse other people, because they have little use for either structure or systems. They tend to change on a whim.

If you work for a Prophet:

- Do not expect him or her to provide specific objectives or instructions. Ask to discuss your objectives and then write your own, based on your discussion.

- Do not expect him or her to follow up on details of your work. Discuss the larger goals toward which you are working.

- Seek out him or her for advice and ideas.

- Be tolerant of his or her latest ideas, even if they seem illogical and inconsistent. Do not confront Prophets about their apparent lack of direction; instead, ask leading questions that will help them shape their brainstorms into practical courses of action.

- Realize that Prophets do not expect you to share their characteristics. In fact, they often appreciate having people around who organize and accomplish their ideas for them.

If Prophets work for you:

- Recognize them for their creative abilities, and reinforce and encourage those talents. Do not demand that they be well organized or conform to standard procedures.

- Listen to them. They need to know that their visionary ideas are important to you. Let them know that within your organization there is room and opportunity for the implementation of their ideas.

- Help Prophets distinguish between their regular jobs and their creative activities. Prophets may need to justify their salaries with mundane work.

- Protect them from Bureaucrats. Remember that in mature organizations Prophets are all too often ignored or eliminated.

- Have patience. Prophets work not for this quarter's results, but for the impact they can have over the long run. Their view is very long range. Insisting on immediate results destroys their creativity.

2. *Barbarians* excel when organizations are struggling to survive or to broaden their base or attempting to diversify. Barbarians see themselves as being in life-or-death struggles to accomplish the Prophet's objectives. High control and direct action appeal to Barbarians, who like to personally lead the troops into battle. They want others to join the team or move out of the way. Barbarians prefer to establish a few simple systems and structures while stressing a high degree of task flexibility.

If you work for a Barbarian:

- Be prepared for action. Barbarians expect you to act quickly and not to engage in lengthy or detailed planning exercises. Go to the heart of the matter and take action.

- Do not expect to be involved in long meetings or consensus decision making. Barbarians will make the decisions and you will carry them out.

- When Barbarians ask for your input, be completely honest and direct. Do not beat around the bush or give lengthy explanations.

- Go to Barbarians; do not wait for them to come to you. If you want a Barbarian to give you a promotion or different job or if you have an idea, you must seek out him or her and discuss your needs in a straightforward manner.

If Barbarians work for you:

- Be sure that their assignments are appropriate for command and single-minded action.

- Leave no confusion about Barbarians' areas of responsibility and what you expect of them. If you do not establish limits for them, they may run down the road so fast that you will have trouble getting things back under control.

- Take advantage of Barbarians' greatest talents; working in turnaround situations and managing organization units that are growing fast and need quick decisions. If your organization is in decline and needs a revolution, Barbarians—if put in charge—can inject excitement and urgency and can renew the vision.

- Help Barbarians make the transition to the next management stage by encouraging them to involve their people more, to delegate more, and to consider longer-range factors and outcomes.

3. *Builders* are most valuable when successful organizations are confronted by many opportunities for growth and diversification. Builders believe in their organization's products and services. They are interested in the means of production, although they focus their energies on making those means more efficient. They are detail oriented and are concerned with short-range numbers. They initiate their organization's leadership shift from "command" to "collaboration."

If you work for a Builder:

- Offer clear, specific, written objectives. Builders hate surprises and believe that you should have a blueprint for your activities.

- Realize that Builders are not the world's greatest communicators. You can help them by initiating needed communication. Do not expect them to do so.

- Do not expect a great deal of positive reinforcement. Builders take satisfaction from the quality and volume of the products that go out the door and they expect that you will, too.

- Realize that Builders appreciate creativity within bounds. They want better ways to get things accomplished. Builders are more interested in "how" than in "what" or "why."

If Builders work for you:

- Be sure that your measurement and feedback are not based entirely on the short term. Builders already tend toward that direction. You need to help them learn to think in the long term.

- Help them to understand the need for involving people below them in decision making.

- Remember that Builders respond to rewards for improving processes ("how") more than for results ("what").

- Do not burden Builders with too much central-staff help. They like to run their own operations with the greatest possible degree of autonomy. Hold Builders accountable for improvements. Offer help but do not impose it.

4. *Explorers* are similar to Builders, but Explorers place their emphasis on increasing the efficiency of the skills used to produce the organization's products and services. They are the organizational members most in touch with customers. They are highly competitive and enjoy keeping score. Interpersonal relationships are important to Explorers, and they are enthusiastic and intuitive. On the other hand, they hate paperwork and do little or no managing.

If you work for an Explorer:

- You will win points for producing results and gaining new business—things an Explorer understands most.

- Tell him or her about your plans. Explorers want to know that their employees have high objectives and expectations.

- Do not tell him or her what cannot be done or what should have been done. Keep your level of enthusiasm high, and frame your comments in a positive context.

If Explorers work for you:

- Remember that they appear to need your approval more than others do, because they are "out in the wilderness" most of the time. When they come back to the office, they need your praise; let them have it.

- When they seem overly optimistic about their own performance, do not shoot them down. Instead, help them develop more realistic expectations and projections.

- When they want you to spend more time in the field with customers than you can afford, work with them on making the best use of their time.

- When they do not have the best relations with those whose support they need in production, help them understand the importance of these members of their team. Explorers often have difficulty along this line.

5. *Synergists* do not favor a single leadership style. Instead, they incorporate the different styles of leadership required to succeed throughout an organization's life cycle. Synergists seek social unity, balance, teamwork, and continuous improvement of products and services (total quality management). To achieve these goals and foster devel-

opment of the production process, they emphasize positive behavioral reinforcement by using symbols, participative decision making, interpersonal skills, and high levels of technical competence.

If you work for a Synergist:

- Be sensitive to his or her need to blend and balance the characteristics of Prophets, Barbarians, Builders, Explorers, and Administrators.

- Do not expect consistency. Demonstrate flexibility in your own approach to problems.

- Demonstrate ability in teamwork, participation, delegation, and constant improvement of products and services.

- Appreciate the Synergist's need for emphasizing both the material and spiritual aspects of the organization.

If Synergists work for you:

- Reward them for achieving a balance between the preservation of creativity and the need for order.

- Realize that Synergists may want you to increase the amount of time that you spend with personnel in production areas instead of staff areas. Although this is generally a good idea, there is still a need to take care of the administrative aspects of the organization.

6. *Administrators* contribute most when organizations have entered a secure stage, are financially successful, are developing broader markets for their products and services, and are developing more complex internal structure. Administrators believe in efficiency and in maximizing the financial side of the organization. To this end, they stress perfecting management-control systems and tend to take the organization's products and services for granted. They are not effective in dealing with people. They make decisions based on data and spend lots of time seeking "correct" answers. Under Administrators, line managers lose power while staff gains it.

If you work for an Administrator:

- Realize that he or she is more likely to reward you for conforming than for creating.

- Understand his or her essential need for administrative control and discipline. When that control becomes stifling, you must help the Administrator to recognize your situation.

- Recognize who you are and what your ambitions are. If you always work for an Administrator, you can develop the same characteristics, which may or may not be the best for you.

If Administrators work for you:

- Remember that Administrators are good at taking care of details; reward them for that. Also help them to see the larger picture, direction, trends, and reasons. Keep them in touch with what is important to the organization.

- Help Administrators to see their jobs as serving those whose performance should be enhanced by their systems: the Builders and Explorers.

7. *Bureaucrats* are most visible in diversified organizations, where primary products and services are viewed as being mature "cash cows." For Bureaucrats, growth occurs through acquiring younger organizations and cost cutting. Bureaucrats confront no problems that cannot be overcome through sound financial management and controls. They place little emphasis on creativity and are more concerned with numbers than people. Bureaucrats like written reports, and they cultivate the flow of paper. They seek to increase autocratic command throughout their organization, often resulting in overorganization, overspecialization, and a lack of trust between levels.

If you work for a Bureaucrat:

- Remember that the Bureaucrat tends to focus on performance that fits the system, without asking whether it is the right performance. Help him or hereby asking questions that will lead to a consideration of more creative responses.

- As a Bureaucrat needs order and conformity, do not make him or her nervous by being "weird." It is difficult to work for a nervous boss, particularly if you are the one who makes the boss nervous.

- Serve as a buffer for your subordinates. Manage them to produce creative responses without interference from your Bureaucratic supervisor. Do not make your own problem your subordinates' problem.

If Bureaucrats work for you:

- Remember that Bureaucrats are better in staff jobs, not line jobs.

- Make sure that they do not spin a web of stifling systems and structure around others.

- As Bureaucrats constantly complain about others who are violating the sanctity of their systems, learn to ask, "So what?"

- Reward them for developing and managing the most efficient administrative processes. Define "efficient" as meaning the fewest possible staff requiring the least amount of time from line managers.

8. *Aristocrats* are generally most evident when the organization's primary products and services are declining because of a lack of attention, investment, and creativity; when organizational components are being eliminated and divested; and when cash is desperately needed. At these times cynicism permeates all parts and levels of the organization. Aristocrats increasingly surround themselves with expensive tokens of their positions ("perks") and view their primary mission as preventing further organizational erosion. They have an aloof management style and do not like making decisions. If forced to do so, they generally use a highly autocratic style. Their organizations are burdened with excessive layers of management, poor communication, little clarity of mission, low motivation, lots of internal warfare, and ineffective formal structures.

If you work for an Aristocrat:

- Quit.

- If you cannot quit, consider the Aristocrat's objectives but create your own independently. Hope that the Aristocrat's successor appreciates your efforts.

If Aristocrats work for you:

- Encourage them to leave.

- If they will not quit, ask them specific questions about their efforts to improve the organization, the quality of their products and services, and their plans for creative developments. Let them know that their jobs depend on a change in behavior.

Strategic Leadership Styles
Instrument Discussion Guide

Use the following questions to stimulate a discussion in your group:

1. Which of the eight leadership styles do your scores on the Strategic Leadership Styles Instrument suggest that you are most likely to use? In what ways are these styles important to your work?

2. What are your key subordinates' leadership styles? What behaviors could you use to improve your relationships with those people? What behaviors should you avoid using?

3. What are your key peers' leadership styles? What behaviors could you use to improve your relationships with those people? What behaviors should you avoid using?

4. What is your supervisor's leadership style? What behaviors could you use to improve your relationship with that person? What behaviors should you avoid using?

5. What suggestions would you give to the following people about how to relate to you better and what to avoid doing?

    a. Your supervisor

    b. Your peers

    c. Your subordinates

6. Which leadership styles are most needed in your organization if it is to adapt successfully to its changing environment? Which behaviors may need to be de-emphasized?

7. To what extent do the behaviors of your leadership style fit with those most needed by your organization? In other words, is your leadership behavior part of the solution or part of the problem? In what ways?

29 Diagnosing Organizational Conflict–Management Climates

Bob Crosby and John J. Scherer

Summary

There are factors in the "climate" of any organization that can help or hinder third-party efforts to address and manage conflict. Although these climate conditions do not themselves create or resolve conflict, they can be powerful variables in determining how effective an intervention will be. When these factors are favorable, even a moderately skilled third-party consultant, working with moderately skilled participants, can be effective. When they are not favorable, even a highly skilled consultant, working with highly skilled individual participants, is likely to be frustrated.

Uses of the Instrument

Because these climate conditions are so critical, it may be impossible to help a given organization unless the climate conditions are first adjusted. For this reason, it is imperative that these factors be identified and analyzed in terms of the organization in question before a commitment is made to a method of third-party intervention. The Conflict-Management Climate Index presented here is useful in the following initial steps of the consulting process:

1. *Deciding Whether to Accept the Conflict-Management Assignment.* By collecting a sampling of opinion (using the instrument presented here) from organizational members regarding these climate factors, the consultant can generate very useful data to be used in establishing expectations with the client. Whether or not the consultant decides to accept the job, in sharing the instrument data with the client, he or she can provide a great deal of useful information to the organization. This information frequently will indicate a need for deeper, long-term organization development work, beyond the particular crisis intervention.

2. *Sensing Interviews.* The instrument can be used in the sensing-interview stage to collect and organize attitudes of organizational members prior to the introduction of any conflict-management intervention and is an excellent method of gathering data in a new or "cold" group.

3. *Diagnosis of Needs.* Once the data have been collected, the categories themselves become self-explanatory diagnostic guides, thus enabling the third-party consultant to focus on factors that need attention during initial discussions with key members of the client system.

4. *Training Intervention.* The instrument also can be used as a teaching device to introduce the concept of conflict-management climate to members of an organization in such a way that they can learn something about conflict management at the same time that they are diagnosing the organization. This is a very powerful combination of input and output and increases the value of both.

5. *OD Program.* Obviously, the particular crisis for which the third-party consultation is needed can be a symptom of larger, more profound issues in the organization. It is possible for the consultant to use the data generated by the instrument to explain to decision makers why these crises may continue unless something is done about the climate to make it more supportive of effective conflict management.

Thus, when asked to "come and do something on conflict management" for an organization, the consultant can use the instrument to elicit data that will help to determine the significant issues that need to be addressed and the best interventions by which to address them.

A Few Notes on Scoring

The lower the score on this instrument, the less likely conflict-management efforts will be to succeed, unless some climate-changing activities are first carried out. It generally would not be advisable to engage in conflict-resolution projects in organizations in which average scores on this instrument were lower than thirty, without clear and strong commitment on the part of top management to attempt to understand and change the climate factors operating within the organization.

Many of the items on the instrument are derived from Richard Walton's work in the field (Walton & Dutton, 1969), and the authors recommend his book as a companion piece to the use of this measurement device.

Reference

Walton, R.L., & Dutton. J.M. (1969). The management of interdepartmental conflict: A model and review. *Administrative Science Quarterly, 14*, 73–84.

Originally published in *The 1981 Annual Handbook for Faciliatators, Trainers, and Consultants.*

Conflict–Management Climate Index

Bob Crosby and John J. Scherer

Your Name: _____

Organizational Unit Assessed: _____

Instructions: The purpose of this index is to permit you to assess your organization with regard to its conflict-management climate. On each of the following rating scales, indicate how you see your organization as it actually is right now, not how you think it should be or how you believe others would see it. Circle the number that indicates your sense of where the organization is on each dimension of the Conflict-Management Climate Index.

1. Balance of Power

1	2	3	4	5	6

   Power is massed either
   at the top or at the bottom
   of the organization.

   Power is distributed
   evenly and appropriately
   throughout the organization.

2. Expression of Feelings

1	2	3	4	5	6

   Expressing strong feelings
   is costly and not accepted.

   Expressing strong feelings
   is valued and easy to do.

3. Conflict-Management Procedures

1	2	3	4	5	6

   There are no clear conflict-
   resolution procedures
   that many people use.

   Everyone knows about, and
   many people use, a conflict-
   resolution procedure.

4. Attitudes Toward Open Disagreement

1	2	3	4	5	6

   People here do not openly
   disagree very much. "Getting
   along to get along" is the motto.

   People feel free to disagree
   openly on important issues
   without fear of consequences.

5. Use of Third Parties

1	2	3	4	5	6

No one here uses
third parties to help
resolve conflicts.

Third parties are used
frequently to help
resolve conflicts.

6. Power of Third Parties

1	2	3	4	5	6

Third parties are
usually superiors in
the organization.

Third parties are
always people of equal
or lower rank.

7. Neutrality of Third Parties

1	2	3	4	5	6

Third parties are
never neutral, but
serve as advocates
for a certain outcome.

Third parties are always
neutral as to substantive
issues and conflict-
resolution methods used.

8. Your Leader's Conflict-Resolution Style

1	2	3	4	5	6

The leader does not deal
openly with conflict but
works behind the scenes
to resolve it.

The leader confronts
conflicts directly and
works openly with those
involved to resolve them.

9. How Your Leader Receives Negative Feedback

1	2	3	4	5	6

The leader is defensive
and/or closed and seeks
vengeance on those who
criticize him/her.

The leader receives
criticism easily and even
seeks it as an opportunity
to grow and learn.

10. Follow-Up

1	2	3	4	5	6

Agreements always fall
through the cracks;
the same problems must
be solved again and again.

Accountability is
built into every
conflict-resolution
agreement.

11. Feedback Procedures

1	2	3	4	5	6

No effort is made to
solicit and understand
reactions to decisions.

Feedback channels
for soliciting reactions
to all major decisions
are known and used.

12. Communication Skills

1	2	3	4	5	6

Few, if any, people possess
basic communication skills
or at least do not practice them.

Everyone in the organi-
zation possesses and uses
good communication skills.

13. Track Record

1	2	3	4	5	6

Very few, if any, successful
conflict-resolution experiences have occurred in the
recent past.

Many stories are available of
successful conflict resolution
experiences in the recent past.

Conflict–Management Climate Index
Scoring and Interpretation Sheet

Instructions: To arrive at your overall Conflict-Management Climate Index, total the ratings that you assigned to the thirteen separate scales. The highest possible score is 78 and the lowest is 13.

Then compare your score with the following conflict-resolution readiness index range.

Index Range	Indication
60–78	Ready to work on conflict with little or no work on climate.
31–59	Possible with some commitment to work on climate.
13–30	Very risky without unanimous commitment to work on climate issues.

Find your lowest ratings and study the following descriptions or interpretations of the thirteen separate dimensions. As you read the descriptions, think about what specifically might be done (or changed) in other activities described, in order to increase your organization's readiness to manage conflict more effectively.

Climate Factors Affecting
Conflict Management in Organizations

1. *Balance of Power.* Simply stated, is power spread appropriately and realistically throughout the organization, or is it massed at either the top or bottom levels? The ideal is not for everyone to have equal power, but for a general feeling among most members of the organization that they have sufficient influence over the most significant aspects of their work lives. This may include the power to obtain a fair hearing and a realistic response from someone in authority.

This factor is important because it reflects the extent to which communication is likely to be distorted. Research evidence (Mulder, 1960; Solomon, 1960) seems to indicate that when two people perceive their levels of power to be different, they are likely to mistrust any communication that takes place between them. People who perceive themselves as being less powerful than the other party tend to perceive communication from that person as being manipulative or condescending. Those who see themselves as being more powerful experience communication from the less powerful as being devious or manipulative. Ironically, these more powerful persons also perceive collaborative behavior as an indication of weakness on the part of those whom they see as less powerful. These perceptions can make effective conflict resolution all but impossible.

In organizations in which power is massed at the top, it is extremely difficult for the third-party consultant to achieve the neutrality necessary to be effective without appearing to "take sides" with someone at the less powerful end of the organization. In organizations in which power is massed at the bottom, there is frequently so much disrespect for—or even disgust with—top management that it is difficult for the third-party consultant to encourage the more powerful workers to respect or even attend to any collaborative actions that top management may take.

Because an appropriate balance of power within an organization is relatively rare, the third party and the participants involved in the conflict will need to collaboratively seek ways to create a balance of power within the limits of the conflict-resolution episode. The two persons or parties in conflict must understand that the more powerful member is to lend some skills or status to the weaker member for the duration of the intervention and also that the more powerful member may not use that power to punish the subordinate, regardless of the outcome of the conflict-resolution process.

The purpose of this balancing of power between the two parties in conflict is to facilitate the process of discussion and mediation, not to create institutional equals. When the consultation process is finished, the parties involved will return to their usual roles (e.g., the boss will still be the boss and the subordinate will still be the subordinate), and it is essential that everyone involved understand this.

2. *Expression of Feelings.* Conflict management is much easier to achieve in a climate in which open expression of members' feelings—especially when those feelings are strongly negative—is valued. In many organizations, a person will find the expression of strong emotions a costly experience and may be either subtly or openly ostracized or reprimanded for such conduct.

It is easy to see why conflict management is more likely to be successful in a climate in which feelings are valued. In the first phases of any conflict resolution, the expression of feelings on the part of the parties in conflict is extremely important; in fact, the success of the next two steps in the conflict-resolution process, differentiation and integration, is directly related to whether complete and honest communication of emotions has occurred.

3. *Conflict-Management Procedures.* In organizations in which there are clearly defined procedures or channels for conflict resolution, the work of a third-party consultant— whether internal or external to the organization—is obviously much easier. In a system in which there are no clearly defined ways to resolve conflict and in which people do not know what to expect or what to do when conflict arises, the work of the third party is made extremely difficult. When people feel safe in using conflict-resolution procedures, they are more likely to have confidence in the outcome. Conversely, if people

in conflict feel that they are fumbling through it, they are not likely to put much faith in either the acceptability or the reliability of the procedure they have chosen to use. If top management seriously wants to support effective conflict management, then specific procedures must be made known to and accepted by members at all levels of the organization.

4. *Attitudes Toward Open Disagreements.* This factor reflects the attitudes of members of the organization about open disagreement over proposals or issues. Janis' book, *Victims of Groupthink* (1972), vividly describes decision making at the national level and shows how unexpressed reservations can lead to apparently consensual policy decisions with which few of the decision makers are in actual agreement.

In a system in which open disagreement about issues is viewed as disloyalty or insubordination, effective third-party conflict mediation is almost impossible. In such organizations, participants may pretend to agree or to work out differences of opinion without actually allowing themselves to find out how very far apart their views or positions are. Where differentiation is insufficient, integration or long-term conflict resolution is simply not possible.

Organizations that require creativity, such as advertising firms and think tanks, solicit and encourage differences of opinion because the discussions that result make possible insights and solutions that might never be thought of in a climate in which everyone agreed with the first idea suggested.

5. *Use of Third Parties.* A healthy conflict-management climate will encourage people to ask others in the system to act as third-party consultants when conflicts arise. Most organizations have, at least tacitly, established the norm that conflict must be kept "in the family" and not "aired in public." This makes the work of the person who is called in to help extremely difficult. One of the first concerns, then, is to confront the reservations and resistances that people have about working with a third party. In particular, it should be made clear that the use of a third party is not a sign of weakness on the part of the persons in conflict. This can be reinforced merely by using third parties effectively.

6. *Power of Third Parties.* As Walton (1969) points out, it is difficult for someone with hierarchical power to be an effective third party. When subordinates feel that anything they say may later be used against them, it is highly likely that crucial information will not be shared during the confrontation episode. However, these data frequently are the keys to unlocking conflict situations. In a healthy conflict-management climate, a supervisor would encourage subordinates to seek third-party help from someone on their level or even lower in the organization. It is hard for most managers to do this, because they want to be seen as helpful and caring and also because they want to have some control over potentially explosive situations.

7. *Neutrality of Third Parties.* Third parties from within the organization must remain neutral about substantive outcomes, or at least suppress their biases sufficiently to be

effective. When third parties are unskilled and biased about what the outcome of the conflict-resolution process should be, one of the people in conflict is likely to feel "ganged up on," and the person who wins may feel a little bit guilty. Such a "conflict-resolution" process may result in a defusing of the issue but also is likely to cause the significant feelings of the people involved to be submerged, to increase mistrust of management, and to make participants feel a lack of ownership of a solution that they may feel was imposed on them.

In addition, past experience with a biased third party makes it difficult for members of the organization to trust the process in the future. Therefore, the third-party consultant may need to spend a great deal of time and energy in establishing his or her neutrality and credibility with the persons involved.

8. *Your Leader's Conflict-Resolution Style.* The senior people in any organization greatly influence the climate. Walton and Dutton (1969) showed that it is possible to characterize a general style of conflict management in an organization and that the people at the top of the organization set that style by their own behavior. In their "contingency theory" of organization, Lawrence and Lorsch (1969) found that not only could they characterize the way people generally approached conflict but also showed that one particular approach, "confrontation," worked best and was associated with organizational effectiveness. In other words, these researcher/consultants found that the way people approach conflict is not a contingency factor but that there was a "best way": confrontation. It means that conflict is openly recognized when it occurs and the people involved proceed to deal directly with the conflict problem. It means *not* running away, *not* trying to "smooth over" real and important differences, *not* immediately trying to "split the difference," and *not* fighting a win-lose battle. Confrontation implies creative problem solving. When superiors confront conflicts, they are seen as strong and their behavior encourages others to deal directly with problems of conflict.

The model set by those in positions of power has effects on all sorts of subordinate behavior but especially influences how subordinates relate to one another when dealing with conflicts. Even when the supervisor's nonconfrontational style is successfully applied to solve a particular problem, it still weakens the organization's problem-solving and conflict-resolution capacity.

9. *How Your Leader Receives Negative Feedback.* In a conflict situation, there is always great potential for the expression of negative feelings. It is rare, even when conflict is dealt with very effectively, for no negative comments to have been expressed. Such comments may concern the content of the conflict ("I think your approach is unlikely to increase sales as much as mine would") or may relate to how the parties feel on an emotional level ("Your attempts to dominate our ad campaigns are signs of your inflated ego"). Grossly ineffective handling of conflict is associated with an inability to deal with either of these types of negative feedback. Even worse is when the leader or person in authority acts against the other party at a later date, thus gaining "vengeance."

This kind of behavior is associated with other nonfunctional ways of handling conflict, such as not letting the other party know one's true feelings, never letting disagreements get out in the open, and trying to deal with conflict "behind the scenes." The type of persons using these strategies avoid showing anger or any expression at all. Their motto might be "Don't get mad, get even."

No healthy person actually enjoys negative feedback, on either the content or interpersonal level, but effective leaders are able to ignore or fail to respond in kind to personal attacks—while often openly recognizing the feelings expressed by the other party—and are likely to look at content criticism more objectively, to determine whether there really is a sound point to the critique. At our best, we may relatively quickly transfer the kernel of truth in a negative item into positive corrective action. A conflict, for example, over the leader's daily "checkup" on a delegated project might lead this leader to examine and correct the tendency to avoid really "letting go" of an important project.

10. *Follow-Up.* Follow-up procedures and methods of accountability should be built into all conflict-resolution decisions. It is possible to have a highly successful confrontation dialogue between two people, to have them reach intelligent resolutions, and then to have those resolutions disappear between the "cracks" in the relationship or in the organization's busy work schedule. It is extremely important that the last step in the conflict-resolution process specifies:

1. What has been decided?

2. What will be done next and by whom?

3. What checks are there on how and whether it is carried out?

4. What are the expected consequences?

5. How, when, and by whom will the effectiveness of these decisions be evaluated?

When people are used to making sure that planned outcomes are implemented, the work of a third party is made much easier. In places in which problems historically must be solved over and over again, it is necessary for the third-party consultant to train people in follow-up procedures before beginning the conflict dialogue.

11. *Feedback Procedures.* When communication channels exist that can be used to surface disagreements and conflicts, it is obvious that more conflict resolution is possible. This does not guarantee that conflicts are generally resolved effectively, but it is a prerequisite if such effective action is to take place at all. There are many ways by which members of an organization can be given access to and encouraged to use channels for

feedback. When upper levels or those in power are responsive to feedback that indicates conflict problems, then even relatively simple "mechanistic" feedback approaches, such as the old-fashioned suggestion box, can work well. Some years ago, New England Bell Telephone Company instituted an "open lines" program whereby people at lower levels could raise problems by telephoning an anonymous executive ombudsman, with their own anonymity guaranteed. Certainly a situation in which the parties feel free to directly approach one another is the most preferable, but when the overall climate cannot support this, a mechanistic approach, if used responsively, can be a useful and productive step toward changing the conflict-management climate.

One commonly touted action that may not work is the so-called "open-door policy." When lower-level or less powerful individuals actually try to use the open door, they find that the policy exists in name but not in fact—that it is not so easy to get through the door at all, and that, when it is done, the response is overtly or covertly a turn off or "cooling out" process. Furthermore, one is observed in the process and the person using the open door may be labeled as a telltale, a spy, someone who cannot handle his or her own problems, etc. All of these negative factors are characteristic of organizations with poor conflict-management climates, and would not, of course, apply to organizations with good climates, open expression of feelings and disagreements, clear procedures for dealing with conflict, effective use of third parties, etc. As it happens, it is the former type of organization in which a so-called open-door policy is likely to succeed, while such a policy would be laughably unnecessary in the latter type of organization.

12. *Communication Skills.* If people in an organization are accustomed to blaming, criticizing, projecting their own issues onto other people, and scapegoating; if they do not know how to make "I" statements (Gordon, 1970) that clearly communicate how to listen to their own positions; or if they cannot listen empathically (Milnes & Bertcher, 1980; Rogers & Farson, 1977) without forming opinions, then it probably will be necessary to prepare them for confrontation dialogues by training them in communicating and listening in high-stress situations. Of course, it is easier to do conflict-management work in an organization in which the members have received training in communication skills. In that case, the role of the third party is to help the participants to stay "on track" and to coach them in maintaining open communication.

13. *Track Record.* How successful were past attempts to resolve conflict equitably? If there is a history of people being reprimanded or fired for initiating an attempt to resolve a conflict, the third-party consultation may be perceived as "window dressing." On the other hand, nothing succeeds like success, and nothing helps the conflict-management consultant more than an organization with a history of useful and lasting involvement in dealing with conflict.

Conclusion

The conflict-management climate in organizations functions a great deal like the weather. When the weather is good, you can do many more things more enjoyably than when the weather is bad. In the middle of a storm, you can still do many of the things you could do when the weather was good, but it requires much more energy, and the risks of failure are increased. We believe that one of the major skill focuses of consultants to organizations trying to learn to manage conflict is in collaborating with top management in seeking innovative ways to change the weather in the organizations along the dimensions charted in the Conflict-Management Climate Index.

References

Gordon, T. (1970). *Parent effectiveness training.* New York: Wyden.

Harriman, B. (1974). Up and down the communications ladder. *Harvard Business Review, 52,*(5), 143–151.

Janis, J.L. (1972). *Victims of groupthink.* Boston: Houghton-Mifflin.

Lawrence, P.R., & Lorsch, J.W. (1969). *Organization and environment.* Homewood, IL: Richard Irwin.

Milnes, J., & Bertcher, H. (1980). *Communicating empathy.* San Diego, CA: Pfeiffer & Company.

Mulder, M. (1960). The power variable in communication experiments. *Human Relations, 13,* 241–256.

Rogers, C.R., & Farson, R.E. (1977). Active listening. In R.C. Huseman, C.M. Logue, & D.L. Freshley (Eds.), *Readings in interpersonal and organizational communication* (3rd. ed.). Boston: Holbrook Press.

Solomon, L. (1960). The influence of some types of power relationships and game strategies upon the development of interpersonal trust. *Journal of Abnormal and Social Psychology, 61,* 223–230.

Walton, R.L., & Dutton, J.M. (1969). The management of interdepartmental conflict: A model and review. *Administrative Science Quarterly, 14,* 73–84.

30 Why Don't They Do What I Want?
Understanding Employee Motivation

Janet Winchester-Silbaugh

Summary

Managers are often puzzled and frustrated when employees and others are not motivated to support their projects or new ways of doing things. Why won't employees use the new software correctly? Why can't they be more helpful to customers? Why won't suppliers deliver on time? Why doesn't the boss support me in this project? Regretfully, organizations often unwittingly reward people for doing the wrong things. This survey is designed to diagnose when reward structures are causing problems.

Organizations usually think of rewards in terms of money: salary, incentives, and bonuses. But research shows that people are rewarded by many other things: pride in their work, challenging projects, the support of their peers, future opportunities, family needs, and personal goals. Understanding these complex and often conflicting rewards can help managers change their reward systems so that the system supports their goals.

People are motivated by many things, among them pay, job satisfaction, opportunity, pride in their work, family needs, and status. We often think of rewards in terms of money: how much salary people earn or whether they receive a bonus or not. It's easy to forget that people are motivated by a complex set of needs that varies by the person. Of course, needs such as pay and job security are essential for people to come to work. Motivation, however, which encourages people to contribute their reputations, their creativity, and their special talents, comes from intrinsic personal values. Top-performing employees reported in a recent survey (Avery, undated) that they were motivated by a good reputation, important work, appreciation by others, and the opportunity to prove their capability to others much more than they were motivated by money.

Employee motivation is complex, and employers can give conflicting messages. For example, a manager who emphasizes "personal accountability" may send employees powerful messages about the benefit of taking no risks, avoiding blame, or even covering up mistakes. Workplaces that focus on "productivity" may find that employees don't take time to serve customers. Employees who enjoy face-to-face interactions with customers may resist communicating with customers by email and form letters, even when those forms of communication would be very effective. Employees who are proud of their work may not want to use a new procedure because they have not mastered it and see it as reducing their quality of work.

The Why Don't They Do What I Want? Understanding Employee Motivation Survey can be used to help managers analyze the rewards and the costs that each employee associates with a situation. Managers who understand what employees are responding to can find ways to send the right message and reward what they intend to reward.

Theory Behind the Survey

People do things based on their own perceptions of what is important. This survey was based on a combination of many people's ideas on the topic. Goldratt's (1997) work on system constraints showed that there are often conflicting and overlapping constraints on a system. People react to those constraints in equally conflicting and confusing ways. Maslow, through his Hierarchy of Needs (Maslow, 1943), illustrated that not all needs are equal and that needs change over time. Vroom and Yetton (1976) pointed out that a decision will be successful only if it is accepted by the people who must implement it. Kohn (1993) combined many studies to caution that rewards can actually serve as punishment and carry subtle negative messages for people. Ryan and Oestrich's (1998) research into the causes of fear in the workplace showed that people are afraid of the loss of credibility and the damage to their relationships with their bosses if they speak out about common management practices. Vroom, in his Expectancy Theory (Vroom, 1964), said that people are motivated to action if they expect that their actions will be successful and that those actions will lead to a useful result. The Harvard Center for Risk Analysis (Slovic, 2001) found that the perception of a risk, such as for an airplane crash, can be even more important than the statistical chance of an event happening in motivating people to action. I have found the survey presented here to be a useful tool in understanding why people act in seemingly irrational ways.

Administering and Scoring the Survey

This survey can be used as a personal or group tool to diagnose how the reward structure of an organization influences resistance to change. Some suggestions for administration with a group follow.

1. Adjust the survey to fit your particular situation. Add or delete reward categories.

2. Give a copy to each group member to fill out and go over the directions with them for clarity.

3. Write the decision, project, or issue you want the respondents to analyze on the "Issue" line.

4. Tell them to determine who the key stakeholders are for this project or issue. (A stakeholder is any person, organization, or group that has a vested interest in the project or its outcome.) Stakeholders include employees, other departments, government regulators, the public, customers, and suppliers, to name a few. They should write the names of the four or five key stakeholders on the lines titled "Stakeholder."

5. For each stakeholder, they are to write several comments about how this stakeholder may think about this issue. The key is for a respondent to look at the issue from the stakeholder's point of view, to see it through his or her eyes. For instance, if your town is putting in a new intersection with an interstate highway, the local gathering place café may lose business, but may also receive a payment for some of its land (financial and resource impacts). It may lose its status as a neighborhood meeting place (social cost), but the town's payment for part of the property may also give the owner the resources to become an upscale restaurant (professional opportunities). The owner may be both sad to lose the daily conversation with neighbors and excited about the possibilities for a new restaurant (psychological costs and rewards). As you can see, rewards and costs are often contradictory. Include what is most important in your particular situation.

6. Now they should rate each element from the point of view of each stakeholder, using the scale of 1 to 5 shown on the survey. Explain that it is realistic for the same stakeholder to have both positive and negative impacts from the same project. If they don't know what the impacts will be, tell them to put a question mark in the blank.

7. When they have finished, they are to add the scores for each stakeholder. The lower the score, the less support the project has and the greater the risks.

A careful review of the risks that respondents point out will give you practical ideas for reducing problems. Look for important costs for a particular key stakeholder that are not critical for the success of a project.

Interpreting the Results

The following ranges of scores can be used to interpret stakeholders' support for the issue in question.

18–20 Active Supporters/True Believers

- This stakeholder will probably go out of his or her way to support the project, put his or her reputation on the line for the project, convince others that the project is a good one, and come up with creative ways to solve problems. This person may even be willing to make significant sacrifices to make this project work.

- The project is good for these stakeholders. Try to make sure they aren't disillusioned. Don't forget this group, but active supporters alone will not be able to carry the whole project. Support other groups as well.

- These stakeholders are important because they can be the true believers who carry the project through tough times. On the other hand, they can flip to being active resisters if they lose faith in the project's value. The wrath of a spurned supporter can be strong.

14–17 Passive Supporters

- These stakeholders think the project is okay, but may not go out of their way to make it happen. Expect them to work faithfully as long as it doesn't involve a heavy cost of some kind, such as putting their reputation on the line, working overtime during holidays, moving, or taking a different job.

- This group will contribute creative energy, if you can hold these people's support. Make sure they have intrinsic rewards, such as working on an excellent team, training in new areas, pride in doing a good job, or the possibility of job growth.

- These stakeholders are important because they can seed support in other groups. They have more credibility with resistant groups than the true believers do.

8–13   Neutral Stakeholders, Waiting for Results

- These stakeholders start out neutral, but will swing to the negative or positive side, depending on how the project goes and on how other people respond.

- Think about what is rewarding to these stakeholders and build up those aspects of the job. Many stakeholders are in this category, so you must pay a lot of attention to them. Their wait-and-see attitude makes them easy to overlook.

- Neutral stakeholders are important because there are so many of them. Most successful projects require that you gain the support of a significant number of neutral stakeholders.

4–7   Quiet Nonsupporters

- These stakeholders may do a good job at their work, but will notice all the problems with the project and will probably talk about these problems with other people.

- These people have something important to lose. If their reactions are emotional, see what social or psychological costs there may be. Often, employees who are good at their current jobs, but who don't think they will get enough training or time to learn a new system, will be in this category. They will lose a lot of professional pride if they cannot become proficient at the new system. They may become supporters if you can show them a safe path to do well with the project.

- These stakeholders, along with the neutral stakeholders, are the most important swing votes. If you can win their honest support, your chances of success rise dramatically.

0–3   Active Nonsupporters

- There are two kinds of active nonsupporters, vocal and quiet. Both can be just as damaging to a project.

- Develop a clear strategy for dealing with active nonsupporters and then follow it to the end. Listen to their arguments because they may tell you about weaknesses in the project that no one else will. It is important to understand what drives their vehemence against the project. Sometimes you can turn the tide by persuading active nonsupporters; other times, the best you can do is to limit their impact.

- These stakeholders are important because they can polarize opinion and poison the well for many other stakeholders. They will work hard to make their points known, so do not take their actions personally.

To get an overall sense of the resistance you'll face, add the stakeholders' scores together. The lower the score, the less support the project has and the greater the risks. A careful review of the risks will give you practical ideas for reducing problems. Look for important costs for a particular key stakeholder that are not critical for the success of a project.

Ways to Increase Support for a Project

You can decrease the resistance to a project by changing the reward system, especially the subtle costs and rewards. Here are some helpful methods:

1. Make sure managers and employees both have roughly equal benefits and costs. For instance, if employees must work mandatory overtime to complete a project, so must managers. If managers receive rewards for meeting goals, build in commensurate rewards for employees. This balance makes the decision makers more aware of the full cost of their decisions and increases the employees' perceptions of fairness.

2. Ensure that the people who make decisions feel the effects if things go wrong. If they don't feel the pain, they may not notice the changes that need to be made.

3. Rely on many different types of rewards, including a mix of financial rewards (such as an incentive check), social rewards (a celebration to say thanks for a job well done), psychological rewards (noticing employees who are making special contributions), and opportunities for growth (such as training and assigning interesting work). Simply receiving additional money to change a system or do things in a different way is almost never enough.

4. Choose rewards that are important for each stakeholder based on his or her life goals. Treating all people identically will not be treating them fairly, because their goals are different. For some people, overtime to earn extra money for a down payment on a house is important. For others, well-timed time off so they can attend their child's basketball game is critical. For still others, learning that new computer tool is really interesting. The most effective rewards are things that people want, and this will be different for each person.

5. Practice what you preach. Nothing kills support for a project faster than telling your employees to take risks, then criticizing them when things go wrong. If you say you'll get back to someone by Tuesday, make sure you do it. If you say training will be available, make it happen. If you ask for honest feedback, be prepared to hear the bad as well as the good.

References

Avery, D. (undated). *Recruiting for retention* [On-line]. Available: www.shrm.org/whitepapers/documents/default.asp?page=61264.asp [last accessed May 17, 2001]

Goldratt, E. (1997). *Critical chain.* Great Barrington, MA: North River Press.

Kohn, A. (1993). *Punished by rewards.* Boston, MA: Houghton Mifflin.

Maslow, A. (1943, July). A theory of human motivation. *Psychological Review, 50,* 370–396.

Ryan, K., & Oestrich, D. (1998). *Driving fear out of the workplace.* San Francisco, CA: Jossey-Bass.

Slovic, P. (2001). *The perception of risk.* London, England: Earthscan.

Vroom, V. (1964). *Work and motivation.* New York: John Wiley & Sons.

Vroom, V., & Yetton, P. (1976). *Leadership and decision making.* Pittsburgh, PA: University of Pittsburgh Press.

Originally published in *The 2002 Annual: Volume 1, Training.*

Understanding Employee Motivation Survey

Janet Winchester-Silbaugh

Instructions: Use this survey each time you wish to assess the likelihood of encountering employee or other stakeholder resistance to a new process or project or a change in a present process. Write in the name of the issue to be analyzed and then each key stakeholder on the lines provided. Attempt to describe the person's motivation for supporting (rewards) or resisting (costs) the issue. Then rate the impact that the issue would have on each, using the scale from 1 to 5 shown below.

| 1 = strong negative impact; this project is big and bad | 2 = mild but noticeable project is annoying, but not worth putting a lot of energy into blocking | 3 = no noticeable impact; "who cares" OR has an equal negative and positive impact | 4 = mild, noticeable positive impact; a pretty good idea, but not worth too much effort | 5 = strong positive impact; worth going out on a limb for |

Issue to Be Analyzed: _____

Stakeholder Rewards or Costs from the Stakeholder's Point of View

Stakeholder 1: _____

Rewards or Costs in Finances or Resources

Social Rewards or Costs

Impact on Professional Growth or Opportunities

Personal Psychological Rewards and Costs

Total Points for Stakeholder 1: _____

1 = strong negative impact; this project is big and bad	2 = mild but noticeable project is annoying, but not worth putting a lot of energy into blocking	3 = no noticeable impact; "who cares" OR has an equal negative and positive impact	4 = mild, noticeable positive impact; a pretty good idea, but not worth too much effort	5 = strong positive impact; worth going out on a limb for

Stakeholder 2: _____

Rewards or Costs in Finances and Resources

Social Rewards or Costs

Impact on Professional Growth or Opportunities

Personal Psychological Rewards and Costs

Total Points for Stakeholder 2: _____

Stakeholder 3: _____

Rewards or Costs in Finances and Resources

Social Rewards or Costs

Impact on Professional Growth or Opportunities

Personal Psychological Rewards and Costs

Total Points for Stakeholder 3: _____

1 = strong negative impact; this project is big and bad	2 = mild but noticeable project is annoying, but not worth putting a lot of energy into blocking	3 = no noticeable impact; "who cares" OR has an equal negative and positive impact	4 = mild, noticeable positive impact; a pretty good idea, but not worth too much effort	5 = strong positive impact; worth going out on a limb for

Stakeholder 4: _____

Rewards or Costs in Finances and Resources

Social Rewards or Costs

Impact on Professional Growth or Opportunities

Personal Psychological Rewards and Costs

Total Points for Stakeholder 4: _____

Stakeholder 5: _____

Rewards or Costs in Finances and Resources

Social Rewards or Costs

Impact on Professional Growth or Opportunities

Personal Psychological Rewards and Costs

Total Points for Stakeholder 5: _____

Sample Completed Understanding
Employee Motivation Survey

Issue to Be Analyzed: *My customer service representatives don't work very hard to make customers happy. They won't make the extra effort; they just follow the book and no more.*

Stakeholder 1: <u>*My department director*</u>

Rewards or Costs in Resources
My year-end bonus looks good. I'm under budget so far. (5 points)

Social Rewards or Costs
I hate to look stupid in front of the other directors.
My family gets mad when I bring work home at night. (2 points)

Impact on Professional Growth or Opportunities
I've heard the vice president is thinking of leaving. I'll be in good position if my statistics look good. (4 points)

Personal Psychological Rewards and Costs
We do good work in my department. (3 points)

Total Points: <u>14</u>

Stakeholder 2: <u>*The customer service representatives*</u>

Rewards or Costs in Resources
There's never enough help. I'm too tired to care about overtime. Why work too hard? The pay is the same either way. You'd think they'd get a computer system that worked right. (2 points)

Social Rewards or Costs
My kids hate it when I have to work overtime. The last time I went out on a limb for a customer, the boss told me I was wrong. I had to call the customer back and explain why we couldn't do what I said we could do. I felt pretty stupid. (1 point)

Impact on Professional Growth or Opportunities
Mary was promoted last year. I wonder why she was instead of me? The education budget is all used up—again. (2 points)

Personal Psychological Rewards and Costs
I hate to tell customers it will be next week before I can get something done. I was proud of my work before this new director came. (1 point)

Total Points: <u>6</u>

31 Motivational Analysis of Organizations—Climate (MAO-C)

Udai Pareek

Summary

Most organizations have a structure (division of work into units and establishment of linkages among units) and systems (specific ways of managing the major functions of the organization, such as finance, production, marketing, personnel, information, and the relationship with the external environment). Most also have norms (accepted patterns of behavior), values, and traditions; and these three elements constitute the organizational culture. The main actors in the organization are its top leaders; they and the other employees have their own individual needs in addition to those of the organization. All of these organizational components—structure, systems, culture, leader behavior, and psychological needs of employees—interact with one another and create what can be called organizational climate.

Organizational climate can only be discussed in terms of how it is perceived or felt by organizational members. Consequently, a climate may be perceived as hostile or supportive, as conducive to achievement or stifling, and so on. Hellriegel and Slocum (1974, p. 225)—adapting the concepts suggested by Beer (1971); Campbell, Dunnette, Lawler, and Weick (1970); Dachler (1973); and Schneider (1973)—defined organizational climate as "a set of attributes which can be perceived about a particular organization and/or its subsystems, and that may be induced from the way that organization and/or its subsystems deal with their members and environment."

Although most authors have used organizational climate as a descriptive concept, some have used it for classifying organizations into categories. For example, Burns and Stalker (1961) describe organic versus mechanical climates, whereas Likert (1967) proposes four types of climates: exploitative, benevolent, consultative, and participative. Such frameworks generally use described categories. Only one framework, proposed by Litwin and Stringer (1968), emphasizes the effect of organizational climate on the motivation of its members. In a rigorous study Litwin and Stringer simulated three different climates (each fostering, respectively, achievement, affiliation, and power motives) and monitored the effects of these climates on productivity. Because climate affects people's motivation (for example, Likert, 1967), a framework based on motivation seems to be quite relevant in studying organizational climate.

Six Motives Connected with Organizational Climate

Six motives are particularly appropriate in developing a framework that facilitates analysis of the connection between organizational climate and motivation:[1]

1. *Achievement.* This motive is characterized by concern for excellence, competition in terms of the standards set by others or by oneself, the setting of challenging goals for oneself, awareness of the obstacles that might be encountered in attempting to achieve these goals, and persistence in trying alternative paths to one's goals.

2. *Affiliation.* Affiliation is characterized by a concern for establishing and maintaining close, personal relationships; an emphasis on friendship; and a tendency to express one's emotions.

3. *Expert influence.* This motive is characterized by a concern for making an impact on others, a desire to make people do what one thinks is right, and an urge to change situations and to develop people.

4. *Control.* Control is characterized by a concern for orderliness, a desire to be and stay informed, an urge to monitor events and to take corrective action when needed, and a need to display personal power.

5. *Extension.* Extension is characterized by a concern for others; an interest in superordinate goals; and an urge to be relevant and useful to large groups, including society.

6. *Dependency.* This motive is characterized by a desire for the assistance of others in developing oneself, a need to check with significant others (those who are more knowledgeable or have higher status, experts, close associates, and so on), a tendency to submit ideas or proposals for approval, and an urge to maintain a relationship based on the other person's approval.

Twelve Dimensions of Organizational Climate

Likert (1967) proposed six dimensions of organizational climate (leadership, motivation, communication, decisions, goals, and control), while Litwin and Stringer (1968) proposed seven dimensions (conformity, responsibility, standards, rewards, organiza-

---

[1] These six motives are also discussed in "Motivational Analysis of Organizations—Behavior (MAO-B)" by U. Pareek, 1986, in J.W. Pfeiffer & L.D. Goodstein (Eds.), *The 1986 Annual* (pp. 121-133), San Francisco: Pfeiffer.

tional clarity, warmth and support, and leadership). A review of their studies and those of others indicates that twelve processes or dimensions of organizational climate relate specifically to motivation:

1. *Orientation.* The dominant orientation of an organization is the main concern of its members, and this dimension is an important determinant of climate. If the dominant orientation or concern is to adhere to established rules, the climate will be characterized by control; on the other hand, if the orientation is to excel, the climate will be characterized by achievement.

2. *Interpersonal relationships.* An organization's interpersonal-relations processes are reflected in the way in which informal groups are formed, and these processes affect climate. For example, if groups are formed for the purpose of protecting their own interests, cliques may develop and a climate of control may result; similarly, if people tend to develop informal relationships with their supervisors, a climate of dependency may result.

3. *Supervision.* Supervisory practices contribute significantly to climate. If supervisors focus on helping their subordinates to improve personal skills and chances of advancement, a climate characterized by the extension motive may result; if supervisors are more concerned with maintaining good relations with their subordinates, a climate characterized by the affiliation motive may result.

4. *Problem management.* Problems can be seen as challenges or as irritants. They can be solved by the supervisor or jointly by the supervisor and the subordinate(s) concerned, or they can be referred to a higher level. These different perspectives and ways of handling problems contribute to the creation of an organization's climate.

5. *Management of mistakes.* Supervisors' attitudes toward subordinate mistakes develop the organizational orientation, which is generally one of annoyance or concern or tolerance. An organization's approach to mistakes influences the climate.

6. *Conflict management.* Conflicts may be seen as embarrassing annoyances to be covered up or as problems to be solved. The process of dealing with conflicts has as significant an effect on climate as that of handling problems or mistakes.

7. *Communication.* Communication, another important determinant of climate, is concerned with the flow of information: its direction (top-down, bottom-up, horizontal), its dispersement (selectively or to everyone concerned), its mode (formal or informal), and its type (instructions or feedback on the state of affairs).

8. *Decision making.* An organization's approach to decision making can be focused on maintaining good relations or on achieving results. In addition, the issue of who makes decisions is important: people high in the hierarchy, experts, or those involved in the matters about which decisions are made. These elements of decision making are relevant to the establishment of a particular climate.

9. *Trust.* The degree of trust or its absence among various members and groups in the organization affects climate. The issue of who is trusted by management and to what degree is also relevant.

10. *Management of rewards.* Rewards reinforce specific behaviors, thereby arousing and sustaining specific motives. Consequently, what is rewarded in an organization influences the motivational climate.

11. *Risk taking.* How people respond to risks and whose help is sought in situations involving risk are important determinants of climate.

12. *Innovation and change.* Who initiates change, how change and innovation are perceived, and how change is implemented are all critical in establishing climate.

The way in which these twelve dimensions of climate operate in an organization indicates the underlying motive of top management and the principal motive that is likely to be generated and sustained within the organization's population. When the twelve dimensions are combined with the six motives discussed previously, a matrix is formed that can be useful in diagnosing the motivational climate of an organization.

The Instrument

The Motivational Analysis of Organizations—Climate (MAO-C) instrument was developed to study organizational climate, specifically with regard to motivation. The instrument employs the twelve dimensions of organizational climate and the six motives previously described. It consists of twelve categories, each of which includes six statements; each of the twelve categories corresponds to one of the twelve climatic dimensions, and each of the six statements represents one of the six motives. Respondents work individually to rank order the six statements within each separate category according to their perceptions of how much each statement is like the situation in their organization (or unit, branch, division, or department within the organization).

Scoring and Interpretation

Usually organizational-climate instruments require respondents to rate organizational processes, and respondents tend to assign ratings in the middle of the scale provided for this purpose. The MAO-C, in contrast, is based on rankings so that the respondent cannot escape in the "golden middle."

After completing the instrument, the respondent refers to the scoring key to discover which motives are indicated by his or her responses and then transfers rankings of motives to the matrix. Then the respondent adds the numbers in each vertical column of the matrix and writes the totals in the appropriate blanks; each of these totals is the score for the related motive or motivational climate. These scores can range from 12 to 72. Next the respondent refers to the conversion table, locates the total for each motive, and writes the corresponding MAO-C index number in the blank provided. The indexes can range from 0 to 100. The following formula was used to arrive at the index for each motive:

$$\text{Index} = \frac{(S-12) \times 100}{60}$$

For each horizontal row on the matrix representing a dimension of organizational climate, the dominant motive (the one with the highest number in the row) and the backup motive (the one with the next-highest number) are noted in the blanks provided (see the two vertical columns on the extreme right of the matrix). The dominant and backup columns are helpful in diagnosing and in planning action to improve the motivational climate of the organization or unit involved. Finally, the respondent determines which motives appear most often in the dominant and backup columns and writes these motives in the blanks provided for *overall dominant motive* and *overall backup motive.*

An organization may total all respondents' index numbers for each motive and then average the numbers for an overall organizational index of each; or the total of the numbers in each vertical column of the individual respondents' matrices can be added and averaged and the index number written, using the conversion table. The advantage of the index is to show the relative strength of the climate with regard to the motives; the cutoff point is 50. If the index number for a particular dimension is greater than 50, the climate is relatively strong in that dimension; if the index number is less than 50, the climate is relatively weak in that dimension. The index also helps in comparing organizations or units within an organization.

Reliability

Retest reliability of the MAO-C has been reported by Sen (1982) and by Surti (1982).

Validity

Validity studies have not been done for the MAO-C. However, indirect evidence of the instrument's validity has been provided as a result of other research on organizational climate. Research on organizational climate as an independent measure and measures of organizational effectiveness share enough in common to warrant some generalizations. Hellriegel and Slocum (1974) have summarized these generalizations as a significant relationship between climate and both job satisfaction and performance.

Deci (1980) suggested three different kinds of environments as being associated with three different attributional patterns. A "responsive and informational" environment (in the terms of the MAO-C, one that is characterized by achievement and expert influence) has been linked with internality; a "controlling and demanding" environment (one characterized by control and dependency) has been linked with externality; and a "nonresponsive and capricious" environment has been linked with "impersonality."

Organizational environments and climate seem to influence the development of internality. Baumgartel, Rajan, and Newman (1985), using four indices of organizational environment (freedom-growth, human relations, performance pressure, and personal benefit) found clear evidence of the influence of organizational environments on locus of control. They concluded that internality could be developed by creating educational and work environments characterized by freedom to set personal performance goals, opportunity for personal growth, and opportunity to influence important events or conditions.

A regression analysis of data from 320 professional women, using role efficacy as a variable, showed that of the fourteen variables that finally emerged in the regression, organizational climate alone explained about 34 percent of the variance, thereby exhibiting a great effect on role efficacy (Surti, 1982).

Theoretically (see, for example, Litwin & Stringer, 1968), one might predict a negative relationship between organizational effectiveness and climates characterized by affiliation, dependence, and control. Litwin and Stringer (1968) found that an authoritarian climate (referred to in the MAO-C as a "control" climate) produced low job satisfaction and low performance. A climate characterized by achievement, extension, and expert influence might be assumed to be related to higher job satisfaction and performance. Using Litwin and Stringer's instrument, Cawsey (reported in Hellriegel & Slocum, 1974) found higher job satisfaction among insurance personnel who perceived the motivational climate as one of achievement.

One study reported on the administration of the MAO-C to 392 executives of a manufacturing firm (Khanna, 1986). Each executive was instructed to complete the MAO-C by evaluating the climate or culture of his or her specific unit or department (as opposed to that of the entire organization). Correlations were noted between the six perceived motives or motivational climates and measures of organizational effectiveness (consisting of consensus, legitimization, the need for independence, self-control, job involvement, innovation, organizational commitment, organizational attachment, and job satisfaction). The climates were also correlated with total satisfaction, that is, satisfaction with work and with the organization as a whole. No significant correlation was found between the climates and the need for independence, self-control, and innovation. With regard to job involvement, the only positive correlation significant at the .05 level was with an achievement climate.

In the same study there were positive correlations (significant at the .01 level) between five other aspects of organizational effectiveness (organizational commitment, organizational attachment, job satisfaction, total satisfaction, and total effectiveness) and an achievement climate, and there was a negative correlation between these five aspects and a control climate. An extension climate correlated positively with organizational commitment at the .05 level and with job satisfaction, total satisfaction, and total effectiveness at the .01 level. A dependence climate showed no relationship with any measure. An affiliation climate had a negative correlation with job satisfaction at the .05 level and with total satisfaction and total effectiveness at the .01 level. A climate perceived as characterized by expert influence had only one positive correlation (at the .05 level) with organizational attachment. All correlations were in the predicted direction, although more correlations were expected with climates characterized by dependence and expert influence.

Negative correlations might be predicted between role stress and climates perceived as characterized by achievement, extension, and expert influence; and positive correlations might be predicted between role stress and climates characterized by affiliation, dependence, and control. Khanna (1986) correlated climate scores with ten aspects of role stress and total role stress (as reported in Pareek, 1983). Specific correlations between role stress and the various climates were as follows:

- No significant correlation with a climate characterized by expert influence;

- Two positive correlations with an affiliation climate (role erosion at the .01 level and personal inadequacy at the .05 level);

- One positive correlation with a dependency climate (role stagnation at the .01 level);

- Six negative correlations with an extension climate (at the .05 level for inter-role distance, role overload, and role isolation, and at the .01 level for role-expectation conflict, self-role distance, resource inadequacy, and total role stress);

- Negative correlations with an achievement climate at the .01 level for all aspects of role stress except interrole distance and personal inadequacy; and

- Positive correlations with a control climate at the .01 level for all aspects of role stress except personal inadequacy.

Similar results were reported by Sen (1982) and Surti (1982). All of these results were in the predicted directions.

In summary, organizational climate has an enormous influence on organizational effectiveness, role efficacy, and role stress. An achievement climate seems to contribute to effectiveness, satisfaction, and a sense of internality; a climate characterized by expert influence seems to contribute to organizational attachment; and a climate characterized by extension seems to contribute to organizational commitment. All of these climates foster relatively low levels of role stress. A control climate seems to lower role efficacy, job satisfaction, organizational commitment, organizational attachment, and total effectiveness and to foster relatively high levels of role stress. An affiliation climate tends to lower both satisfaction and effectiveness and increase role erosion and feelings of personal inadequacy.

Effectiveness Profiles

The completed matrix provides scores for all six motives tested by the MAO-C. The highest of these scores represents the perceived dominant motive within an organization. The general connections between dominant motives and particular types of organizations are shown in Figure 1.

A combination of an organization's highest or "dominant" score and its second-highest or "backup" score results in a basic characterization of that organization's climate. When the six motives are combined in patterns of dominant and secondary or backup styles, thirty organizational profiles are possible. Brief descriptions of these thirty profiles are provided in the following paragraphs. In each description the first motive noted represents the organization's dominant motive, and the second represents its secondary or backup motive. Some of these profiles are based on studies that have been conducted; others need to be studied to validate the concept. In general, climates dominated by achievement, expert power, and extension are conducive to the achievement of results, whereas climates dominated by control, dependency, and affiliation retard the achievement of results.

Motive	Type of Organization
Achievement	Industrial and business organizations
Expert influence	University departments and scientific organizations
Control	Bureaucracies such as governmental departments and agencies
Dependency	Traditional or autocratic organizations
Extension	Community-service organizations
Affiliation	Clubs

Figure 1. Connections Between Dominant Motives and Types of Organizations

1. *Achievement-Expert Influence.* Employees are involved in and highly stimulated by challenging tasks, and the specialists within the organization dominate in determining these tasks. The organization rewards specialization.

2. *Achievement-Control.* Most employees are involved in challenging tasks, but they face a lot of constraints attributable to rigid procedures and an inflexible hierarchy.

3. *Achievement-Dependency.* In spite of an emphasis on high achievement that is shared by most employees, there is a tendency to postpone critical decisions for the approval of a higher authority. The organization discourages making such decisions without approval from a higher level, resulting in a sense of frustration.

4. *Achievement-Extension.* Employees work on challenging tasks and devote equal attention to the social relevance of these tasks. The organization has a highly developed sense of social responsibility as well as a strong sense of its responsibility to fulfill employee needs.

5. *Achievement-Affiliation.* While employees work on challenging goals, they also form strong groups based on common interests or other factors. The organization pays a lot of attention to maintaining good relations among these cliques.

6. *Expert Influence-Achievement.* The organization places a high value on specialization. The specialists influence most decisions, and they emphasize high work quality and unique contributions.

7. *Expert Influence-Control.* The organization is controlled by experts who employ cumbersome procedures. The result is generally a lack of job satisfaction and low to moderate (rather than high) output.

8. *Expert Influence-Dependency.* The organization has a rigid hierarchy dominated by experts. Decisions are made only at the upper levels of the hierarchy, and bright employees are highly dissatisfied.

9. *Expert Influence-Extension.* Specialists play the major roles in the organization, working in a planned way on socially relevant matters. The organization pays attention to the employees' needs and welfare.

10. *Expert Influence-Affiliation.* Although the organization is dominated by experts, strong groups are formed on the basis of common interests or other factors. Because primary attention is placed on maintaining a friendly climate, results usually suffer.

11. *Control-Achievement.* The organization is bureaucratic, is run in accordance with detailed procedures, and has a clear hierarchy. Quality of work is emphasized, but most employees with an achievement orientation feel frustrated. This climate is sometimes found in public-sector organizations.

12. *Control-Expert Influence.* The organization is a bureaucracy in which specialists' opinions are valued but rules are treated as more important.

13. *Control-Dependency.* A bureaucracy and a rigid hierarchy dominate the organization. Because actions are generally referred to levels above for approval, decisions are

usually delayed. It is more important to follow rules and regulations than to achieve results. The senior employees protect those subordinates who do not make any procedural mistakes. Most government offices function in this way.

14. *Control-Extension.* Although the organization is hierarchical, it emphasizes social concern and attends to the needs and welfare of its employees.

15. *Control-Affiliation.* The organization is hierarchical but places more emphasis on good relations among employees than on results. Informal groups based on relationships are seen as important. Some voluntary organizations are of this type.

16. *Dependency-Achievement.* Respect for those in positions of power is emphasized, and so is achievement. Freedom is granted to employees, with the exception that key decisions are controlled by those in power. Many family-owned organizations have such a climate.

17. *Dependency-Expert Influence.* The organization has a hierarchy, with decisions made by those at higher levels. Experts play an important role in the various aspects of organizational life.

18. *Dependency-Control.* The organization has clear-cut channels of communication and is controlled by a few people who ultimately make all decisions.

19. *Dependency-Extension.* A few people dominate and control the organization and demand respect from all other members. However, they take care of the members' needs; and the organization works in socially relevant areas.

20. *Dependency-Affiliation.* The top managers control the organization and employ their own "in-group" members, who are extremely loyal to these managers.

21. *Extension-Achievement.* The organization strives to be relevant to society and emphasizes the achievement of results. People are selected for their competence and are given freedom in doing their work.

22. *Extension-Expert Influence.* Social consciousness is emphasized by the organization, and experts influence all major decisions.

23. *Extension-Control.* The organization's goals have to do with serving a larger cause; but the structure is bureaucratic, with rules and regulations that are to be followed strictly.

24. *Extension-Dependency.* The business of the organization is community service (for example, education, health, or development). Emphasis is placed on conformity to the policies laid down by the top person or team, to whom all final decisions are referred.

25. *Extension-Affiliation.* The organization's business is community service, and members with similar backgrounds (ideology, specialization, and so on) form strong linkages with one another.

26. *Affiliation-Achievement.* The organization places great importance on relationships and draws people with similar backgrounds. Although the organization values achievement of results and excellence in performance, rewards are given mainly

on the basis of an employee's relationship with the person or persons who are in a position to give such rewards.

27. *Affiliation-Expert Influence.* The organization consists mainly of experts, emphasizes good relations, and either employs people of similar backgrounds or has cliques based on common links.

28. *Affiliation-Control.* Although the organization is concerned with maintaining good relations among members, its form is bureaucratic. (For example, a club with strict rules and procedures might be in this category.)

29. *Affiliation-Dependency.* The organization values the maintenance of friendly relations among members, and one or two people make most decisions. Employees are rewarded on the basis of their closeness to the top person(s).

30. *Affiliation-Extension.* The organization's main goal is to maintain good relations among members, and its work involves socially relevant issues. (The Lions Club and similar organizations might be in this category.)

Use of the Instrument

The MAO-C can be used to diagnose organizational climate from the standpoint of motivation. The focus of the instrument can be perceptions of the overall organizational climate or of individual units, divisions, branches, or departments within the organization. After the instrument has been administered, the respondents may individually use a rating scale to evaluate the operating effectiveness of the climate that has been analyzed. Then the administrator may lead a discussion on the basic characteristics of the different effectiveness profiles represented in the group (see the previous section). Subsequently, the respondents may discuss their individual scores and ratings and then arrive at a consensus regarding the diagnosis and evaluation of the climate, which of the twelve dimensions of organizational climate need improvement, why particular dimensions are weak, and what steps may need to be taken in response.

Another approach is to discuss individual rankings and to develop a consensus regarding the desired rankings of motives and what might be done to affect the perceived climate accordingly. Any specific action ideas that are developed may be presented to top management for discussion, approval, and commitment. Then the agreed-on action steps may be carried out and followed up with monthly reviews to determine the success of implementation.

References

Baumgartel, H.J., Rajan, P.S.S., & Newman, J. (1985). Educational environments and attributions of causality: Some exploratory research findings. *Quality of Work Life, 2*(56), 309–328.

Beer, M. (1971, September). *Organizational climate: A viewpoint from the change agent.* Paper presented at the American Psychological Association Convention, Washington, D.C.

Burns, T., & Stalker, G. (1961). *The management of innovation.* London: Tavistock.

Campbell, J.P., Dunnette, M.D., Lawler, E.E., III, & Weick, K.E., Jr. (1970). *Managerial behavior, performance, and effectiveness.* New York: McGraw-Hill.

Dachler, H.P. (1973). *Work motivation and the concept of organizational climate.* Paper presented at the 10th Annual Eastern Academy of Management Meeting, Philadelphia, PA.

Deci, E.L. (1980). *The psychology of self-determination.* Lexington, MA: Lexington Books.

Hellriegel, D., & Slocum, J.W. (1974). Organizational climate: Measures, research and contingencies. *Academy of Management Journal, 17*(2), 255–280.

Khanna, B.B. (1986). *Relationship between organizational climate and organizational role stress and their impact upon organizational effectiveness: A case study.* Unpublished doctoral dissertation, Banaras Hindu University, Varanasi, India.

Likert, R. (1967). *The human organization.* New York: McGraw-Hill.

Litwin, G., & Stringer, R. (1968). *Motivation and organizational climate.* Cambridge, MA: Harvard University Press.

Pareek, U. (1983). Organizational role stress. In L.D. Goodstein & J.W. Pfeiffer (Eds.), *The 1983 annual* (pp. 115–123). San Francisco: Pfeiffer.

Pareek, U. (1986). Motivational analysis of organizations—behavior (MAO-B). In J.W. Pfeiffer & L.D. Goodstein (Eds.), *The 1986 annual* (pp. 121–133). San Francisco: Pfeiffer.

Schneider, B. (1973). *The perceived environment: Organizational climate.* Paper presented at the meeting of the Midwest Psychological Association.

Sen, P.C. (1982). *Personal and organizational correlates of role stress and coping strategies in some public sector banks.* Unpublished doctoral dissertation, University of Gujarat, Ahmedabad, India.

Surti, K. (1982). *Some psychological correlates of role stress and coping styles in working women.* Unpublished doctoral dissertation, University of Gujarat, Ahmedabad, India.

Originally published in *The 1989 Annual: Developing Human Resources.*

Motivational Analysis of Organizations—Climate (MAO-C)

Udai Pareek

Name: _____ Title: _____

Instructions: Completing this inventory will allow you to evaluate the climate or culture of your organization (or your unit or department, if the administrator of this inventory instructs you to interpret the inventory in this way). Below are twelve categories representing twelve dimensions of organizational climate, and within each category are six statements. You are to rank the statements in each category from 6 (*most* like the situation in your organization or unit) to 1 (*least* like the situation in your organization or unit). *Do not give the same rank to more than one statement.*

Rank   **1. Orientation**

_____   a. People here are mainly concerned with following established rules and procedures.

_____   b. The main concern of people here is to help one another develop greater skills and thereby advance in the organization.

_____   c. Achieving or surpassing seems to be people's main concern here.

_____   d. Consolidating one's own personal position and influence seems to be the main concern here.

_____   e. The dominant concern here is to maintain friendly relations with others.

_____   f. The main concern here is to develop people's competence and expertise.

Rank   **2. Interpersonal Relationships**

_____   a. In this organization most informal groups are formed around experts.

_____   b. The atmosphere here is very friendly, and people spend enough time in informal social relations.

_____   c. In this organization strong cliques protect their own interests.

_____   d. Businesslike relationships prevail here; people are warm, but they get together primarily to ensure excellence in performance.

Rank   **2. Interpersonal Relationships,** *continued*

_____   e. People here have strong associations mostly with their supervisors and look to them for suggestions and guidance.

_____   f. People here have a high concern for one another and tend to help one another spontaneously when such help is needed.

Rank   **3. Supervision**

_____   a. The purpose of supervision here is usually to check for mistakes and to "catch" the person making the mistake.

_____   b. Supervisors here strongly prefer that their subordinates ask them for instructions and suggestions.

_____   c. Supervisors here take pains to see that their subordinates improve personal skills and chances of advancement.

_____   d. Supervisors here reward outstanding achievement.

_____   e. In influencing their subordinates, supervisors here try to use their expertise and competence rather than their formal authority.

_____   f. Supervisors here are more concerned with maintaining good relations with their subordinates than with emphasizing duties and performance.

Rank   **4. Problem Management**

_____   a. People here take problems as challenges and try to find better solutions than anyone else.

_____   b. When problems are faced here, experts are consulted and play an important role in solving these problems.

_____   c. In dealing with problems, people here mostly consult their friends.

_____   d. When working on solutions to problems, people here keep in mind the needs of organizational members as well as society at large.

_____   e. People here usually refer problems to their superiors and look to their superiors for solutions.

_____   f. Problems here are usually solved by supervisors; subordinates are not involved.

Rank   **5. Management of Mistakes**

_____   a. When people here make mistakes, they are not rejected; instead, their friends show them much understanding and warmth.

_____   b. Here the philosophy is that the supervisor can make no mistake and the subordinate dare not make one.

_____   c. Usually people here are able to acknowledge and analyze their mistakes because they can expect to receive help and support from others.

_____   d. When a subordinate makes a mistake here, the supervisor treats it as a learning experience that can prevent failure and improve performance in the future.

_____   e. Subordinates here expect guidance from their supervisors in correcting or preventing mistakes.

_____   f. Here people seek the help of experts in analyzing and preventing mistakes.

Rank   **6. Conflict Management**

_____   a. Most interpersonal and interdepartmental conflicts here arise as a result of striving for higher performance; and in analyzing and resolving these conflicts, the overriding consideration is high productivity.

_____   b. Here conflicts are usually avoided or smoothed over to maintain the friendly atmosphere.

_____   c. Arbitration or third-party intervention (usually performed by experienced or senior people) is sought and used here.

_____   d. In a conflict situation here, those who are stronger force their points of view on others.

_____   e. In resolving conflicts here, appeal is made to principles, organizational ideals, and the larger good of the organization.

_____   f. Experts are consulted and their advice used in resolving conflicts here.

Rank   **7. Communication**

_____   a. After due consideration those in authority here issue instructions and expect them to be carried out.

Rank　　**7. Communication,** *continued*

_____　b. Most communication here is informal and friendly and arises from and contributes to warm relations.

_____　c. People here ask for information from those who are experts on the subject.

_____　d. Relevant information is made available to all who need it and can use it for the purpose of achieving high performance here.

_____　e. People here communicate information, suggestions, and even criticism to others out of concern for them.

_____　f. Communication is often selective here; people usually give or hold-back crucial information as a form of control.

Rank　　**8. Decision Making**

_____　a. While making decisions, people here make special attempts to maintain cordial relations with all concerned.

_____　b. Decisions are made at the top and communicated downward, and people here generally prefer this.

_____　c. People who have demonstrated high achievement have a big say in the decisions made here.

_____　d. Decisions here are generally made without involving subordinates.

_____　e. Decisions here are made and influenced by specialists and other knowledgeable people.

_____　f. Decisions are made here by keeping in mind the good of the employees and of society.

Rank　　**9. Trust**

_____　b. Trusting and friendly relations are highly valued here.

_____　c. Here high value is placed on trust between supervisor and subordinate.

_____　d. The specialists and the experts are highly trusted here.

_____　e. A general attitude of helping generates mutual trust here.

_____　f. Those who can achieve results are highly trusted here.

Rank   **10. Management of Rewards**

_____   b. Knowledge and expertise are recognized and rewarded here.

_____   c. Loyalty is rewarded more than anything else here.

_____   d. The people who are rewarded here are those who help their junior colleagues to achieve and develop.

_____   e. The ability to control subordinates and maintain discipline is afforded the greatest importance in rewarding supervisors here.

_____   f. The ability to get along well with others is highly rated and rewarded here.

Rank   **11. Risk Taking**

_____   b. In risky situations supervisors here strongly emphasize discipline and obedience to orders.

_____   c. In risky situations supervisors here have a strong tendency to rely on expert specialists for their advice.

_____   d. Supervisors here generally go to their superiors for instructions in risky situations.

_____   e. In responding to risky situations, supervisors here show great concern for the people working in the organization.

_____   f. In responding to risky situations, supervisors here take calculated risks and strive above all to be more efficient or productive.

Rank   **12. Innovation and Change**

_____   b. Here innovation or change is primarily ordered by top management.

_____   c. Before initiating innovation or change, supervisors here generally go to their superiors for sanction and guidance.

_____   d. Those who initiate innovation or change here demonstrate a great concern for any possible adverse effects on others (in the organization or outside) and try to minimize these effects.

_____   e. Innovation or change here is mainly initiated and implemented through highly results-oriented individuals.

_____   f. Supervisors here seldom undertake innovations that disturb their existing friendships in the organization or earn the enmity of organizational members.

Motivational Analysis of Organizations— Climate (MAO–C) Matrix Sheet

Instructions: Organizations (and units, branches, divisions, or departments within organizations) tend to be perceived as driven by one or more of six specific motives. The *scoring key* will show you which motives are indicated by your responses on the MAO-C and, therefore, which motives you perceive as driving your organization or unit; then completing this *matrix sheet* will help you arrive at a profile of the general motivational climate of your organization or unit as you perceive it. For example, for the first category or dimension of organizational climate, *Orientation*, if you ranked item *a* as 4, you would look at the scoring key and learn that a indicates the *dependency* motive; then you would refer to this matrix sheet and find the horizontal row that corresponds to Orientation, locate the heading "Dependency," and write the number 4 under that heading in the Orientation row. Follow this process until you have transferred all six of your rankings for each of the twelve categories covered in the MAO-C.

Add the numbers in each vertical column of this matrix and write the totals in the blanks provided; each of these totals is your score for that particular motive. Then refer to the *conversion table*, locate your total for each motive, and write the corresponding MAO-C index number in the blank provided on this matrix sheet.

Next, for each horizontal row on the matrix, which represents a dimension of organizational climate, write the dominant motive (the one with the highest number in the row) and the backup motive (the one with the next-highest number) in the blanks provided (see the two vertical columns on the extreme right of the matrix). The dominant and backup columns are helpful in diagnosing and in planning action to improve the motivational climate of the organization or unit. Finally, determine which motives appear most often in the dominant and backup columns and write these motives in the blanks provided for *overall dominant motive* and *overall backup motive.*

Motives

Dimensions of Organizational Climate	Achievment	Expert Influence	Extension	Control	Dependency	Affiliation	Dominant (Abbreviate as necessary)	Backup (Abbreviate as necessary)
1. Orientation								
2. Interpersonal relationships								
3. Supervision								
4. Problem management								
5. Management of mistakes								
6. Conflict management								
7. Communication								
8. Decision making								
9. Trust								
10. Management of rewards								
11. Risk taking								
12. Innovation and change								
Total Scores							**Overall Dominant Motive**	**Overall Backup Motive**
MAO-C Index								

Motivational Analysis of Organizations—
Climate (MAO-C) Scoring Key

Motives

Dimensions of Organizational Climate	Achievment	Expert Influence	Extension	Control	Dependency	Affiliation
1. Orientation	c	f	b	d	a	e
2. Interpersonal relationships	d	a	f	c	e	b
3. Supervision	d	e	c	a	b	f
4. Problem management	a	b	d	f	e	c
5. Management of mistakes	d	f	c	b	e	a
6. Conflict management	a	f	e	d	c	b
7. Communication	d	c	e	f	a	b
8. Decision making	c	e	f	d	b	a
9. Trust	f	d	e	a	c	b
10. Management of rewards	a	b	d	e	c	f
11. Risk taking	f	c	e	b	d	a
12. Innovation and change	e	a	d	b	c	f

Conversion Table

Score	Index	Score	Index	Score	Index	Score	Index	Score	Index
12	0	25	21	37	41	49	61	61	81
13	2	26	23	38	43	50	63	62	83
14	3	27	25	39	45	51	65	63	85
15	5	28	26	40	46	52	66	64	86
16	7	29	28	41	48	53	68	65	88
17	8	30	30	42	50	54	70	66	90
18	10	31	31	43	51	55	71	67	91
19	12	32	33	44	53	56	73	68	93
20	13	33	35	45	55	57	75	69	95
21	15	34	36	46	56	58	78	70	96
22	17	35	38	47	58	59	78	71	98
23	18	36	40	48	60	60	80	72	100
24	19								

32 The Organizational Readiness Inventory (ORI): Diagnosing Your Organization's Ability to Adapt to the Future

James L. Moseley and Douglas J. Swiatkowski

Summary

Models for business abound today. Most business people can probably name two or three off the top of their heads. These models serve a valuable purpose—to help an organization paint a picture of its future, its optimum state. As any person concerned with performance knows, however, this portrait is only half the picture. A clear snapshot of what the organization looks like now is necessary in order to have something to compare with the optimum future. The Organizational Readiness Inventory (ORI) is a means of doing this.

The authors use the 7S Model developed by Peters and Waterman (1988) and Pascale (1991) and embraced by McKinsey and Company. The model provides seven categories by which an organization can measure its current state and define an optimal future state. The ORI provides the means to measure how the members see the organization currently.

The 7S Model—the basis of this instrument—establishes seven key categories or areas of concentration that an organization should have a handle on in order to be successful. These categories are *strategy, structure, systems, staff, style, shared values,* and *skills,* which are defined in Table 1. These categories were recognized and brought together by Tom Peters and Robert Waterman of McKinsey and Company with the assistance of Robert Pascale and Anthony Athos. The work of Harold Leavitt (the "Leavitt Diamond") was also influential in our thinking. The model concentrates not on technology skills or hard skills, but on those that often are considered "soft." As noted by Peters and Waterman (1988), "All the stuff you have been dismissing for so long as the intractable, irrational, intuitive, informal organization can be managed—soft is hard."

The ORI provides a systematic way to find out how the organization assesses itself based on the seven categories. The "voice" of the organization, for our purposes, refers to the amalgam of the thoughts and opinions of the members of the organization. These do not necessarily reflect the open verbal opinions expressed by the individuals, which are often shaded by fear, politics, and "groupthink." The "voice" of the organization reflects what the individuals feel and believe internally. If administered properly and in an environment of anonymity and trust, the ORI helps to bring out the internal voice of the organization.

Table 1. Definitions of the 7S Categories

Category	Definition
Strategy	Plan or course of action leading to the allocation of a firm's scarce resources, over time, to reach identified goals.
Structure	Salient features of the organizational chart (i.e., functional, decentralized, etc.) and how the separate entities of an organization are tied together.
Systems	Reports that are a matter of procedure and routine processes, such as meetings.
Staffing	Demographic descriptions of important personnel categories within the organization.
Style	How key managers behave in achieving the organization's goals; also, the cultural style of an organization.
Style	Distinctive capabilities of key personnel and the organization as a whole.
Shared Values	The significant meanings or guiding concepts that an organization imbues in its members.

The shell of the ORI instrument is based on the Inventory of Self-Actualizing Characteristics (ISAC) (Banet, 1976). The five-point scale and the data-collection method remain much like the ISAC, but the data-reporting method has been modified to produce data in the aggregate, as opposed to the ISAC, which is an individual inventory with the data intended to be used by the person completing it.

The seventy-seven statements (eleven for each of the seven categories) were derived through a literature and Internet search of the seven topics. The authors looked for themes and common threads and framed statements to reflect them.

Description of the Instrument

The ORI consists of a seventy-seven statement inventory, eleven for each of the seven categories of the 7S Model; a Scoring Sheet; and an Interpretation Sheet. Individuals completing the inventory simply read each statement, reflect on how it pertains to their organization, and choose which of the five responses best fits the organization's current way of doing things. See Figure 1 below for a listing of the responses and their corresponding meanings.

N = The organization has not recognized the issue yet.

S = The organization has begun speaking about the issue.

I = The organization has initiated plans of action and goals around the issue.

W = Work is being done toward goals around the issue.

Figure 1. ORI Rating Scale

The individuals completing the survey do not score their own results. Because the data is intended to be viewed in the aggregate and has no real value to the individual, the administrator does the scoring. Although scoring in this way does require quite a bit of time and effort, it was deemed the better method. In testing the instrument, it was found that it took about thirty minutes to complete the scoring, and the individuals who reviewed the instrument thought that this was too cumbersome for individuals.

The administrator uses the ORI Profile Sheet to obtain a composite score for each of the categories by simply averaging the numeric values of all respondents. This information is then plotted on the ORI Profile Sheet to reflect the rating of the group that completed the survey. The Profile Sheet shows how each of the five categories was scored by the group. The ORI Interpretation Sheet helps to clarify what each of the five ratings indicates about the organization.

Administration of the Instrument

It is highly recommended that this instrument be administered in a facilitated session, as opposed to simply handing them out and requesting that people complete them, for three reasons:

- Using a facilitated session greatly increases the number of respondents who actually complete the instrument.

- A facilitated session allows for a standard explanation to be given to participants about what the instrument is intended to do.

- Questions can be immediately addressed in a facilitated session. Although this is not a guarantee of sounder data, the facilitator may be able to help an individual who otherwise may give up or provide incorrect data.

Anonymity is critical for obtaining unbiased data from the participants. All respondents should receive unmarked envelopes to use for returning the entire instrument when they are done. These should be collected in a receptacle near the exit. One person should be responsible for compiling the scores and recording the data. This person should not be a member of upper management. Great care should go into selecting an individual who is viewed as trustworthy by respondents.

Once the data are compiled, bring the members of the organization together and go over the results both verbally and visually. Allow time for some questions and answers about what the data show and what can be learned. Be sure that everyone hears the same message, and also provide an opportunity to discuss next steps based on the results. Focus groups can also be formed around each of the 7S categories to further explore the results and examine possible courses of action.

Based on the trials with this instrument, a thirty-five to forty-five minute time period should be sufficient to provide some background and have respondents complete the instrument.

Presentation of Theory

The theory behind the instrument (the 7S Model), some background on performance improvement, and information about optimum and desired states should be presented to the respondents *after* they have completed the instrument so that results will not be biased. Some possible ways to share this information follow:

- Because a facilitator is already present, he or she could explain the theory after everyone has completed the instrument. The facilitator can provide some background on the 7S Model, explaining the categories and why are they important. The facilitator could also explain why the data are being gathered and what is going to be done with the results. A downside to this method is that people tend to finish filling out instruments at various paces. If you require people to stay after they are finished, those who finish quickly will probably be bored, while those who are moving more slowly will be likely to feel rushed.

- A small job aid could be handed out to respondents as they leave, giving the necessary information on the theory and what will be done with the data. Add the name of a contact person for additional questions people might have.

Regardless of the way that a presentation of the theory is handled, the respondents must have this information to provide a context for the results when they are shared later with the rest of the organization. Good practice is founded on solid theory.

Scoring the Instrument

It should be noted that the value-added output of this instrument is the aggregate data. Individual scores are of no value. However, if an individual is interested in doing so, he or she can be given a Profile Sheet and an Interpretation Sheet to chart out his or her own scores and interpret them.

Posting the Data

The results can be posted and compared with previous evaluations to show progress for the entire organization. The scores can be presented in a number of ways, either showing:

- Scores for the entire organization, or

- Breakdowns of scores by functional unit (human resources, accounting, marketing, etc.).

Care must be taken that each group contains at least five people to assure anonymity of respondents.

Suggested Uses for the Instrument

The ORI is designed to collect the opinions of organization members in order to find the "voice" of the organization. However, there are other possible uses. The ORI provides an extensive list of diagnostic questions that performance improvement specialists could use to guide an audit. Evidence could be sought in support for each statement, and a decision about what was needed could be made on the basis of the evidence. The

ORI could also be used first with the organization's management team as a self-audit. The scores derived from this self-audit could then be compared with organization-wide results.

Reliability and Validity

The instrument is an informal diagnostic tool, as opposed to a formal data-gathering instrument. There were no formal studies conducted; hence, no data exists to demonstrate reliability or validity. This instrument, however, was piloted with instructional and performance technology professionals and revised based on their feedback.

References

Banet, A.G., Jr. (1976). Inventory of self-actualizing characteristics (ISAC). In J.W. Pfeiffer & J.E. Jones (Eds.), *The 1976 annual* (pp. 70–77). San Francisco: Pfeiffer.

Pascale, R. (1991). *Managing on the edge.* New York: Simon & Schuster.

Peters, T., & Waterman, R. (1988). *In search of excellence: Lessons from America's best-run companies.* New York: Warner Books.

Originally published in *The 2000 Annual: Volume 2, Consulting.*

Organizational Readiness Inventory (ORI)

James L. Moseley and Douglas J. Swiatkowski

Instructions: The following instrument has been designed to help give you information about your organization's readiness to adapt to the future. It has a selection of seventy-seven statements you are asked to respond to by indicating the *present* state of your organization. When responding to the statements, be sure to describe your organization's state *at this time, not what you think it should be or will be in the future.* Do not spend too much time selecting your responses. Your initial reaction to the statements is best.

Read each item and circle the letter to the right of the statement that most accurately describes your organization at this time.

N = The organization has not recognized the issue yet.

S = The organization has begun speaking about the issue.

I = The organization has initiated plans of action and goals around the issue.

W = *Work is being done* toward goals around the issue.

R = *Results are being realized* on work being done around this issue.

1.	The organization values diversity in personnel.	N	S	I	W	R
2.	The organization must stand apart from its competition.	N	S	I	W	R
3.	Managers are involved in coaching and providing feedback to employees.	N	S	I	W	R
4.	Potential for career development is realized.	N	S	I	W	R
5.	Organizational vision is consistent with organizational action.	N	S	I	W	R
6.	Educational activities are linked to business goals.	N	S	I	W	R
7.	There is a drastic shortage of skilled labor.	N	S	I	W	R
8.	The organization cannot be held captive to key people; there must be processes that other people could step up and use.	N	S	I	W	R
9.	Skill requirements today change quickly.	N	S	I	W	R
10.	Employees are empowered to make decisions.	N	S	I	W	R

N = The organization has not recognized the issue yet.
S = The organization has begun speaking about the issue.
I = The organization has initiated plans of action and goals around the issue.
W = *Work is being done* toward goals around the issue.
R = *Results are being realized* on work being done around this issue.

11.	Fewer managers, more teams is the trend.	N	S	I	W	R
12.	The organization views itself as a part of the surrounding community.	N	S	I	W	R
13.	Information is utilized, managed, practiced, and disseminated.	N	S	I	W	R
14.	Employee input is encouraged and listened to.	N	S	I	W	R
15.	Our employees' performance must stand apart from the competition.	N	S	I	W	R
16.	Development is linked to strategies of the organization.	N	S	I	W	R
17.	Processes exist to ensure that things are done right the first time.	N	S	I	W	R
18.	Performance is valued more than placement.	N	S	I	W	R
19.	People who are hired possess necessary skill sets.	N	S	I	W	R
20.	Resources are allocated for employee development.	N	S	I	W	R
21.	Interviews are structured to produce information needed to make sound hiring decisions.	N	S	I	W	R
22.	Laughter and having fun while working are encouraged.	N	S	I	W	R
23.	The organization is able to adapt its core skills to a rapidly changing environment.	N	S	I	W	R
24.	This is an organization that identifies levels of resistance, recognizes the source(s), and takes a proactive approach.	N	S	I	W	R
25.	Retaining employees is beneficial.	N	S	I	W	R

N = The organization has not recognized the issue yet.
S = The organization has begun speaking about the issue.
I = The organization has initiated plans of action and goals around the issue.
W = *Work is being done* toward goals around the issue.
R = *Results are being realized* on work being done around this issue.

26. Rites and rituals of the organization are inte-
grated into employees' lives.   N   S   I   W   R

27. A collaborative versus a competitive atmosphere
exists within the organization.   N   S   I   W   R

28. At the heart of the company values lies company
spirit s.   N   S   I   W   R

29. Internal and external scanning reveals the organization's strengths, weaknesses, opportunities,
and threats.   N   S   I   W   R

30. A mutual and inspiring trust, nurtured by
honest and open communication and equal
opportunity, exists.   N   S   I   W   R

31. Activities are benchmarked and measured
over time.   N   S   I   W   R

32. Reward and recognition systems credit skill
development.   N   S   I   W   R

33. An organization needs a consistent plan of
action.   N   S   I   W   R

34. Performance improvement specialists need to
possess cultural self-awareness.   N   S   I   W   R

35. The organization pursues its business with
honor, fairness, and respect.   N   S   I   W   R

36. When change occurs, the organization enters
into a destabilization process.   N   S   I   W   R

37. Opportunities for advancement exist.   N   S   I   W   R

38. The educational/skills background of its people
reflects the organization's needs.   N   S   I   W   R

N = The organization has not recognized the issue yet.
S = The organization has begun speaking about the issue.
 I = The organization has initiated plans of action and goals around the issue.
W = *Work is being done* toward goals around the issue.
R = *Results are being realized* on work being done around this issue.

39. A performance consultant should view systems
    work as an exercise in forecasting.   N   S   I   W   R

40. Gut feelings and hunches should not be imme-
    diately dismissed, but considered based on the
    experience of the individual asserting them.   N   S   I   W   R

41. Alternative sources of human capital are valued
    (outsourcing, interns, co-ops, etc.).   N   S   I   W   R

42. Training partnerships allow the organization to
    obtain different insights on internal organiza-
    tional issues.   N   S   I   W   R

43. In order to be successful, employee develop-
    ment systems should promote personal growth,
    enrichment, and self-learning.   N   S   I   W   R

44. Positions do not remain vacant for an extended
    period of time.   N   S   I   W   R

45. The organization recognizes that developmental
    activities will pay off over time on the bottom line. N   S   I   W   R

46. Congruence exists between the organization's
    beliefs and actions.   N   S   I   W   R

47. Managing a training function requires famil-
    iarization with the instructional systems design
    (ISD) process.   N   S   I   W   R

48. Repositioning evaluation as an integral part of
    performance improvement can increase its cred-
    ibility, utility, and institutionalization.   N   S   I   W   R

49. Experience levels are recognized and valued.   N   S   I   W   R

50. The organization provides needed "tools" for
    employees to perform at their optimum best.   N   S   I   W   R

N = The organization has not recognized the issue yet.
S = The organization has begun speaking about the issue.
I = The organization has initiated plans of action and goals around the issue.
W = *Work is being done* toward goals around the issue.
R = *Results are being realized* on work being done around this issue.

51. Inputs and outputs of all processes must be
    identified.   N   S   I   W   R

52. The organization is aware of its position in the
    global marketplace.   N   S   I   W   R

53. A competency driven process is used to fill
    vacancies.   N   S   I   W   R

54. Assessment centers identify management and
    executive candidates and observe and assess
    their behavior.   N   S   I   W   R

55. Employee strengths and areas of expertise are
    routinely inventoried, documented, and shared
    with all so other employees know where to turn
    for information and assistance.   N   S   I   W   R

56. Beliefs, values, and wishes drive the way stake-
    holders address the strategic planning process.   N   S   I   W   R

57. Deming's Fourteen Points philosophy provides
    the guidelines for creating an environment for
    a TQM system.   N   S   I   W   R

58. Common visions and common purposes
    contribute to successful market positions.   N   S   I   W   R

59. Obvious trappings of position, reserved parking,
    separate facilities, should not exist.   N   S   I   W   R

60. Managing performance is a way to build synergy
    within organizations.   N   S   I   W   R

61. A climate of supportiveness rather than being
    judgmental fosters an atmosphere conducive
    to learning.   N   S   I   W   R

N = The organization has not recognized the issue yet.
S = The organization has begun speaking about the issue.
 I = The organization has initiated plans of action and goals around the issue.
W = *Work is being done* toward goals around the issue.
R = *Results are being realized* on work being done around this issue.

62. Success depends on an organization's ability
    to deliver a level of excellence respected by
    all who rely on it.   N   S   I   W   R

63. Organizations in tune with their employees
    maintain fairness and ethical standards.   N   S   I   W   R

64. The organization supports organizational
    scanning efforts through analysis of the
    organization, people, and work facts.   N   S   I   W   R

65. Processes in the organization are identified
    and represented in some way (policies, flow
    charts, etc.).   N   S   I   W   R

66. Management should regularly receive frank and
    honest feedback from those they supervise.   N   S   I   W   R

67. Fiscally sound decisions are made to support
    organizational goals.   N   S   I   W   R

68. The organization helps its members establish
    personal development plans.   N   S   I   W   R

69. Staffing needs are integrated with key business
    systems.   N   S   I   W   R

70. Outsourcing or "right sizing" is an issue of
    competency.   N   S   I   W   R

71. Human resource development policies and
    procedures shape the manner in which work
    is accomplished.   N   S   I   W   R

72. Mistakes are expected and are viewed as excellent
    opportunities to learn.   N   S   I   W   R

73. Employees are hired to ensure competitive vision.   N   S   I   W   R

N = The organization has not recognized the issue yet.
S = The organization has begun speaking about the issue.
 I = The organization has initiated plans of action and goals around the issue.
W = *Work is being done* toward goals around the issue.
R = *Results are being realized* on work being done around this issue.

74. The organization commits to the delivery of outputs that have a positive and desired impact on what it contributes to the community.   N   S   I   W   R

75. An organization's ideal vision forms a framework through partnership with clients, stake-holders, and sponsoring and regulatory agencies.   N   S   I   W   R

76. Employees want to perform tasks with pride and want to participate in the organization's survival and improvement.   N   S   I   W   R

77. Employees and managers understand the impact that their decisions have on the organization's processes.   N   S   I   W   R

ORI Scoring Sheet

Directions: In each of the charts below find the question numbers from the survey and place your letter score for that item in the box beneath the item number. Once you have done this for all seven charts, assign the appropriate numerical value to each letter using the following scale:

N = –2 S = –1 I = –0 W = –1 R = –2

Finally, add the values for each chart and place the number you obtain in the box below the chart. For example:

Sample Chart

Question	1	18	25	33	88	46	52	63	68	71	77
Letter	N	W	W	R	S	I	N	S	S	R	W
Value	-2	1	1	2	-1	0	-2	-1	-1	2	1
										Score	0

Strategy

Question	6	16	20	24	31	33	45	52	62	67	75
Letter											
Value											
										Score	

Structure

Question	2	11	18	29	36	42	48	57	64	70	71
Letter											
Value											
										Score	

Systems

Question	8	13	17	21	39	43	47	51	55	65	77
Letter											
Value											
										Score	

Staffing

Question	1	7	19	25	37	38	41	44	53	69	73
Letter											
Value											
										Score	

Style

Question	3	10	14	22	27	34	40	46	59	66	72
Letter											
Value											
										Score	

Skills

Question	4	9	15	23	32	49	50	54	60	68	76
Letter											
Value											
										Score	

Shared Values

Question	5	12	26	28	30	35	56	58	61	63	74
Letter											
Value											
										Score	

ORI Profile Sheet

Directions: Compute the average score in each category by totaling all scores and dividing by the number of respondents. Then plot the results on the following graph.

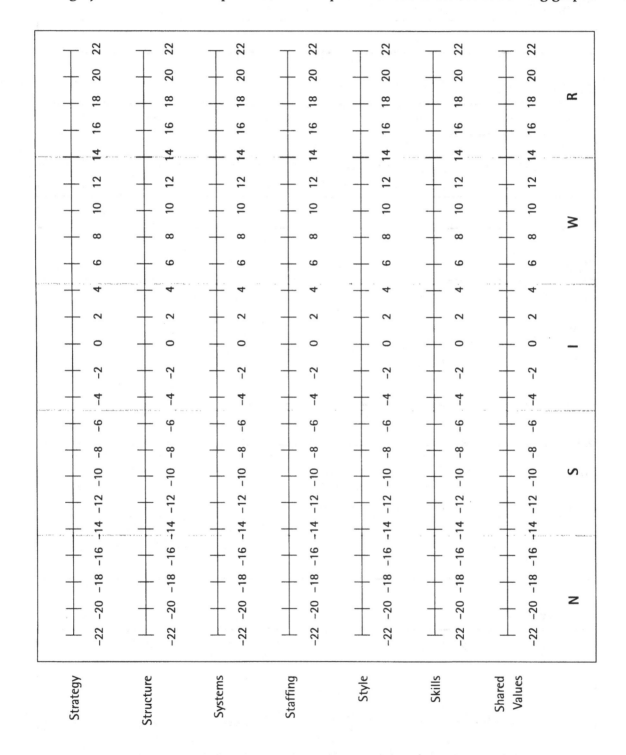

ORI Interpretation Sheet

The following are short explanations of what each answer may mean for your organization. This is not intended as an item analysis, but you may draw your own conclusions about your organization's scores on each category mean.

If Your Score Is N for a Category

The organization has *not recognized the issue yet*. The employees perceive that the organization has not yet even addressed this category of the 7S Model. This could point to many problems and an equal number of solutions. It may be that the organization has not seen the category as significant. It may also be that work is being done in the category, but this has not been clearly communicated to the rest of the organization. Regardless of the cause, receiving an N in any of the seven categories should be a red flag for management.

If Your Score Is S for a Category

The organization has *begun speaking about the issue*. An S rating tells the organization that the employees' perception is that something is at least being discussed. However, an S also could mean that the employees believe talk and only talk is taking place and that there have been no actions to back up the philosophizing. Again, communication could be an issue if the organization has actually put something into practice but done a poor job of informing organization members. Receiving an S should also serve as a warning flag in that the perception of "all talk and no action" on the part of the organization can have negative effects on the employees' willingness to commit to an initiative.

If Your Score Is I for a Category

The organization has *initiated plans of action and goals around the issue*. The employees recognize that the organization is on its way to doing something regarding the category. Plans of action and goals entail allocations of people and time, and in some cases, actual monetary budgets. Receiving an I may also indicate good lines of communication in that the employees are aware of what the organization's plans are. Although receiving an I is better than receiving an N or S on a category, an organization must not allow itself to be complacent and satisfied with an I. Actual activities need to be undertaken and evident to maintain momentum and employee support.

If Your Score Is W for a Category

Work is being done toward goals around the issue. Receiving a W in a category means the employees of the organization see tasks taking place that are designed to help the organization achieve its goals in that particular category. The score tells an organization that the employees see that management is beyond the talking and philosophizing phase and has rolled up its collective sleeves. Again, if employees are aware of the work being done, it may be an indication of a good communication system.

If Your Score Is R for a Category

Results are being realized on work being done around this issue. Receiving an R in a category means that employees of the organization not only have heard the organization speak about an effort, but they have seen the plan and observed the work, and now can see results. This rating not only reveals successful efforts but a strong communication system that celebrates success and is able to help employees make the connections among plans, efforts, and results.

33 The Organizational I-Boundary Inventory:
A Model for Decision Making

H. B. Karp

Summary

Organizations are becoming more complex as they continue to restructure. With this increasing complexity comes a growing concern about how to maintain effectiveness in an ever-changing system. This article presents a model for determining one's personal values and the organization's values, at a given point in time, thus establishing parameters for making decisions in the organizational setting. It is based on two established theories. The first, the Political Savvy Theory, concerns functioning in and as a group. The second theory, the Gestalt Theory, provides a process for increasing self-awareness, with the view toward discovering how one may be stopping oneself from being as effective as possible.

The Organizational I-Boundary Inventory is a sixteen-item instrument that allows the respondents to assess their own values and those of the organization and then compare the two sets of values. The Inventory may serve as a self-assessment instrument; as a foundation for coaching individuals; and as a basis for intra-group analysis and team building.

Organizations are moving toward increasing complexity, as they continue to merge and restructure themselves. Not only are organizational systems becoming larger, but they are becoming more diverse as well, and the guidelines for appropriate effective behavior are becoming less clear as each new change occurs. The dilemma is that the old and established organizational paradigms no longer point to "one best way" to address the problems being faced.

Rod McLuhan's (1964) famous statement that "The medium is the message" may indicate a way to perceive organizations and communications within them. That is, just as systems are in a state of merging and becoming more complex, so must be the theories and applications being developed to understand and cope with them. The Political Savvy Theory and the Gestalt Theory, for example, can be combined and used effectively in determining how best to function in an organization. Applying these practical theories results in a range of appropriate choices that an individual can make in an organizational situation.

Political Savvy Theory

"Political savvy" is a term coined by Billie Lee (1992) to describe what it takes to be effective in today's organizations. Lee's work is based on the initial work of Jinx Melia, whose classic book *Why Jenny Can't Lead* (1986) focused on how women were disempowering themselves in male-dominant systems and what they had to do to become individually more impactful as a political force. Lee took these concepts well beyond the parameters of feminist issues and applied them to effective functioning in large organizations in general. Building on Melia's work, Lee developed the polar concepts of "Bear Fighters" and "Cave Dwellers." Lee stated that, although both concepts are important in organizational functioning, effectiveness in meeting team and organizational objectives now requires a greater emphasis on the attributes that were necessary to be an effective bear fighter in pre-historic times.

From strictly a historical perspective, Bear Fighting characteristics are stereotypically male and aggressive, whereas Cave Dweller characteristics are stereotypically female and nurturing. Bear Fighters, as a group, conform to a totally different set of characteristics and demands than do Cave Dwellers. The function of "bear fighting" is to achieve an objective that cannot be met by a single individual—to function as a team in order to accomplish what is essential for the survival (or success) of everyone in the community (or organization). "Objective" in this sense means a goal that is too large or too complex for any one individual to accomplish successfully, such as fighting and killing a bear. The function of "cave dwelling," on the other hand, is to provide a safe and supportive environment for all community members. The major characteristics of the two types are listed in Figure 1.

The underlying premise of the Political Savvy Theory is that the majority of organizations today operate mostly from a "Cave Dwelling" set of assumptions that have risen from the human relations movement in the 1960s and 1970s, typified by the assumption that good work is a direct result of good working relationships. Lee's assertion is that today's organizations must now incorporate the "Bear Fighter's" assumptions if they are going to survive and prosper. This assumption certainly seems accurate in view of such trends as the global economy, quickly and easily achieved product parity, and the growing emphasis on providing excellent service as the only viable way to compete. Both sets of skills are of equal value, the important thing being that people learn when and how to meet each separate set of needs. As Lee suggests, competent people develop both bear fighting and cave dwelling skills; savvy people know when to use each.

Bear Fighters:

---

1. Put the task before the individual.

2. Operate in an uncontrolled environment, adapting to and using change.

3. Seek accomplishment, minimize risk, and use results as a guide.

4. Compete to get on the team and are admitted based on the team's needs.

5. Form unlimited alliances to accomplish tasks.

Cave Dwellers:

---

1. Put the individual before the task.

2. Operate in a controlled environment, adhering to the rules.

3. Seek safety, avoid risks, and use personal comfort as a guide.

4. Are admitted to the community based on shared values and acceptance.

5. Form a limited number of interpersonal relations within the cave.

Figure 1. Characteristics of Bear Fighters and Cave Dwellers

Gestalt Theory

The word "Gestalt" is German in origin and can be defined as "a clear, emerging figure." Gestalt therapy was developed by Fritz Perls in the clinical setting and has been described by many as "therapy for normal people." It emphasizes the health and development of the entire self. Along with being an approach for strengthening individuals by helping them make better choices, it has also become an approach for increasing individual effectiveness and making changes in organizations.

In the Gestalt view, all human characteristics and capacities operate in polarities, such as hostile/supportive, kind/cruel, or good/evil.

Figure 2 illustrates the entire range for human experience on the aggressive/passive polarity. A "+ 7", at the extreme left, is as aggressive as it is humanly possible to be. Likewise, a "+ 7" at the extreme right is as passive as it is humanly possible to be. Each individual capacity, or sub-boundary, crosses two polarities at two points indicated by the "I."

This example shows the results of the author's Organizational I-Boundary Inventory. The two interior marks represent his sub-boundary on the Aggressive/Passive continuum. That is, a range from 4.7 to 2.8. What this says, in terms of behaviors, is that the author is aggressive enough to go after what he wants that is "unclaimed" by others, at one extreme, but no more aggressive than that, and passive enough to keep a low profile in the face of a direct threat, but no more passive than that. The significance is that these two points describe the extent of his capacity on this continuum and identifies him uniquely. The points define when a "Yes" becomes a "No." When the sub-boundary is added to the hundreds of others that make a person up, the result is that person's "I-Boundary," that distinctive configuration of characteristics and capacities that makes each person absolutely unique and recognizable. Figure 3 displays a sample configuration that includes all eight of the polarities.

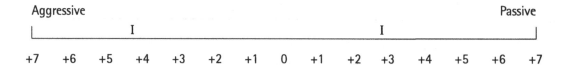

Figure 2. The Aggressive/Passive Continuum

Several assumptions are implicit in the concept of I-Boundary:

1. Because these are capacities only, rather than behaviors, there is no bad way to be or bad capacity to have.

2. The prevailing situation and a person's capacities determine what actions are appropriate or inappropriate, effective or ineffective.

3. Each individual's I-Boundary is so unique that effectiveness lies in being aware of who one is, valuing that uniqueness, and clearly demonstrating that uniqueness to others.

Integration of the Theories

"Political Savvy Theory" and "Gestalt Theory" provide us with a means for becoming more aware of our political and interpersonal effectiveness in the work setting. By changing the designation of "I-Boundary" to "Organizational I-Boundary," and by setting up the poles of the continuum in terms of Bear Fighter/Cave Dweller capacities, we have a means for conducting a "thumb-nail" analysis of what the organization's values are, what the person's values are, and how well the two sets of values are matched.

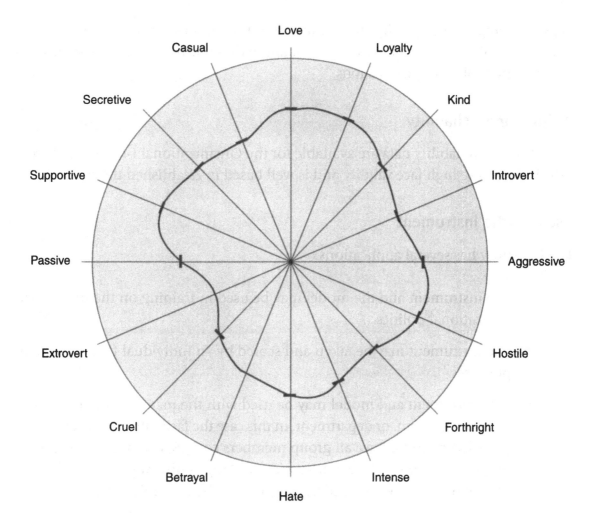

Figure 3. The I-Boundary

The Instrument

The Organizational I-Boundary Inventory is a tool for (1) assessing a respondent's awareness of his or her organization's political environment and (2) measuring the respondent's effectiveness in that environment. The instrument is based on the Political-Savvy Theory and the Gestalt Theory and provides a means for the respondents to assess their own values and the values of the organizational systems in which they operate, and a basis for determining how they may or may not be operating effectively within their systems' political structures.

The instrument makes use of sixteen dimensions, half of which are "bear fighting" or achieving capacities, and the other half being "cave dwelling" or supportive capacities. Each "bear fighting" capacity is paired with its "cave dwelling" counterpart, but the questions are answered separately on a 7-point scale, ranging from "strongly disagree"

(1) to "strongly agree" (7). By answering each question for themselves as well as for how they see their organizations, the participants have a means for comparing their values with those of their organizations.

Validity and Reliability

No validity or reliability data are available for the Organizational I-Boundary Inventory. It does have high face validity and is well based in established theory.

Uses for the Instrument

The Inventory has several applications:

- The instrument and the model may be used in training on the topic of organizational politics.

- The instrument may be taken and scored by an individual for self-analysis purposes.

- The instrument and model may be used with the members of an ongoing work group, team, or department. In this case the facilitator would briefly explain the concept, have all group members complete and score the instrument, and then facilitate a discussion looking at how similar and different the members perceive the political values of their organization.

References

Karp, H.B. (1996). *Personal power: An unorthodox guide to success.* Lake Worth, FL: Gardner Press.

Lee, B. (1992). *Savvy: Thirty days to a different perspective.* Colorado Springs, CO: Billie Lee & Co.

McLuhan, M. (1964). *Understanding media.* New York: McGraw-Hill.

Melia, J., & Lyttle, P. (1986). *Why Jenny can't lead: Understanding the male dominant system.* Sauguache, CO: Operational Politics Inc.

Originally published in *The 1999 Annual: Volume 2, Consulting.*

Organizational I-Boundary Inventory[1]

H. B. Karp

Instructions: The following sixteen statements describe attitudes about organizational life. Respond to each statement below *twice*. First circle the number that best represents your personal view. Then, put an "X" through the number that, in your opinion, represents your organization's view.

1 = Strongly Disagree	3 = Mildly Disagree	5 = Mildly Agree	7 = Strongly Agree
2 = Disagree	4 = Neutral	6 = Agree	

1. In effective organizations, task accomplishment takes precedence over individual well-being. 1 2 3 4 5 6 7

2. It is alright to disregard organizational rules and policies when they get in the way of task accomplishment. 1 2 3 4 5 6 7

3. A manager's primary obligation is the growth and development of his or her people. 1 2 3 4 5 6 7

4. Employees who do not follow and respect organizational guidelines are not good team players. 1 2 3 4 5 6 7

5. Providing an opportunity to achieve is the organization's primary obligation to its staff. 1 2 3 4 5 6 7

6. The most important thing for team members to share is their objectives. 1 2 3 4 5 6 7

7. Providing a safe and secure environment is the organization's primary obligation to its staff. 1 2 3 4 5 6 7

8. The closer the interpersonal relationships of team members, the better. 1 2 3 4 5 6 7

[1] I would like to thank Diane LaMountain, whose assistance was critical in developing this work.

1 = Strongly Disagree   3 = Mildly Disagree   5 = Mildly Agree   7 = Strongly Agree
2 = Disagree   4 = Neutral   6 = Agree

9. In effective teams, agreements are
    openly made and are honored among
    team members.   1   2   3   4   5   6   7

10. Each team member should take care
    of himself or herself before providing
    support to other members.   1   2   3   4   5   6   7

11. Good team members do not ask for, or
    expect, "payment" for favors done other
    team members.   1   2   3   4   5   6   7

12. In terms of providing support, it is
    important that each team member take
    care of his or her teammates first.   1   2   3   4   5   6   7

13. Team members are obligated to state
    clearly and directly what they want or
    need from the group or its members.   1   2   3   4   5   6   7

14. An effective team must be able to work
    in unclear and ambiguous situations.   1   2   3   4   5   6   7

15. Good team members should be able to
    anticipate and respond to the wants and
    needs of their teammates.   1   2   3   4   5   6   7

16. Effective teams should have the ability
    to clarify situations that seem unclear.   1   2   3   4   5   6   7

Organizational I–Boundary Inventory Scoring Sheet

Instructions: Transfer responses from the inventory to the scoring grid below, circling your personal responses to distinguish them from organizational responses. (Note that there are eight polarities represented in the sixteen items; items 1 and 3 are opposite, items 2 and 4 are opposite, and so on.) Next connect the circles. This will yield your individual Organizational I-Boundary (your personal values) in reference to your own Bear Fighter/Cave Dweller capacities. Repeat the procedure for your assessment of your organization's values on each characteristic, using Xs to indicate each score. Connect the Xs to yield an Organizational S-Boundary (S-system) and then compare the two sets of values.

The eight polarities going clockwise from 1, "Task," through 13, "Reliance on Self," are "Bear Fighter" characteristics. These characteristics include: Concern with Task Accomplishment; Commitment to Common Objectives; Willingness To Take Risks; Taking Responsibility for Oneself; Need for Achievement; Valuing Flexibility; Need for Alliances; and Self-Reliance. These are geared to task accomplishment, teamwork, and organizational effectiveness.

Continuing to move clockwise, the remaining eight polarities, beginning with 3, "Nurturance," and ending with 15, "Reliance on Others," are "Cave Dweller" characteristics. These include: the Need To Be Nurturant; Commitment to Commonly Held Values; Following Rules; Respect and Responsibility for Others; the Need for Safety; Valuing Stability; a Need for Close Relationships; and Reliance on Others. These characteristics are geared to providing for the needs of safety, belonging, and caring for others.

Your position on each sub-boundary, for both the Bear Fighting and the Cave Dwelling characteristics, reflects your capacity for responding to that characteristic. Remember that there is no good or bad or right or wrong way to be! Everyone has some needs on both sides.

By connecting the "O"s representing your own view, you obtain an Organizational I-Boundary that describes your "organizational self." By connecting the "X"s you make an Organizational S-Boundary that describes your system. Compare the two boundaries to see where your values are consistent with the organization's and where they may not be.

Organizational I–Boundary
Inventory Interpretation Sheet

The purpose of this inventory is to increase your awareness. Do not make any plans for change yet. If you are taking this survey with other members of your group, department, or organization, compare your perceptions of the organization with theirs. As this inventory and its interpretation are basically subjective in nature, it is up to you to determine their relevance and implications for you. What you intend to do, if anything, is best determined by looking at the results from your survey within the context of your organizational culture. The following points may assist you in deciding what to do with your results.

High Degree of Overlap

Complete, or near complete, overlap between the I-Boundary and the S-Boundary might mean that there is congruence between you and the organization. That is, there is an excellent match between your characteristics and those of the system. If things are progressing well and you have a strong sense of self, then this condition is all to the good.

There are, however, other possible interpretations of such results. For example, if there is a great deal of overlap, it could also indicate the lack of a strong sense of self and that you identify strongly with the organization, at least in terms of functioning within it. This is most typified by the term "Company Man" that was coined in the early 1960s. Typically, these people identify very strongly with the system, are fierce defenders of its values, and look askance at anyone who does not share their views about the organization.

Another interpretation might be that you see yourself as an "outsider." Here the tendency is to mimic the company values, rather than to internalize them, in an attempt to be included more fully by other members of the organization. You will need to determine whether the expression of individual capacities and values you gave is authentic or not.

Little Overlap

A great deal of disparity between the I-Boundary and the S-Boundary might suggest that you do not clearly understand the organization's values. On the other hand, it might indicate that there is too great a difference between your needs and capacities and those of the system. In this situation it may be difficult for you to make a significant contribution. That is, the difference is so great that the organization represents a hostile environment and you may spend more time in self-protection and hiding than in contributing to the organizational objectives.

Issues to Consider

Although there is no prescribed method for analyzing the results of the inventory, there are a few simple ways of being. First, three points disparity between your score ("O") and the system's ("X") on any of the sixteen individual characteristics would indicate the high likelihood of a problem and you should look at those items first. A few of the more obvious possible areas of disparity are listed below.

Alliances Versus Relationships.   What does the organization value as opposed to what you are seeking in the work setting? It may be that you are trying to develop more supportive relationships when what is being demanded are more effective alliances among people who need one another to do the job.

Controlling the Environment Versus Adapting to It.   Understanding the difference between adaptation and control is critical to attaining objectives. Most people in an organization have limited control over conditions and must rely on their ability to adapt to existing conditions, making the best choices from there. However, it is appropriate to challenge rules if they are impeding progress.

Willingness Versus Unwillingness to Negotiate.   Negotiating is an essential set of bear fighting skills that provides a means for attaining a group objective. Cave dwellers are frequently more concerned with liking or disliking the other person, rather than looking at what negotiation with the other person could produce. Often, cave dwellers would prefer not attaining the end if it means dealing with someone they do not like or hold in high personal regard. Bear fighters, in contrast, will engage in negotiation when necessary, regardless of whether they like or dislike the other person.

Risk Taking Versus Risk Avoidance.   Bear fighters attempt to minimize risk, but they are willing to confront it; cave dwellers attempt to avoid it altogether. Rarely can an objective be successfully accomplished without taking some risk.

Teams Versus Friends.   Operating as a team is a necessity when pursuing an object that an individual cannot meet alone. For bear fighters, the sole purpose is goal attainment. Cave dwellers put more emphasis on the process than on the outcome; for them, the purpose of a team is to develop trust, get along well, and work well together. Be clear about the compatibility of assumptions that you make about the nature of teams and those that your organization makes.

34 Innovation Capability Audit

Dave Francis

Summary

The successful management of innovation requires that unique answers be found to the following three key questions:

1. Are we sufficiently innovative?

2. Are we innovative in the "right" ways?

3. If the answer to question 1 or 2 is "no," what needs to be done?

The Innovation Capability Audit assesses an organization's capacity for innovation. The Audit can be used for training or as an organizational survey instrument. It provides a straightforward method for a group to explore the organizational dimensions of innovation and initiate a process of organization development to strengthen innovative prowess. The audit is based on extensive research conducted by the author at the Centre for Research in Innovation Management at the University of Brighton, United Kingdom.

The management of innovation is an important topic. Virtually every management journal regularly has pertinent articles. Organizations that innovate have superior profit and growth performance (Miles & Snow, 1978). Few doubt that there is much innovation to be done: As innovation specialist Professor John Bessant says, "It has been estimated that up to 80 percent of the new products that we will be buying in ten years' time have yet to be invented"(Bessant, 1991).

However, not all innovation adds value. It must be managed to promote functional, not dysfunctional, innovation. Functional innovation is considered to be the application of concepts, ideas, or techniques that enhance the competitive capability of the organization. Dysfunctional innovation, on the other hand, is the investment of resources in costly, unproductive, or distracting initiatives.

Innovation processes are directed toward one or more of four domains—Paradigm, Process, Position, and Product—as shown in Figure 1:

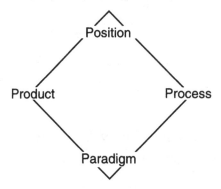

Figure 1. Domains of Innovation

- Innovation can be strategic—redefining the *positioning* of the organization. For example, a chemical company may seek to offer differentiated rather than commodity products. In this case, innovation in product and service must be managed to deliver the new competitive strategy.

- Innovation can be cultural—redefining the dominant *paradigm* of the organization. In this context, a paradigm may be defined as the system of beliefs, mind-sets, values, and practices that define collective thinking processes. For example, a local theater may change its role from being a deliverer of high culture to a center for participative education in the performing arts. In this case, innovation must re-align the beliefs, mind-sets, values, and practices of the entire staff.

- Innovation can introduce or improve *products* in ways that add value for customers and enable the organization's products to be equivalent (preferably superior) to the offers of competing organizations.

- Innovation can introduce or improve *processes* that reduce costs, improve quality, or increase agility.

As an organization innovates, its capacity to learn, adapt, and thrive improves. Further advantage can be gained by mastering fluid forces of change.

Description of the Audit

The Innovation Capability Audit is designed as an organization-wide survey. Its fifty-four items assess an organization's capacity for innovation as measured by eighteen different "innovation drivers." Each item is scored on a six-point scale that describes the extent to which each item is perceived as true.

Validity

The items in this audit are drawn from research and case studies that address the preconditions for organizational innovation. At present, no one universally agreed-on model of innovative capacity exists. However, the Innovation Capacity Audit is designed to be an action-research tool rather than a rigorous data-gathering instrument. Used in this manner, the items are hypotheses that have high levels of face validity.

Administration

The total time required to administer, score, and interpret the Innovation Capability Audit is approximately ninety minutes. Each participant will need a copy of each of the elements of the audit: Innovation Capability Audit, Innovation Capability Audit Scoring Sheet, Innovation Capability Audit Interpretation Sheet, and Innovation Capability Audit Work Sheet. To best facilitate this session, human resource professionals should review leading works on the organizational aspects of innovation (Coyne, 1996; Drucker, 1994; Kanter, 1983; Millson, Raj, & Wilemon, 1992; and Utterback, 1994).

1. *Introduce the session* by saying that innovation is a vital attribute of today's organizations, and the group will examine the extent to which their own organization supports or blocks innovation. This introduction can be illustrated with examples from your own experience.

2. *Distribute the Innovation Capability Audit* and ask each participant to complete it. If necessary, define the organization or part of the organization (for example, a unit or department) being assessed and ensure that participants share a common understanding.

3. *Present a brief lecturette* on the attributes of the innovative organization. The content for this lecturette may be drawn from material in the Innovation Capability Audit Interpretation Sheet.

4. *Distribute the Innovation Capability Audit Scoring Sheet, the Innovation Capability Audit Interpretation Sheet, and the Innovation Capability Work Sheet,* and review their instructions. Ask participants to form subgroups of two to five people, with members of the same organization working together. Ask subgroups to complete the analysis of the audit results.

5. *Invite each subgroup to share at least one insight* gained from the session. These insights should be recorded and posted on a newsprint flip chart.

References

Bessant, J. (1991). *Managing advanced manufacturing technology: The challenge of the fifth wave.* Oxford/ Manchester: NCC-Blackwell.

Coyne, D.W.E. (1996). *Building a tradition of innovation.* Paper presented at the UK Innovation Lecture, London. Published by DTI, London.

Drucker, P.F. (1994). *Innovation and entrepreneurship.* Oxford: Butterworth-Heinemann Ltd.

Kanter, R.M. (1983). *The change masters.* New York: Simon & Schuster.

Miles, R.E., & Snow, C.C. (1978). *Organizational strategy, structure, and process.* New York: McGraw-Hill.

Millson, M.R., Raj, S.P., & Wilemon, D. (1992). A survey of major approaches for accelerating new product development. *The Journal of Product Innovation Management, 9,* 53–69.

Utterback, J.M. (1994). *Mastering the dynamics of innovation.* Boston, MA: HBS.

Originally published in *The 1998 Annual: Volume 2, Consulting.*

Innovation Capability Audit

Dave Francis

Instructions: Innovation is a vital skill, and this audit will help to provide information needed to strengthen innovation in your organization. Please answer each item with care and honesty; the intention is to benefit everyone. Individual results are strictly confidential and will never be identified by name.

The facilitator will define the organization or part of the organization that is the target for review. Please refer to this target as you respond to each item. You may feel that you do not have sufficient knowledge to be objective, but please respond to each statement, even if you give a subjective opinion.

Choose your response based on the following scale:

This statement is true:

1 = To little or no extent	3 = To a moderate extent	5 = To a very great extent
2 = To a slight extent	4 = To a great extent	6 = Totally

1. Top managers take innovation very seriously.   1 2 3 4 5 6

2. This organization's record of gives it real advantage over competitors.   1 2 3 4 5 6

3. If needed, radical changes will be implemented.   1 2 3 4 5 6

4. Creative individuals are well-rewarded.   1 2 3 4 5 6

5. The organization is an early adopter of state-of-the-art technology.   1 2 3 4 5 6

6. This organization is good at getting things done.   1 2 3 4 5 6

7. Employees are empowered to take significant initiative.   1 2 3 4 5 6

8. It is expected that staff at all levels will innovate.   1 2 3 4 5 6

9. Most people here welcome change.   1 2 3 4 5 6

10. Significant resources are invested in developing people.   1 2 3 4 5 6

This statement is true:

1 = To little or no extent	3 = To a moderate extent	5 = To a very great extent
2 = To a slight extent	4 = To a great extent	6 = Totally

11. Technical experts are influential in decision making.

    1   2   3   4   5   6

12. Customers are actively involved in the development of new products.

    1   2   3   4   5   6

13. Extensive collaboration occurs between teams and departments.

    1   2   3   4   5   6

14. People can obtain management's support to implement well-considered initiatives.

    1   2   3   4   5   6

15. Top priority is given to developing new products and processes.

    1   2   3   4   5   6

16. Managers strive to understand new ideas in great depth before making a change.

    1   2   3   4   5   6

17. Decisions about launching new products are taken after very careful analysis.

    1   2   3   4   5   6

18. New ideas are fully driven through, despite setbacks or difficulties.

    1   2   3   4   5   6

19. Senior managers inspire people to be innovative.

    1   2   3   4   5   6

20. Everything we do is part of a strategy to gain competitive advantage.

    1   2   3   4   5   6

21. Top managers give careful thought before making a radical decision.

    1   2   3   4   5   6

19. Senior managers inspire people to be innovative.

    1   2   3   4   5   6

20. Everything we do is part of a strategy to gain competitive advantage.

    1   2   3   4   5   6

21. Top managers give careful thought before making a radical decision.

    1   2   3   4   5   6

This statement is true:

1 = To little or no extent	3 = To a moderate extent	5 = To a very great extent
2 = To a slight extent	4 = To a great extent	6 = Totally

22. Outstanding individuals are highly valued.   1   2   3   4   5   6

23. Our technological strengths and weaknesses have been carefully analyzed.   1   2   3   4   5   6

24. Once a decision is made, initiatives are implemented rapidly.   1   2   3   4   5   6

25. Employees speak up even when challenging important people.   1   2   3   4   5   6

26. Managers and staff identify developing new ideas as a key objective.   1   2   3   4   5   6

27. Almost everyone is 100 percent in support of management's plans.   1   2   3   4   5   6

28. There is a constant search for new ways to define problems.   1   2   3   4   5   6

29. Technical specialists share their knowledge widely.   1   2   3   4   5   6

30. We frequently benchmark how we compare with other organizations.   1   2   3   4   5   6

31. Things get done; there is no unnecessary bureaucracy.   1   2   3   4   5   6

32. People who drive through changes are recognized as heroes.   1   2   3   4   5   6

33. The organization can take an idea and quickly turn it into a product that people want to buy.   1   2   3   4   5   6

34. Those leading a change process can fully describe the advantages and disadvantages.   1   2   3   4   5   6

35. Decisions to support or kill an initiative are taken by managers who really understand the issues.   1   2   3   4   5   6

This statement is true:

1 = To little or no extent   **3 = To a moderate extent**   **5 = To a very great extent**
2 = To a slight extent   **4 = To a great extent**   **6 = Totally**

36. Management insists that only a limited number of initiatives are undertaken at once, to prevent overstretching the organization. 1 2 3 4 5 6

37. The organization's leader is tough on those who seek to block change. 1 2 3 4 5 6

38. New products (or services) really give the customer superior value. 1 2 3 4 5 6

39. Senior management has a recent history of making bold decisions. 1 2 3 4 5 6

40. Exceptional individuals are able to fit into the organization. 1 2 3 4 5 6

41. The organization is investing to develop all the capabilities needed to win in the future. 1 2 3 4 5 6

42. Projects are managed effectively. 1 2 3 4 5 6

43. Personal initiatives are supported, providing people work within guidelines. 1 2 3 4 5 6

44. People are appraised based on their success in being innovative. 1 2 3 4 5 6

45. Everyone is keen to help someone with a creative suggestion. 1 2 3 4 5 6

46. We rarely make the same mistake twice. 1 2 3 4 5 6

47. Those with deep technical skills are highly respected. 1 2 3 4 5 6

48. We learn through strong links with partners, industry associations, universities, and consultants. 1 2 3 4 5 6

49. The way the organization is structured helps not hinders innovation. 1 2 3 4 5 6

This statement is true:

1 = To little or no extent **3 = To a moderate extent** **5 = To a very great extent**
2 = To a slight extent **4 = To a great extent** **6 = Totally**

50. People with ideas can win the resources they need.   1   2   3   4   5   6

51. Departments involved in developing new products or processes work closely together.   1   2   3   4   5   6

52. This organization is striving to be truly world class in every aspect of performance.   1   2   3   4   5   6

53. When it is important, decisions are made quickly.   1   2   3   4   5   6

54. Top managers take personal responsibility for major initiatives.   1   2   3   4   5   6

Innovation Capability Audit Scoring Sheet

Instructions: Transfer your responses for each item on the Innovation Capability Audit to the answer grid that follows. Add the scores in each horizontal column and enter them in the "Total" column.

Topic	Item Score			Total
Ia. Innovating Leadership	1	19	37	
Ib. Provides Strategic Advantage	2	20	38	
Ic. Prudent Radicalism	3	21	39	
IIa. Exceptional Individuals	4	22	40	
IIb. Full Competencies Portfolio	5	23	41	
IIc. Capable Implementation	6	24	42	
IIIa. Selective Empowerment	7	25	43	
IIIb. Innovation Demanded	8	26	44	
IIIc. High Enrollment	9	27	45	
IVa. Continuous Learning	10	28	46	
IVb. Respect for Mastery	11	29	47	
IVc. Fruitful Linkages	12	30	48	
Va. Apt Organizational Form	13	31	49	
Vb. Supported Champions	14	32	50	
Vc. High-Performing New Product/Process Development	15	33	51	
VIa. Guiding Mental Maps	16	34	52	
VIb. Sound Decision Processes	17	35	53	
VIc. Resourced Initiatives	18	36	54	

Innovation Capability Audit Interpretation Sheet

Unblocking Innovation in Your Organization

Developing innovation capability in an organization is complex and challenging. Eighteen dimensions of innovation capability can be identified, as shown on the wheel diagram (Figure 2) and defined in the sections that follow. Each dimension can serve as a driver or as a blockage (that is, a cleared blockage becomes a driver). Each organization has to find ways of overcoming blockages and transforming them into drivers.

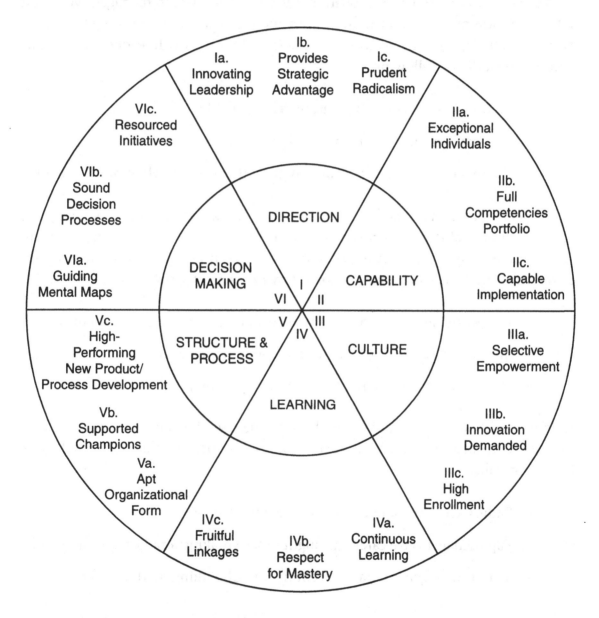

Figure 2. Drivers of Organizational Innovation

Interpretation Guidelines

Begin by reading the descriptions that follow about the eighteen innovation drivers. Share your scores from the Innovation Capability Audit with the other members of your subgroup. In particular, identify low-scoring dimensions and assess their importance to your organization, using the Innovation Capability Audit Work Sheet. Then plan what you need to do to confirm the diagnosis and work on innovation blockages.

Dimensions of Innovation Capability

Ia. *Innovating Leadership.* The organization is led assertively by top managers who share a driving vision of the organization's future and create a context within which innovation thrives. The key characteristics of organizations in which leaders promote innovation include the following:

- Senior managers take innovation very seriously.

- Top managers inspire people to be innovative.

- The organization's leaders are tough on those who seek to block change.

Ib. *Provides Strategic Advantage.* The organization has a well-developed strategy that identifies the capabilities, technologies, products, services, and processes necessary for continued competitive advantage. Organizations in which innovation promotes competitive advantage demonstrate the following characteristics:

- The organization's record of innovation is superior to its competitors.

- Innovation is directed to achieving competitive advantage.

- New products (or services) provide the customer with superior value.

Ic. *Prudent Radicalism.* Bold and far-reaching changes will be made but only after great thought. Organizations that combine radicalness and prudence are identified by the following traits:

- Radical changes can be quickly implemented.

- Top managers give careful thought before making a radical decision.

- Senior management has a recent history of making bold decisions.

IIa. *Exceptional Individuals.* Exceptional individuals are recruited, rewarded, respected, and retained. The following are key characteristics of organizations that recruit, retain, and motivate exceptional individuals:

- Creative individuals are well rewarded.

- Outstanding individuals are highly valued.

- Exceptional individuals fit into the organization.

IIb. *Full Competencies Portfolio.* The organization continuously develops the capabilities needed to support a stream of innovation. The key characteristics of organizations that have a full portfolio of competencies include the following:

- The organization is an early adopter of state-of-the-art technologies.

- Technological strengths and weaknesses have been carefully analyzed.

- The organization is investing to develop all of the capabilities needed to win in the future.

IIc. *Capable Implementation.* Innovative ideas can be quickly and effectively implemented. Organizations that can put new ideas into action share traits such as the following:

- The organization is good at getting things done.

- Once a decision is made, initiatives are implemented rapidly.

- Projects are managed effectively.

IIIa. *Selective Empowerment.* The management philosophy of the organization supports able individuals to take initiatives. The following are key characteristics of organizations that encourage empowerment without losing control:

- Employees are empowered to take significant initiatives.

- Employees speak up even when important people are challenged.

- Personal initiatives are supported, providing people work within guidelines.

IIIb. *Innovation Demanded.* Everyone is expected to innovate. Organizations that expect innovation can be identified by the following indicators:

- It is expected that staff at all levels will innovate.

- Managers and staff have key objectives to develop new ideas.

- People are appraised based on their success in being innovative.

IIIc. *High Enrollment.* People actively support innovation initiatives. The organizations that enroll staff in innovation demonstrate the following characteristics:

- People welcome change.

- Almost everyone supports management's plans.

- Employees help people with creative ideas.

IVa. *Continuous Learning.* Challenge and learning are continuous processes. The key traits of organizations that learn continuously include the following:

- Significant resources are invested in developing people.

- There is a constant search for new ways to define problems.

- The organization rarely makes the same mistake twice.

IVb. *Respect for Mastery.* Those who have in-depth specialist knowledge help to guide the organization forward. A respect for mastery in organizations is demonstrated by the following characteristics:

- Technical experts are influential in decision making.

- Technical specialists share their knowledge widely.

- Those with in-depth technical skills are highly respected.

IVc. *Fruitful Linkages.* The organization is outward looking. Cooperative links are maintained with the outside world (including customers, consultancies, trade associations, standards organizations, suppliers, universities, joint-venture partners, and so on). These are win-win collaborations. When organizations construct fruitful linkages, they show the following traits:

- The organization actively involves customers in the development of new products.

- The organization frequently benchmarks how it compares with other organizations.

- The organization learns through strong links with partners, industry associations, universities, consultants, and so on.

Va. *Apt Organizational Form.* The structure and form of the organization helps not hinders the innovation process. Organizations that are structured for innovation demonstrate the following tendencies:

- There is a extensive collaboration between teams and departments.

- Things get done; there is no unnecessary bureaucracy.

- The way the organization is structured helps not hinders innovation.

Vb. *Supported Champions.* Those who can make things happen are enabled and supported. The key characteristics of organizations that support champions include the following:

- People obtain management's support for well-considered initiatives.

- People who drive through changes are recognized as heroes.

- People with ideas can win the resources they need.

Vc. *High-Performing New Product/Process Development.* There are effective processes for managing new product/process development. Organizations that have effective processes for developing new products and processes share the following traits:

- Top priority is given to developing new products and processes.

- The organization takes ideas and quickly produces products that people want to buy.

- Efforts are concentrated on launching new products that really attract customers.

VIa. *Guiding Mental Maps.* Innovations are directed by a theory of what needs to change and how. Effective conceptual maps for planning change are demonstrated by the following characteristics:

- Managers strive to understand new ideas in great depth before making a change.

- Those leading a change process can fully describe the advantages and disadvantages.

- The organization is striving to be truly world class in every aspect of performance.

VIb. *Sound Decision Processes.* Timely and wise decisions are taken about initiatives. The key characteristics of organizations that have effective decision-making processes include the following:

- Decisions about launching new products are taken after very careful analysis.

- Decisions to support or kill an initiative are taken by managers who really understand the issues.

- When it is important, decisions are made quickly.

VIc. *Resourced Initiatives.* Innovation projects are owned by senior managers and driven through. Organizations that provide initiatives with the necessary resources show the following indicators:

- New ideas are fully driven through, despite setbacks or difficulties.

- Management insists that only a limited number of initiatives are undertaken at once, to prevent overstretching the organization.

- Top managers take personal responsibility for major initiatives.

Innovation Capability Audit Work Sheet

Instructions: Determine the three *lowest* topic scores for yourself and for your subgroup's average. To determine your subgroup's average, combine individual totals for each topic and divide by the number of members in the subgroup, as follows:

Topic	My Score	Score of Other Subgroup Members (list)	Total of Subgroup Scores (My Score + Scores of Other Subgroup Members	Average Score (Total + Number of Subgroup Members)
Ia. Innovating Leadership				
Ib. Provides Strategic Advantage				
Ic. Prudent Radicalism				
IIa. Exceptional Individuals				
IIb. Full Competencies Portfolio				
IIc. Capable Implementation				
IIIa. Selective Empowerment				
IIIb. Innovation Demanded				
IIIc. High Enrollment				
IVa. Continuous Learning				
IVb. Respect for Mastery				
IVc. Fruitful Linkages				
Va. Apt Organizational Form				
Vb. Supported Champions				
Vc. High-Performing New Product/Process Development				
VIa. Guiding Mental Maps				
VIb. Sound Decision Processes				
VIc. Resourced Initiatives				

My Lowest Scores:	
Topic	Score
Topic	Score
Topic	Score

My Subgroup's Lowest Scores:	
Topic	Score
Topic	Score
Topic	Score

The innovation blockages (those with the lowest scores) are probably the major issues your organization has to face. These results need to be verified by discussion and further evaluation. In your subgroup, select *one* probable blockage to discuss. Look back in the explanation section at the characteristics of organizations that do not have that blockage and discuss the following questions:

1. Is this a real blockage for us?

2. Is it important? Why or why not?

3. Why does the blockage occur?

4. What can we do to unblock this indicator within the next ninety days?

35 Organizational Norms Opinionnaire

Mark Alexander

Summary

In any organization various norms of behavior influence the effectiveness and job satisfaction of the employees. Norms can be positive (by supporting the organization's goals and objectives) or negative (by promoting behavior that works against organizational goals).

This opinionnaire is designed to identify these organizational norms and to divide them into the following ten categories:

1. organizational/personal pride

2. performance/excellence

3. teamwork/communication

4. leadership/supervision

5. profitability/cost effectiveness

6. colleague/associate relations

7. customer/client relations

8. innovation/creativity

9. training/development

10. candor/openness

Suggested Uses

The opinionnaire can be used for several purposes: team building, management development, and organization assessment and diagnosis. For team-building purposes, group profiles can be developed through a consensus-finding process and used to identify problems. Similarly, a study of the norms and their effects on individual motivation and behavior is helpful in management development.

An especially valuable use is for organizational assessment and diagnosis. By measuring norms in each of the ten categories to see whether they are positive or negative, an organization can develop its own "normative profile." In effect, this normative profile is a statement of the strengths and weaknesses of the organization on a behavioral level. Thus, the organization can use the Organizational Norms Opinionnaire as a basis for initiating changes in work-group norms and behavior.

Although the items in the opinionnaire are phrased to be as generally useful as possible, the facilitator should feel free to adapt them to fit a particular situation.

Background Reading

Alexander, M. (1977). Organizational norms. In J.E. Jones & J.W. Pfeiffer (Eds.), *The 1977 annual*. San Francisco: Pfeiffer.

Originally published in *The 1978 Annual Handbook for Faciliatators, Trainers, and Consultants.*

Organizational Norms Opinionnaire

Mark Alexander

Instructions: This opinionnaire is designed to help you determine the norms that are operating in your organization. The opinionnaire asks you to assess what the reaction of most people in your organization *would be* if another person said a particular thing or behaved in a particular manner. For example, the first item reads: "If an employee in your organization were to criticize the organization and the people in it . . . most other employees would . . ."

To complete this statement, choose one of the following five alternatives:

A = Strongly agree with or encourage it
B = Agree with or encourage it
C = Consider it not important
D = Disagree with or discourage it
E = Strongly disagree with or discourage it

Choose the alternative that you think would be the most common response to the action or behavior stated and place the letter corresponding to that alternative in the blank space following each item. Complete all forty-two statements in the same manner, being as honest as possible.

Most other employees would:

If an employee in your organization were to . . .

1. criticize the organization and the people in it. _____

2. try to improve things even though the operation is running smoothly. _____

3. listen to others and try to get their opinions. _____

4. think of going to a supervisor with a problem. _____

5. look at himself or herself as being responsible for reducing costs. _____

6. take advantage of a fellow employee. _____

7. keep a customer or client waiting in order to look after matters of personal convenience. _____

A = Strongly agree with or encourage it
B = Agree with or encourage it
C = Consider it not important   **Most other**
D = Disagree with or discourage it   **employees**
E = Strongly disagree with or discourage it   **would:**

8. suggest a new idea or approach for doing things.   _____

9. actively look for ways to expand his or her knowledge
    in order to be able to do a better job.   _____

10. talk freely and openly about the organization and
    its problems.   _____

11. show genuine concern for the problems that face the
    organization and make suggestions about solving them.   _____

12. suggest that employees should do only enough to get by.   _____

13. go out of his or her way to help other members of the
    work group.   _____

14. look at the supervisor as a source of help and
    development.   _____

15. purposely misuse equipment or privileges.   _____

16. express concern for the well-being of other members
    of the organization.   _____

17. attempt to find new and better ways to serve the
    customer or client.   _____

18. attempt to experiment in order to do things better
    in the work situation.   _____

19. show enthusiasm for going to an organization-
    sponsored training and development program.   _____

20. suggest confronting the supervisor about a mistake
    or something in the supervisor's style that is creating
    problems.   _____

21. look at the job as being merely eight hours and the
    major reward as the paycheck.   _____

A = Strongly agree with or encourage it
B = Agree with or encourage it
C = Consider it not important
D = Disagree with or discourage it
E = Strongly disagree with or discourage it

Most other employees would:

22. say that there is no point in trying harder, as no one else does.

    _____

23. work on his or her own rather than work with others to try to get things done.

    _____

24. look at the supervisor as someone to talk openly and freely to.

    _____

25. look at making a profit as someone else's problem.

    _____

26. make an effort to get to know the people he or she works with.

    _____

27. sometimes see the customer or client as a burden or obstruction to getting the job done.

    _____

28. criticize a fellow employee who is trying to improve things in the work situation.

    _____

29. mention that he or she is planning to attend a recently announced organizational training program.

    _____

30. talk openly about problems facing the work group, including personalities or interpersonal problems.

    _____

31. talk about work with satisfaction.

    _____

32. set very high personal standards of performance.

    _____

33. try to make the work group operate more like a team when dealing with issues or problems.

    _____

34. look at the supervisor as the one who sets the standards of performance or goals for the work group.

    _____

35. evaluate expenditures in terms of the benefits they will provide for the organization.

    _____

36. always try to treat the customer or client as well as possible.

    _____

A = Strongly agree with or encourage it
B = Agree with or encourage it
C = Consider it not important   **Most other**
D = Disagree with or discourage it   **employees**
E = Strongly disagree with or discourage it   **would:**

37. think of going to the supervisor with an idea or
    suggestion.   _____

38. go to the supervisor to talk about what training he or
    she should get in order to do a better job.   _____

39. be perfectly honest in answering this questionnaire. _____

40. work harder than what is considered the normal pace. _____

41. look after himself or herself before the other members
    of the work group.   _____

42. do his or her job even when the supervisor is not around. _____

Organizational Norms Opinionnaire Score Sheet

Instructions: On the ten scales below, circle the value that corresponds to the response you gave for that item on the questionnaire. Total your score for each of the ten categories and follow the indicated mathematical formula for each. The result is your final percentage score.

I. Organizational/Personal Pride

Item	Response				
	A	**B**	**C**	**D**	**E**
1	−2	−1	0	−1	+2
11	+2	+1	0	+1	−2
21	−2	−1	0	−1	+2
31	+2	+1	0	+1	−2

Total Score _____ $\div$ 8 $\times$ 100 = [   ] **% Final Score**

II. Performance/Excellence

Item	Response				
	A	**B**	**C**	**D**	**E**
2	+2	+1	0	−1	−2
12	−2	−1	0	+1	+2
22	−2	−1	0	+1	+2
32	+2	+1	0	−1	−2
40	+2	+1	0	−1	−2

Total Score _____ $\div$ 10 $\times$ 100 = [   ] **% Final Score**

III. Teamwork/Communication

Item	Response				
	A	**B**	**C**	**D**	**E**
3	+2	+1	0	−1	−2
13	+2	+1	0	−1	−2
23	−2	−1	0	+1	+2
33	+2	+1	0	−1	−2
41	−2	−1	0	+1	+2

Total Score _____ ÷ 10 × 100 = [   ] **% Final Score**

IV. Leadership/Supervision

Item	Response				
	A	**B**	**C**	**D**	**E**
4	+2	+1	0	−1	−2
14	+2	+1	0	−1	−2
24	+2	+1	0	−1	−2
34	+2	+1	0	−1	−2
42	+2	+1	0	−1	−2

Total Score _____ ÷ 10 × 100 = [   ] **% Final Score**

V. Profitability/Cost Effectiveness

Item	Response				
	A	**B**	**C**	**D**	**E**
5	+2	+1	0	−1	−2
15	−2	−1	0	+1	+2
25	−2	−1	0	+1	+2
35	+2	+1	0	−1	−2

Total Score _____ ÷ 8 × 100 = [   ] **% Final Score**

VI. Colleague/Associate Relations

Item			Response		
	A	**B**	**C**	**D**	**E**
6	−2	−1	0	+1	+2
16	+2	+1	0	−1	−2
26	+2	+1	0	−1	−2

Total Score _____ ÷ 6 × 100 = [   ] **% Final Score**

VII. Customer/Client Relations

Item			Response		
	A	**B**	**C**	**D**	**E**
7	−2	−1	0	+1	+2
17	+2	+1	0	−1	−2
27	−2	−1	0	+1	+2
36	+2	+1	0	−1	−2

Total Score _____ ÷ 8 × 100 = [   ] **% Final Score**

VIII. Innovation/Creativity

Item			Response		
	A	**B**	**C**	**D**	**E**
8	+2	+1	0	−1	−2
18	+2	+1	0	−1	−2
28	−2	−1	0	+1	+2
37	+2	+1	0	−1	−2

Total Score _____ ÷ 8 × 100 = [   ] **% Final Score**

IX. Training/Development

Item	Response				
	A	**B**	**C**	**D**	**E**
9	+2	+1	0	−1	−2
19	+2	+1	0	−1	−2
29	+2	+1	0	−1	−2
38	+2	+1	0	−1	−2

Total Score _____ ÷ 8 × 100 = [   ] **% Final Score**

X. Candor/Openness

Item	Response				
	A	**B**	**C**	**D**	**E**
10	+2	+1	0	−1	−2
20	+2	+1	0	−1	−2
30	+2	+1	0	−1	−2
38	+2	+1	0	−1	−2

Total Score _____ ÷ 8 × 100 = [   ] **% Final Score**

Organizational Norms Opinionnaire Profile Sheet

Instructions: For each of the ten scales, enter your final percentage score from the score sheet and then plot that percentage by placing an "X" on the graph at the appropriate point. (Negative percentages are plotted to the left of the center line and positive percentages are plotted to the right.) Next, connect the "X"s you have plotted with straight lines. The result is your Organizational Norms profile.

Scale	Final Score	−100%	−50%	0%	+50%	+100%
I. Organizational/ Personal Pride						
II. Performance/ Excellence						
III. Teamwork/ Communication						
IV. Leadership/ Supervision						
V. Profitability/ Cost-Effectiveness						
VI. Colleague/ Associate Relations						
VII Customer/ Client Relations						
VIII. Innovation/ Creativity						
IX. Training/ Development						
X. Candor/ Openness						

36 Mentoring Skills Assessment

Michael Lee Smith

Summary

Before the Industrial Revolution, apprenticeship programs played an important role in career development. However, circumstances changed, and the programs were all but lost outside of trade unions. Similarly, informal mentoring was more common earlier this century, when job positions were less competitive. It seems that society has come full circle. We are experiencing major changes in how business is conducted, so we need a system that will support and foster the growth of the workforce. Well-designed mentoring programs can fill this need.

Mentoring programs can increase an employee's chances to progress in an organization. Having a mentor enables one to build on strengths and shore up weaknesses within the context of a relationship that supports success. Mentoring also complements both teams and learning organizations.

The Mentoring Skills Assessment identifies fifteen actions around which mentors and mentees can establish expectations and negotiate actions to allow the mentoring process to be as positive in results as it is in promises.

Mentoring itself is not new. In Greek mythology, Mentor was the friend and adviser of Odysseus and teacher of his son, Telemachus. The word mentor since has come to mean a trusted counselor or guide.

Mentoring Programs

Mentoring programs are found in many settings, including education, small and large businesses and the military (Gunn, 1995; Loeb, 1995; Rothman, 1993; Sullivan, 1992). Mentoring has always been present in the business environment, usually to help new employees learn about their organizations and for all employees to learn new skills

(Silver, 1996; Smith, 1994). These programs are even more necessary when new skills are needed to cope with the modern workplace. This is especially true today, because one can expect the skills one has to be obsolete in three to five years (Nocera, 1996). In addition, mentoring is needed as an alternative to the security and care taking that is no longer part of organizational life (Gunn, 1995).

Mentoring programs may be formal (with corporate sponsorship) or informal (spontaneous or with few guidelines). Either can be effective, although most sources suggest that formal programs are more effective (Gaskill, 1993; Rubow & Jansen, 1990; Wright & Werther, 1991). Regardless of the program's formality, it is possible that mentoring can make the difference in an individual's success or failure in an organization.

A survey of 1,250 prominent men and women conducted by the consulting firm of Heidrick and Struggles found that one of the factors contributing to the respondent's success was being involved in a mentoring relationship. Nearly two-thirds of the respondents reported having had a mentor (Murray, 1991).

Regardless of the program's formality, many benefits can derive from mentoring, such as the following (Alleman, 1989; Bloch, 1993; Geiger-Dumond & Boyle, 1995; Howe, 1995; Loeb, 1995; Murray, 1991; Wright & Werther, 1991):

- Helping newly hired or promoted employees become fully productive and understand the organization's expectations, policies, and resources in a compressed time frame

- Career guidance.

- Low-cost transfer of skills.

- Decreased turnover.

- Creation of future leaders.

- Greater job satisfaction.

- Increased learning for the mentor and mentee.

- Improved organizational climate.

- Positive affirmative action results.

- Increased productivity.

- Improved recruitment efforts.

- Increased ability to manage relationships more effectively.

Three good sources of guidance on designing mentoring programs are Kram (1985), Murray (1991), and Phillips-Jones (1993a).

The Mentoring Relationship

The essence of mentoring is the relationship between mentor and mentee. For most participants, this relationship is different from any others they have within their organizations. It is a helping relationship, with learning and growth as the expected outcomes for the mentee. Often, the mentor experiences these same benefits, which is why the mentor should not usually be the mentee's supervisor. Mentor and mentee must be able to negotiate roles, communicate effectively, set goals, actively listen, manage conflict, and more.

In addition to the interpersonal skills mentioned previously, the mentoring relationship also requires mutual trust, openness, and a willingness to attempt new behaviors. Such behaviors are often new to the mentoring pair, but the relationship is crucial for success. The role each will play as the relationship develops must be clear. To allow it to develop without guidance will put the mentoring relationship in jeopardy. According to Zachary (1994), "the preparation of the relationship by both partners together is critical for development of naturally satisfying relationships."

The Assessment

The mentor and mentee versions of the assessment are designed to facilitate the development of an effective mentoring relationship. Each consists of fifteen actions or behaviors that are expected to take place during any successful mentoring relationship. The mentor/mentee is asked to indicate if each of the mentoring actions should take place (yes or no), how often it should occur (occasionally, regularly, or often) and how important each is to the mentoring relationship (hardly needed, somewhat needed, needed, highly needed, essential).

The mentors and mentees complete their respective assessments prior to their first meeting or before a mentoring program orientation. In this way, their expectations are not influenced by the orientation session (e.g., in terms of what should occur, who should do what, and the importance of each event or behavior). Their individual feelings about "what," "how often," and "importance" are captured before they meet as a mentoring pair. The individual responses then are the source for negotiating expectations as mentor and mentee.

Validity and Reliability

No statistical validity and reliability data are available on the mentoring assessments. However, they have face validity, because their purpose is to prepare for the first meeting between mentor and mentee.

Administering and Scoring the Instrument

Begin by distributing the appropriate versions of the Mentoring Skills Assessments to mentors and mentees. If an orientation session is scheduled, copies of the completed assessments should be sent to the session facilitator in advance. If no orientation session is scheduled, mentors and mentees should set a time to meet and mutually acceptable deadlines for completing the assessments.

Interpretation of Results Prior to Program

When the mentoring assessments are prepared prior to the orientation session for a formal mentoring program, the facilitator "scores" the assessments by simply adding and averaging the mentor and mentee responses independently for each item.

The sample results reported here are from a session of twenty-five mentors and mentees. The facilitator should look at the mentoring actions for which there is agreement between mentors and mentees and for which there are differences. Agreement indicates mutual expectations and, therefore, the actions are likely to happen. Disagreement, on the other hand, indicates items for which negotiation needs to take place early in the relationship. Without negotiation, the differences between mentor and mentee present potential problems for the development of the relationship.

The facilitator's analysis serves as an example of what the mentors and mentees should do when they first meet and compare their individual responses.

In the absence of an orientation session, a letter should accompany the assessments that describes the mentoring process, the program goals, the role of the mentoring coordinator, and whatever resources are available for use, such as self-awareness questionnaires, books, tapes, and so on.

Part One

First, the facilitator should review the percentage of mentors and mentees who responded "yes" to each item. The items in the sample that are marked with an asterisk are the ones that should be noted and discussed.

In this example, there is general agreement that most of the actions should take place. Any action with 15 percent or greater disagreement between mentors and mentees or an action with less than 80 percent "yes" responses from either group should be highlighted and discussed. In this example, items F, G, and K would be highlighted and discussed, as follows.

F. Discuss company politics: 80 percent mentors vs. 100 percent mentees. Mentees uniformly expect to discuss "politics" within the organization. Twenty percent of the mentors do not agree. The mentors can be very helpful to the mentees regarding who has power and who does not, what the organization really considers to be important, and

	Mentor		Mentee
	92 percent	A	100 percent
	100 percent	B	92 percent
	92 percent	C	100 percent
	92 percent	D	92 percent
	100 percent	E	92 percent
*	80 percent	F	100 percent
*	100 percent	G	75 percent
	100 percent	H	100 percent
	100 percent	I	92 percent
	100 percent	J	100 percent
*	67 percent	K	67 percent
	92 percent	L	83 percent
	92 percent	M	83 percent
	100 percent	N	92 percent
	100 percent	O	100 percent

other aspects of the organization that the mentee can benefit from, instead of making "political" mistakes.

G. Discuss/share information about detailed job tasks: 100 percent mentors vs. 75 percent mentees. The mentors all agree they should give detailed information (advice) about the mentee's job. Mentees apparently are less willing to have mentors go into detail. Level of detail aside, mentoring in the work environment should have the job as a prime area for attention, not just personal goals or interpersonal skills. This area will have to be discussed carefully so that each is comfortable with just how involved in job details the mentor should become. Mentors are not usually expected to tell mentees exactly how to do their jobs, but asking questions about objectives, plans, and progress is expected. Mentors are expected to coach mentees, but the level of detail is something for negotiation. (If the mentor does not know the mentee's specific job or discipline, he or she is expected to find sources in the organization for such information when the mentee needs it.)

K. Ask for feedback on how others view me: 76 percent mentors vs. 67 percent mentees. Many mentors and mentees do not expect the mentors to ask mentees about how they (the mentors) are perceived in the organization. One could decide not to do this. However, one of the benefits for the mentor is to receive feedback from the mentee that he or she is not likely to obtain any other way.

Part Two

The second analysis is of the differences and similarities between mentor and mentee responses regarding how often the actions should take place and how important they are to the mentoring relationship. The results for the sample are shown below with plus signs (+) where there is basic agreement and minus signs (–) where there is disagreement. The items with an asterisk are the ones that are different enough to discuss. (Of course, the areas of similarity should receive some mention also to show how much agreement exists, which is a positive indicator of a successful mentoring relationship.)

Any response difference of .5 or more in frequency and .7 or more in importance should be noted for discussion. In this sample, J and M have "significant" differences in both frequency and importance. Action H has a difference in frequency only. The discussion might take the following form:

H. Explore mentee's strengths and weaknesses.

- Frequency: mentors 1.8, mentees 2.3

- Importance: mentors 3.9, mentees 3.9

Mentors and mentees agree that this is one of the most important actions for mentors during mentoring. However, mentors do not think it should happen as often as do the mentees. This may indicate a reluctance by mentors to talk about weaknesses. Few people have trouble talking about strengths or receiving feedback about them. The mentoring relationship is one in which it should be safe to talk about weaknesses. The lack of feedback and consequent lack of development in areas of one's weaknesses, whether job skills, interpersonal skills, or non-technical skills, should be the subject of mentoring meetings. Having an opportunity to explore areas that need development or that could interfere with job or career success is the purpose of mentoring.

J. Give feedback that is positive and negative regarding mentee's jobs plans, progress, and performance.

- Frequency: mentors 1.9, mentees 2.4

- Importance: mentors 3.6, mentees 4.3

This mentor action is similar to H but is specific to giving feedback about job plans, progress, and performance. Both mentors and mentees believe that it is important. In fact, it is the most important action (at 4.3) for the mentees. Mentors see it as taking place less often then mentees. Again, this may reflect a reluctance by mentors to give specific feedback (although it is regarded as needed during mentoring). Mentors should be prepared to give such feedback, and mentees will need to show their willingness to receive the feedback by asking for it. It may feel awkward at first, but mentees must speak up if they want the feedback. Mentors will not find such willing recipients of coaching in their normal job interactions.

M. Meet at least once a month.

- Frequency: mentors 1.2, mentees 2.4

- Importance; mentors 2.6, mentees 3.9

The responses to this item reflect a busy workplace. Commitment is needed by both parties to meet frequently enough for a mentoring relationship to develop and continue. Mentees think it is very important to meet at least once a month. Mentors are less certain about the need, as evidenced by their responses at 2.5 importance and 1.2

	Frequency			Importance		
	Mentor	Mentee		Mentor	Mentee	
(+)	2.1	2.2	A	3.7	3.8	(+)
(+)	1.6	2.0	B	3.3	3.4	(+)
(+)	1.6	1.6	C	3.3	3.8	(-)
(+)	2.1	2.0	D	4.1	3.9	(+)
(+)	2.0	2.2	E	3.5	3.8	(+)
(+)	1.3	1.5	F	2.2	2.7	(-)
(+)	2.0	2.3	G	3.6	3.9	(+)
(-)	1.8	2.3	*H	3.9	3.9	(+)
(+)	2.1	2.0	I	3.4	3.1	(+)
(-)	1.9	2.4	*J*	3.6	4.3	(-)
(+)	1.2	1.4	K	2.3	2.0	(+)
(+)	2.0	2.2	L	3.4	3.6	(+)
(-)	1.2	2.4	*M*	2.5	3.9	(-)
(+)	1.9	2.3	N	3.1	3.5	(+)
(+)	1.8	1.9	O	3.6	3.7	(+)

frequency. The program will not work without regular meetings. In fact, mentors and mentees will probably need to meet more frequently at the beginning. After getting to know each other, once a month may be sufficient. The frequency of meetings will, of course, depend on each mentoring pair's negotiation, but a time commitment must be made. In fact, that is why it is best for the mentee to handle the agenda setting and meeting arrangements, as he or she is usually more interested in the relationship.

Part Three

All actions for which either mentors or mentees rate importance below "3" should also be discussed, if they have not been discussed previously. In the example, all of the actions for which mentor or mentee rated importance below "3" (F, K, M) were noted for discussion, because it is assumed that most mentoring relationships will include all fifteen actions on the Mentoring Skills Assessment. Once the mentor and mentee negotiate their relationship, they can decide whether and how often any of the actions should take place. None of the actions, however, should be rejected too easily (which could happen if both parties scored an item below "3" and just ignored it).

References

Alleman, E. (1989, Winter). Two planned mentoring programs that worked. *Mentoring International, 3*(1), 7.

Bloch, S. (1993). The mentor as counselor. *Employee Counseling Today, 5*(3), 10.

Gaskill, L.R. (1993, Winter). A conceptual framework for the development, implementation, and evaluation of formal mentoring programs. *Journal of Career Development, 20*(2), 148–155.

Geiger-Dumond, A., & Boyle, S. (1995, March). Mentoring: A practitioner's guide. *Training & Development, 49*(3), 54.

Gunn, E. (1995, August). Mentoring: The democratic version. *Training, 32*(6), 64–67.

Howe, E.S. (1995, February). The benefits of mentoring. *Pennsylvania CPA Journal, 2,* 16.

Kram, K.E. (1985). *Mentoring at work.* Glenview IL: Scott, Foresman.

Loeb, M. (1995, June). The new mentoring. *Fortune, X*(11), 213.

Murray, M. (1991). *Beyond the myths and magic of mentoring.* San Francisco Jossey-Bass.

Nocera, J. (1996, April 6). Living with layoffs. *Fortune, 6,* 73.

Phillips-Jones, L. (1993a). *Mentoring program coordinator's guide.* Grass Valley, CA: Coalition of Counseling Centers.

Phillips-Jones, L. (1993b). *The mentors and proteges.* Grass Valley, CA: Coalition of Counseling Centers.

Rothman, H. (1993). The boss as mentor. *Nation's Business, 81*(4), 66–67.

Rubow, R., & Jansen, S. (1990, July). A corporate survival guide for the baby bust. *Management Review, 79*(7), 52.

Silver, S. (1996, March 24). Flatter organizations require new skills. *The Star-Ledger*, p. 55.

Smith, M.L. (1994, March/April). Creating business-development talent through mentoring. *Journal of Management in Engineering, 10*(2), 44–47.

Sullivan, C.G. (1992). *How to mentor in the midst of change.* Alexandria, VA: Association for Supervision and Curriculum Development.

Wright, R.G., & Werther, Jr., W.B. (1991). Mentors at work. In R.B. Frantreb (Ed.), *Training and Development Yearbook 1992/1993.* Englewood Cliffs, NJ: Prentice-Hall.

Zachary, L. (1994, October). Mentoring relationships: Tools for partner participation. *Mentor, 6*(4), 6.

Originally published in *The 1998 Annual: Volume 2, Consulting.*

Mentoring Skills Assessment: Mentee Version

Michael Lee Smith

Name: _____ Location: _____

(Check One): Newly hired or promoted _____ Current employee _____

Instructions: For each of the items that follow, you will need to decide the answer to the following three questions and place check marks in the appropriate columns:

1. Should this activity take place? (Yes or No)

2. How often should this activity take place? (Occasionally, Regularly, or Often)

3. How important is this activity? (Hardly Needed, Somewhat Needed, Needed, Highly Needed, Essential)

| Take Place? | | Frequency | | | Item | Importance | | | | |
Yes	No	Occasionally (1 point)	Regularly (2 points)	Often (3 points)		Hardly Needed (1 point)	Somewhat Needed (2 points)	Needed (3 points)	Highly Needed (4 points)	Essential (5 points)
_____		1	2	3	A. A mentor gives information on the roles and responsibilities of being an employee here.	1	2	3	4	5
_____		1	2	3	B. A mentor shares his or her experiences of making transitions or of being new here.	1	2	3	4	5

	Take Place?		Frequency				Importance			
	Yes	No	Occasionally (1 point)	Regularly (2 points)	Often (3 points)		Hardly Needed (1 point)	Somewhat Needed (2 points)	Needed (3 points)	Highly Needed (4 points)	Essential (5 points)
C. A mentor discusses careers at this company.	___	___	1	2	3		1	2	3	4	5
D. A mentor discusses my personal career goals.	___	___	1	2	3		1	2	3	4	5
E. A mentor discusses/shares information about job problems and solutions.	___	___	1	2	3		1	2	3	4	5
F. A mentor discusses company politics.	___	___	1	2	3		1	2	3	4	5
G. A mentor discusses/shares information about detailed job tasks.	___	___	1	2	3		1	2	3	4	5
H. A mentor explores my strengths and weaknesses.	___	___	1	2	3		1	2	3	4	5
I. A mentor acts as a sounding board for my issues and concerns.	___	___	1	2	3		1	2	3	4	5
J. A mentor gives feedback that is positive or negative regarding my job plans, progress, and performance.	___	___	1	2	3		1	2	3	4	5

Take Place?		Frequency			Item	Importance				
Yes	No	Occasionally (1 point)	Regularly (2 points)	Often (3 points)		Hardly Needed (1 point)	Somewhat Needed (2 points)	Needed (3 points)	Highly Needed (4 points)	Essential (5 points)
___	___	1	2	3	K. A mentor asks me how others perceive him or her.	1	2	3	4	5
___	___	1	2	3	L. A mentor meets with me at least once a month.	1	2	3	4	5
___	___	1	2	3	M. A mentor takes me to meetings, job sites, negotiations, or sales calls.	1	2	3	4	5
___	___	1	2	3	N. A mentor encourages me to speak up, take initiative, and not be satisfied with the status quo.	1	2	3	4	5
___	___	1	2	3	O. A mentor periodically evaluates the mentoring relationship.	1	2	3	4	5

Mentoring Skills Assessment: Mentor Version

Michael Lee Smith

Name: _____ Location: _____

(Check One): Newly hired or promoted _____ Current employee _____

Instructions: For each of the items that follow, you will need to decide the answer to the following three questions and place check marks in the appropriate columns:

1. Should this activity take place? (Yes or No)

2. How often should this activity take place? (Occasionally, Regularly, or Often)

3. How important is this activity? (Hardly Needed, Somewhat Needed, Needed, Highly Needed, Essential)

Take Place?		Frequency			Item	Importance				
Yes	No	Occasionally (1 point)	Regularly (2 points)	Often (3 points)		Hardly Needed (1 point)	Somewhat Needed (2 points)	Needed (3 points)	Highly Needed (4 points)	Essential (5 points)
___	___	1	2	3	A. A mentor gives information on the roles and responsibilities of being an employee here.	1	2	3	4	5
___	___	1	2	3	B. A mentor shares his or her experiences of making transitions or of being new here.	1	2	3	4	5

| | Take Place? | | Frequency | | | Item | Importance | | | | |
	Yes	No	Occasionally (1 point)	Regularly (2 points)	Often (3 points)		Hardly Needed (1 point)	Somewhat Needed (2 points)	Needed (3 points)	Highly Needed (4 points)	Essential (5 points)
	__	__	1	2	3	C. A mentor discusses careers at this company.	1	2	3	4	5
	__	__	1	2	3	D. A mentor discusses the mentee's personal career goals.	1	2	3	4	5
	__	__	1	2	3	E. A mentor discusses/shares information about job problems and solutions.	1	2	3	4	5
	__	__	1	2	3	F. A mentor discusses company politics.	1	2	3	4	5
	__	__	1	2	3	G. A mentor discusses/shares information about detailed job tasks.	1	2	3	4	5
	__	__	1	2	3	H. A mentor explores the mentee's strengths and weaknesses.	1	2	3	4	5
	__	__	1	2	3	I. A mentor acts as a sounding board for the mentee's issues and concerns.	1	2	3	4	5
	__	__	1	2	3	J. A mentor gives feedback that is positive and negative regarding the mentee's job plans, progress, and performance.	1	2	3	4	5

	Take Place?		Frequency			Importance				
	Yes	No	Occasionally (1 point)	Regularly (2 points)	Often (3 points)	Hardly Needed (1 point)	Somewhat Needed (2 points)	Needed (3 points)	Highly Needed (4 points)	Essential (5 points)
K. A mentor asks the mentee how others perceive the mentor.	___	___	1	2	3	1	2	3	4	5
L. A mentor meets with the mentee at least once a month.	___	___	1	2	3	1	2	3	4	5
M. A mentor takes the mentee to meetings, job sites, negotiations, or sales calls.	___	___	1	2	3	1	2	3	4	5
N. A mentor encourages the mentee to speak up, take initiative, and not be satisfied with the status quo.	___	___	1	2	3	1	2	3	4	5
O. A mentor periodically evaluates the mentoring relationship.	___	___	1	2	3	1	2	3	4	5

37 Organizational–Type Inventory

Manfred F.R. Kets de Vries, Danny Miller, and Gaylord Reagan

Summary

Organizations mirror the styles of their chief executive officers. Strategies, structures, and cultures all bear the imprint of executives' personalities. In some cases top managers (and their organizations) are composed, open, engaged, stimulating, and thoughtful. In other cases, top managers (and their organizations) are dramatic, suspicious, detached, depressive, or compulsive. Executives can produce organizations that boast tremendous success, such as IBM or 3M or Hewlett-Packard; or, given the existence of certain vulnerabilities and biases, executives can gravely damage their organizations. The first step in avoiding or combating a problem in executive-management style is to confirm its presence by identifying the type of organization that the executive has built.

The Inventory

Theoretical Framework

In the book *Unstable at the Top: Inside the Troubled Organization*, Kets de Vries and Miller (1987) describe five patterns that result from problem personalities in top management:

1. The dramatic organization;

2. The suspicious organization;

3. The detached organization;

4. The depressive organization; and

5. The compulsive organization.

These patterns can produce disastrous consequences for their host organizations. Kets de Vries and Miller (1987) contend that by identifying an organization's dominant pattern, one can either avoid these consequences or detect and overcome them:

> Too often the problems in unsuccessful organizations come about because . . . top executives get stuck in a specific scenario . . . from which they are unable to disentangle themselves . . . . Obsessions motivate a need to control; fears breed suspicion; dramatic behaviors lead to grandiosity. The executives hold fast to archaic, unhealthy, counterproductive activities that once proved effective or pleasant for them, but that no longer seem to be working. The result is a general ossifying of the organization . . . . When this happens, it can all but completely cancel out the company's effectiveness. (pp. 195–196)

Kets de Vries and Miller (1987, p. 199) caution readers that only a "disposition toward self-discovery and exploration can provide organizations with insight into their counterproductive behaviors. And only in this way can a new, effective configuration evolve, one in which the individual pieces complement each other, one that is in tune with the market." Finally, they write (1987, p. xiv) that this framework applies " . . . mainly where decision-making power and initiative reside largely in the chief executive. But in healthy organizations, and where power is dispersed . . . there tend to be fewer extremes, less uniformity in culture, structure, and strategy, and as a result, fewer problems."

Reliability and Validity

The Organizational-Type Inventory is designed for use as an action-research tool rather than as a rigorous data-gathering instrument. Applied in this manner, the inventory has demonstrated a high level of face validity when used with audiences ranging from executive managers to nonmanagement personnel.

Administration

The following suggestions will help facilitators to administer the inventory:

1. Before respondents begin completing the inventory, discuss the five organizational patterns identified by Kets de Vries and Miller.

2. Distribute copies of the Organizational-Type Inventory, and read the instructions aloud as the respondents follow. Resolve any questions at this time.

3. Urge respondents to avoid overanalyzing their choices. For each item, each respondent should record an initial impression by checking either the "Yes" box or the "No" box, indicating his or her response to each question in each

of the five pattern categories. Then each respondent should circle the number indicating his or her reaction to the attribute described in each question.

4. Ask respondents to wait to score their instruments until all respondents have finished.

5. After scoring their inventories and discussing the resulting scores, respondents should prepare brief answers to Steps 2 through 5 on the interpretation sheet. These answers provide a useful entry point to the processing of the inventory.

Scoring

Each respondent should be given a copy of the Organizational-Type Inventory Scoring Sheet. Using the scoring sheet, respondents should first record the number of "Yes" choices they made within each of the five pattern categories. Then they should record their "No" choices in a similar manner. Finally, respondents should record the total of their "Reaction" choices for each of the pattern categories.

The pattern(s) with the most "Yes" choices best describes the respondent's organization as the respondent perceives it. Specifically, if a respondent checked half or more of the "Yes" boxes within a pattern, that person is probably working in that type of organization. However, if a pattern receives only one or two "Yes" choices, the respondent is probably not working in that type of organization.

"Reaction" scores are used to determine the kind of organization that respondents should seek out or avoid. A low reaction score for a given pattern suggests that the pattern is regarded favorably by the respondent. Conversely, a higher score suggests that the respondent regards the pattern unfavorably.

Respondents may find it easier to interpret their reaction scores if they first convert those scores into numeric averages for each pattern. Averages nearer "1" suggest a favorable reaction, whereas averages nearer "3" indicate an unfavorable reaction.

Interpretation and Processing

When respondents finish scoring their inventories, the facilitator should distribute copies of the interpretation sheet. The interpretation sheet contains brief descriptions of each of Kets de Vries and Miller's five patterns. The descriptions provide information about the characteristics, strengths, weaknesses, and needs of each pattern and offer brief prescriptions for overcoming problems associated with the patterns. While reading this information, respondents should remember that organizations (and individuals) generally do not fall into a single pattern. It is normal for organizations (and individuals) to be hybrids.

Some groups find it useful to prepare a large copy of the scoring sheet on newsprint. In this case the facilitator polls individual respondents about the "Yes"/"No" and reaction scores that they assigned to each of the five patterns. The shared results then form the basis for a group discussion.

The brief answers that respondents wrote for Steps 2 through 5 on the interpretation sheet should also be discussed at this point. The facilitator should allow sufficient time to cover this information, as it provides respondents with an opportunity to apply Kets de Vries and Miller's model to their organization. Special attention should also be devoted to discussing the effects of the organizational weaknesses described in the interpretation sheet and to identifying ways to mitigate those effects. This is a good opportunity for respondents to begin forming a group action plan.

While respondents process the results of their inventories, it is important for the facilitator to encourage them to view their collective results in a positive manner. Once respondents identify their organization in one or more of the five patterns, there is an understandable tendency for the ensuing discussion to become somewhat negative. Respondents should be aware of Kets de Vries and Miller's (1987, p. 196) admonition that all organizations share elements of several of the styles, ". . . each of which tends to become more pronounced under varying circumstances. There is cause for concern only if one style takes over and consistently dominates all aspects of an organization's life." In addition, the authors point out that it is possible for organizations to influence the personalities of top managers. For example, failing organizations can depress previously successful executives. Also, Kets de Vries and Miller note that it is possible for the weaknesses of one pattern to be canceled out by the strengths of another pattern.

Uses of the Inventory

The Organizational-Type Inventory is designed to accomplish the following objectives:

1. To identify the presence (or absence) of the five patterns within respondent organizations;

2. To encourage discussion of the impact of identified patterns on respondent organizations;

3. To initiate discussions about the appropriateness of respondent pattern preferences within the context of an organization's short- and long-term viability;

4. To help differentiate respondent preferences for the five patterns; and

5. To stimulate planning designed to increase individual and organizational-group use of healthy, positive patterns.

References

Kets de Vries, M.F.R. (1980). *Organizational paradoxes: Clinical approaches to management.* London: Tavistock.

Kets de Vries, M.F.R. (Ed.) (1984). *The irrational executive.* New York: International Universities Press.

Kets de Vries, M.F.R., & Miller, D. (1984). *The neurotic organization.* San Francisco: Jossey-Bass.

Kets de Vries, M.F.R., & Miller, D. (1987). *Unstable at the top: Inside the troubled organization.* New York: New American Library.

Miller, D., & Friesen, P.H. (1984). *Organizations: A quantum view.* Englewood Cliffs, NJ: Prentice-Hall.

Zahznik, A., & Kets de Vries, M.F.R. (1985). *Power and the corporate mind* (rev. ed.) Chicago: Bonus Books.

Originally published in *The 1994 Annual: Developing Human Resources.*

Organizational–Type Inventory[1]

Manfred F.R. Kets de Vries, Danny Miller, and Gaylord Reagan

Instructions: For each of the numbered items in patterns A to E below, check "Yes" or "No"; then refer to the following three-point scale and circle the number that indicates your reaction to that condition (or the lack of that condition).

1 = Favorable   2 = Neutral   3 = Unfavorable

Pattern A	Yes	No	Reaction
1. Is power within your organization highly centralized in the hands of the chief executive?	☐	☐	1 2 3
2. Is there a very strong organizational culture in which everyone at the managerial level sees things in essentially the same way?	☐	☐	1 2 3
3. Is the chief executive "put on a pedestal" by many employees?	☐	☐	1 2 3
4. Is there suppression of dissent and contrary opinions by getting rid of or ignoring "rebels?"	☐	☐	1 2 3
5. Does the chief executive seem overburdened with work because he or she tries to do everything himself or herself?	☐	☐	1 2 3
6. Are there many grandiose and risky ventures that deplete organizational resources?	☐	☐	1 2 3
7. Does the chief executive make decisions rapidly and without consulting other people?	☐	☐	1 2 3
8. Is the organization rapidly diversifying, introducing many new products or services, or expanding geographically in a way that depletes organizational resources?	☐	☐	1 2 3
9. Does the chief executive appear to be vain or egotistical?	☐	☐	1 2 3

---

[1]This instrument is based on *Unstable at the Top: Inside the Troubled Organization* by Manfred F.R. Kets de Vries and Danny Miller, 1987, New York: New American Library.

1 = Favorable   2 = Neutral   3 = Unfavorable

	Pattern A, *continued*	Yes	No	Reaction
10.	Are sycophants the main ones being promoted?	☐	☐	1 2 3
11.	Does most information flow down rather than up the hierarchy?	☐	☐	1 2 3
12.	Does the strategy of the organization reside mainly inside the chief executive's mind?	☐	☐	1 2 3
13.	Are growth and expansion pursued seemingly for their own sake?	☐	☐	1 2 3

Pattern B

		Yes	No	Reaction
1.	Is there an atmosphere of suspicion and distrust in the organization?	☐	☐	1 2 3
2.	Do managers blame external "enemies" (regulators, government, competitors) for the organization's problems?	☐	☐	1 2 3
3.	Is there a strong emphasis on management information systems to identify inadequacies and assign blame?	☐	☐	1 2 3
4.	Are there organizational "spies" who inform top managers about what is happening at lower levels?	☐	☐	1 2 3
5.	Is organizational loyalty a big factor in assessing personnel performance?	☐	☐	1 2 3
6.	Does the chief executive have a "siege mentality," constantly defending against perceived external attacks?	☐	☐	1 2 3
7.	Is the organization's strategy focused more on copying other organizations than on trying new, unique approaches?	☐	☐	1 2 3

1 = Favorable   2 = Neutral   3 = Unfavorable

Pattern B, *continued*	Yes	No	Reaction
8. Is there much secrecy regarding performance information, salaries, decisions, etc.?	☐	☐	1 2 3
9. Does the organization's strategy vacillate too much according to external conditions?	☐	☐	1 2 3
10. Is there excessive risk avoidance in the organization?	☐	☐	1 2 3
11. Is the organization too unfocused?	☐	☐	1 2 3

Pattern C

	Yes	No	Reaction
1. Is the organization badly split, with much disagreement among the various functional areas or divisions?	☐	☐	1 2 3
2. Does political infighting occur very often?	☐	☐	1 2 3
3. Is the chief executive somewhat reclusive, refraining from personal contact and preferring to communicate by memo?	☐	☐	1 2 3
4. Is there a "leadership vacuum" in the organization?	☐	☐	1 2 3
5. Do decisions get delayed for long periods of time because of squabbling?	☐	☐	1 2 3
6. Do the personal ambitions of managers take dramatic precedence over broader organizational goals?	☐	☐	1 2 3
7. Are strategies badly fragmented, vacillating between one approach and another according to which senior manager is favored by the chief executive?	☐	☐	1 2 3
8. Is the chief executive too busy with outside matters to pay much attention to the organization and its business?	☐	☐	1 2 3

1 = Favorable   2 = Neutral   3 = Unfavorable

	Yes	No	Reaction
Pattern C, *continued*			
9. Do very few decisions emanate from the top of the organization as things just drift along?	☐	☐	1 2 3
10. Is it difficult to perceive what the chief executive really wants?	☐	☐	1 2 3
Pattern D			
1. Is there a feeling of helplessness to influence events on the part of the chief executive or the key top managers?	☐	☐	1 2 3
2. Has the organization stagnated while other, similar organizations have advanced?	☐	☐	1 2 3
3. Are the organization's products or services antiquated?	☐	☐	1 2 3
4. Is there very little "scanning" of the organization's environment?	☐	☐	1 2 3
5. Are work facilities poor and inefficient?	☐	☐	1 2 3
6. Are the organization's strategies very narrow and resistant to change?	☐	☐	1 2 3
7. Is there a lack of action, an atmosphere of "decision paralysis"?	☐	☐	1 2 3
8. Do many young, aggressive managers leave the organization because of the stifling climate and the lack of opportunity for advancement?	☐	☐	1 2 3
9. Is there extreme conservatism when it comes to making capital expenditures?	☐	☐	1 2 3
10. Do bureaucratic rules set long ago replace communication and deliberation in decision making?	☐	☐	1 2 3

1 = Favorable   2 = Neutral   3 = Unfavorable

	Pattern E	Yes	No	Reaction
1.	Is the organization very bureaucratic, filled with red tape, regulations, formal policies and procedures, and the like?	☐	☐	1 2 3
2.	Is there a tendency for precedents to decide issues more than analysis or discussion?	☐	☐	1 2 3
3.	Has strategy remained essentially unchanged for many years?	☐	☐	1 2 3
4.	Is the organization slow to adapt to trends in the marketplace?	☐	☐	1 2 3
5.	Does the chief executive hoard power?	☐	☐	1 2 3
6.	Is the chief executive overly concerned with one or two elements of strategy (efficiency, productivity, quality, costs) to the exclusion of most others?	☐	☐	1 2 3
7.	Did a former chief executive leave a strategic legacy that is held to be sacrosanct by current managers?	☐	☐	1 2 3
8.	Are strategies very precisely articulated, down to the last detail?	☐	☐	1 2 3
9.	Do information systems provide too much "hard" and too little "soft" data on customer reactions, trends, etc.?	☐	☐	1 2 3
10.	Does the chief executive prefer subordinates who follow directives very precisely and refrain from arguing?	☐	☐	1 2 3
11.	Is there a great emphasis on position and status?	☐	☐	1 2 3

Organizational–Type Inventory Scoring Sheet

Instructions:

1. Count the number of "Yes" checks for each pattern, and enter each total below.

2. Count the number of "No" checks for each pattern, and enter each total below.

3. Add the numbers circled under "Reaction" for each pattern, and enter each total below.

Name of Pattern	Number of "Yes" Checks	Number of "No" Checks	Reaction Total
Pattern A: "The Dramatic Organization"			
Pattern B: "The Suspicious Organization"			
Pattern C: "The Detached Organization"			
Pattern D: "The Depressive Organization"			
Pattern E: "The Compulsive Organization"			

<u>Organizational–Type Inventory Interpretation Sheet</u>[1]

Step 1

Determine which pattern collected the most "Yes" responses. If you checked only one or two "Yes" boxes within a pattern, you probably *are not working* in that type of organization. However, if you checked half or more "Yes" boxes within a pattern, you probably *are working* in that type of organization.

Pattern A: "The Dramatic Organization"

Characteristics

- Has strong leader who is idealized by subordinates
- Has leader who is the primary catalyst for subordinates' morale and initiatives
- Exhibits very centralized policy making (in hands of impulsive, hyperactive leader)

Strengths

- Can create momentum needed to take organization through start-up phase
- Has ability to rebound after failures and to continue moving forward
- Comes up with ideas to revitalize the organization

Weaknesses

- Lacks a consistent strategy
- Sometimes lacks necessary controls
- Tends to avoid consulting with, or getting feedback from, lower levels

Needs

- Distribute authority—empowerment, delegation
- Codify a clear strategy
- Establish a clear hierarchy
- Provide controls and coordination

---

[1]The concept of this interpretation sheet is based on *Unstable at the Top: Inside the Troubled Organization* by Manfred F.R. Kets de Vries and Danny Miller, 1987, New York: New American Library.

- Scan the organization's environment

- Scale down huge projects

- Review core business

- Sharpen focus—get rid of worthless propositions

Prescription

- Plant both feet firmly on the ground

Pattern B: "The Suspicious Organization"

Characteristics

- Has fight-or-flight culture

- Lacks trust—emphasis placed on intimidation and uniformity

- Is reactive, conservative, overly analytical, secretive

Strengths

- Shows good knowledge of events inside and outside the organization

- Avoids dependence on a single market segment/customer

- Provides positive opportunities for growth and diversification

Weaknesses

- Lacks a concerted and consistent management strategy; falls victim to "groupthink"

- Has reactive, piecemeal, contradictory, distrustful atmosphere

- Experiences high staff turnover because of insecurity and disenchantment

Needs

- Foster trust and break down communication barriers

- Establish a participative culture

- Break down "policing" systems

- Pursue strategic themes

- Create distinctive competencies

Prescription

- Develop a unified strategy and sense of mission

Pattern C: "The Detached Organization"

Characteristics

- Lacks warmth and emotion

- Engages in jockeying for power—lots of conflict and insecurity

- Demonstrates strategic thinking dominated by indecisive, inconsistent, narrow perspectives

Strengths

- Has middle managers who play an active role

- Shares variety of points of view in formulating strategies

- Has individual managers who take initiative

Weaknesses

- Lacks leadership

- Exhibits inconsistent or vacillating strategy

- Decides issues by political negotiating rather than on the basis of facts

Needs

- Get a senior manager willing to provide active leadership

- Establish active coordinating committees

- Discourage parochial interests

- Reward overall organizational performance

- Pursue strategic themes

- Create distinctive competencies

Prescription

- Consider the whole

Pattern D: "The Depressive Organization"

Characteristics

- Lacks initiative—lots of passivity and negativity

- Lacks motivation—leadership vacuum

- Drifts, with no sense of direction—inward focused

Strengths

- Generally enjoys an excellent reputation for past successes

Weaknesses

- Tends to live in the past, when things were good for the organization

- Focuses on supplying dying markets/customers/products/services

- Has apathetic and inactive senior management

Needs

- Seek new leadership that is focused on new markets/customers/products/services

- Prune unpromising or older ventures

- Obtain resources for organizational reorientation and renewal

- Find new opportunities in identified markets

- Scan the organization's environment

Prescription

- Challenge the status quo

Pattern E: "The Compulsive Organization"

Characteristics

- Is rigid, directed inward, insular

- Fosters submission, lack of creativity, and insecurity in subordinates

- Focuses on one aspect of a strategy (quality, efficiency, cost cutting); is unable to switch focus quickly

Strengths

- Possesses fine internal controls

- Has a tightly focused strategy

- Exhibits efficient operations

Weaknesses

- Is too attached to tradition

- Responds inflexibly and inappropriately to customer/market demands

- Stifles creativity and influence of middle managers

Needs

- Conduct creativity seminars

- Change selection practices

- Become open to suggestions from lower levels

- Scan markets for problems and opportunities

- Respond better to customer needs

- Get rid of bureaucratic structures

Prescription

- Wage a battle against control

Step 2

Write brief answers to each of the following ten questions. Use specific examples where possible. Do your answers to these questions help you to understand why you classified your organization within the pattern(s) you did? In the book *Unstable at the Top: Inside the Troubled Organization*, Kets de Vries and Miller point out that organizations falling into one or more of these patterns can be very unpleasant places to work and will be unlikely to change without extreme pressure from within to do so.

1. How would you describe your organization's environment?

2. What does your organization stand for? What are its goals?

3. What are your chief executive's "dreams?"

4. What aspects of your organization's functioning are important to its senior leaders? What makes them excited, angry, happy?

5. How are crises and "critical incidents" dealt with in your organization?

6. What kind of people do well in your organization?

7. What measures of performance are used in your organization? What are the criteria for rewards and punishment?

8. What are the criteria for selection, promotion, and termination in your organization?

9. What kind of organizational "war stories" and "rituals" exist in your organization? What are the "taboos?"

10. How would you describe your organization's structure?

Step 3

By totaling your reaction scores for each pattern, you can determine the kind of organization that is most comfortable for you. The higher your reaction score is for a given pattern, the more unfavorable that pattern appears to you. What do your scores suggest? Are you and your organization a "good fit?" Write your answers to these questions in the space that follows.

Step 4

Kets de Vries and Miller identify five "cultural blockades" to adaptation that influence the strength of an organization's culture as well as its resistance or receptivity to change. Which of these blockades exist in your organization, and what needs to be done to make sure that they produce positive results?

1. Adverse (or favorable) impact of senior leaders' legacy

2. Similarity (or dissimilarity) of views within groups whose membership is highly stable

3. Lack (or presence) of employee commitment to overall goals and procedures

4. Presence (or absence) of organizational conflict and distrust

5. Climate of stagnation (or change)

Step 5

Kets de Vries and Miller identify seven "organizational blockades" to adaptation that must be eliminated. Which of these blockades exist within your organization, and how can they be mitigated? For each blockade that you identify as applicable to your organization, use the space provided under the suggestion to jot down notes about steps you might be able to take.

Excessive Bureaucracy

- *Suggestion:* Identify and combat unnecessary rules, regulations, and procedures with the support of top management.

Inadequate Information Systems

- *Suggestion:* Question the relevance of reports, and ask whether the system truly enlightens the organization about emerging trends.

Uneven Distribution of Power

- *Suggestion:* Maintain constant vigilance and an awareness of the abuses of power.

Overexplicit Planning

- *Suggestion:* Constantly update plans, goals, objectives.

Overly Narrow Goals and Strategies

- *Suggestion:* Create alternative plans and contingency plans.

Reliance on Past Success

- *Suggestion:* Critically evaluate present strategy, information systems, power distribution, and so forth.

Limited Resource Availability

- *Suggestion:* Keep track of the flow of resources. Determine how many failures can be tolerated.

About the Editor

Jack Gordon is the former chief editor of *Training* Magazine. His articles and columns on workplace training have appeared in *The Wall Street Journal, San Diego Chronicle, Minneapolis Star Tribune*, and *Learning & Training Innovations*. He has written on other subjects for numerous publications, including *The Economist, The Journal of Law & Politics*, and *Independent Banker*. He has served as editor for books in the "Pfeiffer's Classic Activities" series, including Developing Leaders, Building Better Teams, Managing Conflict at Work, and Interpersonal Communication.

Pfeiffer Publications Guide

This guide is designed to familiarize you with the various types of Pfeiffer publications. The formats section describes the various types of products that we publish; the methodologies section describes the many different ways that content might be provided within a product. We also provide a list of the topic areas in which we publish.

FORMATS

In addition to its extensive book-publishing program, Pfeiffer offers content in an array of formats, from fieldbooks for the practitioner to complete, ready-to-use training packages that support group learning.

FIELDBOOK Designed to provide information and guidance to practitioners in the midst of action. Most fieldbooks are companions to another, sometimes earlier, work, from which its ideas are derived; the fieldbook makes practical what was theoretical in the original text. Fieldbooks can certainly be read from cover to cover. More likely, though, you'll find yourself bouncing around following a particular theme, or dipping in as the mood, and the situation, dictate.

HANDBOOK A contributed volume of work on a single topic, comprising an eclectic mix of ideas, case studies, and best practices sourced by practitioners and experts in the field.

An editor or team of editors usually is appointed to seek out contributors and to evaluate content for relevance to the topic. Think of a handbook not as a ready-to-eat meal, but as a cookbook of ingredients that enables you to create the most fitting experience for the occasion.

RESOURCE Materials designed to support group learning. They come in many forms: a complete, ready-to-use exercise (such as a game); a comprehensive resource on one topic (such as conflict management) containing a variety of methods and approaches; or a collection of like-minded activities (such as icebreakers) on multiple subjects and situations.

TRAINING PACKAGE An entire, ready-to-use learning program that focuses on a particular topic or skill. All packages comprise a guide for the facilitator/trainer and a workbook for the participants. Some packages are supported with additional media—such as video—or learning aids, instruments, or other devices to help participants understand concepts or practice and develop skills.

- *Facilitator/trainer's guide* Contains an introduction to the program, advice on how to organize and facilitate the learning event, and step-by-step instructor notes. The guide also contains copies of presentation materials—handouts, presentations, and overhead designs, for example—used in the program.

- *Participant's workbook* Contains exercises and reading materials that support the learning goal and serves as a valuable reference and support guide for participants in the weeks and months that follow the learning event. Typically, each participant will require his or her own workbook.

ELECTRONIC CD-ROMs and web-based products transform static Pfeiffer content into dynamic, interactive experiences. Designed to take advantage of the searchability, automation, and ease-of-use that technology provides, our e-products bring convenience and immediate accessibility to your workspace.

METHODOLOGIES

CASE STUDY A presentation, in narrative form, of an actual event that has occurred inside an organization. Case studies are not prescriptive, nor are they used to prove a point; they are designed to develop critical analysis and decision-making skills. A case study has a specific time frame, specifies a sequence of events, is narrative in structure, and contains a plot structure—an issue (what should be/have been done?). Use case studies when the goal is to enable participants to apply previously learned theories to the circumstances in the case, decide what is pertinent, identify the real issues, decide what should have been done, and develop a plan of action.

ENERGIZER A short activity that develops readiness for the next session or learning event. Energizers are most commonly used after a break or lunch to stimulate or refocus the group. Many involve some form of physical activity, so they are a useful way to counter post-lunch lethargy. Other uses include transitioning from one topic to another, where "mental" distancing is important.

EXPERIENTIAL LEARNING ACTIVITY (ELA) A facilitator-led intervention that moves participants through the learning cycle from experience to application (also known as a Structured Experience). ELAs are carefully thought-out designs in which there is a definite learning purpose and intended outcome. Each step—everything that participants do during the activity—facilitates the accomplishment of the stated goal. Each ELA includes complete instructions for facilitating the intervention and a clear statement of goals, suggested group size and timing, materials required, an explanation of the process, and, where appropriate, possible variations to the activity. (For more detail on Experiential Learning Activities, see the Introduction to the *Reference Guide to Handbooks and Annuals*, 1999 edition, Pfeiffer, San Francisco.)

GAME A group activity that has the purpose of fostering team spirit and togetherness in addition to the achievement of a pre-stated goal. Usually contrived—undertaking a desert expedition, for example—this type of learning method offers an engaging means for participants to demonstrate and practice business and interpersonal skills. Games are effective for team building and personal development mainly because the goal is subordinate to the process—the means through which participants reach decisions, collaborate, communicate, and generate trust and understanding. Games often engage teams in "friendly" competition.

ICEBREAKER A (usually) short activity designed to help participants overcome initial anxiety in a training session and/or to acquaint the participants with one another. An icebreaker can be a fun activity or can be tied to specific topics or training goals. While a useful tool in itself, the icebreaker comes into its own in situations where tension or resistance exists within a group.

INSTRUMENT A device used to assess, appraise, evaluate, describe, classify, and summarize various aspects of human behavior. The term used to describe an instrument depends primarily on its format and purpose. These terms include survey, questionnaire, inventory, diagnostic survey, and poll. Some uses of instruments include providing instrumental feedback to group members, studying here-and-now processes or functioning within a group, manipulating group composition, and evaluating outcomes of training and other interventions.

Instruments are popular in the training and HR field because, in general, more growth can occur if an individual is provided with a method for focusing specifically on his or her own behavior. Instruments also are used to obtain information that will serve as a basis for change and to assist in workforce planning efforts.

Paper-and-pencil tests still dominate the instrument landscape with a typical package comprising a facilitator's guide, which offers advice on administering the instrument and interpreting the collected data, and an initial set of instruments. Additional instruments are available separately. Pfeiffer, though, is investing heavily in e-instruments. Electronic instrumentation provides effortless distribution and, for larger groups particularly, offers advantages over paper-and-pencil tests in the time it takes to analyze data and provide feedback.

LECTURETTE A short talk that provides an explanation of a principle, model, or process that is pertinent to the participants' current learning needs. A lecturette is intended to establish a common language bond between the trainer and the participants by providing a mutual frame of reference. Use a lecturette as an introduction to a group activity or event, as an interjection during an event, or as a handout.

MODEL A graphic depiction of a system or process and the relationship among its elements. Models provide a frame of reference and something more tangible, and more easily remembered, than a verbal explanation. They also give participants something to "go on," enabling them to track their own progress as they experience the dynamics, processes, and relationships being depicted in the model.

ROLE PLAY A technique in which people assume a role in a situation/scenario: a customer service rep in an angry-customer exchange, for example. The way in which the role is approached is then discussed and feedback is offered. The role play is often repeated using a different approach and/or incorporating changes made based on feedback received. In other words, role playing is a spontaneous interaction involving realistic behavior under artificial (and safe) conditions.

SIMULATION A methodology for understanding the interrelationships among components of a system or process. Simulations differ from games in that they test or use a model that depicts or mirrors some aspect of reality in form, if not necessarily in content. Learning occurs by studying the effects of change on one or more factors of the model. Simulations are commonly used to test hypotheses about what happens in a system—often referred to as "what if?" analysis—or to examine best-case/worst-case scenarios.

THEORY A presentation of an idea from a conjectural perspective. Theories are useful because they encourage us to examine behavior and phenomena through a different lens.

TOPICS

The twin goals of providing effective and practical solutions for workforce training and organization development and meeting the educational needs of training and human resource professionals shape Pfeiffer's publishing program. Core topics include the following:

    Leadership & Management

    Communication & Presentation

    Coaching & Mentoring

    Training & Development

    e-Learning

    Teams & Collaboration

    OD & Strategic Planning

    Human Resources

    Consulting

What will you find on pfeiffer.com?

- The best in workplace performance solutions for training and HR professionals

- Downloadable training tools, exercises, and content

- Web-exclusive offers

- Training tips, articles, and news

- Seamless on-line ordering

- Author guidelines, information on becoming a Pfeiffer Affiliate, and much more

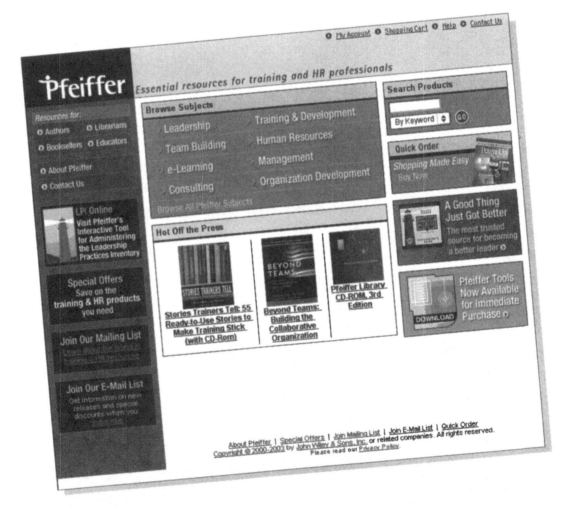

Discover more at www.pfeiffer.com

Customer Care

Have a question, comment, or suggestion? Contact us! We value your feedback and we want to hear from you.

For questions about this or other Pfeiffer products, you may contact us by:

E-mail: **customer@wiley.com**

Mail: **Customer Care Wiley/Pfeiffer**
10475 Crosspoint Blvd.
Indianapolis, IN 46256

Phone: **(US) 800-274-4434** (Outside the US: 317-572-3985)

Fax: **(US) 800-569-0443** (Outside the US: 317-572-4002)

To order additional copies of this title or to browse other Pfeiffer products, visit us online at **www.pfeiffer.com.**

For **Technical Support** questions call **(800) 274-4434.**

For authors guidelines, log on to www.pfeiffer.com and click on "Resources for Authors."

If you are . . .

A **college bookstore, a professor, an instructor, or work in higher education** and you'd like to place an order or request an exam copy, please contact jbreview@wiley.com.

A **general retail bookseller** and you'd like to establish an account or speak to a local sales representative, contact Melissa Grecco at 201-748-6267 or mgrecco@wiley.com.

An **exclusively on-line bookseller**, contact Amy Blanchard at 530-756-9456 or ablanchard @wiley.com or Jennifer Johnson at 206-568-3883 or jjohnson@wiley.com, both of our On-line Sales department.

A **librarian or library representative**, contact John Chambers in our Library Sales department at 201-748-6291 or jchamber@wiley.com.

A **reseller, training company/consultant, or corporate trainer**, contact Charles Regan in our Special Sales department at 201-748-6553 or cregan@wiley.com.

A **specialty retail distributor** (includes specialty gift stores, museum shops, and corporate bulk sales), contact Kim Hendrickson in our Special Sales department at 201-748-6037 or khendric@wiley.com.

Purchasing for the **Federal government**, contact Ron Cunningham in our Special Sales department at 317-572-3053 or rcunning@wiley.com.

Purchasing for a **State or Local government**, contact Charles Regan in our Special Sales department at 201-748-6553 or cregan@wiley.com.